Baptism in Times of Change

CHURCH OF SWEDEN
Research Series

§

The Church of Sweden Research Series promotes research investigating the intersections of church, academy, and society. Its focus is on theology that is in lively conversation with the pressing issues of the world today, both from an academic and from an ecclesial perspective. What is the role of the churches in ever changing ecological, political, cultural, social and religious contexts? How is Christian teaching and practice affected by these changing currents? And how is the Lutheran tradition evolving amid such challenges? Through monographs and anthologies, the series makes available Swedish and Scandinavian scholarship in the English-speaking world, but also mirrors the worldwide connections of the Church of Sweden as part of its own identity.

General editor of CSRS (since 2020): Michael Nausner

VOLUMES PUBLISHED

1. Göran Gunner, editor, *Vulnerability, Churches and HIV* (2009)
2. Kajsa Ahlstrand and Göran Gunner, editors, *Non-Muslims in Muslim Majority Societies with Focus on the Middle East and Pakistan* (2009)
3. Jonas Ideström, editor, *For the Sake of the World. Swedish Ecclesiology in Dialogue with William T. Cavanaugh* (2010)
4. Göran Gunner and Kjell-Åke Nordquist, *An Unlikely Dilemma. Constructing a Dialogue Between Human Rights and Peace-Building* (2011)
5. Anne-Louise Eriksson, Göran Gunner, and Niclas Blåder, editors, *Exploring a Heritage. Evangelical Lutheran Churches in the North* (2012)
6. Kjell-Åke Nordquist, editor, *Gods and Arms. On Religion and Armed Conflict* (2012)
7. Harald Hegstad, *The Real Church. An Ecclesiology of the Visible* (2013)
8. Carl-Henric Grenholm and Göran Gunner, editors, *Justification in a Post-Christian Society* (2014)
9. Carl-Henric Grenholm and Göran Gunner, editors, *Lutheran Identity and Political Theology* (2014)
10. Sune Fahlgren and Jonas Ideström, editors, *Ecclesiology in the Trenches. Theory and Method Under Construction* (2015)
11. Niclas Blåder, *Lutheran Tradition as Heritage and Tool* (2015)
12. Ulla Schmidt and Harald Askeland, editors, *Church Reform and Leadership of Change* (2016)
13. Kjell-Åke Nordquist, *Reconciliation as Politics. A Concept and its Practice* (2016)

14. Niclas Blåder and Kristina Helgesson Kjellin, editors, *Mending the World? Possibilities and Obstacles for Religion, Church, and Theology* (2017)
15. Tone Stangeland Kaufman, *A New Old Spirituality? A Qualitative Study of Clergy Spirituality in the Nordic Context* (2017)
16. Carl Reinhold Bråkenhielm, *The Study of Science and Religion. Sociological, Theological, and Philosophical Perspectives* (2017)
17. Jonas Ideström and Tone Stangeland Kaufman, editors, *What Really Matters. Scandinavian Perspectives on Ecclesiology and Ethnography* (2018)
18. Dion Forster, Elisabeth Gerle, and Göran Gunner, editors, *Freedom of Religion at Stake. Competing Claims Among Faith Traditions, States, and Persons* (2019)
19. Marianne Gaarden, *The Third Room of Preaching. A New Empirical Approach* (2021)
20. André S. Musskopf, Edith González Bernal and Maurício Rincón Andrade, editors, *Theology and Sexuality, Reproductive Health, and Rights. Latin American Experiences in Participatory Action Research* (2022)
21. Karin Johannesson, *Thérèse and Martin. Carmel and the Reformation in a New Light* (2023)
22. Harald Hegstad with Steinunn Arnþrúður Björnsdóttir, Magnus Evertsson, Jonas Adelin Jørgensen, and Jyri Komulainen, editors, *Baptism in Times of Change. Exploring New Patterns of Baptismal Theologies and Practices in Nordic Lutheran Churches* (2025)

Baptism in Times of Change

Exploring New Patterns of Baptismal Theologies and Practices in Nordic Lutheran Churches

Edited by
HARALD HEGSTAD, with
STEINUNN ARNÞRÚÐUR BJÖRNSDÓTTIR,
MAGNUS EVERTSSON,
JONAS ADELIN JØRGENSEN,
and JYRI KOMULAINEN

◥PICKWICK *Publications* · Eugene, Oregon

BAPTISM IN TIMES OF CHANGE
Exploring New Patterns of Baptismal Theologies and Practices
in Nordic Lutheran Churches

Church of Sweden Research Series 22

Copyright © 2025 Trossamfundet Svenska kyrkan (Church of Sweden). All rights reserved. Except for brief quotations in critical publications or reviews, no part of this book may be reproduced in any manner without prior written permission from the publisher. Write: Permissions, Wipf and Stock Publishers, 199 W. 8th Ave., Suite 3, Eugene, OR 97401.

Pickwick Publications
An Imprint of Wipf and Stock Publishers
199 W. 8th Ave., Suite 3
Eugene, OR 97401

www.wipfandstock.com

PAPERBACK ISBN: 979-8-3852-2871-3
HARDCOVER ISBN: 979-8-3852-2872-0
EBOOK ISBN: 979-8-3852-2873-7

Cataloguing-in-Publication data:

Names: Hegstad, Harald, editor. | Björnsdóttir, Steinunn Arnþrúður, editor. | Evertsson, Magnus, editor. | Jørgensen, Jonas Adelin, editor. | Komulainen, Jyri, editor.

Title: Baptism in times of change : exploring new patterns of baptismal theologies and practices in Nordic Lutheran churches / edited by Harald Hegstad, Steinunn Arnþrúður Björnsdóttir, Magnus Evertsson, Jonas Adelin Jørgensen, and Jyri Komulainen.

Description: Eugene, OR: Pickwick Publications, 2025. | Church of Sweden Research Series 22. | Includes bibliographical references.

Identifiers: ISBN 979-8-3852-2871-3 (paperback). | ISBN 979-8-3852-2872-0 (hardcover). | ISBN 979-8-3852-2873-7 (ebook).

Subjects: LCSH: Baptism. | Lutheran Church—Doctrines. | Infant baptism.

Classification: BV811.2 B15 2025 (print). | BV811.2 (ebook).

VERSION NUMBER 03/21/25

Scripture quotations from the New Revised Standard Version of the Bible, copyrighted © 1989 by the Division of Christian Education of the National Council of Churches of Christ in the United States of America and are used by permission

Scripture taken from the New King James Version (NKJV). Copyright © 1982 by Thomas Nelson, Inc. Used by permission. All rights reserved.

Scripture taken from the American Standard Version is in the public domain.

Cover photo: Outdoor baptism in Sápmi. Photographer: Aina Bye.

Contents

List of Figures and Tables | x
List of Contributors | xiii

Introduction | 1
—*Steinunn Arnþrúður Björnsdóttir, Magnus Evertsson, Harald Hegstad, Jonas Adelin Jørgensen, and Jyri Komulainen*

Part I: *Empirical Studies*

1 Baptism in Numbers in the Nordic Lutheran Churches 2009–2022 | 9
 —*Andreas Sandberg and Josephine Ganebo Skantz*

2 Infant Baptism in an Individualized Culture: Examining the Reasons Why Norwegian Parents Baptize Their Children | 25
 —*Tore Witsø Rafoss*

3 Churching Alone? New Patterns in the Use of Baptism in Denmark | 38
 —*Karen Marie Sø Leth-Nissen*

4 The Changing Role of Baptism in Finland: Parents' Attitudes toward Baptism According to a Baptismal Survey | 62
 —*Hanna Salomäki*

5 Infant Baptism in a New Context | 83
 —*Ingegerd Sjölin*

CONTENTS

Part II: *Practices*

6 "We Thank You for the Gift of Baptism": A Comparative Analysis of the Gift Motif in Baptismal Liturgies in the Nordic Countries | 101
—*Karin Tillberg*

7 Prímsigning: Exploring the Context of a Ritual for Infant Blessing | 120
—*Steinunn Arnþrúður Björnsdóttir and Kristján Valur Ingólfsson*

8 Bless or Baptize Children? Some Ecumenical Reflections | 136
—*Terje Hegertun*

9 The Postponed Baptism: The Experience of Being Baptized Prior to Confirmation | 152
—*Berit Weigand Berg*

10 Drop-in Baptism in a Norwegian Context: Results of a Qualitative Study | 167
—*Stein Ellinggard*

11 Folk-Church Ecclesiology—Always in the Making | 181
—*Sunniva Gylver*

Part III: *Communication*

12 Communicating about Baptism in Finland in the 2020s | 201
—*Laura Kokkonen*

13 On Communicating about Baptism: Perspectives from Baptism Projects in the Diocese of Lund | 219
—*Lena Andersson*

14 Baptism in Times of Change: The Need for Targeted Marketing | 236
—*Ingeborg Dybvig*

Part IV: *Theology*

15 The Meaning of Baptism in Our Time: Resources for a Contemporary Lutheran Baptismal Theology | 257
—*Harald Hegstad*

16 "I Consecrate You, Water": Arctic Baptismal Practices and Indigeneity under Climate Change | 272
—*Sigríður Guðmarsdóttir*

17 Naming and Belonging: Some Aspects of Baptism in the Sámi Tradition | 288
—*Lovisa Mienna Sjöberg*

CONTENTS

18 A Future with Hope: New Perspectives on Baptism in Times of Planetary Emergency | 301
    —*Anna Karin Hammar*

19 A Baptismal Theology for Imperfect People with Unfinished Faith | 319
    —*Niels Henrik Gregersen*

20 Baptism as an Ecclesiological and Ecumenical Demarcation: An Orthodox Reading from the Finnish Context | 338
    —*Pekka Metso and Ari Koponen*

Appendix: Learning Points from the Joint Nordic Lutheran Project "Baptism in Times of Change" | 358

Tables and Figures

Chapter 1

Figure 1. Church members by percentage of population in Nordic countries 2009–2022. *Sources: Danmarks statistik, Statistics Iceland, Statistics Norway, Suomen evankelis-luterilainen kirkko, Svenska kyrkan*

Figure 2. Percentage baptized among all live births in Nordic countries 2009–2022. *Sources: Danmarks statistik, Statistics Iceland, Statistics Norway, Suomen evankelis-luterilainen kirkko, Svenska kyrkan*

Figure 3. Percentage baptized among all live births in Denmark, Finland, Norway, and Sweden 2019–2022. *Sources: Danmarks statistik, Statistics Norway, Suomen evankelis-luterilainen kirkko, Svenska kyrkan*

Figure 4. Percentage of executed baptisms compared to estimated baptisms in Denmark, Finland, Norway, and Sweden for 2020, 2021, and 2022. *Sources: Danmarks statistik, Statistics Norway, Suomen evankelis-luterilainen kirkko, Svenska kyrkan*

Figure 5. Percentage of executed baptisms compared to estimated baptisms in all of Denmark, Finland, Norway, and Sweden 2020–2022. *Sources: Danmarks statistik, Statistics Norway, Suomen evankelis-luterilainen kirkko, Svenska kyrkan*

Figure 6. Number of baptisms in percentage of live births by diocese, with the highest and lowest percentages of baptisms, in Denmark, Finland,

Norway, and Sweden in 2019. *Sources: Danmarks statistik, Statistics Norway, Suomen evankelis-luterilainen kirkko, Svenska kyrkan*

Figure 7. Number of baptisms in percentages of estimated baptisms by diocese, with the highest and lowest percentages of baptisms, in Denmark, Finland, Norway, and Sweden in 2020, 2021, and 2022. *Sources: Danmarks statistik, Statistics Norway, Suomen evankelis-luterilainen kirkko, Svenska kyrkan*

Chapter 2

Figure 1. Percentage of Norwegian newborns being baptized in the Church of Norway 1960–2022. *Source: The Church of Norway and Statistics Norway*

Figure 2. Reasons for baptizing in 2012 and 2019. *Sources: Religion 2019 (N = 1943) and Religion 2012 (N = 2,257). Percentages reflect those who answered "important" or "very important."*

Table 1. Church attendance. *Source: Religion 2019. Possible responses were provided in answer to the question, "How often do you attend church services or religious meetings?" (N = 2,347: only members of the Church of Norway)*

Table 2. Reasons for baptizing and frequency of church attendance. *Sources: Religion 2019. Percentages reflect those who answered "important" or "very important" (N = 1,943)*

Figure 3. Reasons not to baptize. *Sources: Religion 2019. Percentages reflect those who answered "important" or "very important" (N = 531)*

Chapter 3

Figure 1: Evangelical Lutheran Church of Denmark: Membership and use of church for life stage rituals 2007–2024. *Sources: Data from the Danish Statistical Office and the Center for Pastoral Education of the ELCD*

Table 1: Background information on interviewees from 2015 and 2020 studies on the decision to opt in or out of baptism among parents of younger children. *Source: Two Danish interview studies*

TABLES AND FIGURES

Chapter 4

Figure 1. Respondents' views regarding the importance of religious rituals in connection with the birth of a child: Baptism survey (N = 1,029) percentages. *Source: The Church Research Institute in Finland. Baptismal Survey 2019*

Table 1. Respondents' views concerning the extent to which others influenced the decision to seek baptism for a child. Proportions answering "very greatly" and "greatly" in percentages (N = 1,039). *Source: The Church Research Institute in Finland. Baptismal Survey 2019*

Table 2. Decision to seek baptism in the immediate circle and to seek baptism for one's own child in percentages (N = 1,029) *Source: The Church Research Institute in Finland. Baptismal Survey 2019*

Table 3. Parents' views on when the decision to seek baptism for a child was made in percentages (N = 1,029). *Source: The Church Research Institute in Finland. Baptismal Survey 2019*

Figure 2. Reasons to baptize a child in families where at least one child was baptized in percentages (N = 776). *Source: The Church Research Institute in Finland. Baptismal Survey 2019*

Figure 3. Reasons for not having a child baptized for parents with an unbaptized child or children in percentages (N = 223). *Source: The Church Research Institute in Finland. Baptismal Survey 2019*

Chapter 5

Figure 1. Percentage of members of the Church of Sweden of the entire population and the proportion of baptized children of all born. *Source: Svenska kyrkans statistikdatabas*

Figure 2. Percentage of baptized children where one or both parents are members of the Church of Sweden in 1992 and from 2006 to 2021. *Sources: Alwall and Sjölin, Kyrkostatistik, 97 and Svenska kyrkans statistikdatabas*

Contributors

Lena Andersson is a pedagogical development worker and project manager for baptism at the Diocesan Office of the Church of Sweden in Lund. She has worked with questions regarding baptism in the Church of Sweden for more than 15 years on all levels of the church: local, regional and national.

Berit Weigand Berg is a pastor in the Evangelical-Lutheran Church of Denmark and presently works as a development consultant at Kirkefondet. She is currently a PhD student at the Protestant Theological University (PThU) in the Netherlands. She is involved in a research and development project focusing on the church of tomorrow, including issues regarding youth in church and baptism.

Steinunn Arnþrúður Björnsdóttir has a PhD in Practical Theology, with her interests centering on how churches respond to changing environments and conditions in their work and missions. She is an ordained minister in the Evangelical-Lutheran Church of Iceland and a sessional lecturer at the University of Iceland.

Ingeborg Dybvig was until recently the Director of Organizational Development for the Church Council of the Church of Norway. From 2015 to 2022, she held the position of Director of Communications for the Church Council. She holds a Master of Rhetoric from Aarhus University.

CONTRIBUTORS

Stein Ellinggard was until his retirement a parish priest in the Bakklandet and Lademoen congregation in Trondheim, Norway. In 2021, he received a one-year scholarship from the Bishops' Conference in the Church of Norway ("Olavsstipendet") to conduct research on drop-in baptism.

Magnus Evertsson works as an ecumenical officer at the Church of Sweden's head office in Uppsala. Before that, he served as a countryside parish priest for a long time. His doctoral thesis in New Testament Studies, presented at Lund University, explores Lukan parables and their reception in homiletic guidelines aimed at the Church of Sweden clergy.

Niels Henrik Gregersen is professor of systematic theology at the Faculty of Theology, director of the Center for Science and Faith at the University of Copenhagen, and a member of the Baptismal Commission of the Evangelical-Lutheran Church in Denmark (2023–2026). Among other endeavors, he coined the term "deep incarnation" and has written extensively on the concept.

Sigríður Guðmarsdóttir is professor of practical theology at Faculty of Theology and Religious Studies, University of Iceland in Reykjavík. Her research is in practical and constructive theology, which she considers from eco-theological, Indigenous, gendered, and Arctic perspectives.

Sunniva Gylver is bishop of the Diocese of Oslo in the Church of Norway. She has served as a parish pastor in several inner-city congregations in Oslo. For many years, she has participated in interfaith dialogue and has published several books. Gylver has been affiliated with MF Norwegian School of Theology, Religion and Society as a lecturer and researcher.

Anna Karin Hammar is a Lutheran minister in the Church of Sweden with a PhD in systematic theology from the University of Uppsala. Her international experience includes working for the World Council of Churches, in addition to close collaboration with Palestinian and South Sudanese Christian Communities.

Terje Hegertun is professor emeritus at MF Norwegian School of Theology, Religion and Society in Oslo, Norway. He has conducted research and published in the areas of Pentecostal theology, ecclesiology, ecumenism, and ethics.

CONTRIBUTORS

Harald Hegstad is professor of systematic theology at MF Norwegian School of Theology, Religion and Society in Oslo, Norway. His research and publications focus on ecclesiology, Lutheran dogmatics, and sacramental theology. He is presently the elected leader of the National Church Council of the Church of Norway.

Kristján Valur Ingólfsson is bishop emeritus of Skalholt, former assistant professor in practical theology at the University of Iceland, and chairman of the Liturgical Committee of the Evangelical-Lutheran Church of Iceland, a position he has held since 1997.

Jonas Adelin Jørgensen, PhD, currently serves as a secretary of the Interchurch Council of the Evangelical-Lutheran Church of Denmark. Previously, he was a lecturer at the University of Copenhagen and a general secretary of the Danish Mission Council. His special interests are missiology, ecumenism, and contextual theology in contemporary Christianity.

Laura Kokkonen, PhD, is a sociologist of religion. In her research, she has primarily focused on the marketing communication and branding used by Finnish Lutheran and Orthodox churches. Her other areas of interest include, for example, the effects of commercialism on contemporary beliefs.

Jyri Komulainen currently works as a chief specialist in the Church Institute for Research and Advanced Training in Helsinki. He is Docent of Dogmatics at the University of Helsinki and has extensively studied interfaith issues, with special emphasis on Hinduism and Catholic Christianity.

Ari Koponen is a Doctor of Theology and a visiting researcher at the University of Eastern Finland, Joensuu. His research focuses on philosophical theology, theological aesthetics, and ecological issues. He has represented the Orthodox Church of Finland in a variety of ecumenical settings.

Karen Marie Sø Leth-Nissen is a researcher at the Center for Pastoral Education and Research of the Evangelical-Lutheran Church of Denmark. She holds a PhD in Church Sociology and has conducted research on the changing relationship between churches and people. She served as a parish pastor for ten years.

CONTRIBUTORS

Pekka Metso is professor of practical theology at the University of Eastern Finland, Joensuu. He also holds the title of Docent of Practical Theology at the University of Helsinki. Ecumenical relations and engagements of the Orthodox Church of Finland are among his various research interests. Metso has represented the Orthodox Church of Finland on various domestic and international ecumenical occasions since the 1990s.

Tore Witsø Rafoss is a researcher at KIFO, Institute for Church, Religion, and Worldview Research. He obtained a PhD in Sociology from the University of Oslo. His research is focused on cultural sociology and religion. He has published on topics such as cultural trauma, religion, and non-religion in Norway, as well as societal and public responses to terrorism.

Hanna Salomäki is the Director of the Church Institute for Research and Advanced Training in Finland. Her main field of research is the sociology of religion, especially religiosity and religious movements.

Andreas Sandberg, PhD, is a human geography researcher at the Church of Sweden's Central Church Office Unit for Research and Analysis. His main areas of interest are church affiliation and socioeconomic and demographic changes in the Church of Sweden's membership body over time, with a special focus on religious customs and participation, as well as how the Church of Sweden's parishes react and adapt to the ever-changing environment surrounding them.

Lovisa Mienna Sjöberg is an associate professor of practical theology at VID Specialized University in Tromsø, Norway. She has conducted research in the field of Sámi theology and ethics. Her research interests and publications are primarily situated within the fields of ethics and theology in Sámi oral traditions and Sámi church history.

Ingegerd Sjölin holds a Doctor of Theology degree in the field of sociology of religion. She has conducted research on the Church of Sweden and has primarily published works related to baptism, communion, and worship. She is now retired but has previously served as a parish priest, the head of the Pastoral Institute in Lund, and as a theological secretary for the Church Handbook Project.

CONTRIBUTORS

Josephine Ganebo Skantz, MA, is a sociologist of religion and a former analyst at the Church of Sweden's Central Church Office Unit for Research and Analysis. She is currently pursuing a PhD in civil society reseach at Marie Cederschiöld University. Her research explores changes in church affiliation, religious practice, and the role of religion in civil society.

Karin Tillberg is the theological secretary of the service books for the Church of Sweden, at the Central Church Office. She received her PhD in Hebrew Bible Exegesis from Uppsala University. Her research interests focus on critical theory and extend across the fields of biblical studies and liturgy, the political and liturgical use of the Bible, and liturgy and language.

Introduction

Steinunn Arnþrúður Björnsdóttir, Magnus Evertsson, Harald Hegstad, Jonas Adelin Jørgensen, and Jyri Komulainen

In the Nordic region, five nation-states are united culturally and socially through a shared history. This common history has led to the development of five societies that share many similarities while also exhibiting strong differences in their characteristics. A common denominator in the Nordic region is the religious history. In the sixteenth century, the region became part of the Lutheran Reformation, a development that led to the emergence of Lutheran state churches in the later five nation-states. The position of Lutheran Christianity as the state religion corresponded to a majority and monopoly situation, where adherence to the Lutheran Church and participation in ecclesial rites were compulsory and even prescribed by law.

However, Finland is a special case, because with regard to its Eastern location, it has served as a meeting point for Latin and Orthodox traditions. During the nineteenth century, when Finland, with its Lutheran majority, belonged to the Russian Empire, the Lutheran Church even obtained an autonomous position in its relationship to the Orthodox sovereign. To this day, Finland has two national churches, Lutheran and Orthodox, although the latter embraces only one percent of the Finnish population.

Lutheranism's status as a monopoly religion belongs to the past. With one exception (Denmark), the state church system is also a part of history. Nordic societies today are religiously pluralistic, with a broad spectrum of beliefs and non-beliefs represented within a framework of religious freedom. In general, secularization has reduced the relative importance of church and religion in societies. Religious pluralization has, among other factors, been fostered by the influx of immigrants from all parts of the world.

Nevertheless, despite this increasing secularization and religious pluralization, the five former Lutheran state churches (still a state church in Denmark)—the Evangelical-Lutheran Church of Iceland (Þjóðkirkjan), the Church of Norway (Den norske kirke), the Church of Sweden (Svenska kyrkan), the Evangelical-Lutheran Church of Finland (Suomen evankelis-luterilainen kirkko), and the Evangelical-Lutheran Church in Denmark (Folkekirken)—still hold a majority position as faith communities, meaning that more than half of the population in all the five countries are members of one of these churches. The churches still have a visible role in the life of Nordic societies, which includes their custodianship of historical church buildings and thus of a national cultural history and identity. In such roles, the churches are often referred to as "folk churches" by themselves and others. The exact content of this concept might vary according to the context, but it often refers to the ideal of being a church open to everyone, with low participation thresholds. How this ideal might be balanced with the need to have a distinct identity in a religiously pluralistic setting is frequently debated.

Traditionally, most newborns in Nordic societies were baptized as infants and thus became part of the church early on. Letting one's child be baptized was, until recently, the dominant tradition in all the Nordic countries. For a newborn to be baptized not only implied becoming a member of the church, but also a part of society. Free church movements, with a Baptist understanding of "believer's baptism," challenged the tradition of infant baptism, even though they still practiced baptism at a later age. Of course, a growing number of adherents to non-Christian religions did not practice baptism. An increasing number of people with a non-religious worldview also weakened the baptismal tradition. However, in recent years, there has been a growing tendency for church members themselves to choose not to baptize their children. This development poses a severe challenge to Nordic Lutheran churches. It raises questions not only about the position of baptism, but also of the churches themselves, as baptism is the main entry point for membership.

Churches have met this challenge in various ways. For instance, churches have analyzed the factors behind their own development, communication strategies, baptismal practices, and theologies. This development has also been the subject of social scientific and empirical research. Between 2020 and 2022, the Nordic folk churches conducted a joint study project, entitled "Baptism in Times of Change." The project aimed to gather and analyze existing materials and practices and stimulate joint reflection, discussion, and ecumenical learning in the Nordic region among researchers, practitioners, and church leaders. This was done by developing an extensive annotated bibliography of relevant material related to baptism in the Nordic region that had been disseminated over the last two decades. The project also included a series of webinars focusing on various sub-themes. Materials from the project are publicly available at https://churchesintimesofchange.org/. A set of recommendations from a concluding consultation is also printed as an appendix in the present volume. Not only was this study a joint Nordic project, but it was also a cooperative effort of the Lutheran World Federation (LWF), in the sense that the participating churches were all Nordic members of the LWF, and the outcome of the project fed into an LWF study process on Lutheran identity.

As a follow-up to this project, the research group members took the initiative to compile the present book. Taking the role of editors, they invited a number of authors to contribute to exploring developments in the role of baptism in Nordic folk churches. These authors were asked to address various aspects of this theme based on their specific areas of expertise.

The book is divided into four sections, the first of which analyzes the present circumstances based on empirical data. In the first chapter of the book, *Josephine Ganebo Skantz* and *Andreas Sandberg* evaluate the statistical data related to baptism in Nordic Lutheran churches. Among other factors, they examine the effects of the COVID-19 pandemic on baptismal numbers. The other chapters in this section examine a variety of factors behind this development. Why do parents allow their children to be baptized, or why won't they? As these chapters show, we are here talking about changing cultural and religious patterns. While *Tore Witsø Rafoss* presents results from an empirical study from Norway, *Karen Marie Sø Leth-Nissen* reports data from Denmark, and *Hanna Salomäki* from Finland. In her chapter on developments in Sweden, *Ingegerd Sjölin* interprets this recent trajectory from a longer historical perspective, focusing on how changing conceptions of the child have affected views on baptism.

In a changing cultural and religious context, churches are adapting their practices related to baptism by revising old ones and introducing new alternatives. The second section on practices analyzes some of these adaptations and innovations. The most basic baptismal practice of all is, of course, the baptismal liturgy itself. In her article, *Karin Tillberg* performs a comparative analysis of liturgies in Nordic churches, focusing on the role of the gift motif. A question that has been discussed in recent years is whether churches should offer a blessing ceremony for children who are not baptized, even if the parents want them to be connected to the church. In their work, *Steinunn Arnþrúður Björnsdóttir* and *Kristján Valur Ingólfsson* present a ritual for infant blessing developed in the Icelandic church, while also arguing that using such a practice does not reduce the importance of baptism itself. Pentecostal theologian *Terje Hegertun* provides an ecumenical perspective in his contribution to this section, arguing for a more flexible approach to such blessings in churches baptizing infants.

Of course, not everyone is baptized as a child, and the baptism of youth and adults has continued to become more common. This is especially relevant to processes of confirmation, in which unbaptized youth are baptized before they are confirmed. In this vein, *Berit Weigand Berg* reports on a study of pre-confirmation baptism and discusses how best to avoid a situation in which the baptism becomes a minor event compared to confirmation. In recent years, "drop-in-baptisms" have even been introduced in Nordic churches. Through such an event, people who wish for themselves or their children to be baptized may show up without prior registration. In light of this phenomenon, *Stein Ellinggard* reports on a study of drop-in-baptisms in Norway. To round out this section, it is essential to consider how the practice of baptism in a culturally and religiously pluralistic context challenges basic presuppositions in traditional ecclesiological practices. In her chapter, *Sunniva Gylver* draws on her experiences as a pastor in inner-city Oslo and argues for the importance of dialogue regarding baptismal and ecclesial practices.

Decreasing baptismal numbers have led churches to reconsider and revise their strategies and means of communicating about baptism. This is the theme of the third section on communication. The first chapter is written by *Laura Hanna Kokkonen*, who analyzes communication about baptism on the part of the Finnish Lutheran Church. The authors of the following two chapters have themselves been responsible for communication strategies in their own respective contexts: *Lena Andersson* in the Lund diocese in Sweden and *Ingeborg Dybvig* in the Church of Norway.

The last section of the book deals with baptismal theology. How could a theology of baptism be developed that is relevant to the contemporary situation without losing its rootedness in inherited Christian insights? In the first chapter, *Harald Hegstad* points to the understanding of baptism as a sign and argues that it could be a possible starting point for developing a Lutheran and ecumenical baptismal theology for today. An essential insight that emerges in subsequent chapters is the necessity of connecting baptismal theology to the ecological challenges of our time. A further insight is the relevance of indigenous theologies in this context. In her chapter, *Sigriður Guðmarsdóttir* emphasizes the connection between the water used in baptism and the holiness of all waters. Later, *Lovisa Mienna Sjöberg* reflects on name giving traditions among the indigenous Sámi people in the context of baptism and connects it with the task of mourning an unborn, dead-born or unbaptized child. The ecological crisis is also the background of the following chapter by *Anna Karin Hammar*, who argues for a new narrative within baptismal theology rooted in a sacramental worldview and a theology of creation.

In the next chapter, *Niels Henrik Gregersen* shows how baptismal theology of baptism is not only about the *what* of baptism, but also the *who*. Here, he warns of the danger of faith perfectionism and argues for a theology of baptism that includes unfinished faith. The last contribution in the book is a reminder that a Lutheran theology of baptism must be developed within an ecumenical horizon. In their chapter, *Pekka Metso* and *Ari Koponen* discuss the role of baptism as an ecclesiological and ecumenical demarcation in the context of Orthodox theology when encountering Lutheranism in Finland.

Working through these various chapters has shown us that baptism is not an isolated theme, but rather a prism of the many issues that churches have to deal with in today's societies. The changing religious and cultural contexts in Nordic societies have challenged the churches' own understandings of their respective identities and missions in profound ways. Such challenges should not be isolated from internal questions that the churches must consider. Rather than leading to self-centeredness, churches should ask how they can best contribute to a sustainable future for the planet and its inhabitants, and how this might be rooted in God's gifts of baptism.

Part I

Empirical Studies

1

Baptism in Numbers in the Nordic Lutheran Churches 2009–2022

Andreas Sandberg *and* Josephine Ganebo Skantz

THE PURPOSE OF THIS chapter is to take an overarching look at the quantitative development in baptism rates in the Nordic countries from 2009 to 2022, with a focus on several indicators for the development in these regions, as well as the effects of the COVID-19 pandemic in Sweden, Norway, Denmark, and Finland.[1] To achieve this objective, comparable statistics were analyzed to determine the similarities and differences in how the tradition of baptism has developed during this time on both the national and regional levels in these countries. With baptism acting as a requirement for membership in Nordic Lutheran churches, rather than parents' affiliation alone, the practice of baptism has become intrinsically tied to future trends in church membership. This chapter also contains a discussion of previous research into parents' motives for baptizing and the importance of religious ceremonies in marking the birth of a child, with the aim of nuancing the possible reasons behind decreasing baptism rates in Nordic Lutheran churches.[2]

---

1. The baptism rate was calculated by dividing the number of baptisms by the number of live births within a specified area for a certain year.

2. Iceland is only included in the overarching comparisons of membership and baptism rates. This is in part due to lack of comparable data with the other Nordic

Nordic churches are currently facing declining membership rates, as the influx of new members through baptism and reentering or joining from another church does not keep up with the numbers of those choosing to exit the church or passing away. This means that membership rates will in turn affect the number of baptisms that take place. The key to understanding the future membership trends of Nordic churches therefore lies in examining the development of baptisms. Though in 2022, Sweden saw the lowest rate in membership of the Church of Sweden, comprising 53 percent of the total population, a look at the decreases in membership over 2010–2022 show that Sweden's 26 percentage-point decrease was matched by a decrease in Norway of 21 percentage points, Iceland of 23 percentage points, and Finland of 17 percentage points (2010–2021). Denmark stands out with a decrease of only 10 percentage points over the same time period (see Figure 1).[3]

To produce a reliable comparison between the countries, a number of key variables need to be standardized. Even though the time of year at which annual baptism rates are recorded varies, this is irrelevant, as the important variable here is changes in baptism rates over time in the different countries, rather than changes in each year. This same issue emerges with the COVID-19 pandemic, as the focus should be on the overall changes in development in a particular country compared to previous years. The standard measure of the baptism rate in all countries was the total number of baptisms in a year divided by all live births during the same year. While a comparison of these baptism rates with those of affiliated live births would have added an interesting nuance to the comparison, the lack of cohesion in the available statistics does not make a just comparison possible at this time.[4] The statistics used have been collected from a number of sources affiliated with the different

---

countries and (in part) the small population of Iceland, which makes a diocesan breakdown essentially impossible.

3. Danmarks statistik, "Medlemmer af folkekirken"; Suomen evankelis-luterilainen kirkko, "Medlemsstatistik 1999–2022"; Statistics Iceland, "Populations by religious and life stance organizations 1998–2023"; Statistiska sentralbyrån: Statistics Norway, "Den norske kirke; Medlem og tilhørige i Dnk i prosent av antall innbyggere (prosent)"; Svenska kyrkan, "Svenska kyrkan i siffror."

4. The Church of Sweden's baptism statistics include the baptism rate of live births with at least one parent who is a member of the church, in addition to the rate among live births overall. This latter rate is not easily accessible for the other Nordic churches.

Nordic churches, and in this chapter, data for all five Nordic countries are presented for the years 2009–2022.⁵

Figure 1. Church members by percentage of population in Nordic countries 2009–2022. Sources: *Danmarks statistik, Statistics Iceland, Statistics Norway, Suomen evankelis-luterilainen kirkko, Svenska kyrkan*

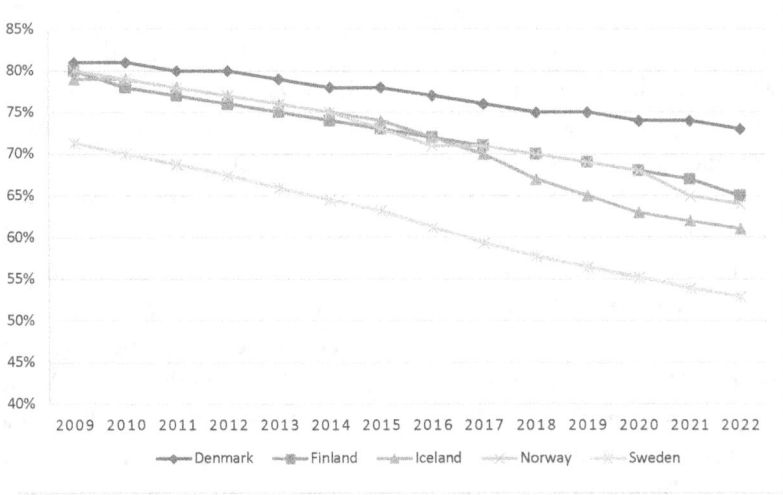

MOTIVES TO BAPTIZE OR NOT BAPTIZE ONE'S CHILD

The influences behind the decision of whether or not to baptize one's child have been the subject of several Nordic studies. In the field of baptism and the religiosity of young adults, two main factors appear to weigh heavily on both the decision to baptize one's child and to even remain a member of the church at all: whether an individual perceives themselves as Christian, and whether they have a positive impression of the church in question.⁶ This positive impression is primarily formed when the person comes into contact with the church through activities aimed at children and confirmation reading.⁷ Participation in church activities es-

---

5. Björnsdóttir, "Baptism in Iceland"; Danmarks statistik, "Kirkelige handlinger"; Statistiska sentralbyrån: Statistics Norway, "Døpte i prosent av antall fødte (prosent)"; Suomen evankelis-luterilainen kirkko, "Medlemsstatistik 1999-2022"; Svenska kyrkan, "Svenska kyrkan i siffror."

6. Høeg and Gresaker, *Når det rokkes*.

7. Nielsen, "Changing Patterns?"

sentially leads to an increase in the degree of perceived participation.[8] In Norway, a majority of respondents in a survey covered by a 2015 report claimed that the child becoming part of the church was an important factor influencing the choice to baptize, something that ties in with the previous discussion of the intrinsic relationship between baptism and membership in Nordic churches.

While a weak relationship with the church is a natural cause for not baptizing one's child,[9] other factors may influence the decision to abstain, such as a confirmed parent with a weak relationship choosing not to baptize because of the second parent's desire to refrain.[10] The importance of a strong relationship with the church, paired with a sense of belonging to one's parish, serves as a strong indicator of continued membership, which in turn affects the decision to baptize.[11] In both Finland and Sweden, members of the church are more likely than the general public to indicate the importance of marking the birth of a child with a religious ceremony, with 73 percent of members reporting such sentiments compared to 60 percent of the public in Finland (2019), and 51 percent of members in Sweden compared to 39 percent of the public (2022). In Norway, 53 percent of members reported such feelings in 2012, an interesting fact to consider given Norway's higher baptism rate compared to Sweden. Survey studies from Denmark, Norway, and Sweden all indicate that tradition-based motives are more common than religious ones. Baptism can be conceived of as a pleasant tradition, a custom in one's family, or a beautiful ceremony, each of which served as a tradition-based motive in these surveys.[12] Meanwhile, it was less common for the decision to baptize to be based on social pressure from the extended family or on religious motives.[13] However, one Swedish study did discuss the framing of religion and tradition as a juxtaposition and argued that tradition does not necessarily equate to a secular motive, but rather serves as a means of leveraging tradition to frame

---

8. Klintborg and Ganebo Skantz, "Gudstjänst," 47–64.
9. Høeg and Gresaker, *Når det rokkes*.
10. Høeg and Gresaker, *Når det rokkes*.
11. Niemelä, "No Longer." Bromander and Jonsson, *Medlemmar i rörelse*.
12. Høeg and Gresaker, *Når det rokkes*.

13. Examples of religious motives being: Having a Christian faith, wishing for the child to grow up to be Christian, and I believe that baptism gives the child God's protection.

and discuss religion in the secular context.¹⁴ This is crucial to consider, as motivations for religious ceremonies become more centered on personal choice and preference rather than tradition, with Sweden seeing a trend toward rural confirmation candidates reporting individualized preferences that have previously been more common in urban areas.[15] With confirmation rates seeing a faster decrease in rural areas, paired with the knowledge that regional baptism traditions and whether the parents are confirmed are the strongest indicators of whether a child will be baptized, it is likely to assume that regional differences in baptism traditions are also likely to decrease in the future.[16]

BAPTISM DEVELOPMENT IN THE NORDIC COUNTRIES 2009–2022

The trend of declining baptism rates is universal among the Nordic countries, with all five seeing an average decrease between 1.5 and 1.9 percentage points per year between 2009 and 2022 (see Figure 2). In absolute numbers, this equates to a decrease from 208,000 baptisms in 2009 to barely 146,000 baptisms in 2019 in total for all five countries. Until 2017, the differences in the decrease rate were relatively small, but in 2018 and 2019 the decrease rate slowed down in Denmark while continuing to persist in the other four counties (see Figure 2). The outbreak of the COVID-19 pandemic in 2020 and subsequent restrictions on public gatherings saw a steep decrease, with only 114,000 baptisms taking place in Nordic countries that year, with Sweden seeing the most drastic decrease.[17] A certain recuperation was observed in 2021 and 2022, though to varying degrees in the different countries, with Finland's recovery being weaker compared to the other Nordic countries. Even if the long-term trend of declining baptism rates is relatively uniform, the differences between the countries remain high and have not changed much over the last decade. In 2009, there was a difference of 27 percentage points between Denmark and Sweden, a change that has essentially remained unchanged 13 years later. At the same time, Finland has exhibited a somewhat sharper decrease compared to Norway's slower. This paired with a slow recuperation for Finland after the pandemic,

14. Sandberg et al., *Dop i förändring*, 122.
15. Fransson, *Tradition, eget val eller vänners?*
16. Fransson and Ganebo Skantz, *Trender i Svenska kyrkans konfirmandverksamhet*.
17. Baptism rates for Iceland are not available beyond 2019.

compared to Norway's quite successful one, contributed to a nearly equal baptism rate in the two countries by 2022. Furthermore, Denmark's baptism rate, which is similar to that of Finland, has seen a successful post-pandemic recuperation, leading to a greater difference between the two of 14 percentage points in 2022. Up until 2018, Iceland saw a developing baptism rate similar to that of Norway; the baptism rate had decreased from 68 percent in 2009 to 52 percent in both countries. However, as shown in Figure 2, the negative effects of the COVID-19 pandemic in Iceland are highly visible, as it had a much greater impact than that seen in not only Norway, but also Denmark and Finland.

However, this method of comparing baptism traditions in Nordic countries is flawed due to the considerable demographic differences between them. Nevertheless, these differences in baptism rates can be partially explained by comparing the sizes of their populations of foreign origin, which in turn affect the percentage of the population affiliated with the church and in turn baptizing their children. Since the Nordic countries have seen a great variation in immigration trends, the extent of which has varied significantly over the course of the twentieth and twenty-first centuries, the number of children born with an affiliation to the Evangelical-Lutheran Church can be expected to, in theory, vary a lot between the countries. Accordingly, a more comparable measure would be the baptism rates of church-affiliated live births, with at least one parent being a member of the church. Therefore, the discrepancy between, for example, Sweden, with an affiliation rate of 53 percent of the population, and Finland, with a corresponding rate of 67 percent with the Evangelical-Lutheran Church, would be significant when compared to baptism rates based on all births, which are unfortunately not available.[18]

---

18. For comparison in 2019, 65 percent of all live births with at least one parent being a member of the Church of Sweden were baptized, compared to 40 percent of all live births in the same year.

Figure 2. Percentage baptized among all live births in Nordic countries 2009–2022. Sources: Danmarks statistik, Statistics Iceland, Statistics Norway, Suomen evankelis-luterilainen kirkko, Svenska kyrkan

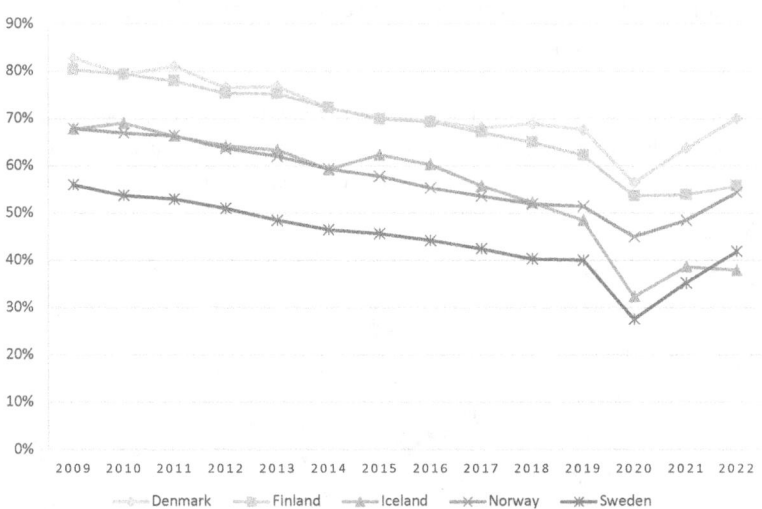

DEVELOPMENT DURING THE COVID-19 PANDEMIC

The role of the baptism as a social tradition in many Nordic countries became highly noticeable when the national restrictions on public gatherings were introduced at the start of the COVID-19 pandemic in 2020. Figure 3 shows the development of baptism rates in the different countries, where the impact of the introduction and subsequent lifting of restrictions can be seen in 2020–2022. Denmark and Sweden stand out as the two countries where the consequences of the restrictions were most noticeable, especially during the first year of the pandemic, where in both countries, the baptism rate fell by 12 percentage points during this year. In Finland and Norway, the decrease was more limited at eight and six percentage points, respectively. In the following years of 2021 and 2022, the baptism rates recuperated in both relative and absolute numbers in all four countries. The extent of this recuperation has, however, varied—with the exceptions of Finland and Iceland, still not having returned to the rates of 2019 in 2022, while the other three countries saw increased birthrates as early as 2021.[19] The development was continually

19. This increase in percentage becomes indicative of recuperations from the previous year, since the children that would have been baptized, the previous year would

strong in Denmark, Norway, and Sweden, where by 2022, baptism rates had recuperated to levels on par with those seen in the years leading up the pandemic. However, such rates increased only marginally in Finland, a nation that in 2022 still found themselves six percentage points below their own 2019 level.

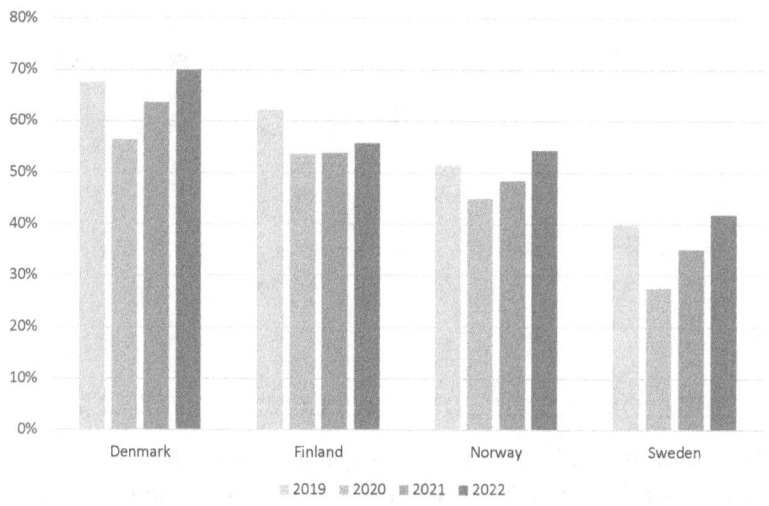

Figure 3. Percentage baptized among all live births in Denmark, Finland, Norway, and Sweden 2019–2022. Sources: *Danmarks statistik, Statistics Norway, Suomen evankelis-luterilainen kirkko, Svenska kyrkan*

Another way to showcase the consequences of the COVID-19 restrictions is to study the development of baptisms in absolute numbers and compare these to the simple prognosis of expected baptism rates if the pandemic had not happened. Between 2009 and 2019, there was a total decrease of 63,000 baptisms in the Nordic countries,[20] which translates to roughly a 30 percent reduction. The Nordic countries saw an average decrease of 3.5 percent per year in the years leading up to the pandemic. This rate varied quite a bit between the counties, with Denmark seeing an average decrease of 2.2 percent per year and Finland 5.2 percent. The number of baptisms decreasing more rapidly in Finland compared to the other countries is most likely due to, in part, to the significant decrease in child births during this period, which declined from

---

have been included in the following instead.

20. Iceland is not included in these numbers.

roughly 60,000 to 45,000 live births between 2009 and 2019, a decrease of 25 percent. Similarly, although to a lesser extent, Norway has also seen a decrease in the number of children born. Denmark and Sweden, in contrast, have seen a relatively stagnant development during the same period, varying only by a few percentage points.

By comparing the development in baptism rates in relative numbers, the differences between the countries become clearer. In Denmark, the baptism rate has decreased by an average of 1.5 percentage points per year, Finland by 1.8 percentage points, and Norway and Sweden by 1.6 percentage points, respectively. Assuming that changes in the baptism rate were consistent during the years 2020–2022, a simple prognosis shows how many baptisms would have taken place if not for the COVID-19 restrictions. In Figure 4, the relationship between the baptisms that actually took place and those that would have taken place during regular circumstances is presented. It can be discerned that the number of baptisms was most heavily affected in Sweden, where the executed baptisms accounted for only 72 percent of the predicted number for 2020. In the other three countries, this percentage ranged between 86 and 90. Even with this method of mirroring the development of the baptism rate during the pandemic years, Finland stands out as the country where recovery has been the weakest in the following years, even if the initial loss during the first year of the pandemic was relatively minor compared to the one in Sweden. In Sweden, though, the recuperation has been much stronger, particularly during 2022, when the number of executed baptisms exceeded the prognosis for that same year by 20 percent. In summarizing the development over the past three years, however, we see that Norway alone has seen a recuperation strong enough to both reach and exceed the number of baptisms that would have been executed according to the prognosis (see Figure 5). This stands in contrast to the recuperation in Sweden, for example, which was still not strong enough by 2022 to compensate for the massive drop seen in 2020. Expressed in absolute numbers, roughly 7,000 expected baptisms never took place in Sweden during this time. In Finland, the corresponding number of lost baptisms is 5,900, and in Denmark, 1,900. In Norway, however, the number of executed baptisms exceeded the prognosed number by almost 1,600.

PART I: EMPIRICAL STUDIES

Figure 4. Percentage of executed baptisms compared to estimated baptisms in Denmark, Finland, Norway, and Sweden for 2020, 2021, and 2022. *Sources: Danmarks statistik, Statistics Norway, Suomen evankelis-luterilainen kirkko, Svenska kyrkan*

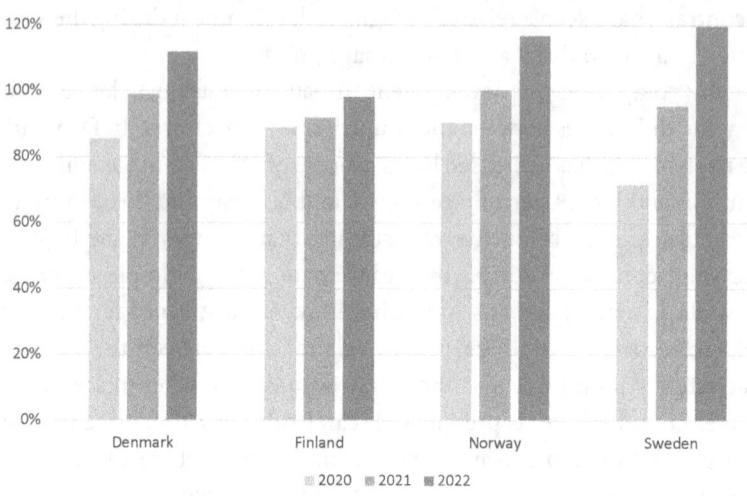

Figure 5. Percentage of executed baptisms compared to estimated baptisms in all of Denmark, Finland, Norway, and Sweden 2020–2022. *Sources: Danmarks statistik, Statistics Norway, Suomen evankelis-luterilainen kirkko, Svenska kyrkan*

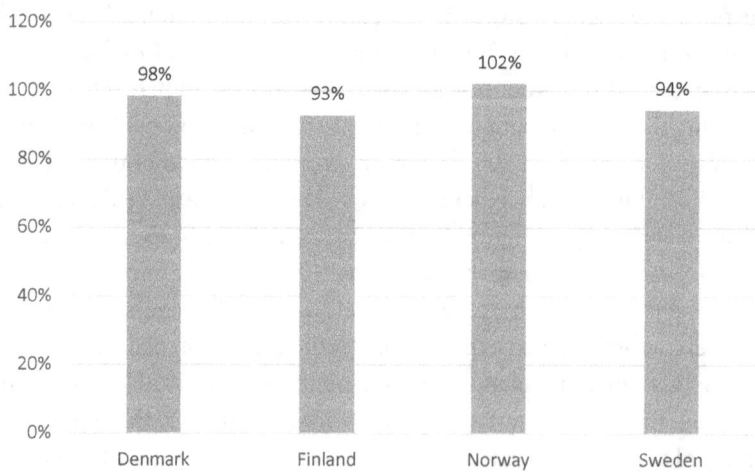

It can thus be concluded that the differences in adherence to baptism traditions that have been observed over a considerable time appear to be unchanged. There was still a 26 percentage-point difference between Denmark and Sweden in 2022, one that was practically the same a decade ago. The development during the years dominated by the COVID-19 pandemic, 2020–2022, affected the countries in somewhat dissimilar ways. In the inter-Nordic comparison, the weaker development in Finland has led to Norway catching up in terms of baptism frequency in these years. Beyond this, the Nordic countries are generally characterized by declining baptism trends, the differences between which are relatively small.

REGIONAL DIFFERENCES WITHIN THE NORDIC COUNTRIES

As discussed in the previous section, there are considerable differences between the countries in terms of the annual baptism rate, and behind the statistics presented at the national level are significant regional differences in each of the four countries.[21] Figure 6 shows the highest and lowest baptism rates among the dioceses in each of the four countries. Expressed in percentage points, the regional differences are the greatest in Norway, where there is a 43 percentage point difference between the Oslo and Møre dioceses. However, Sweden, with the lowest baptism rate among the Nordic countries, showed a significantly smaller difference between the dioceses with the highest and lowest baptism rates. Common among all four countries is that the baptism rate is the lowest in urban areas, while the highest rates occur in dioceses that predominantly cover rural areas. The large variations in percentages between the different dioceses are most likely a reflection of the significant variation not only concerning the tradition of baptism between the different dioceses, but also in the religious customs more generally within those areas. However, the differences are also a reflection of the demographic shifts between rural and urban areas. The percentage of the population with immigrant backgrounds, who, for obvious reasons, are rarely members of the church, is higher in the urban and capital areas compared to the rest of the country in all four cases.

---

21. Regional numbers were not available for Iceland.

Figure 6. Number of baptisms in percentage of live births by diocese, with the highest and lowest percentages of baptisms, in Denmark, Finland, Norway, and Sweden in 2019. Sources: Danmarks statistik, Statistics Norway, Suomen evankelis-luterilainen kirkko, Svenska kyrkan

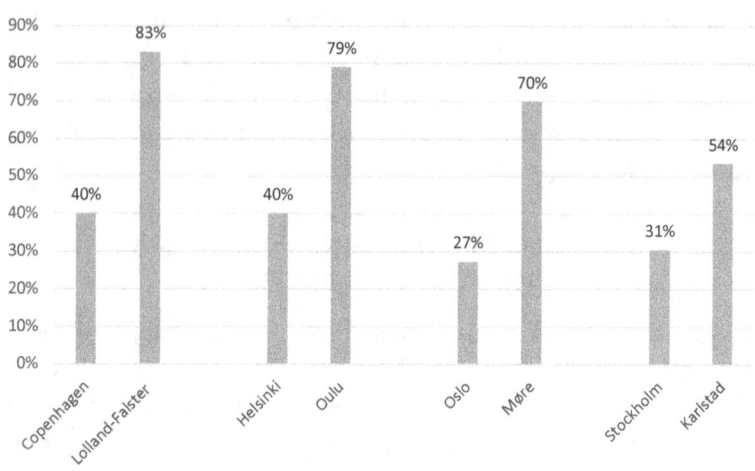

REGIONAL DIFFERENCES DURING THE COVID-19 PANDEMIC IN 2020–2022

The restrictions on public gatherings that were introduced at the outbreak of the COVID-19 pandemic in 2020 had different effects on baptism rates on both national and regional levels in Nordic countries, with the most drastic decreases in baptism rates being observed in the capital areas. The highest decrease was in Stockholm the diocese, where the number of baptisms in 2020 was only 66 percent of the amount forecasted for the year, translating to a 34 percent decrease from the year before. A normal year, based on the development over the last decade, would have seen roughly 7,300 baptisms in the Stockholm diocese in 2020; instead, this number was 4,800. In absolute numbers, 2,500 baptisms never took place because of the restrictions. Helsinki and Copenhagen also saw a drastic decrease in baptisms, with 21 and 22 percent fewer being performed compared to the prognosis for 2020, respectively. Oslo, in contrast, saw a less drastic decrease at only 11 percent. In rural dioceses, the effect of the pandemic was more limited, though the Karlstad diocese did not follow this trend in Sweden (see Figure 7). The Møre diocese in Norway seemed to have experienced very limited effects of the pandemic's restrictions, exhibiting only a small decrease of three percent during 2020 that was compensated by a strong recovery during 2021 and 2022. However, urban dioceses did see a recovery following the pandemic years, when the baptism rates exceeded the prognosis for 2022 in all dioceses, except Helsinki. Overall, though, it was only in the Norwegian dioceses where the total number of baptisms for 2020–2022 exceeded the prognosis for the period under normal circumstances (see Figure 8). The Danish and Swedish dioceses were close to this level, with 94–98 percent of baptisms being performed compared to the prognosis for these three years.

In conclusion, pandemic restrictions have affected developments in the number of baptisms to varying extents on both the regional and national levels for the four countries. Based on the number of baptisms not performed, Helsinki had it worst, with 1,600 expected baptisms not being performed during this three-year period. In Stockholm, roughly 1,100 baptisms were not performed, and in Copenhagen, there were barely 600. Oslo stands out as a clear exception in this context, with roughly 600 more baptisms than the prognosis for the same period. Even in the dioceses outside of the capital regions, a significant number of baptisms were likely never carried out due to the pandemic, primarily for dioceses in Sweden and Finland. In Denmark, the decrease was relatively low in most cases, while the strong development in Norway contributed to more baptisms than expected, based on the previous decade's development.

PART I: EMPIRICAL STUDIES

Figure 7. Number of baptisms in percentages of estimated baptisms by diocese, with the highest and lowest percentages of baptisms, in Denmark, Finland, Norway, and Sweden in 2020, 2021, and 2022. *Sources: Danmarks statistik, Statistics Norway, Suomen evankelis-luterilainen kirkko, Svenska kyrkan*

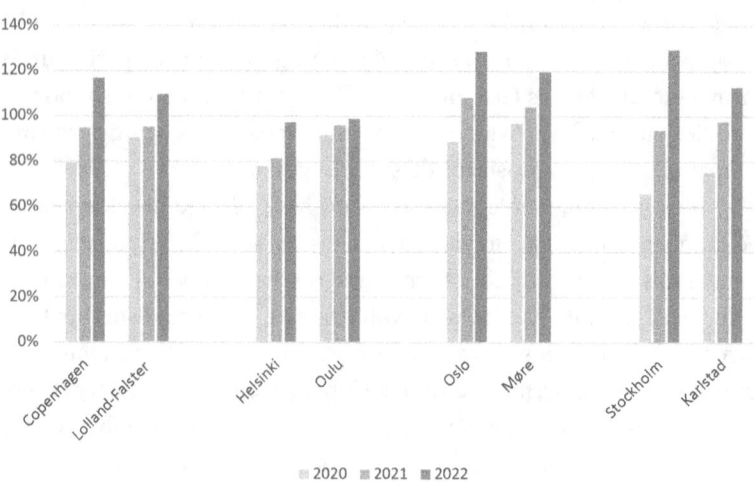

Figure 8. Number of baptisms in percentages of estimated baptisms by diocese, with the highest and lowest percentages of baptisms, in all of Denmark, Finland, Norway, and Sweden in 2020–2022. *Sources: Danmarks statistik, Statistics Norway, Suomen evankelis-luterilainen kirkko, Svenska kyrkan*

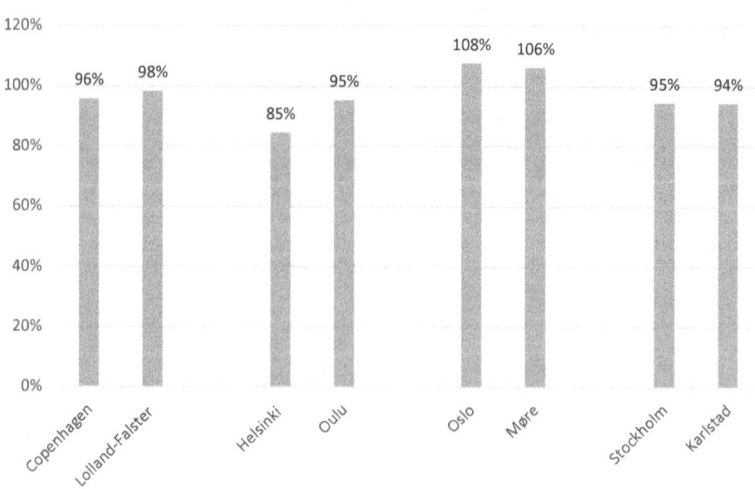

CONCLUSION

Essentially, it can be assumed that developments in baptism rates in Nordic countries are indicative of future developments in church membership. Sweden spearheaded the secular development when the baptism rate of all children born fell below 50 percent as early as 2012, meaning that in 2022 the choice to baptize one's child had been a minority behavior for 10 years. In the same year of 2022 the membership rate for men in Sweden dropped below the 50 percent mark, a percentage that no other Nordic countries had passed. However, the current trends show that this appears to remain only a matter of time, with Sweden only being 10–20 years ahead. The COVID-19 pandemic might have sped things along, with only Norway seeing a full recuperation of the baptism rate compared to the prognosis. Finland, in particular, has seen a delay or possibly a lack of recuperation. Furthermore, the analysis shows that the regional differences support previous studies showing that urban areas exhibit weaker baptism traditions, with the geographical trends being a stronger indicator of secular cultures compared to the more well-established Christian traditions in rural areas. In summary, the baptism trends for the different dioceses and countries can serve as indicators of both the baptism preferences of new parents and the religious culture overall, though Sweden is already seeing diminishing differences in confirmation traditions between urban and rural areas. This indicates that geographic differences in traditions of pastoral services might be diminishing with urban traditions taking precedence. Strong regional traditions are not necessarily a guarantee for future baptism rates, but the relatively strong recuperation in Denmark, Norway, and Sweden does show that for some parents, baptizing one's child is worth the wait.

BIBLIOGRAPHY

Björnsdóttir, Steinunn Arnþrúður. "Baptism in Iceland: Development in Baptism in the Last Two Decades." *Churches in Times of Change*. https://churchesintimesofchange.org/background/baptism-in-iceland.

Bromander, Jonas, and Pernilla Jonsson. *Medlemmar i rörelse: En studie av förändringar i Svenska kyrkans medlemskår*. Uppsala: Svenska kyrkan, 2018.

Danmarks statistik. "Kirkelige handlinger." https://www.dst.dk/da/Statistik/emner/borgere/folkekirke/kirkelige-handlinger.

———. "Medlemmer af folkekirken." https://www.dst.dk/da/Statistik/emner/borgere/folkekirke/medlemmer-af-folkekirken.

PART I: EMPIRICAL STUDIES

Fransson, Sara. "Tradition, eget val eller vänners?—ungas förändrade motiv och förväntningar." In *Konfirmation i förändringens tid: En rapport om konfirmander och ledare 2007–2022*, edited by Sara Fransson. Stockholm: Svenska kyrkan, 2023.

Fransson, Sara, and Josephine Ganebo Skantz. "Trender i Svenska kyrkans konfirmandverksamhet." In *Konfirmation i förändringens tid: En rapport om konfirmander och ledare 2007–2022*, edited by Sara Fransson. Stockholm: Svenska kyrkan, 2023.

Høeg, Ida Marie, and Ann Kristin Gresaker. *Når det rokkes ved tradisjon og tilhørighet.* Oslo: KIFO Rapport nr 2, 2015.

Klintborg, Caroline, and Josephine Ganebo Skantz. "Gudstjänst, unga vuxna och delaktighet." *Nyckeln till Svenska kyrkan* (2022) 47–64.

Nielsen, Marie Vejrup. "Changing Patterns? Occasional Consumers of New Activities in Old Churches." *Nordic Journal of Religion and Society* 28 (2015) 137–53.

Niemelä, Kati. "No Longer Believing in Belonging: A Longitudinal Study of Finnish Generation Y from Confirmation Experience to Church-Leaving." *Social Compass* 62 (2015) 172–86.

Sandberg, Andreas, and Josephine Ganebo Skantz, and Ingegerd Sjölin. *Dop i förändring.* Uppsala: Svenska kyrkan, 2019.

Statistics Iceland. "Religious Organisations: Populations by Religious and Life Stance Organizations 1998–2023. The Evangelical Lutheran Church of Iceland." https://px.hagstofa.is/pxen/pxweb/en/Samfelag/Samfelag__menning__5_trufelog__trufelog/MAN10001.px/table/tableViewLayout1/?rxid=2578fdfc-a5c6-43c5-b247-7a419a6a03d3.

Statistiska sentralbyrån: Statistics Norway. "Den norske kirke: 12025: Utvalgte nøkkeltall kirke, etter region, statistikkvariabel og år. Døpte i prosent av antall fødte (prosent)." https://www.ssb.no/statbank/table/12025/tableViewLayout1/.

———. "Den norske kirke: 12025: Utvalgte nøkkeltall kirke, etter region, statistikkvariabel og år. Medlem og tilhørige i Dnk i prosent av antall innbyggere (prosent)." https://www.ssb.no/statbank/table/12025/tableViewLayout1/.

Suomen evankelis-luterilainen kirkko. "Medlemsstatistik 1999–2022." https://www.kirkontilastot.fi/viz.php?id=239.

Svenska kyrkan. "Svenska kyrkan i siffror." https://www.svenskakyrkan.se/statistik

Witsø Rafoss, Tore. *Et religiøst landskap i endring.* Oslo: KIFO Rapport nr 2, 2016.

2

Infant Baptism in an Individualized Culture
Examining the Reasons Why Norwegian Parents Baptize Their Children

Tore Witsø Rafoss

THE BACKGROUND FOR THIS chapter is the decline in the number of children being baptized. In 1970, 96 percent of all newborn Norwegian children were baptized in the Church of Norway. However, 52 years later—in 2022—the number had decreased to 54 percent. This is a dramatic societal and religious change in a relatively short period, which can actually be considered a symptom of a larger trend: the secularization process that is taking place in Norway, Scandinavia, and several other parts of the world.

This chapter will focus on why Norwegian parents today choose to baptize their children. Using unique survey data from 2019, I will examine this issue in some detail, and then raise some questions about the future of infant baptism in a culture that increasingly emphasizes the importance of the autonomous individual.

BACKGROUND AND RELEVANT RESEARCH

A large amount of scholarly literature exists on religious changes in the Western world, much of which is occupied with how and to what degree religion is changing or declining. The so-called "secularization thesis" states that societies, as they become modernized, will necessarily become more secularized. This thesis has been heavily debated and criticized.[1] Nevertheless, there is no doubt a strong historical momentum toward secularization in many countries, including Norway. The steady decrease in the percentage of children being baptized is in itself a strong indicator of this. As we can see from Figure 1, since 1960, there has been a continual decrease in the percentage of newborns in Norway who have been baptized.

This decrease in national numbers is *partly* a result of immigration to Norway. Many immigrants come from countries where the majority of the population belongs to non-Christian religions, such as Islam, Buddhism, or Hinduism. There is, of course, no reason to believe that a significant number of these immigrants will choose a Christian baptism for their children. However, the influx of immigrants can only explain *some* of the decisions not to baptize. A more important reason is probably the fact that Norwegians in the period since 1960 have become less religious[2]—but this is not the whole story either. Another key factor to consider is that people have started to believe in and practice religion in a different, more individualistic manner. Much research points to the fact that it has become more commonplace to think that one should not "blindly" follow church doctrine, but instead find one's own unique path to religion and spirituality.[3] As we will see, this has consequences for whether and why parents choose to baptize their children.

---

1. The classic statement of this thesis can be found in Berger, *A Rumor of Angels*. For a critical discussion, see Dobbelaere, *The Meaning and Scope of Secularization*. For a discussion of secularization in the Norwegian context, see, for example, Chapter 1 and Chapter 12 in Botvar and Schmidt, *Religion i dagens Norge*.

2. Furseth, *From Quest for Truth to Being Oneself*.

3. See, for example, Furseth, *From Quest for Truth to Being Oneself*; Repstad, *Religiøse trender i Norge*; Watts, *The Religion of the Heart*.

Figure 1. Percentage of Norwegian newborns being baptized in the Church of Norway from 1960–2022.[4] *Source: The Church of Norway and Statistics Norway*

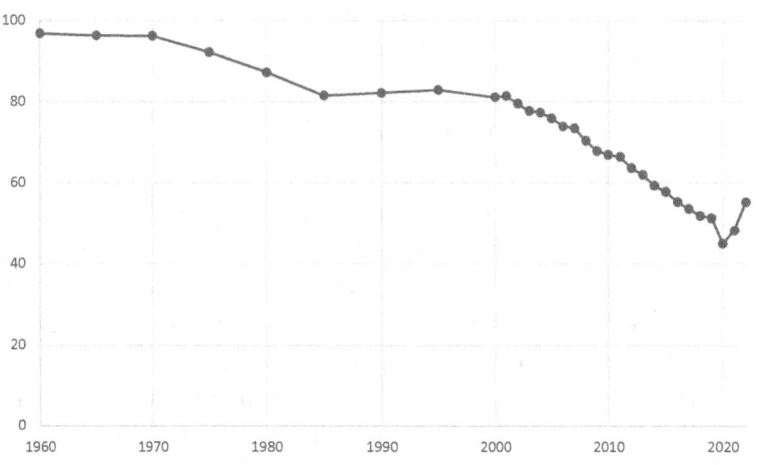

There has been quite a bit of research on baptism in the Nordic countries and in Norway over the last couple of decades.[5] Especially important in Norway has been the contributions from Høeg[6] and Høeg and Gresaker.[7] I will draw on some of these contributions in the discussion below.[8]

DATA AND METHOD

The analysis in this chapter will build on the results of a large survey designed by KIFO: Institute for Church, Religion, and Worldview Research and disseminated in 2019. The survey, named "Religion 2019," was

---

4. The dip in 2020 and 2021 and consequent increase in 2022 is partly a result of the COVID-19 restrictions and the subsequent backlog of baptisms when the restrictions were lifted.

5. See, for instance, Klemmetsby, "Hvorfor de valgte bort dåpen"; Leth-Nissen and Trolle, *Dåb eller ej?*; Rafoss, *Et religiøst landskap i endring*; and Austnaberg, *Utfordringar for prestar og undervisningsmedarbeidarar i dåpsarbeidet i Den norske kyrkja*.

6. See Høeg's works entitled, "Dåp som overgangsrite," "Barnedåp—en sterk tradisjon i et moderne samfunn," "*Velkommen til oss*," "Kjønn og folkelig dåpsteologi," and "Dåpsliturgi og aktørers erfaringer med dåp."

7. Høeg and Gresaker, *Når det rokkes ved tradisjon og tilhørighet*.

8. The "Churches in Times of Change" project has produced a helpful annotated bibliography that contains "entries on statistics, practice, education, campaigns, liturgy, theology, social science and empirical studies on baptism in the Nordic region." The bibliography is available here: https://churchesintimesofchange.org/annotated-bibliography-and-database-on-materials.

answered by 4,024 people and distributed by Kantar. "Religion 2019" was based on a previous study from 2012 ("Religion 2012"), also distributed by Kantar (N = 4001). Both the 2019 and 2012 surveys are considered to be representative of the Norwegian population.[9]

REASONS FOR BAPTIZING

We will first examine why people choose to baptize their children. In "Religion 2019," 62 percent of the respondents reported that they had children. Among the respondents with children, as many as 78 percent said that their child or children are baptized, 2 percent reported having both baptized and non-baptized children, and the remaining 20 percent revealed that their child or children are not baptized. It is important to note that the respondents to the survey were from 18 to 89 years old. This means that some might have just had their children baptized, while others' children may have been baptized many decades in the past. When we look at reasons to baptize (and not to baptize), it is essential to consider the entire age-span of the population.

In both "Religion 2019" and "Religion 2012," respondents who had baptized their children were asked why they had done so. These respondents were presented with a list of reasons and asked how important they were. Figure 2 sums up the percentages who answered "important" or "very important" for the different options. The figure shows a clear hierarchy of reasons, which remained more or less the same in 2012 and 2019. The most frequently reported reasons for baptizing were related to tradition, customs, and the importance of having a beautiful ceremony. Also important was the idea that "baptism gives the child a better opportunity to choose for themselves later in life," and that the child acquires godparents through this process.

Lower on the list of reasons are what we can label "religious reasons," which included the importance of the child being part of the church, the Christian faith of the parent, growing up as a Christian, becoming a child of God, and securing God's protection. The least important reason was pressure from one's family, spouse, or partner.

---

9. As with all surveys of this kind, there are several limitations. Specifically, there are reasons to believe that people with higher education were oversampled, and those of immigrant backgrounds were undersampled.

Figure 2. Reasons for baptizing in 2012 and 2019. Sources: *Religion 2019* (N = 1943) and *Religion 2012* (N = 2,257). Percentages reflect those who answered "important" or "very important."

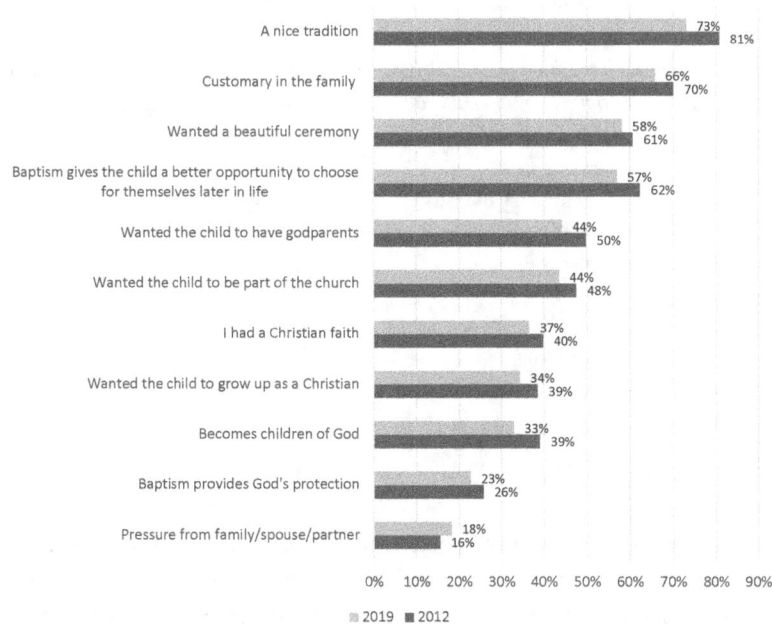

It is worth noting that tradition and customs were the most important reasons for choosing to baptize a child. This needs to be understood in the context of the Church of Norway, which for many is an important symbol of tradition and continuity with the past. We know[10] that many members of the Church of Norway seldom or never use the church and do not strongly identify with Christian beliefs—with these members sometimes being labeled somewhat derisively as "Tradition-Christians" or "Ritual-Christians." These terms refer to members who seldom visit the church—maybe only for a Christmas service or events like baptisms or weddings. At the same time, there is a smaller group of members that does use the church regularly and that holds beliefs corresponding with the church's tenets.

Looking at the data from 2019 for respondents reporting that they were members of the Church of Norway (Table 1), only six percent of members claimed that they visited the church monthly or weekly. The

10. Høeg and Gresaker, *Når det rokkes ved tradisjon og tilhørighet*, 21.

vast majority of members (77 percent) visited the church only yearly. The data also show that the frequency of visits strongly corresponds with other Christian practices and Christian beliefs (analyses of these correlations are not included here).

Table 1. Church attendance. Source: *Religion 2019*. Possible responses were provided in answer to the question, "How often do you attend church services or religious meetings?" (N = 2,347: only members of the Church of Norway)

Frequency of visits	Percentage
Never	17
Yearly	77
Monthly	4
Weekly	2
Total	100

The objective here was to determine whether there was a connection between the different types of church goers and the reasons to baptize. Table 2 shows that this was in fact the case.[11] For the minority who visited the church monthly and weekly, the "religious reasons" for baptism were much more important. This illustrates one of the main characteristics of the "folk church" of Norway (and the other Nordic countries), which is the fact that the church caters to many different types of members and users. Even though the "religious reasons" for baptism are, *on average,* less vital, they are very important to a minority of active church attenders.

---

11. In Table 2, I have reported the responses for all participants, including non-members of the Church of Norway. This is because people may have baptized their children without themselves being a member of the Church of Norway (or any other Christian denomination).

Table 2. Reasons for baptizing and frequency of church attendance. Sources: *Religion 2019*. Percentages reflect those who answered "important" or "very important" (N = 1,943)

	Never	Yearly	Monthly	Weekly	Total
Pressure from family/spouse/partner	35	15	4	9	18
Baptism provides God's protection	2	23	67	63	23
Process of becoming child of God	5	33	93	82	33
Wanted the child to grow up as a Christian	5	35	93	87	34
Adhered to Christian faith	6	38	94	93	37
Wanted the child to be part of the church	13	46	92	80	43
Wanted the child to have godparents	22	47	70	70	44
Baptism would give the child a better opportunity to choose for themselves later in life	36	62	67	59	57
Wanted a beautiful ceremony	40	64	62	40	58
Customary in the family	49	70	72	60	66
A nice tradition	46	80	83	63	73

REASONS NOT TO BAPTIZE

The survey also included another set of questions for parents who decided *not* to baptize their children. These parents were presented with a list of reasons why they did not baptize and asked how important they were (Figure 3).

PART I: EMPIRICAL STUDIES

Figure 3. Reasons not to baptize. Sources: *Religion 2019*. Percentages reflect those who answered "important" or "very important" (N = 531)

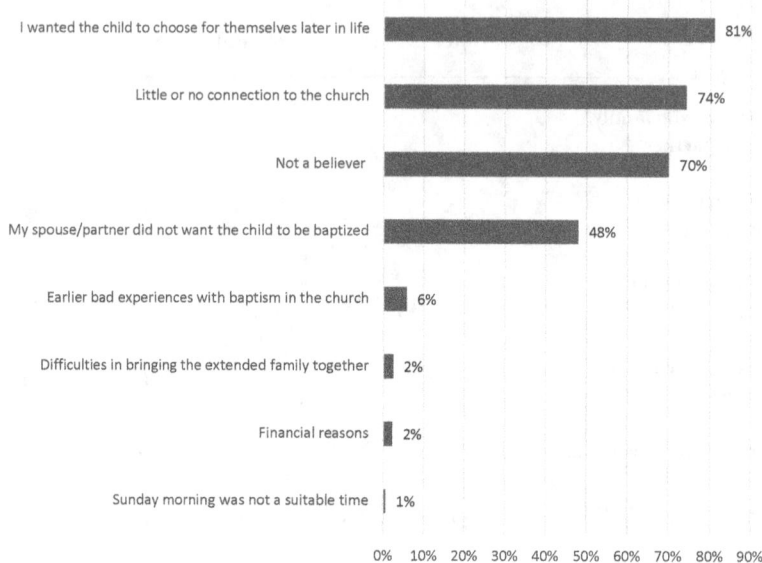

Beginning with the least important reasons, the findings indicate that practical reasons for not baptizing one's children were not important. For instance, almost no one claimed that the time (Sunday morning) was a problem, and very few reported that economic reasons were important (even though it can be expensive to have a dinner or celebration in conjunction with a baptism). A few also responded that it was difficult to bring the extended family together. Only six percent claimed that they did not baptize because of previous bad experiences with baptism.

Much more important than these factors is that the spouse or partner did not want the child to be baptized. Almost half of the respondents claimed that this was an important or very important reason why their children were not baptized. Among the most important reasons were two of a religious nature: that the parent was not a believer, and that respondent had little or no connection to the church. Finally, the most important reason was that the parent "wanted the child to choose for themselves later in life," with as many as 81 percent of parents claiming that this was important or very important. This finding is elaborated on below.

COMPARING PARENTS' REASONS FOR AND AGAINST BAPTIZING

In comparing the reasons provided by the two groups of parents, some interesting symmetries and asymmetries emerged. First, when parents chose to baptize, religious reasons were among the *least* important, but when they chose *not to* baptize, religious reasons were among the *most* important, but in the negative sense that *not* having a religious belief and *not* having a connection with the church were reasons not to baptize.

Second, only 16 percent (in 2019) reported that "pressure from family/spouse/partner" was an important or very important reason to baptize their children, while as much as 48 percent said that the fact that a "spouse/partner did not want the child to be baptized" was an important or very important reason *not* to baptize. This may indicate that it is more common to feel pressured *not* to baptize than to baptize by a partner.

However, what many parents had in common, regardless of their choice to baptize or not, was that they valued the child's autonomy and ability to make his or her own choice. As we have seen, the most important reason *not* to baptize is that the parent "wanted the child to choose for themselves later in life." However, one of the most important reasons for parents to baptize a child was similar, insofar as "baptism gives the child a better opportunity to choose for themselves later in life."

INFANT BAPTISM IN AN INDIVIDUALIZED CULTURE

While the differences and similarities in the reasons provided are themselves illuminated, they should be understood with reference to the fact that certain ideas about individual choice are becoming more dominant in Western culture.

Countless historians, sociologists, and philosophers have pointed out how individualism is a dominant force in the modern world. For example, the philosopher Charles Taylor has analyzed how Western culture holds a strong idea that authentic and ethical choices must be rooted in autonomous and rational individuals. In many of his books, Taylor examines in great detail how individuals have gradually come to see themselves as distinct and separate entities that increasingly value individual rights and autonomy.[12] Taylor maintains that while this em-

---

12. Taylor, *Sources of the Self*; Taylor, *The Ethics of Authenticity*; Taylor, *A Secular Age*.

phasis on individual autonomy and self-determination may be liberating, it can also be isolating, leading to a potential loss of deeper moral and spiritual orientations. Nevertheless, the main thrust of modern society remains geared toward individualism.

Individualism is often seen as connected to an ideal of authenticity. In *The Ethics of Authenticity*, Taylor acknowledges widespread critiques against this particular ideal, in that it promotes narcissism and subjectivism and contributes to a breakdown of moral values. However, Taylor argues that an ethic of authenticity is not inherently self-centered. When understood correctly, it can be a valuable source of moral insight. Taylor believes that authenticity is not just an individual undertaking, but rather an orientation that is deeply intertwined with society. He thus suggests that to realize one's authentic self, one needs to be in communion with others, which alludes to the social nature of authenticity. Still, an "ethic of authenticity" is qualitatively different from more community-oriented ethics, wherein obligations to a community (e.g., religious, national, professional, etc.) supersede the interests of the individual.[13]

Taylor's analyses have a great historical and philosophical scope. In his many works, he ultimately tries to identify, think through, and explain the great religious and cultural shifts that have shaped modern society. Accordingly, his thoughts might have some relevance for this small examination of baptism in Norway. Our findings thus far suggest that parents' thoughts about the authentic and individual rights of their children are a strong factor that influences the choice they make regarding baptism. There have also been several qualitative studies of parents who have chosen not to baptize their children, even though they themselves are members of a church. In all of these studies, many parents emphasized the child's autonomy and right to choose for themselves. In a Danish study by Leth-Nissen and Trolle, six out of nine families that had chosen not to baptize had made this decision because they wanted the child to be able to make his or her own choice. Leth-Nissen and Krabbe cite one informant as saying, "It is deliberate [that] my children are not baptized, and it is precisely because they must be allowed to choose for themselves."[14]

In a related study, Klemmetsby interviewed seven parents who were members of the Church of Norway but who had chosen not to baptize

13. See Graff-Kallevåg, "Baptism in a Secular Age," for a discussion on how to apply Charles Taylor's thoughts to the theology of baptism.

14. Leth-Nissen and Trolle, *Dåb eller ej?*, 53 (my translation).

their children. Klemmetsby concluded that these parents also had strong ideas about the autonomy of their children:

> But unlike in the previous generation, one no longer follows the traditions regarding baptism. It is instead important to follow one's convictions regardless of what others may think. Then, one leaves it up to the children themselves to eventually choose baptism later on. Children's autonomy is thus perceived as important. Thinking like this is natural, given the ideals of the individualistic and subjectivist society we now live in.[15]

Høeg and Gresaker[16] and I[17] have also made similar observations. All this points to the fact that many church members who choose not to baptize have become something like secular Baptists: the child, when old enough, should make their own conscious and authentic choice. Even some parents who are themselves Christians believe that it would be wrong to make this choice on behalf of their child.

The problem with this—from the Church of Norway's point of view—is that such an orientation undermines the entire practice of infant baptism and, to a certain degree, the foundation for the "folk church" of Norway and its membership base. Many types of communities and organizations struggle with how to cater to their members in an age where individualism and freedom are dominant values. For the Church of Norway, however, this problem might be especially acute. The church is in a fundamental way—theologically, practically, organizationally, and even economically—based on the practice of infant baptism. As we have seen, this practice is, for a significant number of parents, no longer compatible with the dominant ideology of our time, which places strong emphasis on the right and obligation for the individual to make his or her own authentic, autonomous choices.

Even when parents choose infant baptism, one of the most important reasons (as we saw above) is that "baptism gives the child a better opportunity to choose for themselves later in life." This might at first glance seem paradoxical, but many parents likely identify with this statement, because they may believe that if the child wants to continue belonging to the church, they can determine this for themselves later on. If the child then wants confirmation in the church, they can do this without having

---

15. Klemmetsby, *Hvorfor de valgte bort dåpen*, 434 (my translation).
16. Høeg and Greasker, *Når det rokkes ved tradisjon og tilhørighet*, 116.
17. Rafoss, *Et religiøst landskap i endring*, 23.

to be baptized, so in this sense, the parent is facilitating a choice the child can make for themselves later on. Claiming that "baptism gives the child a better opportunity to choose for themselves later in life" might also be a means of framing infant baptism in a way that is more compatible with a modern individualistic ideology.

As noted earlier in this discussion, it was found to be more common for a parent to feel pressure *not* to baptize than to baptize. We cannot say for certain, based on this data, why this is the case. However, one hypothesis might be that when parents disagree on whether to baptize a child, the parent who does *not* want to baptize has a stronger argument, in the sense that this parent can align himself or herself with the ideology of the autonomous child. While the most common reasons for choosing to baptize a child were that it was "customary in the family" and "a nice tradition," such references to tradition and customs are the antithesis to a modern, individualist ideology. A central part of this ideology is that people should make their own choices—often in spite of tradition and custom. It might therefore be difficult for a parent to use tradition-based reasons to argue against what, for many, is a creed: the idea that only autonomous individuals can make authentic choices.

BIBLIOGRAPHY

Austnaberg, Hans. "Utfordringar for prestar og undervisningsmedarbeidarar i dåpsarbeidet i Den norske kyrkja." *Scandinavian Journal for Leadership and Theology* 5 (2018).

Berger, Peter L. *A Rumor of Angels: Modern Society and the Rediscovery of the Supernatural*. Garden City: Anchor Doubleday, 1970.

Botvar, Pål Ketil, and Ulla Schmidt, eds. *Religion i dagens Norge: mellom sekularisering og sakralisering*. Oslo: Universitetsforlaget, 2010.

Dobbelaere, Karel. "The Meaning and Scope of Secularization." In *The Oxford Handbook of the Sociology of Religion*, edited by P. B. Clarke, 599–615. Oxford: Oxford University, 2011.

Furseth, Inger. *From Quest for Truth to Being Oneself: Religious Change in Life Stories*. Frankfurt: Lang, 2006.

———. *Religionens tilbakekomst i offentligheten? Religion, politikk, medier, stat og sivilsamfunn i Norge siden 1980-tallet*. Oslo: Universitetsforlaget, 2015.

Graff-Kallevåg, Kristin. "Baptism in a Secular Age." *Dialog* 56 (2017) 251–59.

Høeg, Ida Marie. "Barnedåp—en sterk tradisjon i et moderne samfunn." *Nytt norsk kirkeblad* 30 (2002) 10–17.

———. "Dåp som overgangsrite. En analyse av dåpens offentlige og private riter." *Prismet* 52 (2001) 54–62.

———. "Dåpsliturgi og aktørers erfaringer med dåp." *Nytt norsk kirkeblad* 41 (2013) 33–37.

———. "Kjønn og folkelig dåpsteologi." *Din: Tidsskrift for religion og kultur* 12 (2011) 65–80.

———. "Velkommen til oss." *Ritualisering av livets begynnelse.* Doktorgrads-avhandling: Universitetet i Bergen, 2008.

Høeg, Ida Marie, and Ann Kristin Gresaker. *Når det rokkes ved tradisjon og tilhørighet. Nedgang i oppslutning om dåp i Oslo bispedømme.* KIFO Rapport 2015: 2. Oslo: KIFO, 2015a.

———. "Når det rokkes ved tradisjon og tilhørighet. Perspektiver på nedgangen i oppslutning om dåp." *Luthersk kirketidende* 150 (2015) 427–29.

Klemmetsby, Svend. "Hvorfor de valgte bort dåpen." *Luthersk kirketidende* 150/18 (2015) 430–34.

Leth-Nissen, Karen Marie Sø, and Astrid Krabbe Trolle. *Dåb eller ej? Rapport om småbørnsforældres til- og fravalg af dåb. Det teologiske Fakultet.* Publikationer fra Det Teologiske Fakultet 59, 2005

Rafoss, Tore Witsø. *Et religiøst landskap i endring. Oppslutning om dåp på Østre Romerike.* KIFO Rapport 2016: 2. Oslo: KIFO, 2016.

Repstad, Pål. *Religiøse trender i Norge.* Oslo: Universitetsforlaget, 2020.

Taylor, Charles. *The Ethics of Authenticity.* Cambridge: Harvard University, 1992.

———. *A Secular Age.* Cambridge: Harvard University, 2007.

———. *Sources of the Self: The Making of the Modern Identity.* Cambridge: Cambridge University Press, 1989.

Watts, Galen. "The Religion of the Heart: Spirituality in Late Modernity." *American Journal of Cultural Sociology* 10 (2022) 1–33.

3

Churching Alone?

New Patterns in the Use of Baptism in Denmark

Karen Marie Sø Leth-Nissen

With this chapter, I try to answer the following question: In Denmark, where 71.4 percent (2024) of the population are members of the Evangelical Lutheran Church of Denmark (ELCD), why has the share of baptized infants declined to 56 percent of the birth cohort?[1]

Two main factors have changed Denmark's religious landscape. The first is the shifting demography. Since the 1960s, we have seen waves of migrants coming to Denmark for work, safety, or both.[2] Becoming part of the ELCD has not been relevant to most of them. Even if they so desired, language remains a barrier, as being a Danish speaker is still an essential requirement for many local parish congregations. Today, approximately 14 percent (2024) of the Danish population are made up of non-Danish migrants, only a fraction of whom are members of the ELCD.[3] Children born to migrants and their descendants are less likely

---

1. These rates refer to children born in 2022. See Center for Pastoral Education and Research of the ELCD, "Church Statistics on Baptism."
2. Poulsen et al., *Religiøsitet 1*, 80–81.
3. Poulsen et al., *Religiøsitet 1*, 86.

to be baptized in the ELCD, and this influences the broader share of infant baptisms in the nation.

The second factor—the focus of this chapter—is the changing attitudes toward baptism among parents, who as members of the church may still opt out of baptism for their children.[4] Looking closer for explanations of the parents' changing relationship to church, I employ the theories of Grace Davie (on the shift from obligation to choice) and Per Pettersson (on the shift from long-term to short-term consumption), both scholars from the research field of religious change.[5] The theories of Davie and Pettersson underlie the concept of *churching alone*, for which I have generated hypotheses to test on empirical data.[6]

The analysis in this chapter focuses on the individual level and builds on material derived from several studies. The main data come from two empirical studies on parents' choice of whether to baptize their children, namely Leth-Nissen and Trolle's *Dåb eller ej?* (Baptism or not?) from 2015 (with 2014 survey data and interviews), and Leth-Nissen's *Dåb i dag* (Baptism today) from 2020. Additional quantitative data come from a 2020 survey with over 4,000 respondents conducted at the Center for Pastoral Education of the ELCD and published in Poulsen, Trolle, Larsen, and Mortensen's *Religiøsitet og forholdet til folkekirken 2020* (Religiosity and affiliation to the ELCD) in 2021.

CHURCH MEMBERSHIP AND THE USE OF RITUALS

A total of 71,4 percent of the Danish population are members of the ELCD (2024).[7] While a majority of the members use the church for life stage rituals, burials, weddings, and confirmations, the numbers are slightly decreasing. 81 percent of all the deceased in Denmark receive a burial from a church or chapel with a pastor from the ELCD, and almost two-thirds of youths have a confirmation in the ELCD.[8] The number of

---

4. Poulsen et al., *Religiøsitet 1*, 93–94.

5. Davie, "Religion in 21st Century"; Davie, *Religion in the 21st Century*; Pettersson, *Kvalitet*.

6. Parts of the analysis and discussion in this chapter have been published in Leth-Nissen, *Churching Alone*; Leth-Nissen, "Churching Alone—folkekirken"; Leth-Nissen, "Traditionen til forhandling."

7. Center for Pastoral Education and Research of the ELCD, "Church Statistics on Membership."

8. Center for Pastoral Education and Research of the ELCD, "Church Statistics on Burials." Center for Pastoral Education and Research of the ELCD, "Church Statistics on Confirmation."

infant baptisms, however, is decreasing more than those of other rituals. Specifically, we have seen a rapidly declining trend in baptism numbers over the last two decades. In 1990, 81 percent of a cohort of newborns was baptized within their first year of life, a number that drastically shifted down to 56 percent by 2022.[9] Figure 1 presents data on the population share of members and the use of church for life stage rituals.

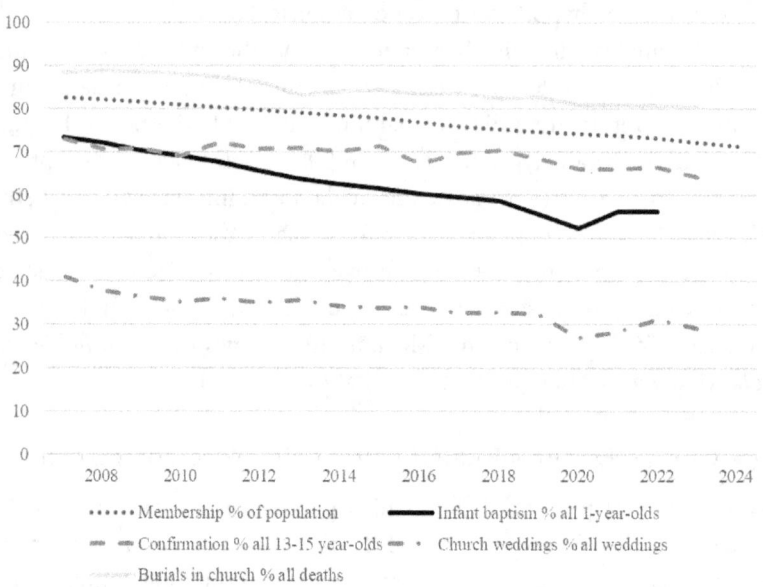

Figure 1: Evangelical Lutheran Church of Denmark: Membership and use of church for life stage rituals 2007–2024. *Sources: Data from the Danish Statistical Office and the Center for Pastoral Education of the ELCD*

The numbers presented in the figure show that the relationship between the Danish population and the ELCD is still strong. The ELCD is a church that is woven into society and has until now been part of the mental backdrop for most Danes.[10]

SCANDINAVIAN BAPTISM STUDIES

Empirical studies focusing on baptism in a Danish context are a relatively new phenomenon. Salomonsen's study on religion in Denmark,

---

9. Center for Pastoral Education and Research of the ELCD, "Church Statistics on Baptism."

10. Gundelach et al., *I hjertet*, 234.

published in 1971, included baptism among many other subjects and found that while parents felt obliged to baptize their children, they did not feel the same way about teaching their children about Christianity.[11] Peter B. Andersen, Nadja Ausker, and Peter La Cour showed how church attendance at the age of 12 declined from 36 percent of all 12-year-olds in the cohort born in 1919–1927 to seven percent of the cohort of 1964–1972.[12] Following Salomonsen's findings, it seems evident that parents have allowed their children to be baptized, but often without supporting their relationship to the church and Christianity.[13] Those who were children in the 1960s and 1970s have now grown up and become parents themselves. How have their practices and attitudes toward the baptism of their children evolved?

The two Danish studies on baptism from 2015 to 2020 both examined these changes in the use of baptism and the factors that explain them.[14] In the broader Scandinavian context, the Danish studies add to two Norwegian studies and one Swedish study on the status of baptism among parents in Scandinavia: *Når det rokkes ved tradition og tilhørighet* (When tradition and belonging is shaken)[15], *Et religiøst landskap i endring. Oppslutning om dåb på østre Romerike* (A changing religious landscape. Use of baptism in Eastern Romerike)[16], and *Dop i förändring: en studie av föräldrars aktiva val och församlingens strategiska doparbete* (Baptism in change: A study of parents' active choice and the congregations's strategic baptism work).[17] Four of the five studies combined a survey and interviews with parents of young children to uncover the reasons behind the choice of having their children baptized or opting out of baptism.[18] I include the findings from the Scandinavian studies in the discussion here when relevant.

---

11. Salomonsen, *Religion i dag*, 175.
12. Andersen et al., "Går fanden i kloster," 106.
13. Leth-Nissen, *Churching Alone*, 190.
14. Leth-Nissen and Trolle, *Dåb eller ej?*; Leth-Nissen, *Dåb i dag*.
15. Høeg and Gresaker, *Når det rokkes ved*.
16. Rafoss, *Et religiøst landskap i endring*.
17. Sandberg et al., *Dop i förändring*.
18. Leth-Nissen's *Dåb i dag* is based solely on interviews.

PART I: EMPIRICAL STUDIES

THEORETICAL FRAMEWORK FOR THE ANALYSIS: CHURCHING ALONE

Churching alone is a concept developed from empirical research into contemporary changes in the ELCD across societal, organizational, and individual levels.[19] In Danish, the word "church" refers to a building or an institution and cannot be used as a verb. Strictly speaking, we cannot speak of *churching*. When I use the word *churching* to identify the changes in the ELCD, I describe the changes in church use over the last few decades (see Figure 1). *Churching* here refers to all the situations in which individuals are connected to the ELCD, such as having their child baptized or their uncle buried, attending Sunday worship, or attending baby hymn singing with their child.[20] Just being a member of the folk church is *churching*, although it may be considered a minimal form of such. Churching can be done alone—not in solitude or loneliness, but in a way that is meaningful to the practicing individual. *Alone* in this context means something like saying, "I want to take part in this event in the church, but I will not promise that you will see me again, and I will not pay for a subscription or become a member of your organization or club." *Churching alone* refers to the ability to take part on your own terms. I argue that the concept of *churching alone* addresses a growing trend at the individual level of the Danish folk church. At the organizational level, this trend of churching alone is supported or even accelerated by a shift toward more market and target-group-oriented activities in parishes and deaneries of the ELCD. To operationalize the concept of churching alone for testing at the individual level, I formulated two main hypotheses by building on the works of Grace Davie and Per Pettersson.[21]

For decades, Davie has been observing major changes in European religion and church life. With her notions of "believing without belonging" (or "belonging without believing") and "vicarious religion," she has effectively described recent movements in European Christianity and

---

19. The introduction to the concept of churching alone follows the work of Leth-Nissen, *Churching Alone, A Study*, 1–4.

20. Many parishes in the ELCD offers the activity of baby hymn singing to parents with children aged 0-1 years. The singing is led by a church musician or a pastor and most often takes place in the nave or choir of the church building. During the activity, the parents learn short versions of well-known hymns and instructed how to sing, dance and play with their children while singing together with the other parents."

21. Davie, "Religion in 21st Century," 282–84; Pettersson, *Kvalitet*, 402–4.

how they have opened up a situation in which choice, more than duty, is the driver behind the use of the church.[22] In her work, Davie shows that while religion used to be imposed or inherited as an obligation, it is now increasingly a matter of choice.[23] Davie ties notions of obligation to tradition, generation, and religion and shows how obligation has shifted into consumption or individual choice.[24] Based on Davie's work, I formulated the first hypothesis of a shift from obligation to choice in individuals' relationships with the church.

In a related vein, Pettersson studied changes in the use of the Church of Sweden and found two main types of relationships with the church, which depended on whether the individual in question was collectively or individually oriented.[25] For the collectively oriented, the church relationship is connected to "collective cultural values" and to culture, history, tradition, and relatives.[26] Such members take part in rites of passage, and to them, the church relationship is part of a wider cultural identity comprising all the contact they have with the church throughout their lifetimes.[27] Pettersson tied the collectively oriented disposition to a long-term perspective, as the decisions these members make toward the use of the church are essentially based on a need for security and coherence. The collectively oriented members generally expect the church to be there when they need it and connect it to security, traditions, solemnity, and silence.[28]

In contrast to this type of member, Petterson found that those who are individually oriented in their church relationship focus on the experience in church, as they emphasize personal needs and choices and evaluate worship and other activities from an individual perspective based on their own interests and feelings.[29] In this sense, Petterson established a connection between the individually oriented church user and a short-term perspective, with decisions based on individual

---

22. Davie, *The Sociology of Religion*, 16; Davie, *Europe: The Exceptional Case*; Davie, "Religion in the 21st Century," 281–82. Davie, "Religion in Europe in the 21st Century," 276.

23. Davie, "Religion in the 21st Century," 284.

24. For the full argument, see Leth-Nissen, *Churching Alone*, 20–22.

25. Pettersson, "From Standardised Offer"; Pettersson, *Kvalitet*, 402.

26. Pettersson, *Kvalitet*, 403–4.

27. Pettersson, *Kvalitet*, 351, 403–4.

28. Pettersson, *Kvalitet*, 351, 403–4.

29. Pettersson, *Kvalitet*, 404.

preferences.[30] Pettersson also found that both types of orientations could be present in the same individual.[31]

Based on Pettersson's work, I thus formulated the second hypothesis of a shift from long-term consumption to short-term consumption connected to church use.[32]

In combining the two hypotheses, my objective was to determine whether a trend toward *churching alone* is present in the data and can explain some of the decline in baptism in Denmark. I thus operationalized the hypothesis of a shift from obligation to choice in the individual's relationship to church as confirmed by the following:

- Interviewees supporting the individual's own choice of religion;
- Parental couples negotiating their choice or rejection of baptism;
- A view of baptism as preliminary; and
- A differentiated church use wherein individuals put together their own "church package."

The hypothesis of a shift from long-term to short-term consumption was confirmed by the following:

- An emphasis on individual orientation and short-term decisions more than collective orientation and long-term decisions in the parents' choice or rejection of baptism.

MATERIAL FOR THE ANALYSIS: SURVEYS AND INTERVIEWS 2015–2020

The relevant material for this analysis on changes in baptism was derived from two parallel rounds of interviews with Danish parents of younger children conducted in 2014–2015 and 2018–2019, as well as two Danish surveys conducted in 2014 and 2020. The two interview studies served as the main body of analytical material for this analysis, while the two surveys contributed to the context and broader perspective of the analysis.

The two Danish interview studies built on the same research design and focused on the decision to opt in or out of baptism among parents of

---

30. Pettersson, *Kvalitet*, 404.
31. Pettersson, *Kvalitet*, 404–6.
32. For a discussion on consumption in connection to church use, see Leth-Nissen, *Churching Alone*, 25–29.

younger children. The first study, consisting of 25 interviews with parents (8 male, 17 female), took place in the metropolitan area of Copenhagen, while the second study comprised interviews with 27 parents (10 male, 17 female) from suburban and rural areas distributed across Denmark.[33] The two groups of interviewed parents followed roughly the same distribution of age, gender, and education, with the caveat that both groups had a higher level of education than the equivalent for the 25–49-year-old age group in the Danish population (see table 1).[34] There were certain distinct differences between the two groups, as fewer of the parents in the metropolitan area were members of the church and less often chose baptism for their child/children (see table 1).[35]

The overview below compares the parents from the two interview studies in terms of basic demographic parameters.

Table 1: Background information on interviewees from 2015 and 2020 studies on the decision to opt in or out of baptism among parents of younger children. *Source: Two Danish interview studies*

Interviews	2015 (metropolitan area)	2020 (suburban / rural area)
Number of parents participating in interviews	25	27
Gender distribution (male/female)	8 male, 17 female	10 male, 17 female
Age distribution	20–50	25–45
Chose baptism for child/children	12	24
Member of the church	15	23
Religious socialization in childhood or youth (church activities, scouting, church choir, etc.)	12	5
Parents with secondary and tertiary education	15	16

33. Leth-Nissen and Trolle, *Dåb eller ej?*, 49; Leth-Nissen, *Dåb i dag*, 35.

34. According to Statistics Denmark, the share of persons with secondary and tertiary education in the Danish population is 27 percent, and in the age group of 25–49-year-olds, the share is 38 percent. In both Danish studies, the share of persons with secondary and tertiary education was 60 percent. See Leth-Nissen and Trolle, *Dåb eller ej?*, 48; Leth-Nissen, *Dåb i dag*, 72.

35. Leth-Nissen and Trolle, *Dåb eller ej?*, 49; Leth-Nissen, *Dåb i dag*, 35.

Interviews	2015 (metropolitan area)	2020 (suburban / rural area)
Parents living in an urban area with over 1,000 inhabitants	25	12
Parents living close to birthplace (max 20 km distance)	2	13

The 2014 survey was distributed to parents across Denmark having children under the age of 18 in the household.[36] With 1,042 respondents, the survey was considered geographically representative. The age span of most of the respondents was 25–55 years. The education level of the respondents was higher than the average for the Danish population, which may have biased the answers, since a higher level of education can be related to less church affiliation.[37] A total of 77 percent of the respondents had their child baptized, 19 percent did not have their children baptized, and four percent had both baptized and non-baptized children.[38]

Across the interviews with parents from metropolitan, suburban, and rural areas, settling down more than 20 kilometers away from one's birthplace more often was associated to opting out of baptism for your child.[39]

The 2020 survey with 4,109 respondents was part of a major study conducted from 2019 to 2022 at the Center for Pastoral Education and Research of the ELCD.[40]

In the next paragraph, I show how the various datasets confirm or refute the hypotheses.

---

36. The survey was conducted by YouGov for the Center for Church Research, University of Copenhagen, and the Danish Bible Society. YouGov conducted 1,042 computer assisted web interviews with persons from the Danish population having children under the age of 18 in the household from December 12–22, 2014.

37. Leth-Nissen and Trolle, *Dåb eller ej?*, 16.

38. Leth-Nissen and Trolle, *Dåb eller ej?*, 17–18.

39. Leth-Nissen, *Dåb i dag*, 80.

40. Published in Poulsen et al., *Religiøsitet 1*, and Leth-Nissen et al., *Religiøsitet*, 2. The survey was conducted by the analysis institute Norstat for the Danish Statistical Office between February 25 and April 6, 2020. Of the 4,109 respondents, 3,217 answered through an online survey, while 892 were interviewed by phone. See Poulsen et al., *Religiøsitet*, 1.

A SHIFT FROM OBLIGATION TO CHOICE

In analyzing the interviews with parents from metropolitan, suburban, and rural areas of Denmark, I found only small traces of obligation regarding the decision of baptism or no baptism. Some parents told that their grandparents hoped for or even expected them to have their child baptized. One mother refused to let her grandmother influence the decision. The mother had—for her grandmother's sake—agreed to her own confirmation when she was young, and this time, she wanted to have her own way.[41] One father knew that his grandparents would be sad if their great-grandchild did not have a baptism. Trying to pay the grandparents respect, he and his wife created an alternative non-faith ritual for the entire family, wherein the child was clad in the family's christening gown.[42] These parents felt an obligation to explain their position on baptism and to create a connection with the older generation in spite of their rejection of the practice of baptism.[43] Such an obligation is different from motivations based on tradition, family, and older generations, as in this case, the parents choose from these traditions. Here, the christening gown functioned as an identity marker connecting the parents to family traditions and relations, even across the rejection of baptism.[44]

No parents reported feeling obliged by their faith to have their children baptized. Most parents identified as non-believers or as believing in their own way and not according to the faith of the ELCD. One parent belonged to a free church, where baptism takes place when the individual is ready to enter a life in God.[45] Furthermore, no parents felt obliged by their church affiliation to have their children baptized. From the data, it is hard to tell whether this had any influence on their decisions. Almost all parents from suburban and rural areas were members of a church and chose baptism. Among the metropolitan parents, some rejected baptism despite their own membership in the church, but non-members (both baptized and non-baptized) more often wanted to reject baptism.[46]

---

41. Leth-Nissen, *Dåb i dag*, 43.
42. Leth-Nissen, *Dåb i dag*, 62
43. Leth-Nissen, *Dåb i dag*, 40.
44. Leth-Nissen, *Dåb i dag*, 86.
45. Leth-Nissen, *Dåb i dag*, 62.
46. Leth-Nissen, *Dåb i dag*, 78.

Many parents, mostly those from suburban and rural areas, explained that tradition was the main factor behind their choice of baptism. However, tradition was not seen as an authentic argument for baptism among parents from metropolitan areas.[47] Does this mean that some parents feel obliged to have their children baptized by tradition? I will discuss the question of tradition later in this chapter.

Individual's Own Choice of Religion—Baptism as Preliminary

The interviewed parents generally expressed that individuals, both children and adults, should make their own choice of religious affiliation. Contrary to the theological understanding of baptism, the parents viewed infant baptism as a preliminary ritual which can only take on its full meaning when or if the child as a teenager wishes to have a confirmation.[48] Other reasons for opting out of baptism for the parents were a reported lack of faith or their affiliation to another faith or a free church.[49] This deferral to individual choice was supported by findings from the 2014 survey, where 51 percent of responding parents opting out of baptism indicated that the main reason was that they wanted the child to decide on their own baptism.[50]

The Scandinavian studies resemble the 2014 Danish survey in terms of the overall results and findings. In the two Norwegian surveys and the Swedish survey, the parents' most frequent reason for opting out of baptism for their children was their wish to leave the decision on religious belonging to the child itself.[51] As in the Danish survey, many of the Norwegian and Swedish informants stated that they were not believers or belonged to a religious community other than the majority Christian church and had therefore opted out of baptism for their children.[52]

---

47. Leth-Nissen, *Dåb i dag*, 78.
48. Leth-Nissen and Trolle, *Dåb eller ej?*, 52.
49. Leth-Nissen, *Dåb i dag*, 78.
50. Leth-Nissen and Trolle, *Dåb eller ej?*, 18.
51. Høeg and Gresaker, *Når det rokkes*, 37, 114; Rafoss, *Et religiøst landskap*, 21–23; Sandberg et al., *Dop i förändring*, 44–47.
52. Høeg and Gresaker, *Når det rokkes*, 37, 114; Rafoss, *Et religiøst landskap*, 21–23; Sandberg et al., *Dop i förändring*, 44–47.

Negotiating the Choice of Whether to Baptize

In the interviews from the 2015 Danish baptism study, some parents living in metropolitan Copenhagen negotiated with each other on the choice of baptism for their child.[53] Here, the individual parent's own preference regarding religion weighed over family considerations and the wishes of the other parent. In the negotiations, the parent with the strongest feelings against or for baptism ended up having the final say on the matter.

The process of negotiation revealed here resembles the findings of the Norwegian interview study. In the Norwegian case, interviews with parents living in the metropolitan area highlighted negotiation as a special feature of the decision-making process regarding whether to opt for infant baptism.[54]

Supporting this further, the Swedish survey found that 13 percent of parents who chose baptism did so because "my partner wanted it," and 16 percent of the parents who had opted out cited the same reason.[55] Opting out of baptism was found to be common among both non-members and members of the church. Rafoss's Norwegian survey on baptism showed that approximately 60 percent of parents who were church members and opted out of baptism said they did so after pressure from their partners.[56] In Høeg and Gresaker's Norwegian survey, 50 percent of church members who opted out of baptism had a partner who either belonged to another religious community or had no affiliation to one.[57]

If we look at the surveys of the Norwegian and Swedish studies, we can see that a larger share of the parents living in a big city had a partner with a different religious background from their own, and this weighed into the final choice regarding infant baptism.[58] Together with the Danish study, these findings suggest a connection between diverse backgrounds of the parents and the negotiation process regarding the baptism.

Parents living in suburban or rural areas in Denmark more often agreed on their choice or rejection of baptism.[59] They showed less of an

53. Leth-Nissen and Trolle, *Dåb eller ej?*, 59–60.
54. Høeg and Gresaker, *Når det rokkes*, 75–77.
55. Sandberg et al., *Dop i förändring*, 42, 46–47.
56. Rafoss, *Et religiøst landskap*, 23.
57. Høeg and Gresaker, *Når det rokkes*, 55.
58. Høeg and Gresaker, *Når det rokkes*, 114; Sandberg et al., *Dop i förändring*, 42, 46–47.
59. Leth-Nissen, *Dåb i dag*, 39.

inclination to negotiate, but to a greater extent, reflected jointly on the choice of whether to baptize their children.[60] These parents shared values and religious backgrounds (religious socialization) to a higher degree than the parental couples living in Copenhagen. Such parents negotiated traditions, choosing from those of their childhood families and trends discovered among friends and on social media.[61]

Differentiated Church Use—An Individual's Own "Church Package"

To a certain degree, parents living in metropolitan Copenhagen put together their own religious package (patchwork religiosity per Dobbelaere), as some of the parents included elements from other religious traditions in their religious practices.[62] Some of them came from other Christian denominations, but parents who were members of the ELCD also mixed elements of different faiths as they found them meaningful.[63] Other parents from the metropolitan area showed a differentiated use of the church, as they had no problem mixing membership and no baptism, or baptism and no membership.[64] In the 2014 survey on baptism, we found the same connections across membership and baptism, as nine percent of parents who were members of the ELCD did not baptize their children, while 37 percent of parents who were not members of the ELCD had baptized all their children.[65] The findings point to the differentiated use of the ELCD. While such use is not mainstream, there is a steady minority using the church without being members, just as some members feel free to reject baptism for their children. The analysis also found a decline in the choice of baptism among parents born after 1970.[66]

Looking at the survey data, we can also see a decline in parents who passed on baptism to their children. Analysis of the data from the 2020 survey showed that for parents who were born in 1981 or younger and who were members of the ELCD, 23 percent did not baptize their children. For

---

60. Leth-Nissen, *Dåb i dag*, 38–39.
61. Leth-Nissen, *Dåb i dag*, 82–87.
62. Dobbelaere, "Towards an Integrated Perspective," 239. Leth-Nissen and Trolle, *Dåb eller ej?*, 59–60.
63. Leth-Nissen and Trolle, *Dåb eller ej?*, 59.
64. Leth-Nissen and Trolle, *Dåb eller ej?*, 53.
65. Leth-Nissen and Trolle, *Dåb eller ej?*, 17.
66. Leth-Nissen and Trolle, *Dåb eller ej?*, 24–25.

the generations older than those born in 1981, the rate of church members not baptizing their children was 8–9 percent or less.[67]

To parents from suburban and rural areas, talk of religion mostly pointed to Christianity, which had been part of their mental backdrop in their childhood and youth.[68] These parents showed a differentiated use of the church by putting together their own "church packages." For instance, one parent who was not baptized himself chose baptism for his son, as he wished for his son to be part of the collective ritual. He himself had wanted to have a confirmation but was too shy as a young man to even raise the question of a baptism. As a result, he felt estranged from his school friends during the year when they had confirmation classes.[69]

Moreover, these parents put together their own package of *traditions*. The analysis thus found that the concept of tradition is transforming, as parents tend to create their own traditions by choosing elements from their respective family traditions, from friends' traditions, and also from other people's traditions (e.g., as seen on Facebook) provided that they feel right.[70]

The analysis also revealed a shift from obligation to choice regarding parents' decisions on whether to baptize their children: Parents showed few signs of feeling obligated toward family, older generations, or their church affiliation. Some felt obliged to explain to their grandparents why they opted out of baptism, but they did not feel obliged to baptize. Many parents put together their own packages of traditions.

- The christening gown served as a symbol of a family relationship and was used in both church and alternative non-faith rituals.
- Parents who chose or rejected baptism both supported the individual's own choice of religion and thought of baptism as a preliminary ritual to confirmation. One parent found the decision regarding baptism too serious for an infant, as an individual should make his or her own choice to live a life in God. In the Danish, Swedish, and Norwegian surveys, the individual's own choice was the main reason for opting out of baptism.

---

67. Poulsen et al., *Religiøsitet 1*, 93.
68. Leth-Nissen, *Dåb i dag*, 76.
69. Leth-Nissen, *Dåb i dag*, 44.
70. Leth-Nissen, *Dåb i dag*, 82–88.

- Parents in metropolitan areas negotiated on whether they should baptize their children. This fits the findings from Swedish and Norwegian studies, the surveys of which showed that parents from metropolitan areas were more likely than other parents to have children with individuals of a different cultural background. This could explain some of the differences in the negotiation processes. In contrast, in the Danish interviews, parents from suburban and rural areas more often had partners with similar backgrounds. Some of them reflected jointly on the choice of baptism, whereas others negotiated.

- Putting together one's own religious package was more common among parents in the metropolitan areas. Parents from metropolitan, suburban, and rural areas showed differentiated church use, as they chose or rejected baptism across their membership status.

LONG-TERM—COLLECTIVE ORIENTATION

Here, I present the findings on parents who emphasized their collective orientation and long-term decisions regarding baptism. Pettersson found that, most often, an individual had both a collective and an individual orientation and made both long-term and short-term decisions.[71] Pettersson defined the collectively oriented as those who made long-term decisions connected to collective cultural values, culture, history, tradition, relatives, and rites of passage.[72]

In the interviews, tradition was mentioned by some parents as a strong argument for their choice of baptism.[73] As I will discuss later, the parents from suburban and rural areas negotiated about which elements from their families they wanted to include in the new tradition they were establishing together. Connected to this, some couples decided on which church building they wanted their new family to belong to and which christening gown their children should use.[74] To one particular couple from a rural area, their connection to a certain church building with a surrounding churchyard made the choice of baptism final. In the churchyard, two of the father's relatives had been buried some years

---

71. Pettersson, *Kvalitet*, 403–4.
72. Pettersson, *Kvalitet*, 403–4.
73. Leth-Nissen, *Dåb i dag*, 40.
74. Leth-Nissen, *Dåb i dag*, 40–41.

before. Thus, in having the baptism in this church building, the father felt like his missing relatives were there for the baptism. As he identified as a non-believer, this made the baptism meaningful to him.[75]

For some parents, the church relationship was part of a wider cultural identity that was built by all the contact they had with the church throughout their lifetime, and the ELCD was part of their mental backdrop.[76] One couple saw their child's baptism as part of a greater existential framework of life, wherein one day, a family would have a funeral in the church, and the next day, parents would have their child baptized.[77]

Many of the parents showed a collective orientation when they looked to the practices of family and friends for inspiration on the choice or rejection of baptism. In the end, the choice was theirs to make, but family and friends still had an impact.[78]

One mother had opted out of church as a young woman. When she and her partner wanted to get married, she found this to be a new opportunity to connect to the church. She wondered whether the local church in the metropolitan area would be the right place to get married. She connected very well with the pastor, and the couple had both their wedding and, later, the baptism of their first child in the local church. Some years later, the couple moved to a rural area in the vicinity of the metropole. They had another child, and this time, they were very clear that they wanted to belong to the local church in the rural area. During her maternity leave, the mother had attended baby hymn singing and established a connection with the new pastor. For the baptism, the couple invited both family and a lot of friends from the metropole. However, the friends disappointed the couple, as they did not care enough to get up early and make it to the baptism in the church, instead only arriving in time for lunch. Only their families attended church.[79] This couple had thus transformed from a mainly individually oriented position to a position of collective values by making more long-term decisions.

As Pettersson writes, the collectively oriented church members expect the church to be there when they need it and associate it with security, traditions, solemnity, and silence. In this vein, one mother

75. Leth-Nissen, *Dåb i dag*, 68.
76. Leth-Nissen, *Dåb i dag*, 52.
77. Leth-Nissen, *Dåb i dag*, 52–53.
78. Leth-Nissen, *Dåb i dag*, 42.
79. Leth-Nissen, *Dåb i dag*, 42.

experienced the baptismal ritual as the presence of God's protection.[80] Another mother felt that her Christian faith connected her to a sense of protection during her fertility treatments and pregnancy. To her, baptism was a powerful and meaningful rite of passage.[81] Others based their decisions on whether to baptize on a need for security and coherence as a form of meaning-making. To some of the parents, the choice of baptism was a way of creating meaning in their lives together, as they agreed that the relationship with the church made them feel safer, and they wanted to pass on this feeling to their child.[82] Some parents chose baptism to explicitly pass on their faith to their child.[83]

All parents were generally positive toward the church. The suburban and rural parents had grown up with the church as part of their mental backdrop (through religious socialization from parents and grandparents), while the metropolitan parents more often had contact with church activities as their main connection to the church and received less religious socialization from their parents.[84] Interestingly, I found no direct connection between religious socialization outside the home in one's youth or childhood and parents' choice of baptism. Eight out of the 12 parents from the metropolitan area had participated in church choirs, scouting, or other activities connected to the church and chose baptism, while four opted out. Five parents had no religious socialization and still chose baptism.[85] Parents from suburban and rural areas had less contact with church activities during their childhood, and only five took part in scouting and church choir, but almost all of them chose baptism.[86]

For some parents, partaking in baby hymn singing symbolized the activation of an otherwise distanced relationship with the church, as they experienced an open and welcoming atmosphere through this activity.[87] Here, a short-term commitment to a church activity—which by most parents was seen as a cultural activity—led to a more collective and long-term relationship.[88] In fact, two mothers, one from the metropolitan area

---

80. Leth-Nissen, *Churching Alone*, 195.
81. Leth-Nissen, *Churching Alone*, 195.
82. Leth-Nissen, *Dåb i dag*, 40.
83. Leth-Nissen, *Dåb i dag*, 40.
84. Leth-Nissen, *Dåb i dag*, 74.
85. Leth-Nissen, *Dåb i dag*, 64.
86. Leth-Nissen, *Dåb i dag*, 64.
87. Leth-Nissen, *Dåb I dag*, 49–50.
88. Leth-Nissen, *Dåb I dag*, 50. Leth-Nissen and Trolle, *Dåb eller ej?*, 68–69.

and one from a suburban area, attended baby hymn singing as a substitute for baptism, which they could not agree on with their partners.[89]

For parents across different geographies, being related to the local community was not itself a determinant of their choice to baptize. For some, baptism was a way of establishing a connection to the local community, as they became familiar with the pastor and began taking part in church activities, such as baby hymn singing.[90] In the same way, taking part in baby hymn singing could lead to knowing the pastor, feeling welcomed, and then choosing baptism.[91]

In the 2014 survey, the answers pointed to baptism being connected to collective values, as the informants reported that their reasons for choosing baptism were "family tradition" (45 percent), "it marks the naming of the child" (45 percent), and "being baptized is part of being Danish"(38 percent).[92] All of these options were based on a collective orientation toward being part of a greater community than just the couple's new family.

The Scandinavian studies resemble the Danish survey in terms of overall results and findings. In the two Norwegian surveys and the Swedish survey, parents' most frequent reason for choosing baptism was "family tradition."[93]

SHORT-TERM—INDIVIDUALLY ORIENTED

Pettersson described the individually oriented as persons with a focus on the experience of being part of the church, thereby emphasizing one's own personal needs and choices. Such individuals evaluate worship and other activities from the perspective of their own interests and feelings.[94]

For one mother, her short-term individually oriented church use of baby hymn singing led to baptism and connecting to the local community.[95] More often for metropolitan parents, the use of baby hymn singing was evaluated as a meaningful cultural activity with the child but did not

---

89. Leth-Nissen and Trolle, *Dåb eller ej?*, 68–69.
90. Leth-Nissen, *Dåb I dag*, 81.
91. Leth-Nissen, *Dåb I dag*, 81.
92. Leth-Nissen and Trolle, *Dåb eller ej?*, 17–18.
93. Høeg and Gresaker, *Når det rokkes*, 37, 114; *Rafoss, Et religiøst landskap*, 21–23; Sandberg et al., *Dop i förändring*, 44–47.
94. Pettersson, *Kvalitet*, 403–4.
95. Leth-Nissen, *Dåb I dag*, 74.

lead to baptism.[96] Some parents from the metropolitan area showed clear signs of individual orientation, as they participated in baby hymn singing without being members of the church.[97]

The parents from the metropolitan area showed more inclinations toward making short-term decisions regarding religious affiliation, as several of them had opted in or out of religion as they found it made sense in their own lives.[98] In contrast, the suburban and rural parents were more likely to carry on with the church relationship in which they had grown up.[99]

Generally, I found that most parents showed both a collective and individual orientation and made long-term and short-term decisions:

- Parents made long-term decisions as they chose which elements of family traditions to pass on. Some chose which church building they wanted their new family to belong to, and this was not necessarily the local church building.
- A family christening gown or having a close relative buried at the churchyard made a baptism meaningful, even for a non-believer.
- Parents were collectively oriented as they looked to family and friends for inspiration, but the choice of baptism and traditional elements to hold onto remained theirs.
- Parents in the suburban and rural areas were more likely to be subject to religious socialization from their families, while parents in the metropolitan area more often received their religious socialization from attending church activities, such as choir or scouting.
- For some parents, the baptism initiated their connection to the local community.
- Attending church activities like baby hymn singing was to some parents a short-term decision, but for others, it led to a connection to the pastor and a baptism in the church.
- Other parents—as part of a negotiation process—substituted the long-term decision of a baptism with the short-term decision of attending baby hymn singing.

---

96. Leth-Nissen and Trolle, *Dåb eller ej?*, 71–74.
97. Leth-Nissen and Trolle, *Dåb eller ej?*, 69.
98. Leth-Nissen, *Dåb i dag*, 74.
99. Leth-Nissen, *Dåb i dag*, 74.

OVERALL FINDINGS AND DISCUSSION

A shift from obligation to choice was present in almost all of the interviews with the parents. However, the shift from collective to individual orientation and from long-term to short-term decisions was not evident in the interviews. Most parents showed a mixed collective and individual orientation in the process of choosing or rejecting baptism for their child. With these findings, I argue that we can see the beginning of a shift toward churching alone, and this explains part of the change in the parents' use of baptism. In the following, I will discuss the mixed collective and individual orientation of the parents by examining the concept of tradition.

Tradition in Transformation

The concept of tradition has become negotiable, as parents have gained a differentiated use of the ELCD. This differentiated use plays out, for example, when a couple of parents opt out of baptism but stay members themselves, or when another parent chooses baptism but no membership for herself. These examples can be captured by the concept of *churching alone*, as it can account for both the shift from obligation to choice (Davie) and the change from long-term to short-term commitment to the church (Pettersson).

In the Danish, Norwegian, and Swedish studies, numerous parents used family tradition as one of the main reasons for their choice of baptism for their child/children. Tradition is an ambiguous term, and like other widely used terms, such as culture, it has been used in so many different ways that, as a theoretical concept, it has become almost impossible to handle, define, and use constructively.[100] In a systematic theological context, *traditio* has been defined as the process itself, namely how *tradita* (i.e., the content of [the Christian or church] tradition) is learned or passed on.[101] During this process, the one who passes on also reinterprets tradition, whereby *tradita* (the content of the tradition) is always undergoing transformation. The content of the tradition is constantly changing during the transmission, which must—in my understanding—occur through narration, conversation, actions, and rituals. This content has a subtle Christian connection, as the individuals and families through the tradition relate to the folk church and the Christianity it preaches. The

---

100. This discussion of tradition follows Leth-Nissen, "Traditionen," 16–20.
101. Percy, *Engaging with Contemporary Culture*, 98.

parents of young children—and the people who surround them—can thus be seen as transformers of tradition, as they are themselves involved in reinterpreting the Christian tradition.

In the following, my outline of the *traditio* process is meant as a kind of generalization and must be understood as a means of initiating broader discussion regarding the changes that we have observed.

The baptism studies showed that the transmission process regarding religion is changing. Previous generations felt obliged to pass on the rituals of holding baptisms, confirmations, weddings, and funerals in church to the next generation. With the generation born in approximately 1950—Generation '68—the transmission weakened. This generation to a lesser extent than the previous ones passed on traditions and affiliation to church to their children. Generally speaking, the Generation '68 felt obliged to have their children baptized to satisfy their parents, but then they effectively withdrew from the *traditio* process.[102] Thus, the *traditio* process stopped being a continuous subject-object relationship between generations. The parents of an infant are thus no longer recipients of *tradita* (the content of the tradition) because the grandparents have disconnected the transmission. According to the interviews, what happens now is that the parents of an infant evaluate the contexts in which they themselves grew up and choose which parts of the traditions they can and will activate and then pass on to their child. I have described the parents of the infant as active and able to make choices as agents in the *traditio* process. However, the term "choice" does not signify here that the parents are completely free to choose. Instead, in my opinion, the parents are set in a situation where they need to orientate themselves within the cross-pressure of competing horizons of meaning (per Taylor) in which they have grown up.[103] Generally, parents today are under pressure from many other horizons of meaning through, for example, their friends, work life, and their lives on social media. These horizons function as a form of background radiation, which the parents are continuously affected by, also when making decisions regarding baptism. The new thing is that the grandparents of the child have stepped back as a horizon of meaning, leaving the parents more to be influenced by other horizons.

The change in grandparents' attitudes to passing on church affiliation was found in the interviews with parents in the Norwegian study,

---

102. Salomonsen, *Religion i dag*.
103. Taylor, *The Ethics of Authenticity*.

where in the same way as described above, grandparents supported the individual's free choice of religion.[104]

Collectively Individualized

When the *traditio* process is characterized by disconnection between generations, one must interpret the interviewees' use of the word "tradition" in a new light. Parents in suburban and rural areas tended to use the word tradition more than those in metropolitan areas. This could lead to the understanding that the parents in the metropolitan areas are far more individualized than those in the rest of Denmark. However, in my view, this understanding would be wrong. The argument I propose is that when the passing on of tradition is broken or under negotiation, and the content of the tradition can be chosen based on how it fits the parents (i.e., a package of tradition), then the parents outside Copenhagen are just as individualized as the parents from the metropolitan area. In other words, they choose to have their children baptized more often than parents in the metropolitan area, but they make an active choice of which parts of the tradition they want to include in their own lives. Furthermore, they only choose for themselves, as the child must later make a corresponding choice at the age of confirmation. Later, in adult life, with a child and a co-parent, a new process of choosing a common tradition package will begin.

In terms of values, the parents in the suburban and rural areas oriented themselves toward their families on both sides more often than the parents in the metropolitan areas. Overall, they tried to balance their own religious wishes with their families' traditions and expectations, and they appeared individualized as they put together their own packages of traditions. With Gundelach, Iversen, and Warburg, I characterize the parents from the suburban and rural areas of Denmark as *collectively oriented individualists*.[105]

BIBLIOGRAPHY

Andersen, Peter B., et al. "Går fanden i kloster, når han bliver gammel? Religiøsitet i lyset af sociale og psykologiske forhold." In *Små og store forandringer. Danskernes værdier siden 1981*, edited by Peter Gundelach, 97–113. Copenhagen: Reitzel, 2011.

---

104. Høeg and Gresaker, *Når det rokkes*, 118.
105. Gundelach et al., *I hjertet*, 193.

PART I: EMPIRICAL STUDIES

The Center for Pastoral Education and Research of the ELCD. "Church Statistics on Baptism." https://www.fkuv.dk/folkekirken-i-tal/daabstal.

———. "Church Statistics on Burials." https://www.fkuv.dk/folkekirken-i-tal/kirkelige-begravelser.

———. "Church Statistics on Confirmation." https://www.fkuv.dk/folkekirken-i-tal/konfirmerede.

———. "Church Statistics on Membership." https://www.fkuv.dk/folkekirken-i-tal/medlemstal.

Davie, Grace. *Europe: The Exceptional Case. Parameters of Faith in the Modern World.* London: Darton, Longman & Todd, 2002.

———. "Religion in 21st-Century Europe: Framing the Debate." *Irish Theological Quarterly* 78 (2013) 279–93. https://doi.org/10.1177/0021140013484432.

———. "Religion in Europe in the 21st Century: The Factors to Take into Account." *European Journal of Sociology* 47 (2006) 271–96. https://doi.org/10.1017/S0003975606000099.

———. *The Sociology of Religion. A Critical Agenda.* 2nd ed. London: Sage, 2013.

Dobbelaere, Karel. "Towards an Integrated Perspective of the Processes Related to the Descriptive Concept of Secularization." *Sociology of Religion* 60 (1999) 229–47. https://doi.org/10.2307/3711935.

Gundelach, Peter, et al. *I hjertet af Danmark: Institutioner og mentaliteter.* Copenhagen: Reitzel, 2008.

Høeg, Ida Marie, and Ann Kristin Gresaker. *Når det rokkes ved tradition og tilhørighet.* Oslo: KIFO, 2015. http://www.kifo.no/doc//RAPPORTER/KIFO%20Rapport%20 2015_2%20Nar%20det%20rokkes%20ved_%20til%20web.pdf.

Leth-Nissen, Karen Marie. "Churching Alone: Folkekirken, de kirkelige handlinger og social kapital i kirkesociologisk perspektiv." In *Tradition og fornyelse*, edited by Enggaard, Nete Helene and Rasmus Nøjgaard, 197–213. Copenhagen: Eksistensen, 2018.

———. *Churching Alone? A Study of the Danish Folk Church at Organisational, Individual, and Societal Levels.* Publications from Faculty of Theology 79. Copenhagen: University of Copenhagen, 2018.

———. *Dåb i dag. Traditionen til forhandling.* Publications from Faculty of Theology 85. Copenhagen: University of Copenhagen, 2020.

———. "Traditionen til forhandling." *Kritisk Forum for Praktisk Teologi* 160 (2020) 7–23.

Leth-Nissen, Karen Marie Sø, et al. *Religiøsitet og forholdet til folkekirken 2020: Bog 2 - Kvalitative studier.* The Center for Pastoral Education and Research of the ELCD, 2022.

Leth-Nissen, Karen Marie, and Astrid Krabbe Trolle. *Dåb eller ej?, rapport om småbørnsforældres til- og fravalg af dåb.* Publications from Faculty of Theology 59. Copenhagen: Center for Church Research, University of Copenhagen, 2015. http://curis.ku.dk/ws/files/144460435/Daab_eller_ej_e_bog.pdf.

Percy, Martyn. *Engaging with Contemporary Culture: Christianity, Theology and the Concrete Church.* Aldershot, UK: Ashgate, 2005.

Pettersson, Per. "From Standardised Offer to Consumer Adaptation: Challenges to the Church of Sweden's Identity." In *Religion in Consumer Society*, edited by Tuomas Martikainen and François Gauthier, 43–57. Farnham, MA: Ashgate, 2013.

———. *Kvalitet i livslånga tjänsterelationer: Svenska kyrkan ur tjänsteteoretiskt och religionssociologiskt perspektiv*. Stockholm: Verbum, 2000.

Poulsen, Jais, et al. *Religiøsitet og forholdet til folkekirken. Bog 1: Kvalitative studier*. Copenhagen: The Center for Pastoral Education and Research of the ELCD, 2021.

Rafoss, Tore Witsø. *Et religiøst landskap i endring. Oppslutning om dåb på østre Romerike*. Oslo: KIFO, 2016. http://old.kifo.inbusinessclients.no/doc//RAPPORTER/KIFO%20Rapport%202016%20med%20omslag_endelig.pdf.

Salomonsen, Per. *Religion i dag, et sociologisk metodestudium*. Copenhagen: Gad, 1971.

Sandberg, Andreas, et al. *Dop i förändring: en studie av föräldrars aktiva val och församlingens strategiska doparbete*. Uppsala: Svenska kyrkan, 2019.

Taylor, Charles. *The Ethics of Authenticity*. Cambridge: Harvard University Press, 1995.

4

The Changing Role of Baptism in Finland
Parents' Attitudes toward Baptism according to a Baptismal Survey

Hanna Salomäki

In Western countries, it has been observed that younger generations have distanced themselves significantly from religious communities. This manifests itself as detachment from religious beliefs, withdrawal from the activities and membership of religious communities, and a decline in private religious practice. In particular, the group that participates in religious activities at an already low level has become even more passive.[1] However, this phenomenon should not be taken as a sign of a decrease in devotional or spiritual questioning. People are still seeking a good and meaningful life, but not necessarily in churches.[2]

The weakening of religion's role is especially evident among young age groups, both in everyday activities and at times of celebration. The broader decline in religious socialization means that many representatives of the younger generation no longer consider the religious rituals that the church or religion offer to be a part of their celebrations of various phases of their lives.[3] Various individual and communal elements are

---

1. Voas, *The Rise and Fall*; Voas and Crockett, *Religion in Britain*.
2. Voas and Watt, "Numerical Change," 13.
3. Voas and Crockett, *Religion in Britain*.

intertwined in these celebrations of turning points, and such celebratory customs reflect society's prevailing values and practices, one's own and one's extended family's traditions, and one's own personal beliefs. Celebrations of the phases of life also entail the making of a choice: the individual decides which elements of their background community to carry on, and which they will not pass on. The Nordic countries' culture of celebration has thus far appeared fairly uniform, although traditions associated with celebration are changing with lifestyle. Recent studies have found that individual choices assume a greater role than previously, including in the various celebrations of the phases of life.[4]

As in other Nordic countries, the Lutheran Church in Finland has played a prominent role in the rituals associated with life's turning points. Even at the beginning of the twenty-first century in Finland, almost all the departed received a church funeral. Ninety percent of the children were baptized, and 70 percent of the couples were married in the church. The Lutheran Church has seen the role of their occasional offices as central: they have been perceived as a significant channel of encounter through which the church has been present in significant moments in Finns' lives. Such ceremonies have reached many Finns, whose participation in the church's other activities has been minimal.[5] Generally, Finns have considered occasional offices to be the main reason to belong to the Lutheran Church. In a 2019 survey, four-fifths of Lutheran Church members considered the church's occasional offices an important reason for belonging to the church. Indeed, the share of those of this opinion was similar in the early 2010s.[6] Generally, changes have taken place more slowly in Finland than in its neighbors.

However, the twenty-first century has seen a change in attitudes toward the services of the church, with only the share of church funerals remaining high, as nine out of ten deceased Finns (95 percent) received a church burial in 2023. In contrast, the proportion of those married in church has been continuously decreasing, as only 39 percent were married in this way in 2023. The proportion of those who are baptized has also continued its rapid decline, with only 56 percent of children being baptized in 2023.

---

4. Vandendorpe, "Funerals in Belgium," 18–33; Pajari, "Kuolema maalla ja kaupungissa."

5. Kääriäinen et al., *Moderni kirkkokansa*, 259.

6. Salomäki, "Worship," 105.

The aim of this article is to analyze the role of religious ceremonies among young adults in Finland. When the role of religion changes in society, individuals also consider rituals in new ways. Against this background, this article examines the process of baptism, including which factors influence the parents' decision to baptize their children. This article is based on a survey conducted among young adults in Finland (2019). First, I will provide an overview of religious changes in Finland and then introduce the research questions and data.

INDIVIDUALIZATION AND OCCASIONAL OFFICES

Participation in occasional offices in Nordic countries is closely associated with membership in folk churches. It has been customary to remain a member of the church while only rarely participating in church events and focusing solely on utilizing occasional offices at life's turning points. This is true, even if the individual does not necessarily consider themselves a believer or does not subscribe to the church's teachings. Ketola has divided Finns into four ideological groups according to how they define their own identities. These include cultural Christians (34 percent), the religious (29 percent), the non-religious (24 percent), and seekers (22 percent).[7] The term "cultural Christian" describes a person who values the church and religion but does not subscribe to the church's teachings.[8] Identification with the different groups varies by generation. For example, the majority of those born in the 1940s consider themselves to be either religious or cultural Christians, but only a small percentage are non-religious. The situation differs for younger generations, with this change being especially evident in those born in the 1980s. A smaller proportion of this age group than any other considers themselves cultural Christians. In fact, one-third of those born in the 1980s and 1990s considered themselves non-religious. The identity of the seeker is also common, especially among those born in the 1980s (according to a *Gallup Ecclesiastica* survey).[9]

Similar results were also obtained in the *European Values Study* (2017) survey. According to this dataset, Finns born in the 1980s and 1990s appeared less religious than those of previous generations. One-third (30 percent) of those born in the 1980s and almost one-fourth (23

---

7. Ketola, "Religious Identities," 68–74.
8. Räisänen, "Ateisti vai kulttuurikristitty?," 97–99.
9. Ketola, "Religious Identities," 68–74.

percent) of those born in the 1990s considered themselves religious, while more than 70 percent of those born in the 1940s felt the same way. Generational differences are therefore remarkable large. The difference between younger and older Finnish women was especially marked, with this generational difference being greater than that in any other European country. Only 19 percent of the youngest cohort of women considered themselves religious, whereas almost nine out of ten (87 percent) of women born in the 1940s identified as religious.[10] The weakening of religiosity was also evident when the current age cohorts of young people were compared with those of the same age in previous generations. The change was especially stark in a comparison of women aged between 15 and 19, as a significantly smaller proportion believed in God and the resurrection of Jesus than those in the same cohort in 2011. The share of those who prayed actively also declined markedly. Interestingly, these changes occurred in a relatively short period.[11]

The above changes can be further examined with the aid of the theory of individualization, which suggests that an individual's religiosity is detached from religious institutions, with the autonomous solutions of the individual being thus emphasized. Churches no longer define the individual's beliefs; instead, individuals construct their own outlooks on life and religious orientation, as well as their own sets of religious beliefs and practices. Christianity may play an important role here but not at the expense of other views. Even if individuals continue to belong to the church, their religious world is both personal and independent.[12] As the authority of religious institutions has decreased, individuals have had more opportunities to decide how to practice religion and what to include in it. In recent studies, religion has been examined from the perspective of the "subjective turn." Religious agency has been seen to have moved closer to individuals and farther from institutions, as religion assumes even more individual forms of a looser bearing. Choices are guided by experience, new technologies, and the crisis in traditional institutions' authority structures.[13]

Many church members view the occasional offices as services provided by the parish. The development of the individualization of religion has been interpreted through the connection between religion

10. Salomäki, "Suomalaisten ikä- ja sukupuolierot," 239–42.
11. Ketola, "Religion and the Cultural Turning Point," 37–39.
12. Pollack, "Religious Change in Europe," 171–84.
13. Hunt, *Religion and Everyday Life*, 28–43, 93–110.

and consumer society: it is thought that religious practitioners behave in the same way as consumers of other services. For example, in the occasional offices, this can be manifested in how more church members now separately assess whether the church's conduct of celebrations associated with the phases of life is self-representative and "self-seeking." In younger generations, reflection on personal autonomous choices can be emphasized precisely because individual choices are especially likely to characterize these generations. In this vein, scholars have assigned generations varying timescales and designations. Ketola has called the generation born between 1980 and 1989 "Generation Y," and those born between 1990 and 1999 have been referred to as "Generation Z." The key defining experience of Generation Y is the idealization of and quest for individuality. Based on this, the generation has also been called the "generation of individual choice." This emphasis on choice is also reflected in religion, where it is typical to believe in "your own way" and the selection of those elements that please you. Accordingly, "Generation Z" has been described as the "generation of uncertainty" and the "online generation of competition and fulfillment."[14]

The average age for giving birth for the first time has continued to rise in Finland. The current average age is about 31 years, and one in four first-time mothers is over 35 years of age.[15] The generational survey's division shows that families are currently established mainly in Generation Y (born 1980–1989) and Generation Z (born 1990–1999).[16] These are the age cohorts that are most critical for church membership, and whose smallest share identifies as religious. The 30–39 age cohort is also that with the lowest church membership. Half (53 percent) belonged to the Lutheran Church in 2019, compared with the Finnish average of 69 percent. Only two-fifths (39 percent) belonged to the church in Helsinki. Overall, Generations Y and Z are most prominent in the age cohorts who have resigned from the church.[17]

---

14. Ketola, "Religion and the Cultural Turning Point," 13–16; Piispa, "Yhdeksän sanaa Y-sukupolvesta," 12–28.

15. "Perinataalitilasto—synnyttäjät, synnytykset ja vastasyntyneet 2019."

16. Piispa, "Yhdeksän sanaa Y-sukupolvesta," 9–32.

17. Sohlberg and Ketola, "Religious Identities and Beliefs," 55–58.

RESEARCH BACKGROUND, TASKS, AND MATERIAL

As described above, the rate of baptism has remained higher in Finland than in the other Nordic countries. The phenomenon of not seeking baptism has already been studied in other countries. Previous research has found that the decision to seek baptism is connected to, among other factors, socioeconomic status, education, place of residence, marital status, and parents' ages. A Norwegian study has shown that a parent's education reduces the likelihood of a child being baptized.[18] Meanwhile, a Danish study demonstrated that baptism is positively correlated with age and education, and a Swedish study revealed that the effect of age was gender-based: the father's age was positively correlated with baptism, whereas the mother's age was negatively correlated. Marital status also had a proven connection with decisions concerning baptism: married parents were more likely to seek baptism for their children than single or cohabiting parents.[19] Several studies have shown that place of residence is connected to the decision to seek baptism, as those who live in rural areas are more likely to have their children baptized than those who live in cities.[20] The decision to seek baptism is connected both to the parents' own religiosity and with customs and traditions. Swedish research has considered parents', especially mothers´, relationships with the church the most significant factor in the decision to seek baptism. The importance of baptism seems to be more connected with traditions, however, than with religious reasons. Still, despite these general patterns, differences between countries have emerged. For example, one's own Christian faith appeared more significant for seeking baptism in the Norwegian study than in the Swedish one.[21]

The rapid decline in the percentage of those baptized has also raised questions in Finland about decisions concerning the baptism of young adults. Information was needed about why some decided to seek baptism for their child and why it was decided not to have a child baptized. Accordingly, the task was defined in terms of the following questions:

18. Høeg and Gresaker, Når det rokkes, 43–44.

19. Lüchau, "Inmeldelse och dåb," 151–75; Sandberg et al., Dop i förändring, 36–40; Jonsson et al., "Who is Baptized," 72–83.

20. Høveg and Gresaker, Når det rokkes, 25–30; Sandberg et al., Dop i förändring, 34–35.

21. Rafoss, Et religiøst landskap, 21–22, 41–42; Høeg and Gresaker, Når det rokkes, 113–19; Jonsson et al., "Who is Baptized," 72–83. Sandberg et al., Dop i förändring, 31–33.

1. How did the respondents feel about the role of religious rituals in celebrations of the various phases of life?
2. What was the process through which respondents decided to seek baptism?
3. Which factors influenced the decision to have a child baptized?

It was decided to select families with reasonably young children for the research group to insure that memories of baptisms would be fresh. Parents of preschool-age children (0–6 years old) were selected as the respondent group. This group's decisions concerning baptism were made in the 2010s, the most significant turning point in the Finnish tradition of baptism.

The data were collected via Norstat's internet panel in February 2019. The survey was conducted in both Finnish and Swedish. Half of the respondents (N = 1,029) were men, and half were women. Sixty-five percent of the respondents belonged to the Lutheran Church, which corresponded well with the average church membership rate in 2019 (69 percent). Three-fourths of the respondents (74 percent) had had their child or children baptized in the Lutheran Church. In addition, three percent had had their child baptized in another Christian church. One-fifth (22 percent) of the respondents had not had their child or children baptized.[22] The questionnaire consisted mainly of multiple-choice questions. Most of the questions of the survey were same as those used in the baptism survey conducted in Norway. This made it possible to compare attitudes of Norwegians and Finns.[23]

ATTITUDE TOWARD RELIGIOUS RITUALS IN CELEBRATIONS OF THE PHASES OF LIFE

The reduced participation in occasional offices reflects a general change in mindset. The baptism survey asked respondents how important they thought it was to include a religious element in celebrations of their various turning points in life. In the group of parents who participated in the baptism survey (average age 35), a religious ritual was considered the most important in connection with death. Three-fourths of respondents (74 percent) considered it important or very important. Three-fifths of respondents (59 percent) saw religious rituals as important

---

22. Baptismal Survey 2019.
23. Rafoss, *Et religiøst landskap*, 64–70.

when getting married, and about the same number (56 percent) when a child was born. The results resemble those of the *Gallup Ecclesiastica* survey (2019), which examined how important the Finnish population generally considered religious rituals to be in celebrations of the various phases of life. Sixty-eight percent of Finns said they considered such rituals important in connection with death, 60 percent in connection with marriage, and 60 percent in connection with the birth of a child (Gallup Ecclesiastica 2019). The survey revealed that those between 30 and 39 years of age were most critical of religion. For example, in this age cohort, more people did not want a Christian burial for themselves (39 percent) than those who did (34 percent).[24]

An interesting observation emerged when examining those who judged religious rituals to be *very* important for the birth of a child among different genders and age cohorts (Figure 1). Among women aged 40 and older, a significantly larger group than men considered religious rituals very important, but among younger age cohorts, the situation was different: the distributions were reversed for those under 30. Young men considered religious rituals significantly more important than women of the same age. A similar observation was made in the *Gallup Ecclestiastica* 2019 survey.[25]

---

24. Salomäki, "Worship," 105–23.
25. Salomäki, "Worship," 107–8.

PART I: EMPIRICAL STUDIES

Figure 1. Respondents' views regarding the importance of religious rituals in connection with the birth of a child: Baptism survey (N = 1,029) percentages. Source: *The Church Research Institute in Finland. Baptismal Survey 2019*

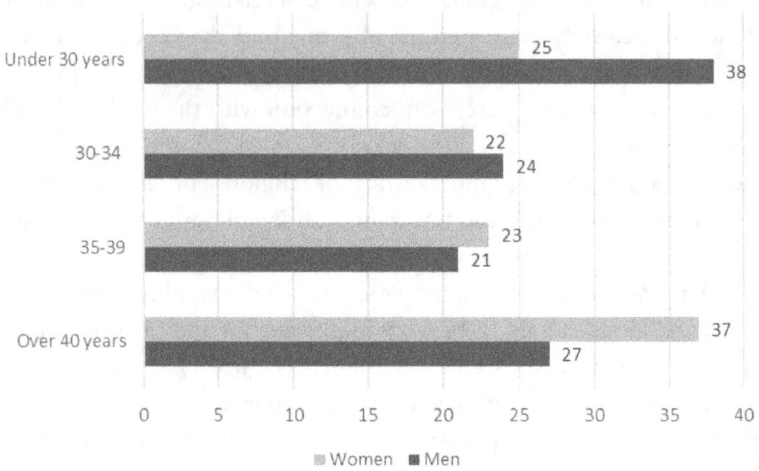

These results are linked with the broader observation that there has been a remarkable change in young generations' religiosity in Finland. Several different research materials show the distancing of young women from the church, including its doctrine, participation in its activities, and private religious practice, while increasing interest in the church and religion has been observed among the youngest cohorts of men.[26] This observation of the change in women's attitudes is relevant to baptism. A previous study found that women were the key group in passing on religious traditions.[27] It can be assumed that young women's critical approach to the Christian faith and reluctance to be identified as religious are strongly reflected in the religious education that occurs in both families and decisions to seek baptism. In the *Gallup Ecclesiastica* 2019 survey, only one-fourth of Finns under the age of 40 considered themselves to have received a religious education at home. Mothers from Generation Z were least interested in passing on the Christian tradition, and among women

---

26. Salomäki, "Suomalaisten ikä- ja sukupuolierot," 236–51; Hytönen et al., *Johtopäätökset*, 251–58; Tervo-Niemelä and Spännäri, "Uskonnollisuuden ja uskonnottomuuden muutos," 59–72.

27. See, for example, Niemelä, *Heikkeneekö uskonnollisuus ikäryhmissä*, 54–57.

under 30, only one-fifth had taught or planned to teach their children to pray in the evening (28 percent of fathers in Generation X).[28]

DECIDING TO SEEK BAPTISM AND THE PEOPLE WHO INFLUENCE IT

Decisions related to an individual's religious life do not occur in a vacuum. Instead, they are greatly influenced by the social environment. Individuals' actions are guided by social norms that reflect common mindsets in society. Values and mindsets change slowly, but the change accelerates after a certain tipping point is reached.[29] In relation to religiosity, this phenomenon may explain the difference in mindsets. Mindsets established for previous generations do not necessarily gain support in younger generations, because the latter's own reference groups may set completely different standards.

The decision to baptize a child is a process that several people close to the individual can influence. When respondents were asked who they believed had influenced their decision to seek baptism, their own spouse emerged as the most important influence (Table 1). Three-fifths of respondents judged that their partner or spouse had influenced the decision to seek baptism greatly or very greatly. Differences between the sexes were observed, as more than one-third of men thought their partner had had a *very* great influence on the decision, whereas only one in four women felt the same way. One-fifth estimated that their own or their spouse's parents had influenced the decision to seek baptism, but others' parents were seen to have had little influence. The influence of friends was generally viewed as quite small.

---

28. Hytönen, "Handing on the Christian Tradition," 184–89.
29. Inglehart, *Cultural Evolution*, 23–24.

Table 1. Respondents' views concerning the extent to which others influenced the decision to seek baptism for a child. Proportions answering "very greatly" and "greatly" in percentages (N = 1,039). Source: *The Church Research Institute in Finland. Baptismal Survey 2019*

	Women	Men	Total
Own spouse/partner	58	65	62
Own parents	19	21	20
Spouse's/partner's parents	15	18	17
Other relatives	9	10	9
Close friends	6	7	6

Parents were also asked how common it was in their immediate circle to seek baptism for a child. The respondents most often judged that almost everyone in their immediate circle had sought baptism for their children, with almost half (46 percent) of the respondents reporting these thoughts. One-fourth (25 percent) estimated that the children in their immediate circle were usually baptized, and an equal proportion (25 percent) indicated that their immediate circle included both those who had sought baptism for their child and those who had not. Only a small number (3 percent) considered that children in their immediate circle were not usually baptized, or that almost no one had sought baptism for their children. Although the respondents did not consider the influence of the immediate circle, except for their partner, to be especially significant, how baptism was perceived within it was strongly reflected in the decision to seek baptism for one's child. If baptism was common in the immediate circle, nine-tenths of respondents also sought baptism for their own children. The smaller the proportion of people in the immediate circle who chose to seek baptism for their child, the less likely it was that one would seek baptism for one's own child. If no children had been baptized in the immediate circle, three-fourths of respondents had made the same decision.

Table 2. Decision to seek baptism in the immediate circle and to seek baptism for one's own child in percentages (N = 1,029) Source: *The Church Research Institute in Finland. Baptismal Survey 2019*

	Yes, in the Evangelical Lutheran Church	Yes, in another Christian church	No	Some children are baptized, some are not	Total
Almost everyone in immediate circle has sought baptism for their children, or children are usually baptized (n = 729)	86	3	10	2	100
Immediate circle includes both those who have sought baptism for their child and those who have not (n = 254)	49	2	47	3	100
Children are not usually baptized in the immediate circle, or almost no one has sought baptism for their children (n = 45)	20	5	74		100

The respondents were asked when they had considered the issue of baptism. The data showed that decisions about baptism were made very early. Two-fifths of respondents and as many as half of the women said they had already made a decision before the relationship with spouse or partner was formed. One-fourth of the respondents had decided during pregnancy, and only one-tenth after the child's birth.

Table 3. Parents' views on when the decision to seek baptism for a child was made in percentages (N = 1,029). Source: *The Church Research Institute in Finland. Baptismal Survey 2019*

	Women	Men	Total
Before the relationship was formed	48	38	43
When getting to know each other	2	5	3
After establishment of relationship	8	13	11
During pregnancy	28	23	25
After child's birth	8	11	9
I can't say/I don't remember	6	10	8

The decision on whether or not to seek baptism was made very early. If the family's children had been baptized, 46 percent had already made the decision before the relationship began. If the child was not baptized, the proportion who had already decided was 39 percent. The younger the respondent was, the less likely they were to have made the decision after the child's birth (only six percent of respondents under 30 had made this decision afterwards).

The results pose a challenge to encouraging long-term relationships with the church. Attitudes toward the church and its rituals have been built over a long period of time. Based on the research, contact with the family after a child's birth is insufficient to convince people of the importance of baptism, for example.

WHICH FACTORS INFLUENCE THE BAPTISM OF A CHILD?

A previous Norwegian study revealed that the decision to seek baptism was primarily justified by traditions, family customs, and the festiveness associated with the baptismal ceremony.[30] These were also the most common reasons among Finnish parents (Figure 2). About 80 percent of parents had considered the tradition of infant baptism, their own family's customs, the role of godparents, and the festiveness associated with baptism to be important or very important in the decision to seek baptism. The festiveness associated with the birth of a child seems especially connected with christenings. In her study, Kauppila

---

30. Rafoss, *Et religiøst landskap*, 21–22.

found that christenings were associated with a richer and more intense palette of emotions than naming ceremonies. Christenings inevitably contain ritual elements that are detached from daily life, whereas naming ceremonies often emphasize a "relaxedness" that can be achieved by the removal of ritual. Thus, the naming celebration does not necessarily differ greatly from everyday life.[31]

Godparents were more important in Finland than they were reported to be in the Norwegian study's findings. Only half of the respondents (54 percent) in the Norwegian study considered having godparents important. Women in Finland especially underlined the importance of having godparents; almost half (46 percent) viewed it as a *very* important reason to seek baptism (against only 25 percent of men). The great importance of godparents also came to the fore in Hytönen's study of baptism, which dealt with Finns' conceptions of baptism and godparents.[32] Although the tradition related to baptism has changed greatly in recent decades, 76 percent of respondents saw baptism as a matter of course in the present study. Half (52 percent) of women and a third (36 percent) of men considered baptism by its nature to be a *very* important factor in seeking baptism for one's child.

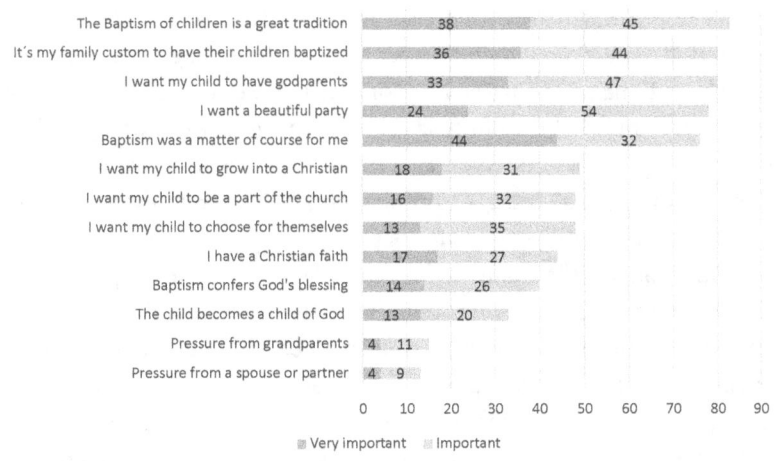

Figure 2. Reasons to baptize a child in families where at least one child was baptized in percentages (N = 776). Source: *The Church Research Institute in Finland. Baptismal Survey 2019*

31. Kauppila, "Ristiäiset, nimiäiset ja tunteet," 85–103.
32. Hytönen, *Maailman tärkein asia*, 272–75.

Various factors associated with faith and religious community were attributed as reasons for seeking baptism by 40–50 percent of the respondents. Reasons associated with faith included that the child could grow up as a Christian and belong to the church. Two-fifths of respondents saw the parents' own Christian faith as a reason for seeking baptism. Parents' own faith played a similar role in the Norwegian study, but it seemed significantly less important for Swedish parents, as only one-third considered it an important reason for seeking baptism. The influence of the immediate circle on the decision to seek baptism was evaluated in the same way as in the Norwegian baptism study.[33] A good tenth of respondents felt the pressure from grandparents to baptize their child. Different genders evaluate the influence of their own partner on the decision in different ways. One-fifth of men (19%) but only six percent of women saw the pressure of a partner as an important reason for having a child baptized. As reported earlier, the majority of parents told in the survey they had made decisions with their spouse or partner, but only a few felt some kind of "pressure" from their partner.

REASONS FOR NOT HAVING A CHILD BAPTIZED

The survey asked families who had not had their child or children baptized which factors had influenced their decisions. Matters related to parents' own relationships with the church and religion emerged as the most significant (Figure 3). Seventy percent of respondents felt it was an important reason that they were not themselves members of the church. The prerequisite for baptism in the Evangelical Lutheran Church of Finland is that at least one of the parents is a member of the Church, and that the child has at least one godparent who is a confirmed and professing member. As in the case above, since it is common for younger age groups to resign from the church, many families do not meet the requirements for baptism.

Additionally, the main reasons included not considering oneself a believer, the weakness of one's bond with the church, and not wanting the church to be involved in one's important celebration. One's own relationship with the church and religion was especially salient, particularly among women. Half (48 percent) of the women (and 38 percent of men) said that not considering themselves believers was a *very* important reason for not having a child baptized. When the role of one's own relationship

---

33. Sandberg et al., *Dop i förändring*, 40–42; Rafoss, *Et religiøst landskap*, 21–22.

with the church was assessed, the differences between the sexes were emphasized even more. Forty-two percent of women considered their own weak relationship with the church to be a very important reason for not having their child baptized, but only a fourth of men (27 percent) felt the same way. These findings are consistent with those of a previous Nordic study, which revealed that parents' own relationships with the church were a significant factor influencing the decision to seek baptism. In particular, the mother's relationship with the church has been found to be of great importance in making the decision to seek baptism. Young adults' images of the church and whether they consider themselves Christians also play an important role in their baptism considerations.[34]

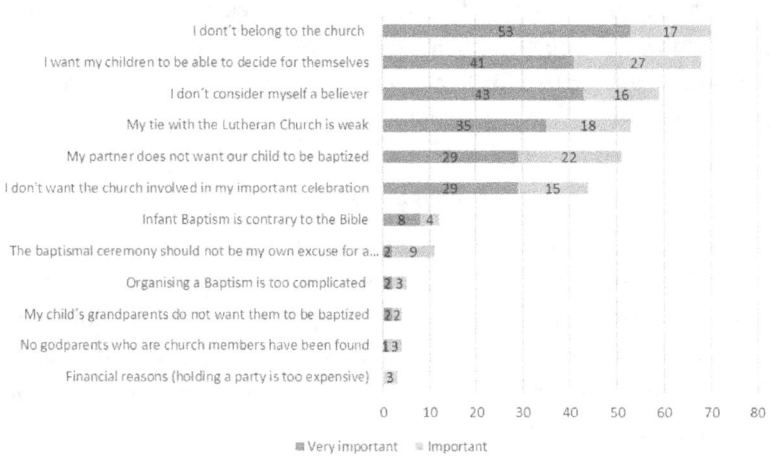

Figure 3. Reasons for not having a child baptized for parents with an unbaptized child or children in percentages (N = 223). Source: *The Church Research Institute in Finland. Baptismal Survey 2019*

Also among the key reasons was the wish to allow the child to make their own decisions about baptism (68 percent). Women and the youngest respondents especially emphasized the child's right to decide for themselves. Half those under 30 thought this was a *very* important reason not to have a child baptized (29 percent of those over 40). Among women, this was considered a *very* important reason by one in two (53 percent), while only one-fourth of men (28 percent) felt the

---

34. Høeg and Gresaker, *Når det rokkes*, 114–16; Sandberg et al., *Dop i förändring*, 119–23.

same way. Interestingly, freedom of choice was used as an argument in both directions: half of the parents whose child had been baptized thought that a reason for seeking baptism was that the child could choose for themselves.

According to the survey, the spouse's opinion was also a very strong factor influencing the decision not to have a baptism, as more than half felt that the spouse's reluctance to have a child baptized influenced the decision. The spouse, therefore, seems to have a significantly stronger influence on the decision not to baptize than to baptize. This view was more common among women (57 percent). However, two-fifths of men (43 percent) considered this an important reason for not having a child baptized. Although the parents justified not having their child baptized by referring to the child's freedom of choice, the parents' own relationships with the church still seemed to be a very important factor.

The survey showed that very few families (4 percent) considered the difficulty of finding godparents to be the reason for not having a child baptized. Moreover, other practical reasons, such as the difficulty of organizing a baptism or financial reasons, were very rarely used as a justification for not having a child baptized.

CONCLUSIONS

This article has examined the factors influencing Finnish parents' decisions to seek baptism, which included attitudes toward the meaning of religious rituals in the celebration of life's phases, the reasons for deciding whether to have one's child baptized, and the process of making that decision. The article is based on quantitative data collected from Finnish parents in 2019.

Based on the findings, the main reasons for baptizing a child were found to be related to traditions and family customs. In contrast, the child is left unbaptized mainly for religious reasons. When parents evaluated the factors influencing the decision to seek baptism, they cited the tradition of infant baptism, their own family's customs, and the festiveness associated with baptism as the most important. Baptism has been one of those rituals that parents in Lutheran countries just pick up without deeper theological reflection. Factors related to the Christian faith were not at the top of the list. Does this also indicate that the number of baptisms will continue to decrease? Is custom a sufficient reason to baptize in such a social environment where baptizing has begun to be the choice of the minority? The theory of individualization emphasizes the detachment of individuals from religious institutions and autonomous, self-directed solutions. In such an environment, the individual builds his or her own religious practices. Accordingly, forms of religion that appear only as external customs are not necessarily attractive.

Another of the study's findings is that the social context greatly influences the younger generation's choices, perhaps even more than the parents themselves realize. The article's finding that families' decisions about baptism largely followed what was happening in their social contexts is also an indication of this emerging pattern. If baptism was the prevailing custom among the closest people, the decision was made to have one's own child baptized. If the closest people did not usually have a child baptized, the great majority of families also left the child unbaptized. Nevertheless, parents themselves mostly believed that only their own spouse and grandparents should influence the decision. The influence of friends was judged to be relatively minor. We are close to a cultural tipping point in Finland, in which being religious will increasingly appear to be a socially atypical identity. In the youngest generations, this point has already been reached, as non-religiosity is a socially acceptable way of determining one's relationship with religion.[35] It can be assumed that this trend also significantly affects choices concerning rituals. When the choice to seek baptism is based above all on following an external tradition, it is susceptible to the pressure of change introduced by the social context. As also Voas and Crockett propose, the more the everyday life of the younger generation is distanced from the religious community and its practices, the less likely it is that religious practices will be adhered to, even on festive occasions.[36]

These findings are linked with the change in Finns' relationships with religion observed in other studies. In particular, the generations born in the 1980s and afterward have been found to be breaking away from "cultural Christianity" in Finland. It has been typical of older generations to value their Christian heritage as part of their own culture, regardless of whether they agree with its teachings. Younger generations approach religion differently, as one's own personal experiences and choices are emphasized in a more individualistic approach.[37] This can result in a different

---

35. Hytönen et al., "Conclusions," 259–61.
36. Voas and Crockett "Religion in Britain."
37. Ketola, *Religious Identities*, 71–74; Pollack, *Religious Change in Europe*, 171–84.

way of interpreting the role religion or the church plays in the celebrations of one's own life phases than in previous generations.

Finally, the article highlights the observed changes in religiosity of different genders. Previous research has shown that the religiosity of young women is weakening, while that of young men is strengthening. This finding differs from prior expectations. The results of this article show that change is also taking place in the transmission of religious traditions. In the past, women have been the central mediating group of religious tradition, but the findings of this study show that men under the age of 30 consider religious rituals important when a child is born more often than women. Among the women, the idea that the child can in time make the baptismal decision themselves was emphasized, and this is an important reason for leaving the child unbaptized. At the same time, however, the woman's own relationship with the church greatly influenced her baptism decision. If the woman's own relationship with the church was distant, the child was probably left unbaptized. More research is needed on both the strengthening of men's religiosity and the weakening of women's religiosity in order to explain the process behind the findings.

How should churches respond to the findings of this article? The article confirms observations made in other Nordic countries that the decision to baptize the child reflects an already existing relationship with the church—or the lack of it. If the church wishes to influence baptism decisions, the key is to maintain a long-term relationship with the younger generation. For example in Finland efforts have been made to reinforce Christian identity by adhering to the Polku (pathway) model, which seeks to offer age-appropriate support for children and young people in different phases of life. The research data clearly reveal that the decision to seek baptism is often made years before the child is born, and even before a family is formed. This finding should guide churches to remain in touch with the younger generation in the ever-lengthening period between confirmation preparation and the establishment of a family.

BIBLIOGRAPHY

The Church Research Institute in Finland. *Baptismal Survey 2019*. SPSS-document. (N = 1,029).

Hunt, Stephen. *Religion and Everyday Life*. New Sociology. London: Routledge 2005.

Hytönen, Maarit. "Handing on the Christian Tradition." In *Religion in Daily Life and in Celebration. The Evangelical Lutheran Church of Finland, 2016–2019*, edited by

Hanna Salomäki et al., 184–223. Tampere: Publications of the Church Research Institute 65: 2021. Kirkon julkaisut (evl.fi)

———. *"Maailman tärkein tapahtuma"—suomalaisten käsityksiä kasteesta ja kummiudesta*. Tampere: Kirkon tutkimuskeskuksen verkkojulkaisuja 63: 2020. 697af03a-0550-04d4-8b92-079f05f378f1 (evl.fi).

Hytönen, Maarit et al. "Conclusions." In *Religion in Daily Life and in Celebration. The Evangelical Lutheran Church of Finland, 2016-2019*, edited by Hanna Salomäki et al., 257–72. Tampere: Publicationss of the Church Research Institute 65: 2021. Kirkon julkaisut (evl.fi).

Høeg, Ida Marie, and Gresaker, Ann Kristin. "Når det rokkes ved tradisjon og tilhørighet." *KIFO Rapport 2015: 2*. Oslo: KIFO, 2015.

Inglehart, Ronald F. *Cultural Evolution. Peoples Motivation are Changing and Reshaping the World*. Cambridge: Cambridge University: 2018.

Jonsson, Pernilla, et al. "Who Is Baptized? A Study of Socioeconomic, Regional and Gender Differences in Child Baptism in the Church of Sweden, 2005 and 2015." *Nordic Journal of Religion and Society* 33 (2020) 72–86.

Kauppila, Helena. "Ristiäiset, nimiäiset ja tunteet—tunteiden ilmaiseminen nimiäisiä ja ristiäisiä käsittelevissä blogikirjoituksissa." In *Kasteen polulla. Kasteen ja kummiuden teologiaa ja käytäntöjä*, edited by Maarit Hytönen, 70–107. Tampere: Kirkon tutkimuskeskuksen julkaisuja 136: 2021.

Ketola, Kimmo. "Religion and the Cultural Turning Point." In *Religion in Daily Life and in Celebration. The Evangelical Lutheran Church of Finland, 2016-2019*, edited by Hanna Salomäki et al., 12–44. Tampere: Publications of the Church Research Institute 65, 2021. Kirkon julkaisut (evl.fi).

———. "Religious Identities and Beliefs are Diversifying." In *Religion in Daily Life and in Celebration. The Evangelical Lutheran Church of Finland, 2016-2019*, edited by Hanna Salomäki et al., 67–90. Tampere: Publications of the Church Research Institute 65: 2021. Kirkon julkaisut (evl.fi).

Kääriäinen, Kimmo, et al. *Moderni kirkkokansa. Suomalaisten uskonnollisuus uudella vuosituhannella*. Tampere: Kirkon tutkimuskeskus. Kirkon tutkimuskeskuksen julkaisuja 82, 2003.

Lüchau, Peter. "Indmeldelse og dåb i den Danske folkekirke." In *Tal om kirken. Undersogelser af Folkekirkens aktivitet—og deltagersstatistik*, edited by Marie Vejrup Nielsen and Hans Raun Iversen, 151–78. Publikationer fra det teologiske fakultet 57. Kobenhavn: Kobenhavs Universitet. 2014.

Niemelä, Kati. "Heikkeneekö uskonnollisuus ikäryhmissä? Uskonnollinen kasvatus ja sen merkitys uskonnollisuuden selittäjänä." In *Uskonto suomalaisten elämässä. Uskonnollinen kasvatus, moraali, onnellisuus ja suvaitsevaisuus kansainvälisessä vertailussa*, edited by Kimmo Ketola et al., 40–59. Tampere: Yhteiskuntatieteellinen tietoarkisto. 2011.

Pajari, Ilona. "Kuolema maalla ja kaupungissa. Suomalaisen hautajais- ja kuolemankulttuurin muutos 1800-luvun lopulta nykypäivään." *Historiallinen aikakauskirja* 4 (2014) 393–405.

"Perinataalitilasto—synnyttäjät, synnytykset ja vastasyntyneet 2019." Tilastoraportti 48/2020. Tilastokeskus. Perinataalitilasto 2019 (julkari.fi).

Piispa, Mikko. "Yhdeksän sanaa Y-sukupolvesta." Helsinki: Teos, 2018.

Pollack, Detlef. "Religious Change in Europe: Theoretical Considerations and Empirical Findings." *Social Compass* 55 (2008) 168–86.

PART I: EMPIRICAL STUDIES

Rafoss, Tore Witsø. "Et religiøst landskap I endring." *KIFO Rapport 2016*: 2. Oslo: KIFO. 2016.

Räisänen, Heikki. "Ateisti vai kulttuurikristitty?" *Vartija* (1996) 97–99.

Sandberg, Andreas et al. *Dop i förändring*. Uppsala: Svenska kyrkan, 2019.

Salomäki, Hanna. "Suomalaisten ikä- ja sukupuolierot uskonnollisuudessa." In *Spiritualiteetti 2020-luvun Suomessa*. Eds. Salminen, Veli-Matti & Huttunen, Niko. 228–57. Tampere. Helsinki: Kirkon tutkimuskeskuksen julkaisuja 137. 2022.

———. "Worship, Church Ceremonies and Christian Holidays." In *Religion in Daily Life and in Celebration. The Evangelical Lutheran Church of Finland, 2016–2019*, edited by Hanna Salomäki et al., 91–135. Tampere: Publications of the Church Research Institute 65, 2021. Kirkon julkaisut (evl.fi).

Sohlberg, Jussi, and Kimmo Ketola. "Religious Identities and Beliefs are Diversifying." In *Religion in Daily Life and in Celebration. The Evangelical Lutheran Church of Finland, 2016–2019*, edited by Hanna Salomäldrars ki et al., 45–66. Tampere: Publications of the Church Research Institute 65, 2021. Kirkon julkaisut (evl.fi).

Tervo-Niemelä, Kati, and Jenni Spännäri. "Uskonnollisuuden ja uskonnottomuuden muutos ja siirtyminen sukupolvelta toiselle suomalaisissa perheissä." In *Millenniaalien kirkko. Kulttuuriset muutokset ja kristillinen usko*, edited by Sini Mikkola and Suvi-Maria Saarelainen, 51–78. Helsinki: Suomen ev. lut. kirkon tutkimusjulkaisuja 139.

Vanderdorpe, Florence. "Funerals in Belgium: The Hidden Complexity of Contemporary Practices." *Mortality* 5 (2000) 18–33.

Voas, David. "The Rise and Fall of Fuzzy Fidelity in Europe." *European Sociological Review* 25 (2009) 155–68.

Voas, David, and Alasdair Crockett. "Religion in Britain: Neither Believing nor Belonging." *Sociology* 39 (2005) 11–28.

Voas, David, and Laura Watt. *Numerical Change in Church Attendance: National, Local and Individual Factors*. London: The Church of England, 2014. http://www.churchgrowthresearch.org.uk/UserFiles/File/Reports/Report_Strands_1_2_rev2.pdf.

5

Infant Baptism in a New Context

Ingegerd Sjölin

TIME NEVER STANDS STILL. This applies to society, life circumstances, and perceptions. Baptism was statutory in the Swedish Church Act of 1686, and all children were baptized in Sweden until the nineteenth century, although customs and practices had changed over the centuries. A new society began to take shape during the nineteenth century, as a large part of the population moved to market towns and cities. Old customs were abandoned, and new ways of thinking and patterns of action emerged in an urbanized and industrialized society. At the end of the century, the legal paragraph on baptism became obsolete. A changed view of children and baptism had broken through. The combined effect was that not all children were baptized.

Sweden became a multi-religious and multicultural society during the latter part of the twentieth century and further into the twenty-first century. Many families now have a creed different from the Christian one, and it is therefore natural that far from all children are baptized. Children gradually gained a stronger position and clear rights during the latter part of the twentieth century and into the twenty-first century. One expression for this is the United Nations Convention on the Rights of the Child (UNCRC), which was ratified by Sweden in 1990 and became the law in 2020. According to the UNCRC, children have the right, based on their maturity, to make decisions about their own lives. Some parents choose not to have their children baptized as infants because they believe that the child should be allowed to decide on his or her own baptism. Thus, a changing view of the child has contributed to fewer baptisms.

In many churches, there are paintings and epitaphs in which the entire family is depicted. Paintings from the seventeenth century usually portray adults and children in the same way, with the children looking like miniature adults. These paintings provide insight into how children were viewed at this time. In the upper echelons of society, children were seen as future heirs to property and social status. To manage this inheritance, a certain education and upbringing were required.[1]

Almost 400 years later, in 2012, an exhibition was shown at Säftstaholm Castle in Vingåker, Sweden, entitled *Se mig!* (See me!). The artist, Berta Hansson (1910–1994), first a primary school teacher and then a full-time artist, contributed to the exhibition with several children's portraits. On the nature of this exhibition, she wrote the following:

> See me! It's the child within the child that I'm interested in. The universal. What is the same in all children, no matter what race they belong to. The big-eyed. The young. The expectant. What life will soon inflict violence upon. I don't mean that I'm trying to paint the happy child, as I don't believe much in that. But I do believe in the unaware child. The child who trusts us adults, and who believes that we are as wise and knowledgeable as we pretend to be.[2]

The view of children has changed from seeing them as small adults, or future adults, to understanding them based on their own premises. Baptism and children have been intertwined for millennia in the Christian church, and the view of children has influenced how the significance of baptism for children has been perceived. This applies to both religious beliefs and interpersonal relationships, as well as the perspectives of those in power. In this chapter, I will explore this transition in Sweden and how it has affected the views and practices of baptism.

VIEWS OF CHILDREN AND BAPTISMAL PRACTICES IN PREVIOUS CENTURIES

In Sweden, all children were baptized until the nineteenth century. Occasionally, children died unbaptized, but it was not common. Already in

---

1. Sandin, *Synen*.
2. Furborg, *Se mig!* This and other translations of Swedish texts are the author's.

the provincial laws recorded in the fifteenth century, it was stipulated who might perform a baptism if the child's life was in danger in connection with birth. The fear that a child would die unbaptized was deeply rooted in beliefs from the Middle Ages, which persisted until the nineteenth century and to some extent into the early twentieth century. A child who died and was not baptized was considered a heathen, and a heathen child was seen as belonging to the wilderness or wasteland. Such a child did not belong to the Christian sphere and was not allowed a burial in the cemetery.[3] The child would not go to heaven and would remain unsaved. Unbaptized children were essentially referred to as pagans.

In medieval times, people experienced life and the afterlife after death as two worlds, with constant and active two-way communication between them.[4] There was a fear that an unbaptized child who died would return to earth and hurt the family. Such beliefs are portrayed in folklore, even into the early twentieth century, and included visions of unbaptized children being transformed into wolves.[5] Life on earth also included trolls, elves, and other beings, and this world was dangerous for an unbaptized child. It was feared that the unbaptized child would be replaced with a troll; therefore, a fire was kept in the stove all day until the child was baptized, which protected the child from the trolls. Folklore research has records describing these "changelings," a notion used to denote children who had been abducted by trolls and replaced with one of their own offspring. The "changeling" was described in folklore research in the mid-1800s as "a monster with a large head and hump on its back—who constantly cried and could never be satisfied."[6]

Baptism was thus crucial to the child and his or her life. It protected the child against evil in this world and also ensured that the child would be blessed if it died. This was at a time when infant and child mortality rates were high. It was therefore understandable that it was important to baptize the child as soon as possible after birth.

As early as the eighteenth century, the first scientific objections came to taking children who were only a few days old to church, regardless of the weather, for baptisms. The botanist and zoologist Carl Linnaeus wrote, "It is very important for the rural people to have their children baptized in the church. They carry the child to the church, even

---

3. Sjölin, *Dopsed i förändring*, 59.
4. Sjölin, *Dopsed i förändring*, 51.
5. Sjöin, *Dopsed i förändring*, 52
6. Sjölin, *Dopsed i förändring*, 54.

in the coldest winter, to be baptized with ice-cold water, often when the sutures are still open."[7] Carl Linnaeus represents the new scientific age in which a child's health was considered more important than an early baptism. At this time, the views of children and baptism had begun to change based on new scientific insights.

Accordingly, Archbishop Lindblom published a revised catechism in 1810:

> Question No. 310: "Are the children without salvation?"
>
> The answer: "No, they have not, by willful unbelief and sin, been able to lose God's general grace through Jesus Christ."[8]

In the liturgical handbooks in the Church of Sweden until 1811, exorcisms and expulsion, renunciation, and repudiation of the devil were included in the baptismal service. The godparents answered for the child during baptism. However, in the baptismal services of 1811, both the exorcisms and the repudiation of the devil were removed. This was an expression of a new view of children and baptism. This revision did not reflect the general population's views on children and baptism, but rather that of the upper classes. In the upper classes, the trend was increasingly shifting toward waiting with respect to baptism. During the nineteenth century, the beliefs that originated in the Middle Ages began to lose their grip, and they ultimately gave way entirely in the early twentieth century. In light of such changes, the author Selma Lagerlöf wrote a fairytale about changelings in 1915.[9] In this sense, the idea that children could be exchanged by trolls came to be more or less relegated to the world of fairytales.

The changes were extensive during the nineteenth century, especially for children. Previously, only children in the upper social strata received an education. In the broader population, children were seen as laborers in the family, as everyone needed to get food on the table.[10] When people increasingly moved from the countryside to market towns and cities, the conditions changed. Industrialization and urbanization brought many new forms of work, and education, regardless of social affiliation, became necessary. In 1842, public elementary schools were introduced

---

7. Sjölin, *Dopsed i förändring*, 80.
8. Sjölin, *Dopsed i förändring*, 102.
9. Titel: Bortbytingen/The Outcast; see Sjölin, *Dopsed i förändring*, 55.
10. Sandin, *Synen*.

in Sweden. This meant that the state participated in raising children in a way that it had not done before. Before, it was the family that had been responsible for the children's education and upbringing. The church's part in education at that time was such that all children, before they were allowed to go to communion, would be expected to read the essential parts of the Catechism. As a state church, the Church of Sweden became largely responsible for the public elementary schools. The curriculum consisted of reading, writing, arithmetic, biblical history, and catechism.

According to the 1686 Church Law, it was necessary to be baptized within eight days to live in Sweden. Being Swedish and being baptized were essentially the same thing, and baptism was a civic duty. Exceptions were made for centuries for foreigners who contributed professional skills of various kinds. When new religious movements began to establish themselves in the mid-1800s, many medieval beliefs were no longer adhered to. This made it possible for Baptist movements to proliferate. Within the larger Baptist movement, only those who confessed their faith were baptized (i.e., believer's baptism). Conflicts arose between the Church of Sweden and Baptist families, the latter of whom refused to have their children baptized. To address this issue, the children were forcibly baptized with the help of the local sheriff. After several forced baptisms, the Strängnäs diocese's judicial chapter asked the Royal Majesty if forced baptism was really to be carried out. The answer came on September 23, 1863, when it was stated that baptism was still a civic duty. However, the view regarding the enforcement of this rule had changed. It was through guidance and loving teaching that parents were encouraged to have their children baptized, and not through coercion.[11]

In 1864, the age for baptism changed from eight days to within six weeks.[12] Just over 20 years later, in 1887, a regulation was introduced that made the paragraph on mandatory baptism obsolete.[13] As a result, some children were not baptized, and in 1910, nearly 48,000 people were not baptized. Ten years later, in 1920, the number of unbaptized had risen to just over 77,500. The proportion of unbaptized continued to increase, and in 1930, there were just over 125,500 unbaptized in Sweden. Of these unbaptized, just under 111,500 were over the age of two and made up 1.9 percent of the population.[14] The number of

11. Sjölin, *Dopsed i förändring*, 141.
12. Sjölin, *Dopsed i förändring*, 179.
13. Sjölin, *Dopsed i förändring*, 179.
14. *Svenska kyrkans årsbok 1938*, 262.

unbaptized individuals differed between the various dioceses. In those dioceses where the Baptist movement had been successful, there were generally more unbaptized children.[15]

The views on children and baptism in Sweden changed, as shown above, to a great extent during the nineteenth century. From being a life-critical event both for this life and the afterlife and a mandatory legal obligation, baptism had now become more of a religious matter that belonged to the family's private sphere.

MEMBERSHIP AND BAPTISM

From 1952, it became possible to leave the Church of Sweden and not register elsewhere. Until then, it would only have been possible to leave the church to become a member of another denomination. After 1952, membership in the Church of Sweden belonged to the private sphere. Children automatically became members if, at birth, they had at least one parent belonging to the Church of Sweden.[16] Decades of debate on whether the Church of Sweden should be a state church included a discussion of whether a child could become a member at birth. Many in the church supported the view that baptism should be the basis for membership. Since January 1, 1996, the main way to become a member of the Church of Sweden has been through baptism, but parents can also register the child as a member without their being baptized.[17]

In the Church of Sweden's yearbook of 1964, baptism rates for the various dioceses are reported. This period covers a large part of the 1950s and the beginning of the 1960s. The baptismal rate for the entire country was 89.1 percent of newborns.[18] Just over 10 percent of those born in the 1950s were not baptized but became members if either of their parents belonged to the Church of Sweden. This meant that there was an increasing number of members who were not baptized. In recent centuries, Sweden has alternated between being an emigrant country and an immigrant country. After the Second World War, industry went into high gear, and people came from different parts of Europe to work and invest in Sweden, most of whom were Christians. In the 1980s,

---

15. *Svenska kyrkans årsbok 1938*, 262.

16. If the parents were not married, their child become a member of the Church of Sweden if the mother was a member.

17. Kyrkoordningen 29 kap 1–2 §.

18. *Svenska kyrkans årsbok 1964*, 188.

immigration increased, with people coming from Europe, as well as from Lebanon, Iran, and Chile. When Yugoslavia disintegrated into civil war during the 1990s, many of its residents sought refuge in Sweden.[19] Some of them belonged to other Christian churches, and some had a creed that differed from the Christian one. A new Sweden with people of different creeds emerged. Now, it was no longer possible to expect all newborns to be baptized. Until 1988, over 90 percent of the population were members of the Church of Sweden. Given the possibility from 1952 to leave the church alongside the early years of labor immigration, this is a very high figure and shows a quite uniform Sweden from an ecclesiastical point of view. Moving forward to 2000, 82.9 percent were members of the Church of Sweden.[20] During the 2000s, Sweden's population increased from 8.9 million to 10.5 million by the end of 2022. Immigration has continued to increase, with immigrants from a variety of EU countries, such as Poland, and refugees fleeing war and oppression in countries such as Iraq, Afghanistan, Somalia, Syria, and Ukraine.[21]

Figure 1. Percentage of members of the Church of Sweden of the entire population and the proportion of baptized children of all born. *Source: Svenska kyrkans statistikdatabas*

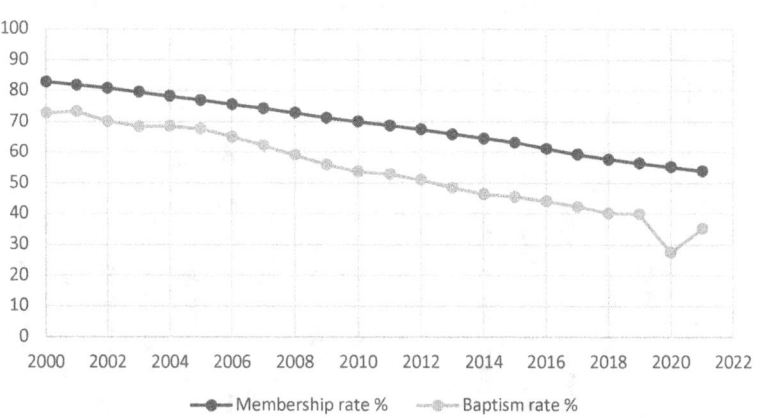

The fact that the number of members of the Church of Sweden has decreased with immigration is a natural consequence of the population

19. Statistikmyndigheten, SCB, *Sveriges folkmängd från 1749 och fram till idag*.
20. https://www.svenskakyrkan.se/statistik
21. https://www.scb.se/hitta-statistik/artiklar/2017/sveriges-folkmangd-fran-1749-och-fram-till-idag

PART I: EMPIRICAL STUDIES

situation. This, in turn, has greatly affected the frequency of baptism. In a multi-religious society, it may be the case that one parent is a Christian and a member of the Church of Sweden, while the other is of another faith. Accordingly, baptism may not be relevant in such circumstances. Living in a multi-religious context, where few are baptized, can lead to not electing to have one's child baptized. In addition, in today's society, there are many who have no faith, and in such cases, baptism may not be seen as essential.

In 1992, 90.4 percent of church-affiliated children were baptized. Fourteen years later, in 2006, 83.2 percent of the children whose parents were members of the Church of Sweden were baptized. This is a decrease of just over seven percentage points. During the same period, the proportion of members of the Church of Sweden decreased from 87.9 percent in 1992 to 75.6 percent in 2006, a decrease of just over 12 percentage points. In an environment where fewer and fewer belong to the Church of Sweden, the practice of baptism is also declining among those members who have children.[22]

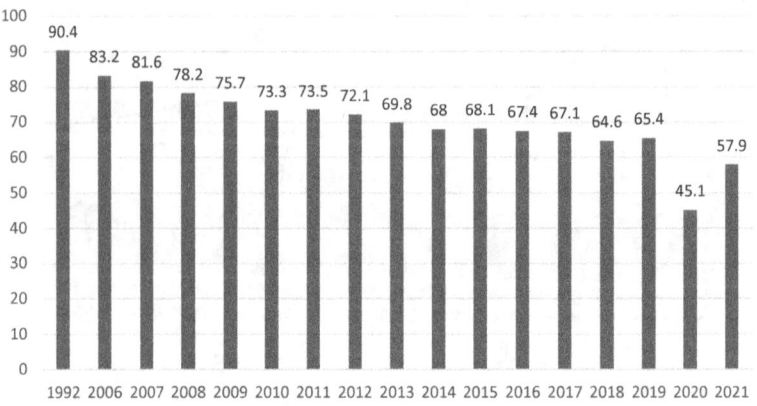

Figure 2. Percentage of baptized children where one or both parents are members of the Church of Sweden in 1992 and from 2006 to 2021. Sources: *Alwall and Sjölin, Kyrkostatistik, 97 and Svenska kyrkans statistikdatabas*

Another explanation for why members may not allow their children to be baptized could be that they were not baptized themselves. Many of those who became parents today were born before 1996 and became members by birth, and 10 percent of this group was not baptized.

22. Alwall and Sjölin, *Kyrkostatistik*, 97 and Svenska kyrkans statistikdatabas.

A CHANGED PERSPECTIVE ON CHILDREN: TWO PERSPECTIVES

Two twentieth-century authors have illustrated the new perspectives on children that emerged during that century. First, the century began with Ellen Key publishing the book *The Century of the Child*,[23] in which she wrote the following:

> But the only correct starting point, as far as a child's education in becoming a social human being is concerned, is to treat it as such, while strengthening its natural disposition to become an individual human being.[24]

According to Key, the child was to be the starting point and the center, both in terms of upbringing and pedagogy. Essentially, the goal was for the child to become an individual human being. Key's thoughts on pedagogy and upbringing had a great impact on society at that time, and her book was ultimately translated into 26 languages.

The other author is Astrid Lindgren. Lindgren made her debut in the 1940s, and she adhered to the following motto: "Children should be loved for their own sake—not for their benefit."[25] In the story of Emil in Lönneberga, the people of Katthult collect money so that Emil's parents could send the prankster to America. When they come to hand it over, the parents do not accept the money. Emil's mother says, "Emil is a sweet little boy. We love him just the way he is."[26] The model for Emil was Lindgren's own father, Samuel August, who was born in 1875.[27] Until 1902, parents were required by law to spank their children when they had done something wrong.[28] Accordingly, Emil runs to the carpentry shed to avoid being punished by his father. There, Emil hasps the door from the inside, and his father hasps it from the outside. A win-win solution. While the father cannot get around to spanking him, he still controls the length of Emil's stay in the carpentry shed through the hasp from the outside. After 1902, it was no longer an obligation to spank children, but rather a right. It was not until 1979 that corporal punishment for children was banned in Sweden, the first country in Europe to do so. The

---

23. Key, *The Century of the Child*.
24. Key, *The Century of the Child*, 107.
25. Sandin, *Synen*.
26. Lindgren, *Emil i Lönneberga*.
27. Lindgren, *Historien bakom Emil i Lönneberga*.
28. Alfredsson, *Den rättsliga regleringen*, 25.

powers, obligations, and rights of parents had radically changed in many ways during the 20th century. Through her many books, Lindgren provides a picture of how children were viewed and thus also of parenthood, which grew stronger during this period. In Lindgren's works, the child is largely understood as an independent and autonomous individual.

A CHANGED PERSPECTIVE ON CHILDREN— THE CHURCH OF SWEDEN

In the official decisions and documents of the Church, the child is increasingly seen as an independent and autonomous individual. Starting with the Church Handbook of 1986, and even more clearly in the 2017 version, the child is in focus throughout the entire baptismal service. In the Church Handbook of 2017, the child's name is requested at the beginning of the service and is then mentioned in at least six different stages of the baptismal service. As mentioned above, the child is construed as an independent and autonomous individual, and it is precisely this child who is baptized. Starting in 1979, all baptized individuals, regardless of age, were allowed to receive Holy Communion. This was reflected in the Church Handbook of 1986, which included an order for Family Eucharists. The first section of the Church Order, which took effect on January 1, 2000, also emphasizes the unique position of the child:

> In the Christian faith, children occupy a special position and therefore need to be given special attention in the activities of the Church of Sweden.[29]

Through baptism, the child becomes a full member of the Church of Sweden. The baptized child can also receive the church's other sacrament, the Holy Communion. The child thus obtains the right to vote in the Church of Sweden from the age of 16. Since 2013, no decisions may be made in the Church of Sweden, either in parishes and dioceses or at the national level, without a child impact assessment having first been carried out. The view of the child in the Church of Sweden is essentially based on Mark 10:13-16:

> People were bringing children to him in order that he might touch them, but the disciples spoke sternly to them. When Jesus saw this, he was indignant and said to them, "Let the children come to me; do not try to stop them; for it is to such

---

29. Kyrkoordningen för Svenska kyrkan, Inledning.

as these that the kingdom of God belongs. Truly I tell you, whoever does not receive the kingdom of God as a child will never enter it." And he took them up in his arms, laid his hands on them, and blessed them.[30]

Jesus sees the children and understands that they belong to the kingdom of God. He also shows that children are role models for adults when it comes to the possibility of receiving the kingdom of God.

A CHANGED PERSPECTIVE ON CHILDREN— THE CONVENTION ON THE RIGHTS OF THE CHILD

The established perception of children changed during the twentieth century, as exemplified through references to Swedish literature, changes in Swedish law, and developments within the Swedish Church. The extent of this transformation was much broader than just one country, as it occurred throughout a significant part of the world. The UNCRC, established in 1989, reflects an altered perspective on children that transcended international boundaries. A total of 196 countries have signed the UNCRC. The Convention was ratified in 1990 and adopted as a law in Sweden in 2020.[31] The UNCRC contains four main principles:[32]

- Article 2. All children have the same rights under this convention, without discrimination of any kind.
- Article 3. The best interests of the child shall be a primary consideration in all actions concerning them.
- Article 6. Every child has the right to life, survival, and development.
- Article 12. Children capable of forming their own views have the right to express those views freely in all matters concerning them, with due regard to their age and maturity.

The fourteenth article establishes the right of children to the practice of religion. The UNCRC gives children the right to their own spiritual life and the opportunity to be part of the faith and tradition to which they belong through their families.

---

30. The Bible New Revised Standard Version, NRSV.

31. *Konventionen om barnets rättigheter med strategi för att stärka barnets rättigheter i Sverige.*

32. *UNCRC Convention on the Rights of the Child.*

PART I: EMPIRICAL STUDIES

A CHANGED PERSPECTIVE ON CHILDREN— A CHALLENGE FOR PARENTS

The view of the child as an independent subject that emerged during the twentieth and twenty-first centuries has affected the decisions that parents make on behalf of their children. Generally, parents prefer to wait until the child can make their own decisions. The book *Dop i förändring* presents a survey that provides some answers as to why some choose not to baptize their children.[33] Just over half of the parents who did not choose baptism responded that they did so to let the child decide. Other reasons mentioned may have strengthened that resolve. Just over four in ten said they were not religious, and just over one-fifth stated that they had a weak affiliation with the Church of Sweden. Nearly one in 10 reported that baptism was not a tradition in their family or among their relatives, and it was possible that they themselves were not baptized. Sixteen percent had skipped baptism because their partner did not want it to be performed. Additionally, some just did not have the energy to organize a baptism, and others chose to skip it for economic reasons, since arranging a baptism celebration can be costly.[34]

The baptismal service is the church service in the handbook that offers the greatest opportunities for the worshipping congregation to participate actively. One of the parents, godparents, or someone else in the baptismal congregation is invited to answer the name question, say the Thanksgiving prayer, read Bible texts, participate in the laying-on of hands during the prayer of deliverance, pour baptismal water, and say the intercessory prayer. Additionally, a question can be posed to the parents after the creed if they want to have their child baptized. For a parent who did not grow up in the Church of Sweden and thus is not baptized or confirmed themselves, it may be unfamiliar to "confess" their faith in front of family and friends, such as by saying the Thanksgiving prayer:

> God (in gratitude over the miracle of life we have gathered here).
>
> Thank you for N.[35]
>
> Thank you for our lives which we may share with each other.
>
> Thank you for the trust you have shown us and for the gift you have bestowed on us.

---

33. Sandberg et al., *Dop i förändring*, 47.
34. Sandberg et al., *Dop i förändring*. 47.
35. N. is used in place of a person's name.

Give us tenderness, steadfastness, and calm.

Help us to share your love with N/her/him/the children for whom we have been given responsibility. In the name of Jesus. Amen.[36]

If one does not have a close relationship with the Church of Sweden or the Christian faith, it could be strange to openly pray to God and read Bible passages in front of loved ones. As a parent, one may decide not to have their child baptized for this reason.

Based on a view of the child as an independent subject, parents may want their child to be able to decide on his or her own baptism. The baptism in the Church of Sweden is based on the Gospel of Mark, where it is stated that children belong to the kingdom of God. In baptism, this is brought to life. Even a small child has his or her own relationship with God that can be deepened and grown. This remains a challenge for the Church of Sweden to communicate to today's parents.

A CHANGED PERSPECTIVE ON CHILDREN— A CHALLENGE FOR THE CHURCH OF SWEDEN

On several occasions, proposals have been made within the Church of Sweden, and motions have been submitted to the Church Meeting to introduce a blessing ceremony as a complement for those who do not want their children to be baptized.[37] In the Church of Sweden, the child has a special status, as described above. In the Bishops' Letter, entitled "Leva i dopet" it says the following:

> Baptism is more than child blessing and naming. Sometimes parents hesitate to have their child baptized, but still want the child to take part in a church ceremony. Perhaps they see child blessings as a first step toward baptism. To pray for an individual child or to bless it is obviously good and right, but to design a ritual for blessing children is not consistent with our church

---

36. *Kyrkohandbok för Svenska kyrkan, Del I*, urval på engelska franska spanska tyska.

37. This was an issue discussed at the Church Meetings in 2002 and 2003. The statement of the Board of Education, LN 2003:21y, and the Church Meeting Motion 2006:68, concerned the agreement between the Church of Sweden and the Mission Covenant Church of Sweden. The Worship Committee's report in 2006:6 provided a detailed reflection on baptism and child blessing in light of the ecumenical agreement between the Church of Sweden and the Mission Covenant Church of Sweden.

tradition. The biblical motive for baptizing infants is found in the Gospel of Mark 10:13-16.[38]

Introducing a blessing ceremony instead of baptism, or as a step toward baptism, is thus rejected by the bishops as being inconsistent with the traditions of the Church of Sweden.

The Church of Sweden has another option, though: to allow the child to become a member of the Church of Sweden without baptism. Prior to the introduction of baptism as the basis for membership in 1996, numerous discussions were held at all levels of the Church of Sweden. Most people considered it untenable and incompatible with being a church to require that one be born into the church. In the discussions, opinions were raised suggesting that it might be possible to register one's child while waiting for baptism if the parents wanted the child to decide for themselves. The decision was made that while baptism should be the main pathway to membership, it should also be possible to register the child as a member without it. Few have used this option. One reason is that the Church of Sweden has not actively advertised this option. These days, there are forms on the Church of Sweden's national website, as well as on some parishes' websites, through which a child can be registered as a member of the church.

As not all members were baptized before 1996, there are many members today who are not baptized and will remain so for a long time. Being a member and being a baptized member are not the same thing. All members are eligible to vote in church elections once they turn 16 years old. Members who have a taxable income pay a church fee, but those without the means do not pay anything. However, being a baptized member provides additional opportunities. For instance, baptized members are welcome to receive communion and are allowed to assist the priest in serving it. In times of crisis, a baptized member can perform a baptism, and to be a godparent, one must be baptized. Baptized members can be confirmed and can also be ordained as deacons, priests, or bishops. Baptized members can also serve as churchwardens. To be a member of the parish board, diocesan board, or governing body at the national level, one must be baptized. Additionally, to be an elected auditor or presenter, either in the judicial chapter of a diocese or on committees at the national level, one must be baptized.

---

38. *Leva i dopet*, 73.

All members who are not baptized shall be contacted according to the Church Order, at the latest, before their eighteenth birthday. Those who are registered as members will remain so after their birthday. There are congregations that acknowledge all those who join the Church of Sweden throughout the year and invite them to a special worship service. This can be an opportunity for further congregations if more parents choose to register their child as a member.

INFANT BAPTISM IN A NEW CONTEXT

In this chapter, I have argued that the baptism of infants in the Church of Sweden has been challenged by changing views of the child. The child is now seen as a separate, independent individual from both a societal and a familial perspective. Views of children and parenthood have undergone radical changes over the past 150 years. From being a legal obligation until 1887 and strongly linked to tradition to becoming a means of obtaining family membership in the church, now, for some parents, baptism is increasingly seen as a religious choice that children should make for themselves.

The artist Berta Hansson was quoted as writing, "The child who trusts us adults . . . believes that we are as wise and knowledgeable as we pretend to be." In a multi-religious and multicultural society where children are seen as independent subjects, it is a difficult balancing act to be a parent. What should we choose for our children? What should they be allowed to decide for themselves? Such questions have challenged the institution of infant baptism in the Church of Sweden.

Clearly and generously offering membership to children whose parents want the child to decide for themselves whether they want to be baptized is not an easy path for the Church of Sweden to take. This can lead to promoting the idea that baptism is only for those who confess their faith and not an act of grace. It can also be seen as a way to gain members and thus secure future income. Despite these concerns, such an effort is still a respectable way for the Church of Sweden to meet the individual child on his or her own terms, offer membership, and then maintain continuous contact to share knowledge and experiences of the Christian faith. Hopefully, this could lead to the children themselves wanting to be baptized later in life, perhaps in connection with confirmation. By offering membership, the Church of Sweden respects both the parents and the child and opens up a pathway to a deeper lifelong relationship.

BIBLIOGRAPHY

Alwall, Jonas, and Ingegerd Sjölin. *Kyrkostatistik*. Nyckeln till Svenska kyrkans verksamhet och finanser, SCB-Tryck, Örebro 1994.

Alfredsson, Emil. *Den rättsliga regleringen av barnaga under 1900-talet - en del i civiliseringsprocessen?* Lund University Publications Student Papers, 2014.

Furborg, Lars. *Se mig!* Säfstaholms slott: Vingåker, 2012.

Key, Ellen. *The Century of the Child*. New York: Putnam, 1909.

Kyrkohandbok för Svenska kyrkan, Del 1, i urval på engelska franska spanska tyska. Uppsala, 2022.

Kyrkomöte 2002 och 2003, protokoll och handlingar.

Kyrkoordning för Svenska kyrkan, Lydelse 1 januari 2023.

Leva i dopet. Biskopsbrev, 2011.

Lindgren, Astrid. *Emil i Lönneberga*. Stockholm, 2003.

———. *Historien bakom Emil i Lönneberga*. https://www.astridlindgren.com/se/karaktarerna/emil-i-lonneberga/historien-bakom-emil-i-lonneberga. 2024-02-19.

Konventionen om barnets rättigheter med strategi för att stärka barnets rättigheter i Sverige. Stockholm: Regeringskansliet, 2014.

Sandberg, Andreas, et al. *Dop i förändring - en studie av föräldrars aktiva val och församlingars strategiska doparbete*. Uppsala, 2019.

Sandin, Bengt. "Synen på barnet och barndomen." *Social Politik* (2017). https://socialpolitik.com/2017/03/27/synen-pa-barnet-och-barndomen/.

Sjölin, Ingegerd. *Dopsed i förändring: studier av Örebro pastorat 1710–1910*. Lund: Lund University, 1999.

Statistikmyndigheten, SCB. *Sveriges folkmängd från 1749 och fram till idag*. https://www.scb.se/hitta-statistik/artiklar/2017/sveriges-folkmangd-fran-1749-och-fram-till-idag. 2024-02-19.

Svenska kyrkans årsbok 1938. Svenska kyrkans diakonistyrelses bokförlag. Stockholm, 1937.

Svenska kyrkans årsbok 1964. Diakonistyrelsens bokförlag. Stockholm, 1963.

Svenska kyrkan i siffror. https://www.svenskakyrkan.se/statistik. 2024-02-19.

Svenska kyrkans statistikdatabas.

United Nations Convention on the Rights of the Child (UNCRC), 1989. https://www.ohchr.org/en/instruments-mechanisms/instruments/convention-rights-child. 2024-02-19/.

Part II

Practices

6

"We Thank You for the Gift of Baptism"

A Comparative Analysis of the Gift Motif in Baptismal Liturgies in the Nordic Countries

Karin Tillberg

In the spring of 2023, the Church of Sweden launched a national campaign on baptism. The reason behind the campaign was a motion accepted by the General Synod in 2021. The motion addressed the need to conduct such a campaign in the aftermath of the COVID-19 pandemic, which resulted in a lower number of candidates for baptism. Several dioceses have had regional and local initiatives to increase baptism rates, but the motion in 2021 stressed the need for national outreach due to the severity of the effects of the pandemic on baptism.[1]

In the first phase prior to the launch, the communication department at the Central Church Office conducted surveys among new parents to determine the most effective way to communicate with them about baptism.[2] Since there are so many parish websites and leaflets that communicate that baptism is a gift,[3] one of the main questions in

---

1. Svenska kyrkan, *Kyrkohandbok 2021*.

2. The campaign is described in Swedish on the internal website for employees in the Church of Sweden. See Svenska kyrkan, *Kommunicera dop.*

3. The quotation, "Baptism gives life a meaning that defies meaninglessness. It is a gift that is not based on achievement and that gives a sense of belonging," can be found

the survey was whether the image of baptism as a gift was a meaningful one. Among the results, it was noted that the image did not mean anything to those participating in the survey; rather, it was perceived as an empty image.[4] If we look at the various liturgies in the Nordic churches under survey in this chapter, the gift motif occurs in all of them (the quote in the title of this chapter comes specifically from the Finnish liturgy) and in the letter on baptism from the bishops' conference of the Church of Sweden.[5] On the website on baptism published by the Evangelical Lutheran Church in Finland, one of the first descriptions, just under the heading, is that baptism is a gift.[6] In the *Baptism, Eucharist, and Ministry (BEM)* document, it is among the first things stated on baptism, as "Baptism is a gift of God, and is administered in the name of the Father, the Son, and the Holy Spirit."[7]

What theology are the churches conveying when referring to baptism as a gift? To answer this question, further inquiries into what is embedded in the image of baptism as a gift and how it affects our understanding of baptismal theology are required, as well as how that theology is conveyed in the liturgy. The service orders highlight different tenets of soteriology, depending on the wording of the motif, but not necessarily in conjunction with what a national church teaches on baptism. The semantic notion of "baptism as a gift" and "the gift of baptism" is another illustration of how the image is used in a multifaceted and sometimes contradictory way. The gift motif occurs both in the image of baptism as a gift and in the images of gifts being given at the time of baptism, such as the gift of eternal life and the gift of salvation, as well as in the image of the baptismal candidate—most often a child—as a gift, which is celebrated at the time of baptism. How is the gift motif supposed to be interpreted when used in such diverse ways?

Furthermore, in relation to the national campaign initiated by the Church of Sweden, what does it mean that such an image is so frequently used by the church in various ways, yet does not necessarily convey the significance that those who work in the church attribute to it?

---

in Svenska kyrkan, *Meningen med dopet*.

4. Svenska kyrkan, *Kommunicera dop*. The initial statement reads, "Baptism is a gift which we have received and proceed to give forward, as part of Christ's mission" (translation mine), which is cited in Svenska kyrkan, 2011, 7.

5. Svenska kyrkan, *Leva i dopet*, 7.
6. Evangelisk-lutherska kyrkan i Finland, 2023.
7. World Council of Churches, *Baptism, Eucharist and Ministry*, 1.

In this chapter, I will examine the baptismal liturgies in Lutheran churches in the Nordic countries. While noting some important similarities and differences, I will focus on the gift motif as it occurs in the liturgies. I will then discuss this motif in relation to the anthropological notion of gift giving[8] and show how this concept can help shed new light on the meaning of the gift of baptism and assist in answering the questions I pose in this chapter.

GIFT GIVING AS CONDITIONAL OR ABSOLUTE

The notion of gift giving has played an important role in understanding human societies within the field of anthropology and influences how we comprehend economic and human relations. For the sake of brevity, I will not go into detail regarding the different theories that exist on the nature of gifts and gift giving, but suffice to say, there are a few key aspects of giving that should be outlined here.

For gift giving to occur, there must be a giver and a receiver. The gift has to be presented in an unconditional manner; otherwise, it becomes something else, like a bribe.[9] Still, this supposed unconditional nature of the gift can be questioned, and this is a notion that many scholars have reflected on.[10] For example, it could be argued that a pure gift can never be given without asking for anything in return—not even gratitude.[11] Thus, a gift is always given with the condition that it is received *as a gift*, which then makes it impossible to be pure.[12] Thus, the giver can never give in an absolute manner.

In his seminal discussion on the gift, Marcel Mauss argues that gift giving does not primarily take into account the nature of the gift—that is, to receive the gift is not the same as owning a new item.[13] Rather, gift giving is a process wherein giving and receiving is a movement depending on reciprocity.[14] When someone receives a gift, they do so in a manner that is dependent on how they wish for a gift to be received. For instance, I would accept a gift in the same way that I would wish

---

8. This notion was developed primarily by Marcel Mauss and Jacques Derrida.
9. Horner, *Rethinking God as Gift*, 1.
10. See overview in Hénaff and Morhange, *The Philosophers' Gift*.
11. Horner, *Rethinking God as Gift*, 5.
12. Derrida, *Given Time*, 64, 137.
13. Mauss develops this notion in Chapter 1, Mauss, *The Gift*.
14. Horner, *Rethinking God as Gift*, 10.

someone else to accept the gift I give to them. Inherent in this process is the notion of debt and reciprocity. As I accept a gift, I am indebted to the giver—if only in the form of the giver expecting me to say thank you. For this reason, I would want to give back, or reciprocate, if not to the same person, but in a similar fashion to someone else.[15]

Jacques Derrida uses his notion of deconstruction to examine the concept of gift giving as it is understood in anthropology. He discusses it in a similar way to how he explicates the notions of hospitality[16] and forgiveness.[17] These notions should be understood as existing on a continuum, ranging from the absolute, pure, or unconditional to the conditional.[18] The ideal for Derrida is the absolute, yet this is not possible to actually accomplish. For a gift to truly be given as a gift, there must be no expectation of giving back or even expressing gratitude. Derrida claims that a pure gift exceeds the idea of reciprocity and stands outside the realm of economics.[19] As soon as a dimension of reciprocity or economic transaction informs giving, it simultaneously nullifies the gift.[20] For this reason, the pure gift comes forth as an impossibility.

How can this idea be applied to the gift motif as it occurs in the liturgies? How can it inform our analysis of how the meaning of baptism is conveyed in the liturgy? I will now move on to discussing the liturgies, beginning with an initial summary.

BAPTISMAL LITURGIES IN THE NORDIC COUNTRIES

Denmark

If baptism is celebrated as an independent service, it starts with a prelude, hymn, and baptism sermon. The pastor initiates a canticle of praise and then leads the congregation in a prayer of thanksgiving. The beginning of the prayer gives thanks to God for providing us with baptism, which turns us into children of God and gives us the Holy Spirit, together with the forgiveness of sins and eternal life. The giver is God, and the receiver is not just the baptismal candidate/s, but the whole

---

15. Derrida, *Given Time*, 12.
16. Cf. Derrida och Dufourmantelle, *Of Hospitality*.
17. Derrida, *On Cosmopolitanism and Forgiveness*.
18. The term "pure gift" comes from Malinowski, and "free gift" was proposed by Sahlins; see discussion in Holm, *Gabe und Geben bei Luther*, 8.
19. Henriksen, *Desire, Gift, and Recognition*, 42.
20. Henriksen, *Desire, Gift, and Recognition*, 43.

congregation. The prayer is phrased so that the promise of salvation and what it entails are summarized.

A reading from Scripture follows, first, the Great Commission (Matt 28) and then the Gospel of Jesus and the children from Mark 10. The pastor makes the sign of the cross on the forehead, lips, and chest of the candidate. Then, he/she asks the candidate or the parents about the name. The profession of faith is phrased as questions to the candidate through the words of the Apostolic Creed. The baptism proper then occurs. After the baptism act, the pastor lays his/her hand on the candidate and prays with a phrase reminiscent of the introductory prayer. The pastor then leads the congregation in the Lord's prayer, while at the same time laying his/her hand on the candidate. Then follows an address to the sponsors (i.e., godparents). The pastor can choose the words freely and this is the part of the 1992 liturgy that most pastors have changed.[21] A baptismal hymn follows, after which is the collect prayer of the baptism in the case of an independent baptismal service; otherwise, the collect prayer of the liturgical year is used.[22] The independent service ends with the blessing, recessional hymn, and postlude.

In the Danish liturgy, the gift motif occurs in the prayer at the beginning of the service and has a counterpart in the collect prayer at the end. The prayer expresses gratitude to God for giving us baptism. It elucidates what the gift of baptism entails, namely the forgiveness of sins and eternal life, which stresses the soteriological dimension of baptism but also that the gift of baptism is a gift of the Holy Spirit, and thus a gift that turns the baptismal candidate into a child of God.

Finland

The service begins with an opening hymn, invocation, and greeting, followed by some introductory words. The first alternative mentions the importance of the parents, in that the baptism can occur because God has given the child as a gift to the parents.[23] At the precise moment of the service, God gives salvation as a gift to the candidate.[24]

The content of the second alternative relates to the Gospel of Jesus and the children and how baptism includes the gift of eternal life. The

---

21. Folkekirken, "Sådan foregår dåb i folkekirken," 6.
22. Folkekirken, "Sådan foregår dåb i folkekirken," 7.
23. Evangelisk-lutherska kyrkan i Finland, *Dop*, 5.
24. Evangelisk-lutherska kyrkan i Finland, *Dop*, 5.

giver is Jesus Christ, and the receiver is the child about to be baptized. Thus, the gift motif stands out in two different ways: salvation as a gift from God and baptism as including a gift of eternal life. In the third alternative, baptism is referred to as a rebirth and a washing of sins, and that the baptized is clothed in new life.[25] The eschatological dimension of baptism is thus highlighted, as indicated by the proclamation that "Our Lord Jesus Christ himself has instituted holy baptism to give us a sign and seal of new life."[26]

After a set of questions concerning baptism directed to the parents and sponsors, the gift motif occurs again in one of the alternative prayers: "Our gracious God, for the sake of his son Jesus Christ, has released you from the power of sin, death, and evil. May God give you strength every day to die to sin and live for Christ."[27] Through this phrasing, it becomes clear that the giver is God, the father, and the receiver is the baptismal candidate. I would refer to the image of baptism here as an atonement.

The second section, God's Word, contains readings from Scripture. The pastor then proceeds to hold a short homily. The third section is called the Washing. It begins with a reading of the Great Commission. The Apostolic Creed follows, and then the baptism occurs. The pastor welcomes the child into the local parish and into the church universal at this time. The baptismal candle is presented at this point, followed by a hymn or other type of music. The prayer of intercession follows, and the pastor leads the congregation in the Lord's prayer. The fourth and final section of the service, Conclusion, contains the blessing/benediction, and a hymn.

Iceland

In the Icelandic liturgy, the service begins with the baptismal hymn. After the hymn, the priest addresses the congregation and explicates the baptism, in that through baptism, we become children of God.[28] The priest or reader (it is suggested that it be one of the godparents) then reads from Scripture.

---

25. Evangelisk-lutherska kyrkan i Finland, *Dop*, 6.
26. Evangelisk-lutherska kyrkan i Finland, *Dop*, 7.
27. Evangelisk-lutherska kyrkan i Finland, *Dop*, 19.
28. Þjóðkirkjan, *Skírn á ensku*, 1.

The priest then proceeds to say a baptismal prayer. The first alternative emphasizes baptism as a gift, how it presents the candidate with eternal grace, and that it is a washing and a rebirth. The giver is God, and the receiver is the baptismal candidate. Theologically and soteriologically, the eschatological dimensions of baptism are emphasized, as baptism is construed as opening "the door of grace . . . into the eternal kingdom."[29]

The second alternative shifts the focus and states that the child is the gift. The rest of the prayer concerns the responsibility of those around the child. Baptism is referred to through the phrase, "promise of baptism."[30] Moreover, the parents ask for gifts of warmth and security to care for the child, and the gift received in baptism—with the candidate as the receiver—is that of the Holy Spirit, a gift that will "quicken everything good that you have entrusted to his/her soul."[31]

In the third alternative, the gift of eternal life is at the core of the prayer and baptism, and the act of cleansing is highlighted: "wash him/her in the water of life so that his/her soul may be cleansed, born anew to life in you, clothed in Christ [. . .]."[32] Baptism here functions as a kind of atonement. The candidate is told to grow into salvation, but at the same time, the grace of baptism is mentioned. The giver is God (possibly through Christ), and the receiver is the one being baptized. Then, the priest prays over the font. In the epiclesis, the relationship between the Spirit and the baptismal water is likened to the moment of creation, when the Spirit of the Lord hovered over the waters.

The confession of faith follows, at which time the Apostolic Creed is used. The congregation remains standing for the signing of the cross. After this phase, the priest asks the baptismal question (i.e., the name of the candidate). Then follows the baptism proper. After pouring the water, the priest lays his/her hand on the candidate and prays. This prayer contains phrases that describe the washing away of sins, rebirth, and grace. The priest then leads the congregation in the Lord's prayer, followed by an address, the latter of which is aimed at those who will be in proximity to this child and help her or him secure a Christian upbringing. After the address, a candle may be given, but this is described as optional.

---

29. Þjóðkirkjan, *Skírn á ensku*, 2.
30. Þjóðkirkjan, *Skírn á ensku*, 2.
31. Þjóðkirkjan, *Skírn á ensku*, 2.
32. Þjóðkirkjan, *Skírn á ensku*, 2.

Norway

In the Norwegian variant, the first section, the Gathering, contains a prelude, an entrance hymn, and a greeting. Then, a gathering prayer is prayed. The first alternative describes how baptism is part of the life of a Christian, with the following phrase demonstrating the essence of the prayer: "Give us open minds, thankful hearts, and willing hands, so that we may receive your word, praise you for your goodness, and in word and deed witness your mighty works."[33] The giver is God Almighty, and the whole congregation functions as the recipient. The second alternative stresses the sacramental character of baptism and relates it to both the Eucharist and God's word. The third alternative interprets baptism as that which grants us a place in the home of the church of God and in heaven, thus stressing the eschatological dimension of baptism. The fourth alternative consists of instruction to use another suitable gathering prayer. Then follows the reception of the baptismal candidate(s), which includes a reading of Mark 10.

Next is Section II, The Word. Additional readings from Scripture are performed here. After the readings, the baptismal hymn is sung, and then the priest holds the homily. The third section contains the prayers of intercession. The fourth section, the baptism, begins with a reading of the Great Commission. Then, an address to the sponsors follows, with a description of their task.[34] After that, the renunciation of evil and the confession of faith follow, after which the baptism proper takes place. The name question appears here. As water is poured into the font, a prayer is said in which the gift motif is emphasized in two ways: first, the prayer starts by thanking God "for the waters of baptism, which by your word is a source of grace," and second, that God "in baptism . . . give[s] us the promise of eternal life."[35] The giver is God, but the recipients are all Christians, since this would symbolize the core of salvation, which is the promise of eternal life. The words in the prayer can thus be considered an invitation to baptism and not merely a statement of facts concerning baptized Christians.

After the baptism, the candidate may be presented with a candle, which is given with words explaining that Jesus is the light of the world. The next heading is Prayer and Thanksgiving, and there are three

---

33. Den norske kirke, "Liturgier: Dåp i egen gudstjeneste," 3.
34. Den norske kirke, "Liturgier: Dåp i egen gudstjeneste," 8.
35. Den norske kirke, "Liturgier: Dåp i egen gudstjeneste," 9.

alternatives. The first one includes a prayer for strength for the godparents, the second one gives thanks for welcoming the candidate to the church, and the third one gives thanks for the promise of eternal life. After this prayer, the priest leads the congregation in the Lord's prayer. The fifth section contains an optional canticle of praise, a blessing, and words of dismissal. The service ends with a postlude.

Sweden

In the Swedish context, the service starts with music and/or a hymn. This is followed by introductory words that elucidate the meaning of baptism, and there are three alternatives to choose from. The first alternative is very short and speaks of baptism as living in fellowship with Christ.[36] The second alternative stresses the function of baptism as that which makes us equal with one another and describes the promise as central within the rite of baptism.[37] The third alternative connects baptism with the different persons of the Trinity and explicates the practice as that which is part of God the Creator, which thus provides vindication and forgiveness, blessing, and hope. This is the only alternative that uses the image of the gift and does so in an abstract way. It is baptism itself that is phrased as that which gives; the prayer is not addressed to God or Jesus, and the receiver is the entire congregation, or possibly all Christians. The gift is further described through phrases concerning the different persons of the Trinity:

> Baptism gives joy, the God of Creation is near. Baptism gives vindication, we are given forgiveness.[38] Baptism gives blessing, we are given the Holy Spirit. Baptism gives hope, we get to live, die, and resurrect with Jesus Christ.[39]

The fourth alternative stresses baptism as a means of deliverance from evil and as a form of rebirth.

The prayer of thanksgiving forms the next part of the liturgy. The section begins with a question of the name of the baptismal candidate, and then the Gospel of Jesus and the children is read. Next comes the

---

36. Svenska kyrkan, *Kyrkohandbok 2017*, 173.
37. Svenska kyrkan, *Kyrkohandbok 2017*, 173.
38. N.B. the wording: it does not say "we are forgiven," but rather that "we are given [the gift] of forgiveness." Such a phrase spells out the soteriological motif even if it means that the language is not worded according to ordinary usage.
39. Svenska kyrkan, *Kyrkohandbok 2017*, 173.

prayer of deliverance. In this part, the priest lays his/her hand on the candidate while praying and then makes the sign of the cross on the forehead, lips, and chest of the candidate. Music and/or a hymn follows, and then the Great Commission is read.[40] After the reading, the priest can deliver a sermon, but it can also be held after the blessing. The priest then proceeds to say the baptismal prayer while pouring water into the font. The first alternative emphasizes the importance of water, as that which gives life to the world: "(O) God, we thank you, for in the well of baptism you bring forth water that gives life to the world." The second alternative stresses how we, through baptism, are given a role in the salvation story: "We thank you, for in baptism you give us a share in the life, death, and resurrection of your Son. Thank you for making this water a source of grace."[41] Again, the receivers are all Christians, and not specifically the baptismal candidates. God is a giver, but so is the abstract noun of water as a giver of life.

The Apostolic Creed is read and followed by the question of whether the candidate wishes to be part of such a faith. Then follows the act of baptism and the welcoming into the local parish and into Christ's church universal. As part of the welcoming process, the candidate is presented with the baptism candle, which is lit upon the paschal candle. Sponsors, parents, or other relatives then state the prayers of intercession, and the priest leads the congregation in the Lord's prayer. The Priestly Blessing (Aaron's blessing) and words of dismissal end the service.

GIFTS PRESENTED THROUGH BAPTISM: RECIPROCITY

In the baptismal liturgies presented above, referring to something as a gift or as given is quite common. The baptismal water is likened to the water that gives life, which was already there in creation.[42] Salvation and eternal life are also described as gifts in several of the liturgies. The child to be baptized is described as a gift primarily to the parents, but also to the local parish and to the church universal.

---

40. Svenska kyrkan, *Kyrkohandbok 2021*, 52.
41. Svenska kyrkan, *Kyrkohandbok 2017*, 179.
42. When mentioning the gift of water, the gift of the Spirit is also discussed (e.g., in the Finnish liturgy, see Evangelisk-lutherska kyrkan i Finland, *Dop*, 29). However, I will not develop the notion of the gift of the Spirit in baptism, since this idea is at the core of Christian dogma on baptism, as well as being included in the exegetical discussions on Jesus's baptism in the Jordan. See, for example, Dunn, *Baptism in the Holy Spirit* and Schmemann, *Of Water and the Spirit*.

Because of these various uses, there is a movement in the gift-giving process, as it appears in the liturgy, where the one identified as the giver and receiver shifts. The liturgy is thus shaped as a reciprocal process. Reciprocity is at the core of the anthropological understanding of gift giving. In this vein, Mary Douglas argues that "the gift serves to establish relations,"[43] and that the reciprocal nature of the process engenders relationships between two or more agents, since there is always at least a giver and a receiver present in the process.

Bo Holm has described how reciprocity can be understood along a spectrum or continuum, the poles of which are made up of negative, balanced, and generalized reciprocity.[44] Through this spectrum, we can identify the nature of that which is received or taken—that is, whether it is a bribe or theft (on the negative side) or if it is the exact opposite, like a pure gift (as generalized reciprocity).[45] In comparison, Risto Saarinen discusses the nature of the gift as it relates to theology and differentiates between the economic and donative variants of theological giving.[46] To illustrate this distinction, he refers to the spreading of the gospel among the first listeners, during which "the listeners receive a gift which is not meant to impose immediate duties and tasks on them. Witness and proclamation thus exemplify donative modes of teaching."[47] It is possible to understand "salvation" in a similar manner in the baptismal service order, in that it is not mentioned to generate an immediate response, or to produce expectations.[48] Holm informs us that the spectrum does not concern levels of reciprocity, but rather "different degrees of sociability."[49] Thus, the spectrum helps delineate the relationships between giver, taker, and receiver. What makes the baptismal liturgy even more complex when outlining such relationships is the fact that the gifts being given are not tangible commodities. Abstract nouns, such as water, salvation, and grace, are presented as gifts. Even human beings are presented as such. In the Finnish liturgy, one of the first phrases in the service order is as follows:

---

43. As discussed in Holm, *Gabe und Geben bei Luther*, 81
44. Holm, *Gabe und Geben bei Luther*, 9.
45. Holm, *Gabe und Geben bei Luther*, 80.
46. Saarinen, *Luther and the Gift*, 234.
47. Saarinen, *Luther and the Gift*, 233.
48. Cf. Henriksen, *Desire, Gift, and Recognition*, 40 .
49. Holm *Gabe und Geben bei Luther*, 80.

PART II: PRACTICES

> Dear Christians,
>
> We are here because God has given this child to NN and NN. As his/her parent[s], you have followed Christ's command and brought your child to be baptized. At this occasion, God calls him/her by name to be his/her own and gives salvation as a gift.[50]

Here, the child is described as a gift from God. Accordingly, God is the giver, the parents are the receivers, and the child is the object being given. The section ends with God giving an additional gift: salvation. However, the receiver's role now seems to have shifted to the child, who occupies the position of baptismal candidate. In the first sentence, the reciprocal nature between the giver and receiver is spelled out, insofar as it is stated that the whole reason for the baptism to occur is because God has given the parents a gift (i.e., the child). Because they have received this gift, they have brought the child to be baptized. The gift that the child receives, however, does not require a retort—God does not have any expectations in giving salvation to the child.

The service order does not serve to explain what the gift entails or to whom. In the more general setting of websites or the bishops' letter, I would argue that it is clear that the giver is always God, and the receiver is always the baptismal candidate and, in the case of infant baptism, the parents. However, this is not what transpires in the liturgies. Apart from God, the liturgies refer to the parents as givers when delivering the gift of baptism to their child, and when giving both the local and the universal church a new member. When drawing attention to the image of baptism as a gift and the gifts of baptism, I am simultaneously highlighting that there are both givers and receivers. By doing so, the agents of the liturgy come to the fore. The gift is therefore not just an abstract noun, but the token of the relationship. The anthropological notion of gift giving entails the ability to decline—to say no to the gift—as central to forming a relationship. I will now discuss the gift as conditional or pure as a means of inquiring about whether the agents can say yes or no to each other.

BAPTISM: PURE GIFT OR GIVEN CONDITIONALLY?

To understand the dynamics of gift giving, and the extent to which we can talk of a gift given freely, or in the words of Saarinen, whether the gift is donative or economic, I will now turn to discussing the pure

---

50. Evangelisk-lutherska kyrkan i Finland, *Dop*, 5.

gift and the conditional gift, and how they can be said to appear in the liturgies discussed.

One of the major differences in the Nordic liturgies under survey concerns the role of the renunciation of the devil. In the Danish baptismal liturgy, the creed is worded as a set of questions, which begins with the question of forsaking the devil. The questions are posed to the baptismal candidate and end with the final question of whether she/he wishes to be baptized. In the Norwegian liturgy, as noted above, renunciation can be phrased as both a statement and a question. The phrasing of the renunciation marks it as a collective action when the phrase is in the form of a question to the candidate.

Concerning gift giving, I argue that we can interpret the function of the renunciation as a condition for baptism. In the manual, the alternative "no" is not given; it is only possible to answer "yes" in the liturgical setting of the baptism. To note such a thing might sound truistic; nevertheless, if baptism is supposed to be understood as a gift, it is worth noting that in this case, it is not possible to decline. Thus, the gift of baptism is dependent on renunciation. That this is so is strengthened by the order of the different parts of the service in this section: first comes the renunciation, then the creed, then the question of the name, and then the act of baptism with water. This is not to say that the intention of baptism is conditioned on the renunciation, nevertheless the intention appears as such through the phrasing of the liturgy.

In the Finnish, Icelandic, and Swedish liturgies, there is no component similar to the renunciation. In the Finnish and Swedish orders of service, "evil powers" are addressed in the form of a prayer that the priests say in relation to making the sign of the cross.[51] The sign of the cross is received unconditionally. The question of whether the candidate (or the parents) wishes to be baptized comes after the creed in the Swedish liturgy, and in this case, it is optional. In the Finnish liturgy, a set of questions, with the heading "Questions," is posed to the candidates, parents, and sponsors concerning the desire to baptize and whether they promise to bring up the child in the Christian faith. In the Icelandic liturgy, there is only the question of the name that is asked. Accordingly, baptism is

51. Cf. in the Finnish liturgy, the sign of the cross comes first, which is followed by the prayer asking to release the candidate from the "power of sin, death, and evil"; see Evangelisk-lutherska kyrkan i Finland, *Dop*, 15. In the Swedish liturgy, the prayer comes first and is phrased in a very similar fashion: "God, you alone can save us from all evil, and deliver N from the powers of darkness . . . ," as articulated in Svenska kyrkan, *Kyrkohandbok 2021*, 51.

performed on the condition that they (the candidate and/or the parents) accept the gift—that is, that they want it in the first place. In addition, the Norwegian and Danish liturgies pose renunciation as a condition, which is emphasized by the fact that "no" is not an option.

A liturgy that presents the gift of baptism in an unconditional manner is the Icelandic version, given the absence of questions (or demands) in this case. We can refer to such a gift as a pure gift.[52] A pure gift is given unconditionally, without expecting anything in return. However, the mere fact that the baptismal candidate has shown up can be stated as a condition for the baptism to occur. Still, it is important to note that the fact that baptism can be viewed as a conditional gift does not nullify or denigrate the gift. Rather, inherent in the notion of the conditional gift lies the idea of active agents in the form of both giver and receiver. In the liturgy, we want to express our gratitude, thanksgiving, and praise, rather than accepting the gift in silence.

GIFT AS GRACE: BAPTISM AS A MEANS OF GRACE

The very idea of a pure gift in theological terms brings us to the notion of grace. Jan-Olav Henriksen has suggested that a theological way of speaking about gifts is to speak about grace.[53] This is in many ways indicative of Martin Luther's way of speaking about the gift as part of his theology of justification. Similarly, Luther, in his *Large Catechism*, explains that the gift of baptism is to redeem, as "baptism is that which saves."[54]

Holm discusses how grace can be understood as a pure gift in Lutheran theology,[55] and how a Lutheran understanding of justification has been explained as a pure gift, in the sense that God gives and humans receive.[56] The reason for the gift being pure can be explained through the phrase "grace alone," which is at the core of Luther's theology of justification. As Holm argues, "It is impossible to bribe God with pious

---

52. Derrida expands on Mauss's notion; see Mauss, *The Gift*, 93 and Derrida, *Given Time*, 64.

53. Henriksen, *Desire, Gift, and Recognition*, 40.

54. "Since we know now what baptism is, . . . , we must . . . learn why and for what purpose it is instituted; that is, what it avails, *gives*, and produces. And this also we cannot discern better than from the words of Christ above quoted: 'He that believeth and is baptized shall be *saved*'" in Luther, *The Large Catechism*, art. Cf. ch. VI, art. 32 (italics mine).

55. Holm, *Gabe und Geben bei Luther*, 78.

56. Holm, *Gabe und Geben bei Luther*, 79.

deeds."⁵⁷ God gives us that which we can never run out of, such as grace, salvation, and eternal life, and there is nothing we can give back that can measure up to those gifts. Such statements also occur in several baptismal liturgies. As Saarinen explains, when discussing different theologians' interpretations of Luther's justification theology, "for Luther, the divine gift in justification is unilateral and does not allow for any reciprocity or economy of the gift."⁵⁸ Similarly, Holm challenges the notion of the free, or pure, gift. He argues that when we categorize a gift as free, we are simultaneously stating that it is not given reciprocally. If we receive a gift from God without wanting to reciprocate in some way, we are also preventing ourselves from forming a fellowship with God.⁵⁹

This line of reasoning can be likened to the way the bishops' conference in the Church of Sweden discusses baptism as a gift in their pastoral letter on baptism. There, the image of baptism as a gift is used to elucidate the notion of the so-called prevenient grace, as developed by Einar Billing.⁶⁰ In short, Billing argued that God's grace would reach everyone through the church without a confession of faith *prior* to receiving it.⁶¹ Billing developed this notion in relation to baptism, and it has since served as an explanation for why the Church of Sweden primarily baptizes children rather than practicing infant baptism for reasons concerning original sin.⁶² It is not possible for infants to profess their faith or to otherwise perform in a manner that would earn them God's grace, which makes them a perfect example of how prevenient grace functions.⁶³

When the bishops' letter mentions baptism as a gift, the bishops explain this notion through the idea of prevenient grace, which is considered "the kind of grace that precedes our decisions, actions, and

57. Holm, *Gabe und Geben bei Luther*, 82.

58. Saarinen, *Luther and the Gift*, 264.

59. Holm, *Gabe und Geben bei Luther*, 79; Henriksen, *Desire, Gift, and Recognition*, 42–43.

60. While not his precise phrasing, Einar Billing used the notion of prevenient grace to explain the importance of infant baptism. He does so in a number of writings, but primarily in Billing, *Den svenska folkkyrkan*.

61. Because the parishes in the Church of Sweden were spread geographically throughout the whole country, the gift of grace depended on the limits of the church and was not concerned with the limits of an individual's faith. Cf. Svensson, "Luther i den moderna lutherdomens tjänst," 344.

62. Augustine mentions the "gift of baptism" in relation to the forgiveness of sins: "It is an antidote given us against original sin." See Augustine, *Enchiridion*, ch. XIII, v. 64.

63. Billing, *Den svenska folkkyrkan*, 11.

accomplishments. We baptize infants by trusting in the prevenient grace. Just like the child is carried forth in baptism, we are forever carried by the grace of God."[64] In the terminology used in the present study, prevenient grace can be phrased as a pure gift. Just as infants are not able to profess their faith, nor are they able to express gratitude or reciprocate in some form, the only way humans can respond is through faith.[65] Baptism is the place where humans can present such a gift to God, but it is not necessarily needed in advance. In the baptism service, the candidate has the opportunity to say yes to being in fellowship with God through Christ.

The baptismal candidate is not merely a passive receiver but also someone who takes an active role in the process of gift giving. Just as the letter from the Swedish bishops' conference explains, baptism is a gift that we must give forward. In all the liturgies discussed, the Great Commission is read as motivation, or as words of institution, for baptism. Holm describes it as a process through which "the Christian gives to make the neighbor give."[66] Saarinen similarly argues that it is possible to give something to someone else without losing it for yourself; in other words, in such cases, the gift is understood as donative rather than as part of an economic exchange. To illustrate, he mentions teachers who share their knowledge with their students without ceasing to keep on knowing.[67]

Only God can give salvation, grace, and eternal life, and Christians cannot present each other with the same gift that God gives. There is always a necessary asymmetry between God and humans.[68] Christians can give forward the gift from God through faith, without losing the gift they themselves have received from God. This does not mean, however, that we can accept the gift as pure or that we reciprocate by presenting a pure gift to others. Rather, the idealized notion of the pure gift is maintained, since the giver in this case is God himself, who can be both unconditional in his love and demand that the receivers answer the call of faith.

---

64. Svenska kyrkan, *Leva i dopet*, 37. Cf. p. 16: "Fellowship given as gift and not built on accomplishments."
  65. Holm, *Gabe und Geben bei Luther*, 83.
  66. Holm, *Gabe und Geben bei Luther*, 86.
  67. Saarinen, *Luther and the Gift*, 235.
  68. Holm, *Gabe und Geben bei Luther*, 84.

BAPTISM AS A GIFT: A CONCLUDING DISCUSSION

At the beginning of this chapter, I described the national campaign on baptism that is currently happening in the Church of Sweden. In a conversation with Magdalena Widmark—a communication officer at the Central Church Office—at the start of the campaign, I received information about the focus group study that the communications department had conducted, wherein the questions on the various images used in communication on baptism were posed. During the conversation, she told me about the views that surfaced concerning baptism as a gift, and how the communication department had therefore chosen another image as its main motif. The focus groups are put together so as to mirror the larger community of members in the Church of Sweden, but it is important to note that the people in the focus groups only formed a smaller number. Still, the consequence was that their answers played into the design of a national communications campaign.

What is it about the gift motif that does not resonate with people? To receive or give a gift is a common event for most people. Gift giving almost defines certain holidays, such as birthdays or Christmas. However, this is not the type of gift described in the liturgies analyzed above. It is possible that the only tangible gift to which persons who hear the words of baptismal liturgies can relate is the image of the child as a gift. In a poetic sense, it might also be possible to understand water as the gift of life.

The more soteriological dimensions of baptism as gift, and the gifts received through baptism, are nevertheless not as clear and self-explanatory as they appear in the service order.[69] The theology that surfaces focuses on how that which God gives us does not want for anything in return; in other words, it does not demand that we perform in a certain manner. Several of the prayers in the Nordic Evangelical Lutheran liturgies can be interpreted as versions of the notion of the prevenient grace of Einar Billing, which I discussed above. At the same time, the doctrines of salvation, the eschaton, and sin appear in quite bold letters, especially in the Finnish and Norwegian liturgies. Such concepts are difficult to grasp in the moment of a baptism, where the focus might be on the small child, or children participating in the service, or the joyous nature of the occasion, regardless of the age of the baptismal candidate. As Lutherans, it is important to speak in the people's language so that the congregation truly understands what is happening.

---

69. Norheim, *Practicing Baptism*, 49–53, cf. also 34, 36, 40–41.

However, the church needs to be true to itself and effectively proclaim its own doctrine. When performing a baptism, the priest or pastor need not use explanatory terms to evoke a sense of theological depth. All sacraments are mysteries and need not always be transparent to make sense. The image of baptism as a gift from God, alongside the image of the gifts the one baptized received, need not be spelled out to be meaningful. Furthermore, there are other images that appear in the liturgies that are more difficult to comprehend, such as baptism as a daily dress,[70] but that are indicative of the tradition in which such words appear.

By examining the baptismal liturgies in the Nordic churches through the lens of gift giving, I argue that it is clear that different languages should be used for different settings, and that these uses of language do not necessarily influence each other. The language used in a communications office setting needs to be direct, catchy, and to the point, which is not something that liturgical language should strive for. At the same time, complex theological thoughts and doctrines should not necessarily be the stuff of the service order, but rather form the content of baptismal education. Describing baptism as a gift could be especially illuminating in a liturgical setting, where the congregation's main emotion is gratitude because of the child at its center. Such an emotion informs the way words of gifts are heard. Furthermore, the joy that often accompanies gratitude means that the images that the pastor or priest uses will be interpreted in a positive light.

BIBLIOGRAPHY

Augustine, Saint. *Enchiridion* [Handbook on Faith, Hope, and Love]. Translated by Albert C. Outler. Texas: Christian Classics Ethereal Library, 1955.
Billing, Einar. *Den svenska folkkyrkan*. Andra upplagan utgiven av Samfundet Pro Fide et Christianismo. Stockholm: Diakonistyrelsens förlag, 1963 (1930, 1942).
Den norske kirke. "Liturgier: Dåp i egen gudstjeneste—vedtatt av Kirkemøtet 2017." *Liturgier* (2023). https://ressursbanken.kirken.no/nb-NO/2022/liturgier/#na.
Derrida, Jacques. *Given Time: I. Counterfeit Money*. Translated by Peggy Kamuf. Chicago: University of Chicago, 1994.
———. *On Cosmopolitanism and Forgiveness*. Translated by Mark Dooley and Michael Hughes. Thinking in Action. London: Routledge, 2001.
Derrida, Jacques, and Anne Dufourmantelle. *Of Hospitality*. Translated by Rachel Bowlby. Cultural Memory in the Present. Stanford: Stanford University, 2000.
Dunn, James D. G. *Baptism in the Holy Spirit: A Re-examination of the New Testament Teaching on the Gift of the Spirit in Relation to Pentecostalism Today*. London: SCM, 1970.

70. Cf. Luther 1911/2018.

Evangelisk-lutherska kyrkan i Finland. "Dopet." *Familjefester och helgdagar - dop 16* (2023). https://evl.fi/sv/familjefester-och-helgdagar/dop/.

———. "Kyrkohandboken." *Dop* (2003). https://kyrkohandboken.fi/forr/dop.html.

Folkekirken. "Sådan foregår dåb i folkekirken: liturgi." *Sådan foregår dåb i folkekirken*, 1992. https://www.folkekirken.dk/livets-begivenheder/daab/saadan-foregaar-daab.

Hénaff, Marcel, and Jean-Louis Morhange. *The Philosophers' Gift: Reexamining Reciprocity*. New York: Fordham University, 2019.

Henriksen, Jan-Olav. *Desire, Gift, and Recognition: Christology and Postmodern Philosophy*. Grand Rapids: Eerdmans, 2009.

Holm, Bo Kristian. *Gabe und Geben bei Luther: das Verhältnis zwischen Reziprozität und reformatorischer Rechtfertigungslehre*. Berlin: de Gruyter, 2006.

Holm, Bo. "Luther's Theology of the Gift." In *The Gift of Grace: The Future of Lutheran Theology*, edited by Niels Henrik Gregersen, 78–86. Minneapolis: Fortress, 2005.

Horner, Robyn. *Rethinking God as Gift: Marion, Derrida, and the Limits of Phenomenology*. New York: Fordham University, 2001.

Luther, Martin. *The Large Catechism*. Translated by Henry Eyster Jacobs. Philadelphia: United Lutheran Publication Society, 1911/2018.

Mauss, Marcel. *The Gift: The Form and Reason for Exchange in Archaic Societies*. Translated by W. D. Halls. 1990. Reprint, Routledge Classics. London: Routledge, 2002.

Norheim, Bård Eirik Hallesby. *Practicing Baptism: Christian Practices and the Presence of Christ*. Eugene, OR: Pickwick Publications, 2014.

Saarinen, Risto. *Luther and the Gift*. Studies in the Late Middle Ages, Humanism and the Reformation 100. Tübingen: Mohr Siebeck, 2017.

Schmemann, Alexander. *Of Water and the Spirit: A Liturgical Study of Baptism*. New York: St. Vladimir's Seminary, 1974.

Svenska kyrkan. *Kommunicera dop*, 2023. https://svkyrkan.sharepoint.com/sites/kornet-kommunikation/SitePages/Kommunicera-dop.aspx.

———. *Kyrkohandbok för Svenska kyrkan del I i urval: Antagen för Svenska kyrkan av 2021 års kyrkomöte*. Stockholm: Verbum, 2021.

———. *Kyrkohandbok för Svenska kyrkan: antagen för Svenska kyrkan av 2017 års kyrkomöte. Del 1*. Uppsala, 2018.

———. "Kyrkomötet, ärenden 2021." 2021. https://www.svenskakyrkan.se/kyrkomotet/arenden_2021.

———. *Leva i dopet: brev från biskoparna till Svenska kyrkans präster och församlingar*. Uppsala, 2011.

———. *Meningen med dopet*. 24 11 2022. https://www.svenskakyrkan.se/dop/meningen-med-dopet (accessed 05 12, 2023).

Svensson, Leif. "Luther i den moderna lutherdomens tjänst: Albrecht Ritschl och den svenska Lutherrenässansen." *Svensk Teologisk Kvartalskrift* 97 (2021) 335–50.

Þjóðkirkjan. *Skírn á ensku: The Holy Baptism*. Reykjavík, 2020.

World Council of Churches. *Baptism, Eucharist and Ministry* (Faith and Order Paper no. 111, the "Lima Text"). 1982.

7

Prímsigning

Exploring the Context of a Ritual for Infant Blessing

STEINUNN ARNÞRÚÐUR BJÖRNSDÓTTIR *and*
KRISTJÁN VALUR INGÓLFSSON

THE WORD "PRÍMSIGNING" IN Icelandic (and old Norse) is an adaptation of the Latin term "prima signatio." This custom was recorded in the Sagas and elsewhere and was the name chosen for the ritual of blessing of infants in Iceland in 2009. This chapter discusses the contextuality of such blessings and their position in relation to baptism. Is there a need for a ritual for such blessings, and what status should a formally adopted liturgy have compared to the sacrament of baptism?

In 2009, the liturgical committee of Þjóðkirkjan, the Evangelical Lutheran Church of Iceland (ELCI), received an inquiry regarding the possibility of a ceremonial blessing for a set of parents and their child, for whom there was no mutual agreement regarding baptism. The parents did not share the same faith, but still wanted a blessing for the child. The committee considered the matter and recommended a thanksgiving service for the newborn child and signatio crucis. A brief liturgy of such a blessing was proposed. Although the proposal was accepted by the Bishop of Iceland for trial purposes, it has not been formally adopted in the handbook. The ELCI's liturgical handbook dates back to 1981 and has been under review for several years. This ritual, as well as others discussed in this article, remains under review in the ongoing process of producing a new handbook.

Signatio crucis is a tradition from early Christianity.[1] Other examples of its practice are found in the Nordic literature from the Viking era, when heathens needed this blessing to trade or interact with Christians.[2] It is also referenced in the Hómilíubók, an Icelandic manuscript believed to date back to 1200[3] which discusses those who have had primo signatio. Here, this ritual is called "prímsigning," a clear adaptation of the Latin term "prima signatio." Accordingly, the ELCI chose the term prímsigning for the new liturgical proposal in 2009.

None of the Nordic Lutheran majority churches have a special ritual for such blessings in their handbooks. In the 2011 publication "Leva i dopet" (Living in Baptism)—a letter from bishops to ministers and congregations of the Church of Sweden—a firm stand was taken against such actions having a special ritual.[4] Other Nordic churches have not issued such a statement against the ritual of blessing infants or children.

The different approaches of the Church of Sweden and the ELCI highlight the tensions discussed in this chapter. In all the Nordic majority churches, ministers may respond to requests for the blessings of infants or children, but such acts are seen as a matter of pastoral care. Generally, baptism is the service, liturgy, and sacrament offered to infants and children. However, the number of infant baptisms is declining in all Nordic countries, as can be seen in statistics from the project entitled *Baptism in Times of Change*.[5] Sometimes, children are baptized later on, especially in connection with confirmation. For example, in 2017, 57 percent of newborn children in Norway were baptized in the Church of Norway. That same year, 1,000 confirmands were baptized in the church, as well as 200 older individuals.[6]

The question discussed here is whether there is a need for a ritual of blessing and thanksgiving for a child whose parents do not want or agree on baptism. If so, a further issue to consider is the resulting status

1. St. Augustine, "Confessions," 50.
2. See Uspenskij, "The Baptism of Bones and Prima Signatio in Medieval Scandinavia and Rus," 9–22.
3. "Íslensk hómilíubók" www.heimskringla.no.
4. Church of Sweden, *"Leva i dopet,"* 44.
5. Hegstad, "Comparative Analyses of Statistics."
6. Hegstad, *Dåpen*, 11.

of this ritual. To answer this question, we will first look at the Icelandic ritual that was introduced in 2009, and how it was used. We will then explore the changes in the religious landscape, including baptism, that occurred during the first two decades of this century. In connection with this objective, we look at other rites of passage or blessings that have been discussed and practiced in the ELCI as acts of pastoral care and which are now discussed as formal liturgical services. Focusing on contextuality, we look at the history of baptism, primo signatio, and infant rites and attempt to answer our main question. The discussion is framed within the field of practical theology, using Richard Osmer's description of the four tasks.[7] According to Osmer, the four tasks of practical theology are as follows:

- *Descriptive-empirical task:* This task involves describing the human situation and the cultural and social contexts in which theological reflection takes place. This task is focused on understanding the experiences of individuals and communities and the ways in which they make sense of their world.
- *The interpretive task:* In this case, the task consists of interpreting the meaning of these experiences and contexts in light of Christian tradition and scripture. More specifically, this task is focused on identifying the theological themes and perspectives that can be drawn from these experiences and contexts.
- *Normative task:* Here, theological and ethical norms are brought to bear on the human situation to guide action. In other words, this task is focused on identifying the moral and ethical implications of Christian theology for everyday life.
- *Pragmatic task:* This task involves developing practical strategies and programs for addressing the needs and concerns of individuals and communities. Accordingly, this task is also focused on implementing practical solutions and actions that can help address the problems and challenges faced by people in their everyday lives.

According to Osmer, these four tasks of practical theology are interdependent and should be carried out in an iterative and reflexive manner. In this way, practical theology can be seen as a dynamic and ongoing process of

---

7. Osmer, *Practical Theology*.

engaging with the complexities of human experience and the challenges of the Christian faith in the contemporary world.

The four tasks could also be simply stated with four questions: What is going on? Why is it going on? What ought to be going on? and How might we respond?

In the following section, we will describe the context (i.e., the what and the why) and then move to the normative and pragmatic tasks of considering possible responses.

A RITUAL OF BLESSING

When the Liturgical Committee of the ELCI received the request for a ritual of blessing, they stressed the importance of meeting the wishes of the parents who had different beliefs but still desired to receive a blessing for their child (as was the case in relation to the request). The committee emphasized that this rite was not a replacement for a baptism, and the parents should understand that it would be the child's decision regarding whether to receive baptism later in life. The committee also stressed that the rite could not be performed without the full cooperation of both parents.

As the ritual was not a baptism, it would not be registered in church records, as is done with baptisms, confirmations, weddings, and funerals. Furthermore, the child would not be formally registered in the church—unless the parents decided to take this additional step, despite other misgivings.[8]

Originally, the intended purpose of the rite was to accommodate parents of different religions. It could, however, also be seen as an alternative to baptism if the parents do not want to commit to the latter at this time. In this sense, it could be construed as a step along the way toward the possibility of baptism later. In this respect, the term prímsigning recalls the catechumenate, or the time of learning before baptism.

---

8. It should be noted that the ELCI records baptisms in church books but does not have its own membership records. To record the membership of a child in any religious or life stance association, the parents need to register it with the central registration authority. If a child is born to parents who both belong to the same religious/life stance association, the child will be registered there automatically. It is therefore possible to be a member of the church but not baptized, and also to be baptized but not a registered member.

All the Nordic majority churches are members of the Porvoo Communion,[9] which means that they share an altar and pulpit fellowship with other churches of the Communion. One of the member churches, the Church of England, has Christian-initiation rites, which served as an inspiration for the Icelandic ritual in 2011.[10] The introduction to the Church of England's ritual states that it is for parents who see this event as a preliminary step toward baptism, parents who do not wish for their children to be baptized immediately and for those who do not ask for baptism, but who recognize that something has happened for which they wish to give thanks to God.

The Liturgical Committee of the ELCI had discussed conducting a ritual or prayers in connection with the thanksgiving of a child and issuing a blessing when the request was made. They saw it as important that a Porvoo sister church had taken steps toward conducting a ritual for such a blessing and were inspired by this.

The Icelandic ritual was also seen as a thanksgiving and prayer for a newborn child, accommodating parents with different religious backgrounds who acknowledged that the child may seek to be baptized later in life. The rite could also be performed when the parents wanted to entrust their child to God and ask for the blessings of the church, but still postpone baptism to a later point in time.

The liturgical committee stressed that the rite was not a name-giving ceremony, which is a common part of the baptismal function in Iceland.[11]

The ritual from the Church of England has the following structure:

- Introduction
- Reading(s) and sermon
- Thanksgiving and blessing
- Giving of the gospel
- Prayers
- Ending

---

9. For information on the communion, see http://www/porvoocommunion.org.

10. Church of England, *Rites on the Way*.

11. When the name is given at baptism in the ELCI the pastor registeres the name with the Registers Iceland (Þjóðskrá), as well as in the parish books and digitally with the ELCI.

The Icelandic rite is as follows:

Prayer

"We thank the Lord for the life of this child and the health of the mother during pregnancy. Keep this family in your safety."

Readings

Isaiah 43:1b, 2, 3a, 4a, 5a.

Mark 10:13–16

Reading or Psalm

The minister may address the parents or light a candle as a sign for a future baptism.

The Sign of the Cross

The minister addresses the child by name and states, "Accept the sign of the cross, and may the Lord watch over you from this moment and for all of your days."

Prayer

The Lord's Prayer

Blessing

Since the rituals of blessing are not registered, it is difficult to determine how many such blessings have been performed. At least 29 such blessings have been conducted according to a reply to an open survey sent to pastors in summer of 2023, but not all have used the liturgy provided by the bishop's office.[12] It is possible that not all pastors were aware of that possibility, since it is not in the handbook of 1981, and a new handbook has not yet been published. As mentioned above, the ritual is presented in the proposal for a new handbook.

---

12. A link to a simple MonkeySurvey was posted to the Facebook website of pastors in Iceland. A total of 40 responded, 20% of the 200 members, of which 160 are in active ministry. The survey was posted to see if there had been requests for services of infant blessing. A total of 13 pastors had conducted infant blessings, one or more times. At least seven used their own form. Others got the form from the bishop's office or from a colleague.

PART II: PRACTICES

THE QUEST FOR AUTHENTICITY

The project *Baptism in Times of Change* gathered statistical data on baptism in Nordic folk churches, and it shows a sharp decline in the number of infant baptisms in relation to newborns in the countries.[13] In Iceland, the decline has been noticeable, decreasing from 89 percent in 2000 to 42 percent in 2019. The decline in numbers is also mirrored by the fact that the number of children who are registered in the church at birth has dropped considerably from 80 percent in 2005 to 55 percent in 2019.[14]

In Iceland, research is lacking on the reasons why people choose to have their children baptized or not baptized. Research in Norway[15] and Denmark[16] has shown that "traditional" religiosity is being replaced by a personal choice and is characterized by weaker links to the church and a demand for individual authenticity. "The child should decide for itself" is the foremost reason for not choosing baptism, which underlines a separation from the tradition wherein a shared history and sense of belonging were more decisive factors when baptizing a child. The lack of any connection with the church is another influential reason. The third is religious conviction (e.g., do not believe, cannot say yes to the creed, or have another belief).

These are not traits restricted to baptismal practice or religion in general. The answers have their roots in individualism and the quest for authenticity in decision making.[17] However, it means that the search for the truth or ethics of an action is a search conducted within an individual, and not in the traditions or institutions of society. In other words, the quest for authenticity supports the notion that if I participate in a service, that service must have meaning for me. The Danish theologian Karin Marie Leth-Nissen used the term "churching alone" to describe the changes of attitude in relation to church and traditional religious values in Denmark. The concept coins how individuals no longer feel

---

13. Hegstad, "Comparative Analysis of Statistics."

14. This can in part be explained by changed legislation regarding registration. According to legislation from 2013 every child is registered at birth as belonging to a religious or life stance association if both parents or the custodian parent belong to that association. Before 2013 a child was registered according to the membership of the mother. Increased immigration has also had effect as well as people leaving the church.

15. Hoeg, *Religious Parental Transmission*, 416–34.

16. Leth-Nissen, *Dåb i dag*.

17. See e.g. Taylor, *The Ethics of Authenticity*; Iversen, "Sekulariseringens betydning."

obliged to participate in church rituals, choosing instead to seek rituals that have individual meaning for them.[18]

Both Norwegian and Danish research have pointed to the importance of early socialization in transferring faith or religious heritage, which points to a change that began with the formation of the generation that now has young children. Historically, faith in Iceland was mostly mediated at home, given the rural nature of society that persisted throughout the centuries. Earlier Icelandic surveys on this topic do not exist, but when comparing surveys from 1988 and 2004, we can see that the person who had the strongest religious influence on respondents was the mother. When asked about the strongest religious influence, 50.7 percent of respondents in 1988 mentioned their mother, whereas in 2004, only 36.6 percent reported the same. The function of fathers in this respect also declined, but the role of grandparents as a religious influence was slightly stronger in 2004. This indicates that a change had started by the turn of the century.[19]

At the beginning of the 21st century, the British sociologist Grace Davie and French sociologist Daniéle Hervieu-Léger discussed this transmission of religion as a form of collective memory in their analysis of changes in Europe, alternatively describing the disruption of this transmission as "mutation" of religious memory or a change in the chain of memory.[20] Both agree that we can no longer take for granted that there is a "shared religious memory, held in place by the historic churches."[21] Discussing this in light of secularization theories, Davie and Hervieu-Léger both maintain that the change does not leave a vacuum, and there is thus a need to ask what emerges when this change has taken place.[22]

Looking again at Osmer's methodology, it should be evident that we have mainly been concerned with the "what" and "why." The statistics tell us that there has been a decline in baptismal numbers, and research into the sociology of religion has revealed a disruption in the transmission of religious beliefs. Research on baptism has shown that when religious tradition is mediated, it increases the likelihood of a child baptism. Research has also shown the influence of individualism on traditional religion and the quest for authenticity for the individual

18. Leth-Nissen, *Churching Alone*.
19. Björnsson and Pétursson, *Trúarlíf Íslendinga*.
20. Davie, *Religion in Europe*; Hervieu-Léger, *Religion as a Chain of Memory*.
21. Davie, *The Sociology of Religion*, 61.
22. Davie, *The Sociology of Religion*, 61.

when it comes to religious ceremonies. The following chapters will continue to consider these issues as we look at the normative aspects regarding this particular ritual and the handbook.

RITES OF PASSAGE

A baptism is a sacrament. In the sacrament, the baptized person is reborn of spirit and water and taken into the church of Christ, which is one and holy. But for the people partaking, it is also a rite of passage. In Iceland, baptism is often linked to name giving, the name is traditionally mentioned for the first time in the baptismal service. Baptism then marks the beginning of life and of a new life. We have other rites of passage in churches, including confirmations, weddings, and funerals. These are not sacraments, but are special services for which there is a special ritual. Confirmation is usually conducted during the Sunday service at the ELCI. In Iceland, baptism is encouraged in the Sunday service, but in reality, the majority of baptismal services are conducted outside of the Sunday services, either as a special (and private) service in the church or in a venue outside the church building, which is often a family home. Weddings and funerals are always separate services, not part of the Sunday service.

The decline in the number of infant baptisms and the corresponding increase in the baptisms of youth and adults has created an opportunity for the ELCI to review the baptismal liturgy and develop age-appropriate liturgical services. Working on a new handbook gives the church the capability to adapt to a changed environment, and accordingly, the working document of the new handbook already includes several rituals for the baptism of adults. In the new handbook, we can also find proposals for other rituals that mark a significant moment in people's lives, such as a ritual for the funeral of a stillborn baby. There has also been a call for a ritual in the case of miscarriage, but this has not yet been addressed.[23]

The liturgical committee is also reviewing a request for a ritual for a trans person who was baptized as a child with a given name but who has now taken a new name. The new name signifies that the person is renewed and is his/her true self, usually after a long and difficult struggle. The baptism of that person is still valid, but the request is for a special blessing of this new identity and the new name. Such a blessing could, of

---

23. Handbókarnefnd, *Handbókarefni*.

course, be handled within the sphere of pastoral care, but in this case, the request is for a formal ritual, a formal service in the church.

What would a ritual add to a prayer within the scope of pastoral care? A liturgy reflects the teachings of the church, and this would affirm the church's position as an open and affirming church that welcomes trans people. A liturgy can be celebrated privately, but it is in essence a public statement, an affirmation—in this case of the transformation taking place and the new person as someone to be celebrated and welcomed and needing prayer.

Some churches have already published such liturgies, but with other resource materials and different foci.[24] In many ways, the discussion on the liturgy of transition highlights issues related to the liturgy of blessing or prímsigning. Both rituals are discussed in relation to baptism, both echo calls for new rites of passage in the liturgy of the church, and both are frequently referred to as belonging to the sphere of pastoral care.

Richard Osmer's third question was: What ought to be going on? A decline in baptismal numbers calls for a response from the church and has been the source of different initiatives aimed at counteracting these developments. Several such initiatives were highlighted by the research project *Churches in Times of Change*.[25] In addition, churches are responding to these changes by reaching out to people in communities and offering new ceremonies, such as infant blessings (prímsigning) or other rituals marking a rite of passage.

CONTEXTUAL CHRISTIANITY

Fewer infant baptisms reflect a changing society. A discussion on transgender rituals is also a reminder that the times are changing. As shown above, our churches are responding to these changes. It is within these responses that we can situate the discussion in this chapter, which looks more closely at the underlying context and changes in Christianity that have emerged at different times.

Infant baptism was not the most common form of the practice in early Christianity and is not specifically mentioned in the New Testament.[26] In the Acts of the Apostles, we learn that Lydia was baptized "with her household" (Acts 16:15) and the jailer was baptized "with all

---

24. Puddister, "Transition, affirmation liturgies commended for 12-month study."
25. Churches in Times of Change, http://www.churchesintimesofchange.org.
26. For a discussion on the history of infant baptism, see Hegstad, *Dåpen*, 116–55.

his family" (Acts 16:34). We can thus assume that there might have been other children and infants included, as well as servants and slaves, when the whole household was baptized.

Infant baptism was first specifically mentioned by St. Tertullian (AD 155–220). It is clear from his writing that infant baptism is a known practice, but he argues against it. St. Origen (AD 185–253) also recognizes infant baptism as having been practiced from the times of the apostles, and so does Cyprianus (d. 258).[27] However, baptizing adults in Christian families was also common, as was evident in the childhood of St. Augustine, who speaks of this in his "Confessions," where he notes that when he was a boy, "I was regularly signed with the cross and given his salts, even from the womb of my mother."[28] The rite St. Augustine describes is the same as the one he later cites for catechumenists, who, at the beginning of their study of baptisms, received the cross and salts. This rite could also be repeated. In St. Augustine's case, there is no special mention of formal baptismal study in relation to this rite, but such a process is referenced, for example, in the case of Victorinus,[29] who, seeking baptism, entered the catechumenate, received primo signatio, and initiated his Christian learning and preparation for baptism.

Infant baptism became the general practice after 380 AD, when Christianity became the official religion in the Roman Empire.[30] The expression of the lived faith and the traditions of that faith have thus always been contextual.

Another example of contextuality is linked to the previous discussion on the term prímsigning. In the Viking era in Northern Europe, heathen men who wanted to trade with Christians or be in their service could accept primo signatio, or prímsigning, which enabled them to socialize with Christians, but still keep their own faith. An example can be found in Njals saga, where the priest Þangbrandur travels around the country and his hosts either receive baptism or prímsigning[31] In Egils saga, Egill and his brother Þórólfur receive prímsigning to be able to work for the Christian king Aðalsteinn in England.[32] Furthermore, in the Icelandic Hómilíubók, a collection of homilies, prayers, and

27. Hegstad, *Dåpen*, 120–21.
28. Augustine of Hippo, *Confessions*, 50.
29. Augustine of Hippo, *Confessions*, 187–88.
30. Hegstad, *Dåpen*, 116.
31. *Brennu-Njáls saga*, 200–203.
32. *Egils saga*, https://www.snerpa.is/net/isl/egils.htm. Chapter 50.

teachings on faith and liturgy dating from around 1200 that was mentioned earlier in this chapter, there is a reference to people who have had prímsigning, both in terms of how long they can stay in the church during mass[33] and as a reminder to pray for them.[34]

Prímsigning was no longer needed as a ritual when Christianity became the only religion in the Nordic countries, and infant baptism emerged as the norm. The baptism of infants was decreed by law in Lutheran times; for example, this was accomplished in 1687 in Norway,[35] in Sweden in 1686,[36] and in Iceland in 1685.[37]

Freedom of religion in the nineteenth century did not change the fact that infant baptism was the norm in Nordic countries, and only toward the end of the twentieth century did this begin to change. The decline in numbers has been rapid during this century,[38] as discussed above. This is thus the context in which Nordic churches find themselves at present, as well as many sister churches in secularized Western culture.[39]

In this chapter, we have discussed two new contextual situations in which a request for a new liturgy has been made, both of which are linked to baptism as a religious event and a rite of passage. In both cases, there has not been a consensus in Nordic churches about a formal ritual, even if there is a considerable consensus about the need for a prayer and a blessing in such cases, and that the church should meet this need.

Socially, infant baptism is a rite of passage. In addition to being taken into a holy church, the infant is presented to the congregation—and to its society. The request for the blessing of an infant can truly be a wish for blessing and thanksgiving, but it may also reflect the desire for a formal rite through which the child is presented to present society. As such, members of the church might feel that a new ritual would somehow lessen the importance and prevalence of baptism in people's minds.

33. "Um messuna," *Íslensk hómilíubók*.
34. "Oratio Domini," *Íslensk hómilíubók*.
35. Hegstad, *Dåpen*, 116.
36. Church of Sweden, *Att leva i dopet*, 42.
37. Pétursson, *Kirkjurjettur*, 83–84.
38. Hegstad, "Comparative Analyses of Statistics."
39. The reluctance to publish rituals in the Nordic Lutheran Churches seems to be more salient than it was among sister churches in the British Isles. The Church of England has had such a ritual for some time, as discussed in Chapter 1. The Church in Wales published a ritual in 2015 for the blessing of newborns, which can be used in cases where parents do not agree on baptism. See The Church in Wales, *Prayers for the Thanksgiving of the Birth of a Child*.

However, the prevalence of baptism in our society is already lessening, regardless of any new rituals. This has thus increased the need to reach out to people with the gospel and build bridges toward those parents who have come to shy away from what they see as too restricting or defining, but who would still welcome a blessing. A blessing as a ritual can be seen as a step along the way to baptism that is supported by the church, which is itself facing a new situation in a new context. Meeting parents halfway in preparing the blessing can establish a connection with them and open the door for further encounters.

A CONTEXTUAL HANDBOOK?

The liturgical handbook provides guidance and instructions for conducting liturgical services. The main focus is on the order of service, prayers, and readings, and on the structure of various traditional services, such as baptisms, confirmations, weddings, and funerals. It serves as a valuable resource for ensuring that the liturgy is conducted in accordance with the traditions and practices of a particular denomination or religious community. Generally, the handbook reflects the biblical teachings, the liturgical tradition, and the context of the church.

Liturgical handbooks are used by the clergy, lay leaders, and other participants involved in conducting these services. In this respect, they can be an important tool for maintaining continuity and consistency in worship practices within a religious community over time. However, it is precisely because they are a tool through which to interact with the community that the question of context arises. Which alterations does a changing context call for? How might we respond, for example, to the distinctive challenges that have arisen in the new context of Nordic churches?

As stated earlier, the ELCI has been in the process of reviewing the handbook of 1981. The importance of context can be noted in the handbooks of the last two centuries in Iceland. In the handbook of 1801, the emphasis on the Enlightenment and the importance of teaching and rationalism is especially visible. In the handbook of 1910, and even more so in that of 1934, a liberal theology is evident, and in 1981, there was a sharp turn toward classical liturgy, which has been linked to the liturgical movement of the twentieth century. The most significant change in the wake of the 1981 handbook has been the revival of celebrating Holy Communion as a regular part of the Sunday service.[40]

The current work, in connection with the handbook, stresses the need for new liturgical forms so that the book can fulfill its role of enabling the clergy and others who use it to accurately reflect Christian teachings with consistency. Instead of leaving different circumstances to the sphere of pastoral care, the current direction of the proposed work is toward the development of new guidelines and rituals for various situations. Specifically, there is demand for not only a liturgy for prímsigning and transgender people, but also for many instances of pastoral work, such as pilgrimage, memorial, and prayer services in the wake of trauma in society, or when pastors are called to bless a new house or a ship to name a few.[41]

In this respect, the handbook can be interpreted as both a resource and a tool for clergy and others who need guidance. It acknowledges the context of the church and the need for such tools, thereby increasing consistency in adapting to new contexts.

The question might be raised as to whether having a ceremony of blessing—what we have referred to as prímsigning—could in some way diminish the importance of baptism. The answer given here is that it does not. However, it is still recognized that the baptism of newborns is in decline, and that there is a need to reach out to parents and remain open to new opportunities to connect with them. Such a ceremony of blessing affirms the complexity of our context, in all its pluralism as a multi-religious society, and offers a way to share the word of God in these circumstances. Central to this is the idea that prímsigning is a visible action of blessing that keeps the doors open and the hope alive that this connection might later lead to baptism.

BIBLIOGRAPHY

Arason, Þorgeir. "Handbókin og helgisiðirnir. Hvar stöndum við 40 árum eftir útgáfu síðustu Handbókar?" In *Kirkjuritið*, 22–33. Reykjavík: Prestafélag Íslands/Skálholtsútgáfan, 2021.

Augustine of Hippo. "Confessions." In *The Works of St. Augustine, a Translation for the 21. Century*. Edited by J. E. Rotelle. New York: New City, 1997. https://wesleyscholar.com/wp-content/uploads/2019/04/Augustine-Confessions-vol-1.pdf.

Bjarnason, Sæmundur, ed. "Egils saga." https://www.snerpa.is/net/isl/egils.htm.

40. Arason, *Handbók og helgisiðir*.
41. Arason, *Handbók og helgisiðir*, 30.

PART II: PRACTICES

Björnsson, Björn, and Pétur Pétursson. "Trúarlíf Íslendinga" [The Religious Life of Icelanders]. *Studia Theologica Islandica* 3, 1990.

Church in Wales. *Prayers of Thanksgiving for the Birth of a Child.* https://www.churchinwales.org.uk/en/publications/liturgy/Prayers_for_Birth_of_a_Child

Church of England. *Welcoming Transgender People.* 09/07/2017. https://www.churchofengland.org/news-and-media/news-and-statements/welcoming-transgender-people.

———. *General Synod. An update on 'Welcoming Transgender People' GS 1178.* https://www.churchofengland.org/sites/default/files/2018-01/gs-misc-1178-an-update-on-welcoming-transgender-people-003.pdf.

———. *Pastoral Guidance for Use in Conjunction with the Affirmation of Baptismal Faith in the Context of Gender Transition.* https://www.churchofengland.org/sites/default/files/2019-06/pastoral-guidance-affirmation-baptismal-faith-context-gender-transition.pdf.

———. *Rites on the Way: Approaching Baptism. Thanksgiving for the Gift of a Child.* https://www.churchofengland.org/prayer-and-worship/worship-texts-and-resources/common-worship/christian-initiation/rites-way.

Church of Sweden. "Leva i dopet," *Brev från biskoparna till Svenska kyrkans präster och församlingar.* 2011.

Davie, Grace. *Religion in Europe—A Memory Mutates.* Oxford: Oxford University, 2000.

Davie, Grace. *The Sociology of Religion, A Critical Agenda.* London: Sage, 2013.

Gallup, *Trúarlíf Íslendinga.* Unpublished Survey. 2004.

Handbókarnefnd. *Handbókarefni úr fórum Helgisiðanefndar og Handbókarnefndar 2000—2020 til kynningar á Prestastefnu* 2021. https://docs.google.com/document/d/1P0BFvV6o0XDvx2kqjTg574GwJzc7fHGjIxH2LN_f-6w/edit#/.

Hegstad, Harald. *Dåpen: En nådens kilde.* Oslo: Verbum, 2019.

———. "Comparative Analyses of Statistics." *Churches in Times of Change* https://churchesintimesofchange.org/findings-from-the-project/comparative-analysis-statistics

Hervieu-Léger, Danièle. "Religion as a Chain of Memory." *Nova Religio: The Journal of Alternative and Emergent Religions* 8 (2005) 128–29.

Hoeg, Ida Marie. "Religious Parental Transmission and the Importance of Authenticity." *Mission Studies* 37 (2020) 416–34.

Iversen, Hans Raun. "Sekulariseringens Betydning." *Religionsvidenskabeligt Tidsskrift* 58 (December 2012) 33–49. https://doi.org/10.7146/rt.v0i58.7660.

Íslensk hómilíubók, (Book of Homilies, author unknown, from app. 1200) http://www.heimskringla.no/wiki/Íslensk_hómil%C3%ADubók.

Leth-Nissen, Karen Marie. "Dåb i dag. Traditionen til forhandling." *Publikationer fra Det Teologiske Fakultet* 85 (2020).

———. "Churching Alone: A Study of the Danish Folk Church at Organisational, Individual, and Societal Levels." *Publikationer fra Det Teologiske Fakultet* 79 (2018).

NRK. *Historisk seremoni: Elin og Stein er de første som gjør dette i Norge*, https://www.nrk.no/innlandet/transperson-blir-historisk-i-den-norske-kirke.-skal-markere-overgang-fra-et-kjonn-til-et-annet-1.15547798.Osmer, R. R. *Practical Theology: An Introduction.* Grand Rapids: Eerdmans, 2008.

Pétursson, Jón. *Kirkjurjettur.* 2nd ed. Reykjavík: Unknown publisher, 1890.

Puddister, Matthew. "Transition, Affirmation Liturgies Commended for 12-month Study." *The Anglican Journal*, March 1, 2022. https://anglicanjournal.com/new-gender-blessings-for-trial-use/.
Taylor, Charles. *The Ethics of Authenticity*. Cambridge: Harvard University, 2018.
Thorsson, Örnólfur, ed. *Brennu-Njáls saga*. 5th ed. Mál og Menning: Forlagið, 2008.
Uspenskij, Fjodor. "The Baptism of Bones and Prima Aignatio in Medieval Scandinavia and Rus." In *Between Paganism and Christianity in the North*, edited by Leszek P. Słupecki and Jakub Morawiec, 9–22. Rzezow: Rzezow University Press, 2009.

8

Bless or Baptize Children?
Some Ecumenical Reflections

Terje Hegertun

INDIVIDUAL AUTONOMY HAS BECOME an important value among parents of young children. Therefore, questions have been raised as to whether *baptism can occur later in life or perhaps be replaced by a rite of blessing for the children.* This chapter discusses this dilemma in light of increasing secularization and with the help of a variety of ecumenical insights.

BACKGROUND: FOLK CHURCHES IN A NEW ERA

Many people are inclined to ask what the role of folk churches will be when they lose their cultural and hegemonic religious status. More specifically, do these Nordic churches have the resources needed to face a scenario characterized by declining membership and decreasing support for baptism as one of the church's core practices? These are issues that are being discussed today in attempts to come to terms with the challenges that Nordic folk churches are facing. Alternatively, the question can be phrased like this: how can we interpret our contemporary existence and capture the present through its existential and religious pulse?[1]

---

1. Hammar, *Skapelsens mysterium*, 26.

The term "folk church" can be understood as a church that has a close connection to a people and a nation, which creates "cohesion and understanding when it comes to religious identity and practice," writes Jan-Olav Henriksen in his article "Secularization as the Folk Church's Ambiguous Condition."[2] The encounter with secularization and religious diversity otherwise means that people do not necessarily believe or participate in those religious practices that are exclusively linked to the prevailing thinking within a particular faith tradition, which is understood in this article as the Nordic Lutheran folk church. Social pluralism has already for many years produced signals that there may be other frameworks and interpretations that shape the lives of those who formally are members but do not necessarily share the baptismal theology expressed in liturgical formulations. In postmodernity, the image of God has become more private and thus more speechless.

Henriksen believes that this transformation affects the extent to which folk churches must accept that there is only one specific way of interpreting reality, preaching, and practice.[3] The sociologist Peter Berger is among those who claim that modern social development implies—on an individual level—that one must turn attention away from the world that is objectively given outside us and toward our own subjectivity and a more complex inner world.[4] In other words, pluralization, secularization, and privatization have changed the relationship between religion, authority, and the individual "in a way that opens up more ambiguities."[5] Folk churches, as well as churches of Baptist traditions, have experienced this transformation during the last twenty years or so. Thus, there now exists a transition from religious heteronomy to autonomy, which assigns a more reflexive relationship to religious forms of understanding, according to Henriksen.

A CHANGING PICTURE

While the concept of a "folk church" in Norwegian theology has previously been used to refer to a church that stands in opposition to the religious ideals of various revival movements and free churches, this

---

2. Henriksen, "Sekularisering," 167 (my translation).
3. Henriksen, "Sekularisering," 170.
4. Berger, *The Heretical Imperative*, 22.
5. Henriksen, "Sekularisering," 173, (my translation).

picture is about to change, according to Tron Fagermoen.[6] Today, other ecclesiastical and theological traditions have begun to appropriate the term, which has generated a more ambiguous folk church ecclesiology as a result.

The changes that have arisen in people's relationships to baptism represent a challenge that churches need to address, particularly on theological terms, Fagermoen argues.[7] He maintains that the increase in those who are attending baptismal acts indicates that in recent years, baptism has become more clearly a family event, and a celebration of the child and the family. Therefore, in a future revision of the baptismal liturgy, a clearer focus should be placed on the fact that the child is created in the image of God, and on the joy and gratitude for the child who has been born. In the years to come, it will be important that the liturgy interact with the expectations and life experiences of the families who come to church and ask for baptism. This means that the act of baptism should perhaps have a clear reference to creation theology. Sensitivity to the context in which people live is a basic prerequisite for a theology to be meaningful in our time.[8]

In his work, Fagermoen discusses what it means to live in a pluralistic and multicultural society, where baptism is no longer a matter of course. Not only does it actualize the relationship between baptism and salvation, but it also directs a stronger focus on the relationship between the act of baptism itself and the need for facilitating development, growth, and maturation if one is to live as a follower of Jesus. In other words, baptism can never be seen in isolation from what *follows* the baptismal event. In this vein, the Swedish theologian Anna Karin Hammar has stated that a baptismal theology that wants to be credible in the context of the Church of Sweden, with its strong focus on the integrity of the individual, "needs to deal with the question of whether it is morally justifiable to baptize children who are too young to answer for themselves whether they wish to be baptized or not." In other words, the shift in context from the traditional collective identity to the contemporary individual focus cannot be left unprocessed.[9]

6. Fagermoen, "Et valg mellom visjoner," 5.

7. Fagermoen, "Dåp og antropologi," 91–96.

8. Fagermoen, "Dåp og antropologi," 91. This is in accordance with the position of the Swedish theologian, Anna Karin Hammer, as outlined in in her Ph.D. thesis, *Skapelsens mysterium*, 34.

9. Hammar, *Skapelsens mysterium*, 91–92 (my translation).

The objective, then, which in later years has shifted toward faith education programs, should be understood as encouraging the socialization of the baptized into the life of the church and community of faith. The result is a greater understanding of God's reality and what it means to be united in the faith of Christ.[10] However, it should be noted that these considerations are also relevant to churches that practice child blessings.

Other reflections correspond with the overarching topic of this book project. The current issue of concern is how leaders of Nordic Lutheran churches are reacting to the decline in the number of children being baptized, and what kind of self-reflection is taking place among parents and church members, as well as among church leaders. In my view, secularization, urbanization, and ecumenism play important roles here. As a result of a general pluralism and diversity of opinion, some parents have become unsure as to whether they as parents—on behalf of their children—should decide to let their baptism be a religious and social rite, or whether it is better to wait until the children can decide for themselves. Generally, parents want their children to choose when they get older.[11] It may also be the case that at least one of the parents is influenced by a Baptist understanding of baptism, according to which the conscious choice of the baptizand is of fundamental importance.

However, since many parents who choose not to baptize their children still want to have a relationship with the church for themselves and their families, representatives of Nordic folk churches often ask whether other rituals or connections could be considered fruitful. Among the questions that emerge regarding strategies and new practices enacted in response to the decline is whether *child blessing could be an alternative when parents choose not to baptize.*

According to Hammar, modern families are characterized by the paradox of individualization.[12] At the same time that they want the right to live their own lives, they also have a longing for greater fellowships. In such circumstances, a church environment has the privilege of communicating that families are not alone but rather part of a larger community that together embodies the meaning of what is best for the children.

---

10. Fagermoen, *Reformasjon nå*, 92, 95.

11. The Evangelical Lutheran Church of Iceland has developed a liturgy for the blessings of children. See Chapter 7 in this volume for an expanded discussion of this.

12. Hammar, *Skapelsens mysterium*, 39.

PART II: PRACTICES

SOME SOCIOLOGICAL AND HISTORICAL FACTS

Before I try to answer the central question of this chapter, I will continue with some sociological and historical facts. Part of my observation is that new questions have reached the classical churches in ways comparable to what younger free church movements have already experienced for a long time.[13] Free churches have been forced to foster communities reflecting their own times, wherein ideals of religious freedom and the self-determination of individuals seem to be self-evident values. The folk churches, on their side, have enjoyed being in a privileged situation for centuries, with the result that the great majority of Norwegian children have been baptized based on an established church tradition. This tradition has been relatively unaffected by more modern trends of self-determination and individual autonomy. While in earlier times, infant baptism was mandated by law, the churches of today are now at the mercy of the active choice of the parents on behalf of the children. To a lesser extent, this choice leans in favor of folk churches.[14] Generally, however, individual liberalism has influenced both Baptists and secularized members of folk churches, although at different historical points in time.

When Anabaptism broke out in the 1500s, soon followed by the Baptist movement, it was driven—among other things—not only by a conviction of having the right understanding of what the New Testament text was saying about baptism, but also by modern ideals of religious freedom and the demand for the self-determination of individuals. This development relates to the fact that baptism and salvation are closely interwoven in the New Testament. Both perspectives point in the same direction: the individual should decide for himself or herself. Thus, the national churches hear the same thing: "We will wait for baptism and let our children themselves decide whether they want to be baptized or not." In my view, this position is not necessarily a *no* to baptism; rather, it is a no to the *time* at which baptism may occur. Child blessing, then, may be an opportunity to give parents a sense of belonging to the church while they wait.

It may be a brutal fact, but the situation for the Evangelical Lutheran Church has radically changed compared to its proud history of tradition. About 60 years ago, nearly 100 percent of all Norwegian children

---

13. For an introduction to various aspects of this issue, see the anthology of Sæther and Tangen, *Pentekostale perspektiver*.

14. The situation for the folk church in a Norwegian context is effectively described in Dietrich et al., *Folkekirke nå*.

were baptized. Today, the percentage has declined to approximately 50 percent of all newborns. The decline is greatest in the diocese of Oslo, the capital of Norway, compared to other areas of the country (in 2018, 31 percent of all children became baptized), while the number of adults being baptized has increased.[15] Indeed, it is a demanding task to fight against one's own golden past!

Another more introspective observation is that Christian churches, for a long period of time, have been involved in ecumenical conversations about baptism. Such conversations have given different churches a better theological understanding of what Christian baptism is all about. The polemical tone has been replaced in favor of a more respectful conversation, as the objective becomes one of learning from each other's theological traditions. Other fruits of the increasing contact between church denominations are the existence of cross-concessional families. The result in this case is that you cannot be sure which form of baptism is most appropriate for these families.[16]

Filadelfiakirken in Oslo, the Pentecostal church to which I belong, has recently decided that it will welcome as new members those who have faith, or at least are on their road to personal faith in Jesus as Savior and Lord, based upon the Apostolic Confession, without requiring that everyone be baptized with the same form of baptism. The reason for this change is—among other things—that a high percentage of those who engage in this congregation as volunteers or devoted local leaders have a Lutheran background. Therefore, it becomes difficult to maintain any requirement of re-baptism for those who value the baptism to which they were exposed as children. In short, some members do not see any reason to be baptized again.[17]

I would suggest that the combination of the declining numbers of baptisms, the increased focus on faith education (in Norwegian: trosopplæringsreformen), and a more common understanding of the theological content of baptism together imply that the difference between the historical churches and the free church movements in the north has become smaller. Today, different church bodies can understand each other in better ways than seemingly ever before. They are, so to speak, "in the same boat" when it comes to addressing the challenges that secularization

---

15. "Kraftig nedgang i antall døpte," Statistisk Sentralbyrå (26 February 2024).

16. Different aspects of the baptism debate from an ecumenical perspective can be found in Hegertun, *Nådens gaver*, 176–87.

17. The BEM Declaration discourages churches to perform rebaptism, §13, 4.

and postmodernism represent regarding the way Christian communities meet the spiritual needs of modern families, which ultimately turns on questions about baptism as a transition rite.

ECUMENICAL OBSERVATIONS

Baptism, Eucharist, Ministry, the so-called BEM document, which is one of the best-known papers from the World Council of Churches (WCC), discusses infant baptism and adult baptism as equivalent alternatives, in the sense that both are roads that lead to the church. Here, infant blessing is also mentioned:

> In some churches that unite both infant-baptism and believer-baptism traditions, it has been possible to regard as equivalent alternatives for entry into the Church both a pattern whereby baptism in infancy is followed by later profession of faith, and a pattern whereby believers' baptism follows upon a presentation and blessing in infancy. This example invites other churches to decide whether they, too, could not recognize equivalent alternatives in their reciprocal relationships and in church union negotiations.[18]

The document contains a benevolent mention of the arrangement of child blessings: "Some of these churches encourage infants or children to be presented and blessed in a service which usually involves thanksgiving for the gift of the child and the commitment of the mother and father to Christian parenthood."[19] This leads to some common theological and ecumenical observations upon which Lutherans and Baptists largely agree, observations that may reduce the tension between child blessing and infant baptism.

In his book about baptism, Harald Hegstad is among those who clearly refer to baptism as a "powerful sign" and not only a punctual event.[20] In Hegstad's view, baptism must be seen as an act of God that includes *both* an event and a process. I suggest that both Baptists and Pentecostals have an immediate understanding of this way of articulating the acts of God in the baptismal act. Second, Hegstad emphasizes the close connection between baptism and faith. Luther's position is well known, as he believed that without faith, "baptism is of little use,

---

18. BEM, Commentary 12, 4.
19. BEM, Section IV, § 11, 3.
20. Hegstad, *Dåpen*, 51–55.

even though in itself it is a divine, infinitely rich treasure."[21] Perhaps we could state that there is no baptism without faith, and no faith without baptism. To be baptized is to partake in the gift of salvation, whether this gift is received in faith sooner or later.

Interestingly, the New Testament varies its language when describing the gift of salvation. Some passages indicate that it is received by faith, and others that it is given through baptism (see Acts 2:38; 1 Cor 6:11; Gal 3:2.14.27; Eph 2:8; 1 Pet 3:21). The terms in use are generally interchangeable, which means that both Lutherans and Baptists are "right" in their understandings of baptism. The difference ultimately depends on which approach and theological angle of view are in play. To put this in another way, just as repentance can take the place of baptism, baptism can take the place of repentance. In the same way that Lutherans fear that child blessing may become a substitute for infant baptism, Baptists are afraid of an uncritical infant baptismal practice that may dissolve the relationship between faith and baptism, thereby leading to "an indiscriminate baptismal practice," as stated in the BEM document.

In this Faith and Order document, the WCC also tries to point out special challenges inherent in the two baptismal traditions:

> To overcome their differences, believer Baptists and those who practice infant baptism should reconsider certain aspects of their practices. The first may seek to express more visibly the fact that children are placed under the protection of God's grace. The latter must guard themselves against the practice of apparently indiscriminate baptism and take more seriously their responsibility for the nurture of baptized children to mature commitment to Christ.[22]

There are reasons to problematize baptismal practices that do not take religious education seriously. Correspondingly, there are reasons to problematize practices that do not include baptism in the rite of initiation.[23] Historically, what constituted the church in the long tradition was not only faith nor only baptism. Instead, it was an understanding of baptism that led to confessed faith. This understanding required the clear

---

21. "The Holy Baptism," in *The Large Catechism*.

22. BEM, § 16, 5.

23. For an extensive discussion of the relationship between baptism and faith in the initiation process, see McDonnell, *Christian Initiation*.

recognition that it was not enough to be baptized, as one also needed to live in the grace of baptism as a follower of Jesus Christ.[24]

Third, a general ecumenical insight experienced by many believers in different denominations worldwide is that God truly acts in human life, even outside of a strict sacramental framework. Salvation reaches the believer as a powerful sign, as a promise, and even sometimes as a surprise, but it does not preclude God from acting even before, during, and after baptism. The consequence of this perspective would be to emphasize, in line with what Regin Prenter states, that there is a clear basis in Lutheran thinking that it is the Spirit who makes Christ present in the sacrament.[25] However, the Spirit can also be experienced and expressed in other ways. What this means is that we cannot operate with too narrow categories when discussing the work of the Spirit in the church's sacramental practices, not even when we talk about baptism.

A fourth observation based on the first three is this: If infant baptism to a greater extent than before is the result of a conscious choice on the part of the parents—and not just a social convention or a cultural family event—then we may ask with the patristic theologian Oskar Skarsaune:[26] Perhaps the declining baptismal rates can be a good thing for a folk church? His reflection is that if the church fails to teach those who are baptized, parents' no to baptism may be a sign of increased responsibility. If they feel free not to baptize their children, it may be because they know for themselves that they are not able to lead their children into the Christian faith. They will not make a promise they are unable to keep. A local church must respect that, according to Skarsaune. Only *then* do you take the church, baptism, and non-believing parents seriously.

A THEOLOGY OF THE INFANT BLESSING?

I belong to a church tradition wherein infant blessing is a common act of intercession and a public presentation of the child that is given to the parents and the congregation. The logic is clear: children deserve this starting point. Thus, they become subject to intercession and care through this process. Then, faith education in Sunday school programs and youth gatherings follows. The blessing event emphasizes the great joy and the gift that the child truly is for both the family and the congregation. Within

---

24. Regarding baptism as Christian initiation, see Hegstad, *Dåpen*, 153–55.
25. Prenter, *Spiritus Creator*, 114–80.
26. Skarsaune, *Etterlyst*, 272.

the tradition of Baptist and Pentecostal churches, child blessing consists of a concrete prayer requesting that God must take care of the baby on her or his way to baptism. The blessing is not a substitute for baptism, but rather an expression of the parent's desire for God's blessing over the child's life and future in a special way. Therefore, it should be the interest of all churches to develop a theology and liturgy around child blessings.

What do rituals of intercession and the act of blessing actually entail? Child blessing could very well be regarded as *a covenant act that entails promises of both God's and the church's blessing and care*. The human involved is affirmed and embraced as a child of God and thus a unique and beloved person. According to the Swedish theologian Gustaf Wingren, baptism is a victory of creative life. Baptism does not bring anything new to man beyond God's meaning for creation, which consists of life, freedom, and worship.[27] It is thus possible to develop a theological understanding of child blessings as a manifestation of both the gift of life and a lifelong calling for discipleship. As such, it is both an initiation and a covenant.

One of the most beautiful stories in the Bible is when Jesus forgets all the adults surrounding him and welcomes the children. He makes them models for all believers, takes them in his arms, places his hands on them, and blesses them (Mark 10:13–16). In the kingdom of God, the child has a leading place, and the roles have changed: It is not the children who will be like adults, but the adults who will be like children. The kingdom of God *is* for the children. As a direct transmission of what happened in this remarkable story, the text is read every time child blessings are performed in churches around the world. A priest or pastor takes the child in his or her hands, prays, and blesses both the child and the family who is gathered. Moreover, it has become increasingly common to include godparents in the blessing, as they should have an active and conscious understanding of their role as supporters and interceders. Thus, the external framework is not so unlike what applies when infant baptism takes place.

The question, however, is one of determining what kind of anthropology is behind the child blessing. This seems to be an unsettled question. Baptist theology, from time to time, has been accused of being built on an underdeveloped anthropology. What is common among the churches practicing child blessings is that nobody has yet developed a full-scale

---

27. Wingren, *Credo*, 83, 197–98.

systematic theology about the status of the child. A conscious liturgy has hardly been developed, either. The act only appears to be a beautiful part of the service, but as far as I know, it has not been the subject of any comprehensive systematic-theological clarifications.

A review of the faith basis for the denominations that practice child blessing in Norway reveals that the practice is hardly mentioned in official documents. Thus, no theology or liturgy has been developed for child blessings. However, in an earlier church service manual for the Pentecostal movement in Norway, we can find the following passages connected to child blessing. Specifically, one can engage in free prayer, or,

> Dear Lord Jesus! We pray for a blessing on this child. Thank you for the gift of life. You will preserve ... NN ... and protect him/her from dangers and accidents. Let him/her grow in faith in you and reach the goal you have set for all people: the eternal salvation of the soul. Amen.

One may also pray for the family and for the home. In this case, one can engage in free prayer, or,

> Dear Lord Jesus! You will bless and preserve this home. You have established the family; keep your hand on these dear friends. Thank you for the gift that you have given mother and father. You will give the parents grace and the ability to raise the child in the Christian faith. Amen.[28]

The closest one gets to a basic understanding of a theological clarification is that the child—as created in God's image—is under God's protection and, as such, already *is* a child of God. Baptism, as well as child blessings, reveals a miracle of creation and proclaims the hope of liberation for humankind. A baby becomes blessed in the name of the love of God, who created the world. Interestingly, many of the same perspectives are included in the Swedish liturgy of infant baptism. Here is one example of a thanksgiving in which the parents can pray:

> God, we are here in wonder and gratitude for life. Thanks for NN. Thanks for the life we get to share with each other. Thanks for the gift you give and the confidence you show us. Give us tenderness, firmness, and calm. Help us to give your love to her/him/the children we have been given responsibility for. In the name of Jesus. Amen.[29]

28. *Predikanthåndboken* (my translation).
29. https://www.svenskakyrkan.se/dopsajten/gudtjenstordningen (my translation).

In his book on baptism, Hegstad states that the text from Mark 10 seems to be the basis for the Baptist view of baptism "because it says that the kingdom of God already belongs to the children, [and] baptism is not necessary for them."[30] When these churches perform child blessings, one perceives this act to be in accordance with what Jesus himself did. Obviously, this seems to be a satisfactory scriptural basis. To put this in another way, the practice of child blessing is based on a concrete belief that children already belong to the kingdom of God. That is why free church members bring the children to church and let them be exposed to the teaching and protection program of the church.

In Filadelfiakirken in Oslo, after the blessing, extensive efforts are made to ensure that children are included in the various activities of the church. Older children actively participate in worshipping groups; they partake in the Lord's Supper, and they are included in the comprehensive program for faith education and inclusion.[31] The underlying idea is that when a child is brought to the congregation through the ceremony of child blessing, the whole congregation becomes responsible for an extensive teaching and service program, in line with the Great Commandment (Matt 28), which covers all phases of life, from the cradle to the grave. In this way, child blessings must be understood as something much more than a single event. In fact, the blessing implies congregational responsibility for the entire lifetime. Of course, this is a major challenge for a local church, not least in terms of human resources. Today, Filadelfiakirken in Oslo has several hundred volunteer employees who, together with their leaders, are responsible for everything that must happen to realize the program of MicroFila, which is the name of the children's activity program.

The same liturgy mentioned above from the Swedish church also contains a prayer for the child, which can be used by parents, a priest, or another person. It should be noted that the content of this prayer is practically identical to what can be heard during a child blessing ceremony:

> Let's pray: God of life, we collect our good thoughts, everything we want for NN, and we pray: Let her/him live in faith and grow in security and fellowship, enclosed by the prayer of the congregation. Give her/him hope and courage when life is difficult, the

---

30. Hegstad, *Dåpen*, 119 (my translation).
31. For a deeper understanding of the program, see https://microfila.no/.

power to stand up for others, and the feeling of being carried. In the name of Jesus. Amen.[32]

The perspective that comes out of the story of Jesus and the children (Mark 10) is groundbreaking: in the child, the kingdom of heaven has come near. Whoever receives the child in the name of Jesus welcomes God. Therefore, in the child, creation and salvation are linked.[33] Child blessing underlies the notion that life is stronger than everything that breaks down what is good. In this way, child blessing—both within free churches and in a Lutheran context—can be developed as a doxology, a thanks-for-life, and an expression of God's creative and everlasting presence.

A MORE FLEXIBLE APPROACH?

To face our own time, a more flexible approach is needed, which means that churches must take seriously the fact that today, all church bodies are faced with a more complex population. Representatives of the Nordic folk church should not be too quick to conclude that everyone who is not baptized as a child is lost to the church.[34] In the future, one can expect from these churches a greater variation in the initiation rituals and practices than has been the case so far. My advice is that Nordic churches should consider establishing a liturgy for child blessing in line with the approach of the church of Iceland.

However, the actual position of the folk churches in both Norway and Sweden is that child blessing, in a historical sense, is a "foreign custom." All aspects of the child blessing are already covered by baptism. However, documents from these churches also state that creating a liturgy may provide an opportunity to prepare a ritual that is clearly different from the baptismal liturgy and thus make a more definitive distinction between baptism and child blessing. Nevertheless, none of these churches wants to establish a particular liturgy of child blessing. Indeed, they warn against actively promoting such a ceremony, but any priest can still independently assess whether child blessings could be applicable during the intercession part of the service.[35]

32. https://www.svenskakyrkan.se/dopsajten/gudtjenstordningen (my translation).
33. Hammar, *Skapelsens mysterium*, 121.
34. Hegstad, *Dåpen*, 142–43.
35. See https://www.kirken.no/globalassets/kirken.no/bispemotet/2018/dokumenter/bm-saksdokumenter/bm-20.18-barnevelsignelse.pdf See also https://www.svenskakyrkan.se/filer/Leva%20i%20dopet%20-%20biskopsbrev%20om%20dop%20(x).pdf

The presupposition is that such a practice is not a substitute for baptism but an event of intercession. It should be possible to design a rite for the blessing of children to meet those families who are not opposed to baptism but who want to wait to make such a decision until a later stage of the child's life. At the same time, the churches should consider extending the education program to include parents and godparents. Only in this way can we safeguard the interaction that must exist between the church as both a sacramental and a teaching community, as clearly stated in the Great Commandment (Matt 28).

Some may fear that a more flexible approach will promote further secularization. I do not think so, based on a quick look at those places in the world where the church is growing the fastest. Thus, I think this is an unfounded fear. Throughout the world, churches are growing within those environments that have a comprehensive teaching program linked to Christian initiation, regardless of whether the rite of entry is infant baptism or child blessing.

The necessity of seeing the close link between baptism and education has long been clearly articulated by the Church of Norway. The document *Baptismal Practice and Baptismal Education in the Norwegian Church* states, "It must be a crucial matter to see that the biblical prerequisites for a sound baptismal practice have not failed. If the national church is to continue to maintain its practice of baptism, it must therefore intensively upgrade its baptismal training."[36] In this vein, an extensive faith education reform program was launched in 2004. Furthermore, the new text from Faith and Order ("One Baptism: Towards Mutual Recognition") emphasizes that baptism is situated within the context of lifelong growth in Christ. Even more strongly than in the BEM, baptism is seen as part of a Christian initiation process, preceding the act of baptism and continuing after the act through the baptized individual's incorporation into the Christian community.

In her article " . . . legger vi vårt barn i dine hender . . . " the Norwegian theologian, Hege Fagermoen, discusses the fact that some members of the Church of Norway want to mark their affiliation to the church, while at the same time seeking something other than what is given in baptism. She acknowledges the need for a broader theological conversation about what child blessing means for the view of baptism, and therefore also the view of the church. According to Fagermoen,

---

36. *Dåpspraksis og dåpsopplæring i Den norske kirke*, 94–95.

PART II: PRACTICES

"As a folk church, we must take it as a solid declaration of trust that parents turn to us with their newborn children and want the church as a framework around their children. It is a declaration of trust that we should manage with gratitude and awe."[37]

Perhaps a more clearly designed and theologically grounded arrangement for child blessing could help ensure that the folk church does not see the need to compromise with the church's view of baptism and faith, either in their communication or in practice. First, though, a conversation must be held about how churches in Nordic countries should understand and meet the desire for child blessings.

BIBLIOGRAPHY

Berger, Peter I. *The Heretical Imperative: Contemporary Possibilities of Religious Affirmation*. Garden City, NY: Anchor, 1980.

Dåpspraksis og dåpsopplæring i Den norske kirke: en utredning avgitt til Bispemøtet våren 1982 med bispemøtets vedtak og studieplan for sju samvær. Oslo: IKOs læremidler, 1982.

Dietrich, Stephanie, et al. *Folkekirke nå*. Oslo: Verbum Akademisk, 2015.

Fagermoen, Hege E. "... legger vi vårt barn i dine hender..." In *Luthersk Kirketidende* 154 (2019) 430–431.

Fagermoen, Tron. "Et valg mellom visjoner: en analyse av ulike kirkesyn i kirkevalgkampen 2015." *Tidsskrift for praktisk teologi* 33 (2016) 4–15.

———. "Dåp og antropologi, innledning." In *Reformasjon nå. Luther som utfordring og ressurs for Den norske kirke*, 91–96. Stavanger: Eide, 2016.

Hammar, Anna Karin. *Skapelsens mysterium, Skapelsens sakrament. Dopteologi i mötet mellan tradition och situation*. Uppsala: Uppsala Universitet, 2009.

Hegertun, Terje. *Nådens gaver i gjestfrihetens hus. Kirken som karismatisk og sakramentalt fellesskap*. Oslo: Lunde, 2018.

Hegstad, *Dåpen: En nådens kilde*. Oslo: Verbum Akademisk, 2019.

Henriksen, Jan-Olav. "Sekularisering som folkekirkens tvetydige betingelse." In *Folkekirke nå*, edited by Stephanie Dietrich, et al., 166–78. Oslo: Verbum Akademisk, 2015.

Luther, Martin, "The Holy Baptism." In *The Large Catechism*. https://bookofconcord.org/large-catechism/holy-baptism/.

McDonnell, Kilian, and George T. Montague. *Christian Initiation and Baptism in the Holy Spirit: Evidence from the First Eight Centuries*. Collegeville, MN: Liturgical, 1994.

Predikanthåndboken. Oslo: Rex, 1995.

Prenter, Regin. *Spiritus creator: studier i Luthers teologi*. København: Samlerens, 1946.

Skarsaune, Oskar. *Etterlyst: Bergprekenens Jesus. Har folkekirkene glemt ham?* Oslo: Luther, 2018.

Sæther, Knut Willy, and Karl Inge Tangen (eds.). *Pentekostale perspektiver*. Bergen: Fagbokforlaget, 2015.

---

37. Fagermoen, "... legger vi vårt barn i dine hender..." (my translation).

Wingren, Gustaf. *Credo. Den kristne tros- og livsanskuelse.* Oslo: Gyldendal, 1979.
World Council of Churches. "BEM Declaration." Faith and Order Paper No. 111. Geneva: 1982.
———. "One Baptism: Towards Mutual Recognition. A Study Text." Faith and Order Paper No. 210. Geneva: 2008/2011.

9

The Postponed Baptism

The Experience of Being Baptized Prior to Confirmation

Berit Weigand Berg[1]

EVERY YEAR, A GROUP of young people in Denmark is baptized in Folkekirken (the Evangelical Lutheran Church of Denmark, abbreviated as the ELCD) prior to their confirmation, and while this experience is rather seldom in some parishes, the national numbers point at this as being something more than just an occasional event. Of the youth being confirmed in 2023 approximately 18 percent were baptized in close proximity to their confirmation.[2] These baptisms, and in particular the reasons behind them, were the main motivation for conducting the project "The Postponed Baptism."[3] At the beginning of

1. This article has one primary author responsible for the representation of the study in this chapter. However, leaving the pronoun "we" out of the article would be a vast misrepresentation of the project. At the start of the project, all decisions were made unanimously by the two project leaders (see note 3). For the duration of the project, all reflections were facilitated and to some extent concluded by the project leaders. However, all conclusions were presented to the participating pastors before being presented outside the project, thereby creating a second "we."

2. https://www.fkuv.dk/folkekirken-i-tal/konfirmerede.

3. In Danish: Den udskudte Dåb. A collaborative development project lead by Berit Weigand Berg (Kirkefondet) and Anders Damtoft Kaufmann (Konfirmandcenter Folkekirkens Uddannelses- og Videnscenter). Both theologians and former ministers,

the project, interviews were conducted with youth who had all chosen to be baptized prior to their confirmation, and in some cases also with their parents. This chapter will present their answers, as well as the resulting reflections that arose from their further consideration.[4] Finally, this chapter includes some practical-theological reflections and recommendations based on the project.

BACKGROUND

Two earlier studies on baptism in Demark made it evident that while parents all over the nation actively consider baptism, the tendency toward a "yes" is lower in one particular parish in the southern part of Copenhagen than it is in all other suburban, larger city, and rural parishes.[5] However, in all areas of the country, parents expressed the same idea: that children should make their own decisions. This consideration does not necessarily lead to a "no" regarding baptism. Sometimes, the child is baptized anyway, based on the logic of the parents that the baptism does not really count until it has been confirmed.

The church is experiencing lower baptism rates among infants, and the rates of confirmation are also declining. However, the decline in the number of confirmations is not occurring in a one-to-one linear line with the decline in infant baptism. Each year, a significant number of youths are being baptized prior to their confirmations. From 2007 to 2019, there were a total of 29,038 baptisms among youth in the group aged 13–15 years.[6] This fact has raised several questions, of which two became the main focus of this project: what leads youth to consider being baptized, and how do they experience this practice?

STRUCTURE OF THE PROJECT

As mentioned above, this project arose out of interest in some of the significant statistics combined with the two prior studies, although both have a slightly different focus. Aside from this existing research, the project had

---

they now work as consultants within or on behalf of the ELCD. Berg holds an additional M.A.in Participatory Theology, with a prime focus on youth ministry, which is relevant to this project.

4. A full project report is available in Danish: see Kaufmann and Berg, *Præsentation*.

5. Leth-Nissen and Trolle, *Dåb eller ej*; Leth-Nissen and Berg, *Dåb i dag*.

6. In the age group of 10–12 years, almost 6,000 has to be added to the number, giving a total of around 35,000, or a little less than 2,700 each year.

little else to stand on. It was therefore formed as a preliminary study, and the knowledge presented here is to be interpreted as such.

In particular, two ideas drew our concern while we were designing the project. First, an interview is a life event for the interviewee, as stated by Kvale and Brinkmann.[7] Second, the knowledge produced should be of relevance for pastors from Folkekirken. The overall structure of the project therefore became, due also to the influence of COVID-19, an adapted version of the design thinking methodology.[8] Design thinking is a combined deductive and inductive method applied in a non-linear process consisting of five steps: empathize, define, ideate, prototype, and test. The first step, empathize, becomes the core of the project, as the following four steps all refer to this first step. Inspired by Henk de Roest,[9] we decided to *engage practitioners conducting research on Christian practices* and included pastors in steps two to five as a way of ensuring the project's relevance.

For step one, we wanted to conduct semi-structured interviews with newly baptized confirmands (herein the baptized, even when describing a pre-baptized situation). In line with Kvale and Brinkmann, as well as Moschella,[10] we realized that interviews conducted with questions such as, "how did you experience being baptized?," could become not only a life event in itself but also lead to a pastoral conversation. We decided to think of the interview as part of a circle surrounding the baptism, rather than a detached conversation. This led us to choose the pastor as the interviewer. The baptized would then have received an education regarding baptism, have been baptized, have been confirmed, and now have reflected on this process with the same pastor. We believed that by using the same pastor, who would further advance the work of the project, it would indicated to the baptized that this was indeed the church who was interested in them and their experiences, while at the same time providing the pastors with a legitimate reason to reconnect with those confirmands they had baptized.

Although we conceptualized this as preliminary research, the number of interviews conducted put the study in the category of qualitative

---

7. Kvale and Brinkmann, *Interview*.

8. Design thinking is based on principle described in 1969 by Herbert A. Simon in his book *The Sciences of the Artificial*. Throughout the elaboration of this method, the focus has been on how to bridge the gap between experience and development.

9. Roest, *Collaborative Practical Theology*.

10. Moschella, *Ethnography*.

research.[11] The interviews were not, however, recorded, and the joint reflection was based on notes that each pastor made during the interview, and not on exact quotation. The pastors were asked to fill out a questionnaire shortly after each interview. As we expected a cacophony of voices, and as we felt obliged to secure the anonymity of the interviews, we made the point of not distinguishing one voice from the others and in not making any links to the interviewing pastors.[12]

FINDINGS OF THE INTERVIEWS

From Infancy to the Time of Baptism

In a few of the interviews, the parents also participated, and they presented several reasons why their child was not baptized as an infant. Independent deliberation and family situations were some of these reasons. The answer to what they had done to equip their child to make the choice of being baptized prior to confirmation was unanimously reported as "nothing." Some parents had indeed decided that their children should make the choice themselves, but they had not intentionally facilitated this process. They had exposed their children to baptism and confirmation as a way of taking part in the life events of family and friends, but they had no recollection of having engaged in a conversation about baptism. It was not until the question of confirmation was raised, and they therefore needed to sign their child up for confirmation class and start planning the party, that they addressed the issue of baptism. The answers from the baptized confirmed this. The conversations about baptism and confirmation, which the baptized did have prior to their own ceremony, seem mostly to take place among peers. Among others, elder siblings, cousins, and classmates were mentioned in these interviews. Conversations with the pastors were not mentioned either by the parents or by the baptized.

A Good or a Bad Experience of Baptism

Focusing on the baptism itself, we expected a cacophony of voices, and different voices were indeed found. However, in the joint reflection with the pastors, it became evident that the voices fell into two main groups: those of the baptized, who had a good experience, and those who had

---

11. There were more than 5, and less than 25, as suggested by Polkinghorn, as reported in Bartholomew et al., *A Choir*, 3.

12. Bartholomew et al., *A Choir*.

an insignificant or perhaps even a bad experience. Tuning in closer to these two groups and their answers provided us with a rather interesting insight. Cross-reflections showed a coherency between their experience on the one hand and their understanding of the connection between baptism and confirmation on the other. More will be said about this later, but it is first necessary to elaborate on experience.

The baptized, who claimed that they had a good experience, pointed to the uniqueness and sincerity of the experience. They referred to the event as a special moment, which rose from the things surrounding it, as well as the moment itself. The ritual indeed, but also other elements, seemed to strengthen the experience of the baptism. This included the time spent on their own with the pastor ahead of the baptism, as well as preparing and rehearsing for it. Likewise, taking part in the preparation for the day with their family, participating in the baptism service itself, and the time spent with their families afterwards were also mentioned. Focusing on the actual baptism, they referred to what we came to call the *cocktail effect*.[13] A term borrowed from, for example, biochemistry, the cocktail effect illustrates how while each element has an impact on its own, the combination of the elements can also create a joint impact. The baptized referred to the extended history of the tradition, their preexisting relationships with the pastor, the space that was created for them individually by mentioning their name, and tiny pieces of their vita being included somehow in the liturgy as elements that had an important part to play in what they described as a good experience. When all this fell into place, the baptized talked about their baptism as an important, even transformational, moment.

The importance of this cocktail effect and what happened when it was lacking became evident when considering the answers from those who had an insignificant or bad experience. Being baptized by a pastor who one had no preexisting relationship with, without any kind of preparation or rehearsal, and with room only for a single mentioning

---

13. "When we are exposed to a number of different chemical substances simultaneously, combination effects, also known as 'cocktail effects,' can occur." https://eng.mst.dk/chemicals/chemicals-in-products/focus-on-specific-substances/endocrine-disruptors/combination-effectscocktail-effects/. The term cocktail effect is sometimes used as a synonym for the term bricolage or "byggekloss-spiritualitet" (Graff-Kalleåg and Kaufmann, *Byggekloss-spiritualitet*). With cocktail effect, I refer to a distinct difference between these terms, as it is the pastor, and not the baptized, who becomes the responsible subject in the cocktail effect, in contrast to "byggekloss-spiritualitet" in which it would be the baptized who is seen as the active subject.

of their name, but no pieces of their vita created a space in which the oldness of the tradition or the quality of the music was not enough to create an authentic event. These experiences left the baptized with the understanding that baptism was just an annoying technicality toward the more important confirmation.

Baptism and Its Connection to Confirmation

Turning to the question of the experienced interrelation between baptism and confirmation, as described earlier, the baptized who had a good experience understood baptism as something of its own importance, whereas the baptized with a bad experience understood baptism as a simple technicality before confirmation. In some of the responses, we found an extra dimension. A good experience sometimes left the baptized with a sense or understanding of some kind of meaningful *connection* between the baptism and the confirmation, either as equally important or even with baptism being considered the more important element. On the contrary, a bad experience left the baptized with the feeling that baptism held no real importance. In this case, it was simply a thing that the pastor claimed to be necessary. It appears that the baptized formed a link between their experience of the baptism and their theological reflections on its significance.

Interviews as Theological Reflections on Baptism

Within the ELCD, it is tradition to provide some kind of education prior to baptism. In the case of a baptism prior to confirmation, an established practice is to include this education in the larger confirmation class. The interview, therefore, included questions about what the baptized remembered from this class, which was close to nothing. What the interviews provided instead was a glimpse of a different space of importance: the time after the baptism, and the process of growing into being baptized.

In the pastors' experience, the baptized were willing to talk with them during the interviews. Some even seemed eager and thanked the pastor for the opportunity to talk about the experience. They showed up on time or even early. One was clothed in a way that the pastor understood as "dressed for an important conversation." The occasion might have been just an interview, but the baptized navigated the situation as if it was an important life event.[14] This was confirmed in the

---

14. Kvale and Brinkmann, *Interview*.

conversations, bringing forth two points of relevance. One was that all the conversations about what baptism is thought to be, that the baptized had had with peers and others before the baptism had vanished once the baptism had happened, leaving this conversation with the pastor as the very first on the experience of being baptized. The other was that the baptized while talking to the pastor realized that some of their answers and understanding of their experience and baptism in general were not formed until during the interview.

The lack of post-baptism conversations did not come as a surprise to us. However, the consequences of this lack of conversation did. A lack of conversation generally meant a lack of opportunity to reflect on the experience and impact of baptism. The pastors mostly shared common post-baptism teachings on baptism, such as those included in preachings, Bible-study groups, articles in church newsletters, and so on. They did not engage in individual conversations. Based on these interviews, the pastors recognized that a follow-up conversation, like those in these interviews, might in itself play a cathectic role and become part of the religious formation, perhaps even as a prolonging of the experience itself—not only to the baptized, but also to the pastors.

THE PASTOR

With the inclusion of pastors in the project, we had a unique opportunity to elicit their reflections on the answers. In the following, I will present some of these responses. The participating pastors all recognized that they were not involved in many conversations about whether or not to choose baptism, and they indicated that they would really like to be in these conversations. One of the participating baptized reflected on this and reported two relevant facts in support. First, the pastor visited the school class in June to invite the students to participate in the confirmation class, which was to start in September. However, at the time of this visit, the choice had already been made about whether to be confirmed. Second, at this introduction, the pastor said, "Do not worry if you are not already baptized. We will fix it." This statement often generated worries along the lines of, "Am I baptized? Should I be? Why am I not? What is meant by, 'Will we fix it?'"

Most of the participating pastors had, in some way or another, already been engaged in liturgical reflections about baptism. However, it still came as a surprise to them how much the little details mattered.

Their main reason to add, for example, elements from the vita and extra sign-acts had been to make the situation more relevant for the baptized, and hopefully also more authentic.[15] However, they had not realized that the importance of the sacrament became even more evident to the baptized through these adds-on.

The pastors recognized that their teachings on baptism in confirmation class were based on a more general approach and only seldom included details of the specific baptisms awaiting ahead. A full introduction to and explanation of the ritual only happened in the private preparatory conversations between the pastor and the baptized.

Although prior to the project, we were all aware that reflections could be formed by conversations, the pastors were surprised by the experience that they, too, gained a better understanding of baptism through these conversations. They sensed that they saw new angles of meaning and understood the underlying reality of baptism as an experience, instead of only as a doctrine or a practice. Moreover, the pastors' reflections revealed that the post-baptism discussions were more like theological conversations between peers. In this sense, the post-baptism conversation can transform the baptism into a reality for both the baptized and the pastor, as the experience establishes the new reality in which the baptized has become part of a new "we."

PRACTICAL-THEOLOGICAL REFLECTIONS AND RECOMMENDATIONS

By using design thinking in this project, there was a continuous focus on developing the reported reflections into new products, which could take the form of a new liturgy, a new curriculum, a new behavior, or anything the pastors found relevant. In the following, I will present some of the reflections, recommendations, and suggestions, from the participating pastors and the leaders of the project.

Reflections The church needs to be aware that it is very likely that parents do not intentionally help their children make the decision on whether they should be baptized. This decision seems to be based on what the

---

15. Davids and Rønkilde, *Det, som sker*. Pastors are more likely to add directing remarks, small speeches, and sign-acts than to remove elements from the authorized ritual in the handbook. The only thing that the pastors tend to leave out is the standard question from the liturgy, "Has the child already be baptized at home?"

children experience or pick up along the way (bricolage) and what they hear from peers, such as older siblings, cousins, or friends.

- Some of the baptism experiences were connected to the preexisting relationship between the pastor and the baptized, or the lack thereof. The experienced value of the ritual seems to increase when the pastor is considered "my" pastor.
- The significance of the ritual should not be underestimated. What the pastor invests in it is very likely to be what the baptized decode from it. When the ritual appears authentic and relevant, the theological importance of the baptism becomes not only visible, but also something that can be genuinely experienced.
- Participants should be aware that the ritual begins before the prelude or initial prayer/psalm. The preparation for the ritual and the way the baptized are included in those preparations play an important part in the baptism itself. We borrowed the term "the cocktail effect" as a way of describing this.
- Likewise, the ritual does not necessarily end after the postlude or closing prayer/psalm. A conversation afterwards might cast some light on what happened in a way that leads to a more reflective experience and, through this, a deeper theological understanding of baptism. The church should be aware that such a conversation, which includes questions like, "what did you experience when you got baptized?," and "what does it mean to you to be baptized," likely do not happen naturally with anyone.

The following two considerations report what we have only glimpsed in the reflections. These insights call for further research. However, as we are working along the lines of a preliminary study, we found these insights sufficiently relevant to put forward here:

- There seems to be a risk of creating a discrepancy between the dogma of the church and the experience of the baptized when it comes to understanding the importance of baptism versus confirmation, a discrepancy for which the church also holds responsibility, when, probably for a number of good reasons, it ends up providing a nonauthentic baptism.

- The post-baptism conversation could be a way for the church to establish a theological conversation with the layperson, who, through baptism, has entered into the common priesthood.

To establish further alignment between lived religion, contextual theology, and dogmatic theology, this project identifies several liturgical strategies that can be engaged, which will be presented below.

Recommendations and Suggestions

Based on the insight that the choice for or against confirmation is—according to the baptized—made before the church starts to invite prospective students to the confirmation class, we recommend that the church communicate about confirmation not only a few months ahead, but a year or maybe two before classes begin.

As "my" pastor seems to play an important role in establishing a good experience, we suggest that the same pastor be the one who engages in communicating, meeting, teaching, planning, and baptizing. This does not mean, however, that the pastor has to be the only person involved in all of these steps.

Through this project, we had the unique opportunity to suggest a revised baptism liturgy, as there was an official open public call for reflections and suggestions regarding the liturgy in the spring of 2021.[16] The group of pastors from Aarhus Vestre thus offered the following suggestions:

- There is no need to change the core of the sacrament. If the other elements in the cocktail effect are present at the baptism, including the relationship and preparation, then minor vita elements in the liturgy and perhaps small sign-acts should be sufficient to create the feeling of inclusion among the confirmand. For instance, it may be essential to replace pronouns with names in the ritual.

- To create an inclusive environment, it is relevant to reconsider the choice of readings. Since 1992, Matthew 28, 18–20 and Mark 10, 13–16 have both been mandatory in the ELCD, whether the baptism

16. "Indtil den 26. marts 2021 har det været muligt for enhver, lærd som læg, at indsende indlæg til det, der i folkemunde er blevet kaldt liturgipostkassen, på mailen folkekirkensliturgi@km.dk. Bidrag til debatten har også haft form af kronikker og indlæg i aviser, magasiner, online og trykte tidsskrifter, mens enkelte har udgivet bøger (monografier og antologier) om emnet." See Rønkilde and Engaard, *Systematisering og analyse*.

candidate is an infant, a pre-confirmand, or an adult.[17] As we have learned how even the smallest elements can help the baptized feel recognized and consequently understand the sacrament as relevant, we suggest that Mark 10 be replaced as a mandatory reading, either with a list of suggestions for readings or a selection made by the pastor. Such a mix of mandatory and suggested readings is found, for example, in the funeral liturgy within the ELCD.

- As a way to bridge the gap between the pre-confirmation baptism and the confirmation, we suggest the use of a baptism word—whether it be a piece of Scripture or part of a hymn—which should be read at the baptism and repeated at the confirmation. Baptism words are not part of the authorized ritual and are only used in a few parishes (inspired by Germany). Although not mandatory, confirmation words are mentioned in Ritualbogen. We therefore suggest that the pastor read a baptism word to the newly baptized confirmand right after the baptism blessing and before the Lord's prayer, and that this baptism word is repeated as the confirmation word at the time of the confirmation.

REFLECTIONS

In the following section, I will offer some further reflections on two of the central findings of the project.

The Experience

What the baptized had experienced became the natural starting point of the conversation. The fact that the experiences of the baptism could significantly differ seemed to echo the experiences of the participating pastors. However, the extent to which this experience was linked to the prior relationship between the baptized and the pastor calls for more reflection. The pastors recognized this, but they also saw it as a challenge to their Lutheran understanding of sacraments and ministry.[18] Although

---

17. Prior to 1992, the handbook contained two liturgies: one for children and one for adults. There was only one reading in the liturgy for adults, which was Matthew 28. Due to Danish legislation, pastors are still allowed to use this adult liturgy, which dates back to 1912, even though it is not included in the handbook.

18. This minister-ritual-congregants connection is also found and more fully elaborated on in the work of Kirstine Helboe Johansen, who identifies the pastor as both a visible and magical actor. See Johansen, *Det hellige, almindelige præsteembede*.

reflecting on this issue by no means led to a final conclusion, the pastors recognized that a gap might exist between Lutheran dogmatics and experienced praxis. However, on this occasion, they decided to continue to work with a main focus on the experience. They accepted the prior relationship between pastor and baptized and the role of the pastor in the baptism liturgy as an important element within the cocktail effect. They did not make this choice in order to promote the position of the ministry, but as a way to pay respect to the experience presented to them by the baptized, thereby highlighting this relationship as one of the elements that promotes the experience of baptism as something unique, important, and more than just a technicality. The pastors agreed that the sacrament is not falsified through a bad experience, but that it can lose its authenticity if one or more elements from the cocktail effect are missing.

The Connection

Although the number of confirmands is declining, confirmation is still an important ritual in Denmark. It no longer provides any legal rights, and a lack of confirmation does not cost one any rights, either. This is true within the church, as well as in secular society. An individual can become bishop as well as prime minister without being confirmed. Still, confirmation remains a ritual that holds importance to youth, their families, and the surrounding community. Commercials will be directed to confirmands, smaller towns will hang flags on the community flagpoles on the main street, and special greetings will be sent to the confirmand from their football team, as just a few examples of the ritual's significance.

However, within Lutheran theology, confirmation does not hold sacramental or ecclesial importance. What counts the most is the baptism. Nevertheless, looking at confirmation from the perspective of the confirmand, their parents, and even the practice of the churches themselves tells a different story.[19] Confirmation is important. The question is whether we can tie it more closely to baptism.

The baptized had not been asked to rate their experiences, but it was still possible to detect a link in this respect. Those with good experiences state that the experience of the baptism became important in itself, and not just as a necessary obstacle on the way to confirmation.

---

19. Many churches promote the confirmation with a lot of extra resources, compared to an ordinary service (e.g., with extra decorations in or around the church, such as a flag alley, flowers, balloons, live music, and gifts for the confirmands).

Some—but not all—even reported that the experience of baptism equaled or superseded that of the confirmation, placing a before-and-after awareness of the baptism process.

Those with a bad experience all indicated that baptism held no or only very little importance to them. What mattered to them more was the confirmation. In the case of a bad experience, it seemed as though their lived religious experience and the contextual theology they encountered within their own baptism were rather far from the dogmatic theology of the church. The pastor, or more broadly the church, failed in making the theological importance of baptism available for them in their experience of baptism. The cocktail effect gave them—or confirmed - the understanding of confirmation as the church tradition that is of the most importance and baptism as a technicality. However, in the case of a good experience, the understanding of baptism versus confirmation seems to be somewhat in line with dogmatic theology, at least when it came to baptism.

If it is important to us as a church to maintain a significant link between baptism and confirmation, there seems to be a unique opportunity to do so via the postponed baptism.

CONCLUSION

Within the ELCD, confirmation is not a sacrament. Today, not being confirmed does not hold any consequences. No rights are gained, and no rights are lost, either within the church or outside its walls. However, in order to be confirmed, there is a non-negational requirement for baptism. As the baptism is a sacrament, and confirmation is not, it can be theologically argued that baptism holds higher importance than the confirmation does. In this article, we present the findings indicating that for some confirmands, this is not how they understand the process. For some, the baptism in connection with their confirmation is not experienced as anything other than a technicality that the church finds necessary, but does not necessary itself put a lot of effort into. Hence, this leaves the baptized with the understanding that the baptism does not hold any higher importance for the church

For others, this baptism holds a value of its own. Their understanding is influenced by their experiences. When all the elements of the cocktail, as we call it in this article, were present, they felt the relevance of their baptism, which again formed their understanding of the baptism as not just a box that needed to be checked on the way toward confirmation, but as something more, with its own importance.

As the number of postponed baptisms has been rising, we find it relevant to argue that one way to make the church's teachings of baptism and confirmation align more with the interests of the confirmands, it might be essential to improve their understanding of baptism. This can be done through classroom teachings, but as the newly baptized interviewed for this project let us know, such understanding is very much communicated through how the baptism is prepared and conducted. Furthermore, as the interviews suggest, how and with whom the baptism is reflected on afterwards also play an important role in this process.

The decline in infant baptism is still the most stark in the larger cities in Denmark. Likewise is the increase in postponed baptism. At this point, some parishes only seldom experience a non-baptized confirmand wanting to be confirmed. However, from these interviews, we know that the conversations about baptism prior to confirmation often only take place among peers. We therefore suggest that there should be an awareness of the significance of these conversations within the ELCD to ensure that youth in cities, as well as in rural areas, are able to access such knowledge and make informed decisions.

Baptism prior to confirmation is indeed a matter of technicality. Ultimately, it has to be done if the confirmand wants to be confirmed. However, if the church, the pastor, the confirmand, and other relevant parties put some effort into the preparation, the ritual, and all the other things surrounding the baptism, it might be more likely to become experienced as a moment of change, with a before and after—ultimately, as a moment that matters in itself. This understanding could arise directly from the experience itself, or it could come from post-baptism reflections.

BIBLIOGRAPHY

Baltzarsen, Maj, et al. *Folkekirkens potentialer og barrierer blandt unge voksne.* Analyse & Tal F.M.B.A. 2020.

Bartholomew, Theodore. T., et al. "A Choir or Cacophony? Sample Sizes and Quality of Conveying Participants' Voices in Phenomenological Research." *Methodological Innovations* 14 (2021).

Davids, Iben Munkgaard, and Martin Bendixen Rønkilde. "Det, som sker i dåben, gør os trygge. Dåbspraksis i Haderslev Stift." 2017.

Graff-Kallevåg, Kristin, and Tone Stangeland Kaufmann. *Byggekloss-spiritualitet: en studie av spiritualitet i Den norske kirkes trosopplæring.* Oslo: IKO, 2018.

PART II: PRACTICES

Grube, Kirsten, and Suzette Munksgaard. *"Hvis jeg skulle bruge en præst, skulle han være mere som et menneske end en præst med en titel"—at bygge bro mellem kirkens budskab og unges virkelighed Ungdomshøringer i Aalborg Stift*. Center for Ungdomsstudier, CUR, 2012.

———. *Mere end blot to timer, Evaluering af Alternativ konfirmationsforberedelse i Viborg*. Center for Ungdomsstudier, CUR, 2011.

Johansen, Kristine Helboe. "Det hellige, almindelige præsteembede." *Kritisk Forum for Praktisk Teologi* 121 (2019) 61–72.

Kaufmann, Anders Damtoft, and Berit Weigand Berg. *Præsentation af projektet "Den udskudte dåb."* Konfirmandcenter og Kirkefondet, 2022.

Kvale, Steinar, and Svend Brinkmann. *Interview; det kvalitative forskningsinterview som håndværk*. Copenhagen: Reitzel, 2018.

Leth-Nissen, Karen Marie, and Astrid Trolle. *Dåb eller ej? rapport om småbørnsforældres til- og fravalg af dåb*. Copenhagen: Københavns Universitet, 2015.

Leth-Nissen, Karen Marie, and Berit Weigand Berg. *Dåb i dag. Tradition til forhandling*. Copenhagen: Københavns Universitet, 2020.

Moschella, Mary Clark. *Ethnography as a Pastoral Practice*. Cleveland: Pilgrim, 2008.

Munksgaard, Suzette, and Søren Østergaard. *Mere end blot forberedelsen til en fest?* Center for Ungdomsstudier og Religionspædagogik, CUR, 2008.

Ritualbog—Gudstjenesteordning for Den Danske Folkekirke. Copenhagen: Vajsenhus, 1992.

Roest, Henk de. *Collaborative Practical Theology: Engaging Practitioners in Research on Christian Practices*. Theology in Practice 8. Leiden: Brill, 2020.

Rønkilde, Jette Bendixen, and Nete Helene Enggaard. *Systematisering og analyse af indkomne bidrag til folkekirkens liturgiske drøftelse*. 2021.

10

Drop-in Baptism in a Norwegian Context
Results of a Qualitative Study

Stein Ellinggard

In May 2015, the Lademoen congregation in Trondheim, inspired by the Church of Sweden, invited people to participate in a drop-in baptism. On that day, seven individuals, aged five to 75 years old, were baptized. Since then, many congregations in Norway have invited people to participate in drop-in baptisms, and as a result, many have decided to be baptized. This article presents findings from interviews with parents who baptized their children and adults who were baptized between 2015 and 2020 in drop-in baptisms. It also presents findings from interviews with congregations who planned and implemented drop-in baptisms in their communities.[1]

WHAT IS DROP-IN BAPTISM?

Drop-in baptism is an alternative to traditional baptism. Normally, families or adults contact the church some weeks before a baptism is to be held. The local priest then holds an official meeting, thereby informing and preparing the participants for the Sunday service. However, with a drop-in baptism, there is no prior meeting. The announcement is made

---

1. The article is based on Ellinggard, *Frelst i en fei!*

for a specific time and date, such as a Saturday morning from 10:00 a.m. to 12:00 p.m., during which everyone is invited to come. On the day of the baptism, there will be some people from the local congregation and a priest waiting in the church. The candles will be lit, and the church will be prepared as it would be for a Sunday service. A registration will be conducted to record the interested individual's social security number, check records to prevent re-baptism, and produce a baptism certificate. There will be a short conversation before the baptism, and if there are no sponsors, someone from the congregation may act as a sponsor or witness. The baptism ritual follows the traditional procedure, which includes the blessing and the Lord's prayer, in addition to some hymns and music. After the baptism, there may be a church café celebration, wherein people can socialize and receive additional information.

PRESENTATION OF MATERIAL

My research was based on semi-structured interviews with 15 individuals who participated in drop-in baptisms, six parents with children and nine adults who were baptized. The first group included parents aged 30 to 50 years old, with eight children ranging from one to 11 years old, consisting of one girl and seven boys. In this group, the parents told me that they all had faith in God, except for one father, who reported that he had not believed at all. The adults who were baptized were aged 20–75 years old and included six men and three women. The study also included interviews with 22 individuals aged 35–65 years who work in seven different congregations. Seven personal interviews were conducted with employees and volunteers in these congregations. In two congregations, I conducted focus-group interviews, in which there were 12 priests, five men, and seven women between the ages of 35 and 65. These groups also included three women and one man from the local church counsel. One woman was working for the church office administration. There was one male musician, one female deacon, one female teacher, and two females who worked with children. In this part of the study, the informants were divided into three different types of churches: the forest church, the city church, and the sea church. I will explain the differences between them later. All names were changed in this report.

DROP-IN BAPTISM FROM THE PARTICIPANTS' POINT OF VIEW

Drop-in Baptism Lowers the Barriers!

Despite the church's efforts to lower the barriers to baptism, this study revealed that baptism could still be difficult to arrange. Olav (40) did not baptize his two sons due to his father's death. "I had no energy," he said. Time went by, and it became increasingly complicated to organize baptism. He did not know what to do, since he had no close relationship with a congregation and did not know any priest. He believed that a baptism had to be held during a regular Sunday service, but when he asked his sons, they did not want to participate in that way. This was also the case for adults who wished to be baptized. They hesitated and lacked the courage to seek help. As one elderly woman said, "I did not want to disturb the church." Some did not want religious exposure in public, while others were not interested in the process of preparation. For both families and adults, drop-in baptism was a good solution. "The simplicity was the key," Peter (40) said, who also reported the following:

> A new room was suddenly opened—a place where you could go to the church and do it in front of God's eyes. Drop-in baptism says, "Come as you are; focus on yourself and not on others."[2]

In this way, drop-in baptism was a good fit for their everyday lives and functioned as both a private and personal means of receiving a baptism. Bjorn (45) described his baptism as follows:

> In the chapel, it was very intimate. Just my wife and my children. This was a private moment. Maybe the most private moment in my life. Only me and my faith.

In this sense, it is easy to characterize such drop-in behavior as a form of "fast food" baptism, according to a consumer-oriented logic. According to the Norwegian researcher Ida Marie Høeg, this logic is challenging religious life in Norway today, since "the consumer society leads people to demand beliefs and practices which can stimulate needs, feel enjoyment, and deal with strain and the cost of the marked ethics."[3] This trend has emerged across all of Europe, as noted by researchers such

---

2. All quotes in this chapter come from qualitative interviewes conducted by the author.

3. Høeg, "Religion Parental Transmission," 421.

as Davie,[4] Leth-Nissen,[5] and Pettersson.[6] It is possible to view drop-in baptism as a part of this trend and perhaps a legitimate way of acting in the era of modernity.

Generally, drop-in baptism helps people become baptized without too much discomfort. This could lead us to think that this kind of baptism is not serious enough and is thus akin to shopping in a religious market. This is not the case, though, because when we listen to the stories, we find deep and sincere motivation. In one of his articles about shopping and religion, the French philosopher Bruno Latour wrote that there does not need to be any contradiction between this way of acting as a consumer and practicing religious life in our time.[7] In this view, it can be just as natural to be a consumer in a religious market today as it was in the Middle Ages. If this is true, perhaps the church must also accept the fact that people enjoy being baptized in this way and find it quite meaningful. Lowering the barriers does not necessarily mean that the religious motives of those who participate are any less serious than if the ceremonies were held in a more traditional way.

Drop-in Baptism and Personal Choice

The phenomenon of drop-in baptism incites the question, "Is it the right time for me to be baptized?" The church sets a time, and the participants can make their own personal choices. Among the interviewed adults who were baptized, several referred to earlier experiences as a motivation for baptism. One of them was Tor (45), who considered himself "a church outsider." During a difficult period in his life, he prayed to God and said, "If you help me now, I will go to church and be baptized later." Accordingly, baptism was a personal and deeply profound choice for him, which made the entire process very meaningful, as he had fulfilled his promise to God.

The focus on personal choice is becoming increasingly important for all ages today, as well as for children. In this study, several parents emphasized the importance of respecting their children's choices and wanting to support them. This was the situation for Per (40) and Monica (40), who did not baptize their son as a baby, because Per said he had no

4. Davie, "Religion in Europa."
5. Leth-Nissen, *Churching Alone*.
6. Pettersson, "From Standardised Offer to Consumer Adaption."
7. Latour, "Thou Shalt Not Take the Lord's Name in Vain," 229.

faith. When their son came to them at the age of seven and expressed a desire to be baptized, they agreed to attend a drop-in baptism. Per said, "When he wanted to be baptized, we would find a way to do it." This is a significant point in time, according to Høeg, as the child's integrity, values, and rights are becoming more important and have changed how the parents raise them, including in terms of religiosity. At this point, the parents may hand over the decision-making authority to the child.[8] Such an act reflects the essence of our time, as Charles Taylor points out,[9] by introducing the concept of *authenticity*, which involves loyalty to one's originality and uniqueness.[10] This personal way of acting also has an impact on how we relate to all kinds of rituals. The Swedish researcher Karen Jarnkvist talks about a new paradigm of rituals that must be more personal and meaningful to the participant and give them a sense of satisfaction.[11] The study of drop-in baptism confirms this shift, as in this case, the participants make their own choices, fulfill their own wishes, and give the ritual their own meaning.

Drop-in Baptism as a Rite of Initiation

While personal choice and experience are central in this time of individualization, studies also show that we still want to be part of a community. Baptism helps us achieve this and creates a new sense of affiliation, with an entity such as the local church. According to the Danish professor Anders-Christian Jakobsen, baptism today functions more as a ritual that brings individuals into a new group, rather than as a rite of passage or a change in state.[12]

In this study, Gunn (75) felt that baptism was an important part of being a Christian. When she heard about drop-in baptism, she traveled with her granddaughter and an old friend to a church far from home. In her words, "This was a gift from God to me. Now, I became 100 percent a member of the church." Gunn's perspective on baptism highlights the ritual as an *initiation rite* that provided her with a sense of belonging to the church community. However, baptism may also function in other ways. For instance, consider the case of Liv (35), who did not identify

---

8. Høeg, "Religious Parental Transmission and the Importance of Authenticity."
9. Taylor, *The Malais of Modernity*.
10. Taylor, *The Malais of Modernity* 43.
11. Jarnkvist, "Reflektioner över dop, vigsel og begravning."
12. Jakobsen, "Drop-in-dåb," 51.

herself as a personal Christian. However, after getting married, she became acquainted with a family who strongly emphasized Christian values and felt drawn to them. When she was asked to be a sponsor in a baptism, she was invited to a drop-in baptism event. Liv described her experience as follows:

> When I was baptized, I felt a sense of peace, and many pieces fell into place. I finally found a place where I belonged, and it just felt right.

It appears that for Liv, baptism was not necessarily a deeply personal religious experience or a means of establishing a closer connection to the church, but rather a way to participate in a longstanding tradition that held meaning for her. By being incorporated into this tradition through the act of baptism, Liv was able to find a sense of belonging and connection to a local community that shared her values and beliefs. This experience highlights the role of baptism not just as a religious sacrament, but also as a cultural practice that can provide a sense of continuity and meaning for individuals.

Another example is Ari (50), who had made a long journey, both geographically and culturally, to ultimately settle down in Norway with his wife and children. He wanted to be integrated into Norwegian society, learn the Norwegian language, get in contact with people in the local congregation and community, and secure a good job. At the same time, he wanted to renew his faith. As a result, he attended a drop-in baptism with his children to be baptized together with them. In Ari's words, "I was thinking, 'Now it is time to start anew and create a new relationship with Jesus and God.'" For Ari, the baptism served as both a renewal of his faith and as a rite that helped him and his daughters integrate into the new country of which he wanted to be a part.

The third example here is Peter (40), a family man with kids. Generally, the family is the most important community in many people's lives. In this study, several men spoke about feeling like outsiders in their own families because they were not baptized. When they heard about drop-in baptism, it became a golden opportunity for them. Peter spoke about his motivation for getting baptized and said, "Our family belongs together. The day we separate, I hope to see them again." In this way, baptism brought him closer to his family in both this life and the afterlife.

These examples show us how baptism functions as a ritual that provides people with access to different types of communities and strengthens their sense of belonging and identity; however, it does not always connect them more closely to the local congregation and the church. This is confirmed by Karin Jarnkvist's research in Sweden,[13] as well as that of Enggard and Nøjggard conducted in Denmark. Overall, baptism may connect individuals to various types of communities beyond just those associated with religious institutions.[14] This study also confirms that even though we live in an era of individualism, we still seek to be a part of different kinds of communities. We are living in a kind of collective-oriented individualism, as the Danish theologian, teacher, and writer Hans Raun Iversen calls it,[15] and baptism helps us join in the process.

DROP-IN BAPTISM FROM THE LOCAL CONGREGATION'S POINT OF VIEW

Drop-in Baptism Highlights the Adaptability of the Church

What, then, motivated these local congregations to arrange drop-in baptisms? To better understand their motivation, I took a closer look at the context and identified three types of churches: the forest church, the city church, and the sea church. In the forest church, the number of baby baptisms was still high, and during the COVID-19 period, they offered baptism services on Saturdays for the first time. This was a positive experience and served as a motivation for offering drop-in baptisms. In the city church, there was a significant decline in the number of baptisms. This became a wake-up call. When the bishop encouraged them to adopt a more flexible baptism practice, they decided to offer drop-in baptisms. The goal of the drop-in baptisms was to reverse the decline and enable more families to baptize their children. In contrast, the sea church existed in a pluralistic religious society and was competing with other churches and congregations. Still, the number of baptisms was quite high. However, some families were leaving the congregation to baptize their children in more conservative congregations. Through drop-in baptism, the sea church wanted to show people that they were an inclusive and open-minded church. One of the priests, Kirstin (45), said the following:

We have talked about being visible, and that baptism should be easily available.

Marit (65), one of the volunteers, made a similar remark:

13. Jarnkvist, "Narratives on Ritual Transfer," 108.
14. Enggard and Nøjgaard, *Tradisjon og fornyelse*, 146.
15. Iversen, *Folkekirke-Brugerkirke-Kirke i misjon*,135.

> We want to be a congregation where people who don't feel at home in the church can come to us.

As we can see, there have been some different motives for practicing drop-in baptism, but all wanted to adjust their baptism practices to their local context. For example, consider Knut (55), who worked as a priest in the forest church. According to Knut, "The church should listen more to people and find out where they are." With drop-in baptism and other types of practices outside the Sunday service, he felt that he could interact with the people in a more personal way. In a similar way, Kjersti (40), a priest in the sea church, said that drop-in baptism was the way baptism should be, in that "this is the best way; we must meet people's needs. I think this was the way the baptism was meant to be from the beginning."

Statements like these show us that some folk churches want to be flexible and adaptable to the local context. These observations have been confirmed by other empirical research, such as the study of Elisabeth Tveito Johnsen (2020), which suggests that churches that have experienced growth in their Sunday services have adjusted themselves according to the logic of the service society to reach their goals.[16] New baptism practices, such as drop-in baptism, can be seen as part of this adaptation.

Marketizing in Nordic Folk Churches

Several studies have pointed out that this adaptability has been evident in Nordic folk churches for a long time. According to the Finnish sociologist of religion Per Marcus Moberg, one of the biggest social changes in the West over the last few decades has been connected to the market-driven economy and the rise of the media. Neoliberalism has spread everywhere and established consumption as the ethos of late modernism.[17] Moberg argues that this has also impacted religious organizations and Nordic folk churches.[18] In his analysis of official documents, he found a language characterized by marketization. In his view, discussions about a decline in membership have influenced churches' self-understandings. Which means they acts more like a secular organization in a marked, selling, and buying religious products. Its success depends on high quantity numbers. This effects theology, values, strategy, and vocational understanding.

---

16. Johnsen, "Growt in a Context of Decline."
17. Moberg, *Church, Marked and Media*, 2.
18. Moberg, "Exploring the Spread of Marketization."

Another researcher who has observed these changes is the Swedish sociologist Per Pettersson, who studied the Church of Sweden and noted a close connection between the development of Swedish society, its relationship with the church, and the church's identity.[19] As society had developed into a service-dominated economy, he says, wherein the production of services, the user, and the user's subjective perception and experience had gained more significance,[20] this necessitates flexibility and adaptability from the service provider,[21] and every service must be unique because of the social relations between the individuals involved. These developments also have implications for the church as well, he argues, as its authority and legitimacy are diminishing, and the church is being assessed based on its services. As a result, the church must alter its approach to interacting with members and focus on catering to the religious market.[22] Although Moberg's and Pettersson's analyses do not include the Church of Norway, it is not difficult to find similar words and terms in its official documents that exhibit some of the same tendencies.[23]

Is Drop-in Baptism a Marketizing of Baptism?

Based on these findings, we should be inclined to ask whether drop-in baptism is part of this strategy of marketization. Some statements in the study, such as "the church needs to be more adaptable," "there needs to be more simplicity," and "the church needs to be more on the offering page," seem to be endorsing a kind of marketing strategy, but is this the reality of the situation? In this study, I found little of this kind of thinking in the local communities. Instead, I found a lot of good community-building praxis at play.

In every community, there is an ongoing exchange among its members. Simone Mulier Twibell defines this as the creation of social capital:

> Social ties formed between individuals and groups make it possible for resources to be shared, information to flow, and cooperation to develop in order to facilitate action in society and generate potential personal and communal benefits.[24]

---

19. Pettersson, "From Standardised Offer," 43-47.
20. Pettersson, "From Standardised Offer," 53.
21. Pettersson, "From Standardised Offer," 53.
22. Pettersson, "From Standardised Offer," 49.
23. Borg bispedømmeråd, "Dåp i Borg."
24. Twibell, "Social Capital and the Church," 115.

In her work, Twibell distinguishes between *bonding* and *bridging* social capital. Bonding social capital refers to the process of bringing together individuals who share something in common, such as ethnicity, gender, age, and social class. Such bonding may block out other features. In contrast, bridging social capital refers to social networks that connect people who are different and belong to different communities.[25] In her study entitled *Churching Alone*,[26] Karen Marie Leth-Nissen analyzed the Church of Denmark and made use of this perspective to determine how the members interacted with each other. Her findings revealed that the church primarily connected people who already had a preexisting relationship with each other, which would be the process called bonding.[27] If we look at drop-in baptism, it becomes apparent that the planning period fostered the bonding of social capital. The baptism event was organized by the congregation council, and multiple meetings were held in which different tasks were assigned to members. Bjorg, (60) a leader of the forest congregation, stated the following:

> We were planning who should be with us and how many we needed. We tried to think about how the day would be. Some had to stand in the door and say hello; some had to make coffee, and so on.

Such divisions of labor reinforced the connections between people who had already had a relationship. However, such remarks show that drop-in baptism also has the potential to facilitate the bridging of social capital, since the baptism created new, small communities of people who had not seen each other before. These communities are significant parts of the baptism process, as noted by Kjersti (40) of the sea church:

> I think those who came were especially sensitive to how we met them and how we talked about God and the baptism . . . . and their experiences will stay in their bodies.

Similarly, one of the deacons in the city church described the atmosphere in the church as follows:

> They did not just sit down waiting, but they also stayed in the church after baptism; it was a positive situation.

---

25. Twibell, "Social Capital and the Church," 117.
26. Leth-Nissen, *Churching Alone*.
27. Leth-Nissen, *Churching Alone*, 209.

In this way, drop-in baptism both strengthened the connection between people in the local congregation and bolstered associations between the newcomers. In all this, we see that the motivation was rooted in the provision of diaconal service, indicating that a church that aims to be accessible to its members may be the most successful in this respect. This is also in accordance to Pettersson, who says that his service-oriented perspective can be viewed as diaconal work.[28] Similarly, Moberg contends that, despite the content of official documents, they do not provide a comprehensive picture of what is actually happening in local churches.[29] There is a distance between the National level and the local, were the congregations are directed against the everyday life, meeting people's needs.

Drop-in Baptism and Privatization

Multiple studies indicate that religion has become a more personal matter,[30] and institutional religious practices are declining. With traditions breaking down, and society becoming more diverse and individualistic, people may no longer identify with the traditional concept of infant baptism. One priest from the sea church expressed this as follows:

> There is a sort of conformity in the way we think of baptism. A little child dressed up in a white christening dress . . . but what about those who do not fit into this picture or don't want to fit in?

Essentially, drop-in baptism breaks away from this traditional notion of baptism and makes it accessible to more people. This particular approach has removed the practice of baptism from its traditional setting and transformed it into a more public event carried out within the church community. According to one of the priests from the sea church, "When people come (to drop-in-baptisms), it is not just for creating their own happiness; it is also because the church says, 'This is the place.'" In these places established by the church, distinct communities emerge. Although not all of them may persist for long, they still play a crucial role in the baptism process. This is also in accordance with Leth-Nissen's observations regarding the Church of Denmark and drop-in baptism. She suggests that drop-in baptism may create new small here- and now communities which

28. Pettersson, *Kvalitet i livslånga tjänsterelationer*, 350–51.
29. Moberg and Martikainen, "Religious Change in Market and Consumer Society," 26.
30. Repstad, *Religiøse trender*, 10.

people are being baptized into. This kind of experience may strengthen the bonds between them.[31] It is therefore possible to argue that drop-in baptism has the potential to create more opportunities to bridge social capital, and functioning as a means of *deprivatizing* the existing institutionalization of the practice. This concept, referred to by José Casanova in his book *Public Religion in the Modern World* (1994),[32] describes how religion is becoming an increasingly visible and significant part of public life. In this sense, drop-in baptism elevates baptism out of the private sphere by integrating it into the public sphere, transforming our understanding of its significance, and freeing it from old traditions.

CONCLUSION

This study of drop-in baptism has provided us with more information about the different motives for baptism in Norway. It demonstrates the significance of religious diversity and complexity among people today, as well as the importance of acknowledging the move toward individualization and personal choice. The study also reveals that baptism has shifted from being a rite of passage to a rite of initiation. Through baptism, people strengthen their connections to new communities that may not necessarily be local congregations. Additionally, this study confirms the theory of the new ritual paradigm, in which the individual plays a more central role in baptism. The convenience and the low costs associated with drop-in baptism fit into the daily lives of both parents with young children and adults today. This study shows that this form of baptism can be a natural expression of religious belief for people and should not be dismissed as superficial or unserious. Despite its association with marketization, or strategic thinking more broadly, the local churches appear to have a genuine desire to provide this offering as a diaconal service. Against this background, drop-in baptism may create an opportunity for bridging capital, bringing people together, and renewing our understanding of the ritual.

Overall, drop-in baptism has provided more people with access to the baptism ritual. This practice encourages congregations to become more personally involved with the people, shifting their focus to integration and education in local communities. However, it also challenges the identity of the church, as it is based on an interest in adapting to the

---

31. Leth-Nissen, *Churching Alone*, 210-13
32. Casanova, *Public Religions*.

religious market. This challenge lies at the heart of what it means to be a folk church in Norway today.

BIBLIOGRAPHY

Borg bispedømmeråd. "Dåp i Borg." 2020.
Casanova, José. *Public Religions in the Modern World*. Chicago: University of Chicago Press, 1994.
Davie, Grace. "Religion in Europa in the 21 Century: The Factors to take into Account." *European Journal of Sociology* 47 (2006) 271–96.
Ellinggard, Stein. *Frelst i en fei?!: En kritisk undersøkelse omkring bruken av drop in-dåp i Den norske kirke fra 2015–2020*. Oslo, 2021.
Enggard, Nete Helene, and Rasmus Nøjgaard, eds. *Tradisjon og fornyelse*. Eksistensen, 2018.
Høeg, Ida Marie. "Religious Parental Transmission and the Importance of Authenticity." *Mission Studies* 37 (2020) 416–34.
Iversen, Hans Raun. *Folkekirke-Brugerkirke-Kirke i misjon*. Copenhagen: Eksistensen, 2021.
Jakobsen, Anders-Christian. "Drop-in-dåb—Nogle teologiske overvejelser." In *Drop-in-Dåb*, 47–57. Copenhagen: Eksistensen, 2019.
Jarnkvist, Karin. "Narratives on Ritual Transfer: An Interview Study about the Creation of Civil Ceremonies in Today`s Sweden." *Nordic Journal of Religion and Society* 32 (2019) 106–16.
———. "Reflektioner över dop, vigsel och begravning." In *Nyckeln till Svenska Kyrkan: En skrift om organisation, verksamhet och ekonomi 2018*, 7–17. Uppsala: Svenska Kyrkan, 2018.
Johnsen, Elisabeth Tveito. "Growth in a Context of Decline." *Nordic Jounal of Religion and Society* 75 (2020) 107–40.
Latour, Bruno. "'Thou Shalt Not Take the Lord's Name in Vain': Being a Sort of Sermon on the Hesitations of Religious Speech." *Anthropology and Aesthetics* 39 (2001) 215–34.
Leth-Nissen, Karen Marie. *Churching Alone: A Study of Danish Folk Church at Organisational, Individual, and Societal Level*. Copenhagen: The Faculty of Theology, University of Copenhagen, 2018.
———. "Churching Alone: Folkekirken, de kirkelige handlinger og sosial kapital i et kirkesosiologisk perspektiv." In *Tradition og fornyelse: Teologiske perspektiver på gudstjeneste og liturgi*, 197–213. Copenhagen: Eksistensen, 2018.
Moberg, Marcus, and Tuomas Martikainen. "Religious Change in Market and Consumer Society: The Current State of Field and New Ways Forward." *Religion* 48 (2018) 115.
Moberg, Marcus. *Church, Market and Media: A Discursive Approach to Institutional Religious Change*. London: Bloomsbury Academic, 2017.
———. "Exploring the Spread of Marketization Discourse in the Nordic Folk Church Context." In *Making Religion: Theory and Practice in the Discursive Study of Religion*, 239–59. Leiden: Brill, 2016.
Pettersson, Per. "From Standardised Offer to Consumer Adaption." In *Religion in Consumer Society: Brands, Consumers and Markets*, 43–57. New York: Routledge, 2013.

PART II: PRACTICES

———. *Kvalitet i livslånga tjänsterelationer: Svenska Kyrkan ur tjänsteteoretisk och religionsociologisk perspektiv*. Stockholm: Verbum, 2000.
Repstad, Pål. *Religiøse trender*. Oslo: Universitetsforlaget, 2020.
Taylor, Charles. *The Malais of Modernity*. Sweden: Bengt Nordin Agency, 1991.
Twibell, Simone Mulieri. "Social Capital and the Church: Engaging Virtually for the Sake of the World." *International Bulletin of Misson Resource* 46 (2022) 115–22.

11

Folk-Church Ecclesiology—
Always in the Making

Sunniva Gylver

The Church of Norway is a folk church with a declining membership rate, which, as of 2023, consisted of 64.9 percent of the population.[1] In the most multicultural urban areas, this percentage goes down to about half, and the lowest membership percentage is in a local parish in the diocese of Oslo, which is 21 percent.[2] Serving as pastor in one such area from 2003 to 2013, I experienced that the practice of baptism really challenged my ecclesiological understanding. I asked questions like the following: Who is actually the local church community, and how is it shaped by the Lutheran folk-church practice of baptism? What does the ritual of baptism and the church signify to our members in this context of diversity?

My starting point for this contribution was three personal cases in which baptisms were prepared in this diverse context, which sparked my ecclesiological awareness. By drawing on the elaborate theo-dramatic theory proposed by Urs von Balthasar and Nicholas Healy, as well as an understanding of ecclesiology as a process and conversational practice, as espoused by Claire Watkins, I have been able to reflect upon my

---

1. https://www.ssb.no/kultur-og-fritid/religion-og-livssyn/statistikk/den-norske-kirke.
2. Diocese of Oslo, "Annual Report," https://www.kirken.no/globalassets/bispedommer/oslo/dokumenter/arsmelding%202022.pdf.

understanding of folk church ecclesiology as contextually dependent and always in the making through dialogue.

My conclusion is that the practice of baptism may gain increased significance for local members when they represent a religious minority. In such cases, this practice may contribute to strengthening an ecclesiology of dialogue. Baptism is still a widespread ecclesiological folk church practice, involving a broad range of members and non-members as well. In addition, baptism is a sacrament performed in the midst of the worshipping community. In this context of diversity, baptism highlights and intensifies the complex, ever-changing, blurry, and provisional character of the local folk church community. In doing so, it emphasizes the need for and potential of an ecclesiology of dialogue. Taking advantage of Anne-Louise Eriksson's description of the church as a *responding community*,[3] I suggest that the capacity of the baptism practice is to enable this responding community in a very inclusive way.

CONTEXT

The context of my reflections can be considered diverse for two reasons. First, there is the diversity among the church members believing, practicing, and belonging to the Church of Norway as a folk church. Second, there is the more general religious and cultural diversity of the geographical parish and area.

"Folk church" is an ambiguous term that has held significance for decades in the identity work and ecclesiological discussions of the Church of Norway.[4] It is the central definition of this church in the Norwegian Constitution (§ 16) and in the national vision documents of the church.[5] In this chapter, "folk church" is synonymous with the Church of Norway. It implies a church being present and accessible nationwide and financially supported by the members through public budgets, with significant attendance related to membership, *rites de passage*, and national traditions. The members of the folk church adhere to a broad range of Christian theologies and practices. A folk church, in this view, is expected to maintain a self-understanding anchored in an explicit

---

3. Eriksson, "Besvarande gemenskap," 10–11.

4. Sandvik, *Folkekirken*; Myhre-Nielsen, *En hellig og gangske alminnelig kirke*; Hegstad, *The Real Church*.

5. https://ressursbanken.kirken.no/globalassets/kirken.no/om-kirken/slik-styres-kirken/planer-visjonsdokument-og-strategier/strategi%202022-2029/strategi%20for%20den%20norske%20kirke%202022-2029%20engelsk.pdf.

ecclesiological commitment and identity related to all its members and even further to the entire geographical parish.

For decades, the municipal district of Gamle Oslo (Old Oslo) has been one of the most multicultural and multireligious areas in Norway. When I started working in the local church (Grønland kirke) in 2003, there were three large mosques and a dozen smaller ones within the geographical area of the parish, in addition to several other faith communities of different religions and non-religious life stances. The district also stood out in national statistics due to its poor living conditions, high unemployment, a high share of the population receiving social benefits, high levels of violence, and remarkably high mortality rates.[6]

As a church, we had a significantly lower membership rate than the national average at 32.4 percent. The numbers of baptisms, weddings, and funerals were correspondingly low. In a parish consisting of 15,700 persons, we had one confirmand, 49 people in an average worship service, and three weddings in 2012.[7] Our children and youth activities were attended by groups of whom 90 percent were Muslims. As a local priest in Gamle Oslo, I spent a lot of time on counseling, diaconal work, interfaith dialogue, and diapraxis.[8]

Now, this situation has become the norm in many places. Twenty years back, Gamle Oslo was still an exception. This local ministry gave me a new array of questions, challenges, experiences, and relations. Through the years, I realized that this context triggered my ecclesiological reflections on the following questions: Who was a part of the local church community? How did the practice of baptism influence the shape and understanding of this community? What did it mean to be a minister, a church, and a folk church in this place? Furthermore, I became even more convinced that a refined ecclesiology of dialogue is of utmost importance for the church. In other words, what was needed was a self-understanding based on ongoing conversation with the entire array of local voices both inside and outside the church.

---

6. Barstad, "Levekår i storbyene"; Barstad and Skardhamar, "Utviklingen av levekårene i Oslo indre øst."

7. Årsmelding (Annual Report), Grønland menighet, 2012.

8. In this chapter, diapraxis is used simply to describe interfaith dialogue as expressed in concrete actions. In this concrete context, the local mosque and church have, for instance, been organizing cabin trips, nightwatching in the neighbourhood, gingerbread workshops in Advent, and nativity scene and mosque construction.

During my 10 years of ministry in Gamle Oslo, I regularly wrote in a pastoral diary to process and reflect upon the ministry in a new and different context of diversity. In this contribution, I want to share three personal cases from this diary, all of which occurred in the context of conversations while preparing for baptism. The seminal work of Nicholas Healy in his *Church, World and the Christian Life: Practical-Prophetic Ecclesiology*, as well as Clare Watkins's idea of ecclesiology as a process and a *conversational practice*, are helpful concepts through which to explore my baptism cases and reflect upon an ecclesiology of dialogue—or, in short, a folk church ecclesiology always in the making.

ECCLESIOLOGY OF DIALOGUE

Ecclesiology refers to the study of the identity and mission of the church from a systematic-theological as well as a practical-theological perspective. Our ecclesiology is mediated through the language we use about the church, including metaphors and models for the church, such as, for instance, the body of Christ and the people of God.[9] Furthermore, ecclesiology is also concretized in different artifacts, actions, and relations, the study of which is of equal importance to the discipline.[10]

The increasing cultural-religious diversity of our Nordic societies over the last few decades and the corresponding decrease in national folk churches like the Church of Norway has put the dialogical approach, internally and externally, to the fore. An ecclesiology of dialogue implies to me that such an ongoing conversation with insiders and outsiders of the church is a compulsory part of our thinking, talking about, and attending the church. Dialogue is then to be understood as close to constitutive for the church as a church. As the missiologist Stephen Bevans has said, "The church, mirror of the Trinity, is in its deepest identity a church of dialogue."[11] Fundamentally, the church is based on the intra-divine, inner-trinitarian dialogue and community of love that all of creation is invited to partake in.

An ecclesiology of dialogue assumes an ongoing conversation not only inside God and between God and God's creation, but also between

---

9. Dulles, *Models of the Church*; Ekstrand, *Folkkyrkans gränser*.

10. Hegstad, *Folkekirke og trosfellesskap*; Ideström, *Lokal kyrklig identitet*; Ward, *Perspectives on Ecclesiology and Ethnography*.

11. Bevans, "Ecclesiology and Missiology," 132.

different positions inside the church. This, in turn, needs to be nurtured and challenged by continuous dialogue and diapraxis with outsiders.

Nicholas Healy and His Practical-Prophetic Ecclesiology

I consider the baptism cases that will be treated here as part of a more general praxis of folk church ministry and interfaith dialogue, as they touch on vital questions of religious identity, conversations with "the other," and the identity and mission of the church. I find Healy's practical-prophetic ecclesiology and the ecclesiological discussion following his seminal work, including the contributions of Watkins, helpful in framing and verbalizing such an ecclesiology of dialogue as always in the making.[12]

Healy writes, "I will take it as axiomatic that one's theological view is always preliminary, always open to challenge, assessment and partial or radical alteration by means of dialogue or confrontation with other Christians and non-Christians, as well as with Scripture and the Christian tradition more generally."[13] This commitment to openness and change through dialogue and confrontation is unavoidable in a genuine ecclesiology of dialogue. The main task of ecclesiology, following Healy, is to equip churches to respond carefully to their contexts (everything influencing the life and work of the local church) through critical, theological reflection on its identity.[14] Healy apparently distances himself on the one hand from those emphasizing an understanding of the church as different and counter-cultural, and on the other hand from those coming close to abolishing the distinction between the church and the rest of the world. As such, he seems to reject both exclusivism, particularism, and inclusivism.[15]

Healy's work is an elaborated version of Hans Urs von Balthasar's theo-dramatic theory. According to von Balthasar, there are two possible theological meta-perspectives of our world: the epic and the dramatic, and the relationship between God, the world, and the church should be understood as a drama.[16] The theo-dramatic perspective is an insider participatory orientation, while the epic approach takes an

---

12. Healy, *Church, World and the Christian Life*, 19–21.
13. Healy, *Church, World and the Christian Life*, 2.
14. Healy, *Church, World and the Christian Life*, 22.
15. Healy, *Church, World and the Christian Life*, 77–79.
16. Healy, *Church, World and the Christian Life*, 53–57.

outsider bystander perspective and considers our world as a finished and completely predictable work.

From a dramatic perspective, everything is already included in God's creative and redemptive vision of history, but each person and community is free and responsible for responding in their own ways. Even if the Christian church has a unique role to play in the drama of this world, the Holy Spirit is present and working everywhere, and the church might continue to gain new insights and be surprised by God outside its own realm. The church thus witnesses Jesus Christ in imperfect ways and is always in need of outside voices to become truer in its testimony, and we are all connected through this divine, open-ended drama going on in our world.[17]

I find this theoretical perspective to be fruitful for my baptism case reflection, as it offers helpful analogies and a fitting theological vocabulary. Specifically, this approach sharpens our awareness of the dramatic, diverse, fragmented, conflicted, and provisional character of our reality and might improve the will and ability of the church to acknowledge and respond to it. My overarching perceptions and framing of the three actual baptism cases as part of an ecclesiology of dialogue always in the making are further articulated in the sections below.

Claire Watkins on Ecclesiology as a Conversational Practice

The Catholic systematic theologian Claire Watkins has described ecclesiology as a process and *conversational practice*.[18] In 2010, Helen Cameron, Watkins, and others published a book on theological action research (TAR) and proposed a methodological framework entitled the four voices of theology.[19] This model operates with four theological voices: the normative (referring to Scripture, tradition, confessions, and liturgies), the formal (academic theology), the espoused (the theology articulated in the local church), and the operant (theology expressed in concrete action in the local church). The model emphasizes the significance of inviting all these different voices into the ecclesiological conversation, and in doing so, it acknowledges that the process is *theological all the way through*.[20]

---

17. Healy, *Church, World and the Christian Life*, 66–67.
18. Watkins, "Practicing Ecclesiology," 39.
19. Cameron et al., *Talking About God*, 53–55.
20. Cameron et al., *Talking About God*, 35.

The theology in four voices received a lot of enthusiastic attention in the years following its publication. Nevertheless, the model was criticized for a few reasons, including a simplified understanding of clear-cut voices, an understanding of church that was too traditional, and for giving priority to the normative voice in a way that could threaten the transforming ecclesiological contributions of other voices.[21] In understanding ecclesiology as a process and a *conversational practice*, the question of normativity should always be put to the fore: which voices are heard, and how? Transparency and a power-critical perspective are vital to such a process.

In her more recent work, Watkins elaborates on the model, accounting for an expanded understanding of where to find the church and its relevant, not so clear-cut, theological voices. She emphasizes the mutual interdependence and influence of these voices, and how theology and ecclesiology are always in the making, represented by *epiphanies* created in the conversational practice and space. Watkins gives priority to the normative voice in this hermeneutical process, but based on the term "progress of revelation," borrowed from the Vatican II, she challenges the view that Scripture and tradition are static entities:

> The Tradition that comes from the apostles makes progress in the Church, with the help of the Holy Spirit. There is a growth in insight into the realities and words that are being passed on.[22]

None of these theological voices are perceived as fixed, static entities, nor are our insights into the mysteries of baptism and the church ever complete. This is why a robust ecclesiology is always in the making through dialogue between all the voices present.

CASE REFLECTIONS

In a Lutheran folk church, baptism is ecclesiologically significant. We become members of the church through baptism, and our view of baptism contributes to shaping our ecclesiology. The project of exploring a folk church ecclesiology always in the making in this very multicultural and multireligious context, in my case, was nurtured through dialogue on actual baptisms, which took place in the concrete visits with the parents and sponsors, the performance of the rituals, and, later, in reflective, collegial conversations.

---

21. Graham, "The State of the Art," 177; Ideström and Kaufman, *What Really Matters*, 174–77; Kaufman, "From the Outside," 139.

22. Watkins, "Practicing Ecclesiology," 36–37.

PART II: PRACTICES

To a certain extent, the context was the same for these three actual cases, which are extracted from my pastoral diary that was written during the fall of 2013. They all offer glimpses of conversations that took place while preparing for baptism, in the same church, and with the same pastor. More specifically, they all bring the "who and how" of the local folk church to the fore.

These situations allowed me to confront new and unexpected ecclesiological questions and dilemmas related to how I, as a pastor, and we, as folk church, understand and practice baptism and participate in a church community. I experienced that baptism (including the surrounding conversation and ritual) in this multicultural and multireligious context nurtured identity work and actualized questions concerning what it is to be a church and who the church actually is as a result.

Case 1: What Is Mine?!

With the baby sleeping close by, her mom and I had been talking for a while about the baptism the upcoming Sunday. We were sitting around the kitchen table and touched upon colic, the miracle of life, faith, applications for kindergarten, sibling jealousy, and being a single parent.

Suddenly, the six-year-old girl came storming in. We knew each other because, for a short period, she had been singing in our children's choir in church.

"Sunniva, what is mine?!" I didn't have time to explore what she really meant; then she continued: "Fatima and Khadidja have hijab and Ramadan and all that stuff. What is mine?!"

I hesitated a moment, considering what would be a true and appropriate answer in a family engaged in a standard folk-church religious practice, visibly only attending church for rites de passage and maybe Christmas.

"Well, you are baptized . . ." I uttered.

She beamed. "Of course I am!," she said and ran out again to her friends.

In this first case, the question "What is mine?!" points to the need for religious identity and belonging on the part of the six-year-old, which seems to be activated by the faith artifacts and practices of her Muslim friends. These friends carried their religious identity visibly through their hijabs, and the rules of practice related to Ramadan had concrete implications for meals and activities. My interpretation of her beaming response in the actual situation is that baptism was perceived (rightly so) as the ritual that had made her a part of a faith community, like her friends, and that through this ritual, she had been offered a religious identity and a sense of belonging.

This six-year-old and her family were living in a context of religious diversity, and the children and youth in particular generally spent a lot of time in school and leisure activities and formed close friendships across religious and cultural differences. In my ongoing doctoral work, I interviewed church members in similar contexts and found different generational approaches. The confirmands in my empirical material all had close friends of another religious faith, while the adult church members did not. These young people show how religion and church have become more important to some in this context of diversity. Here, children and youth are always part of an ongoing dialogue across religious borders.

Case 2: Rooted in Two Faith Traditions

Wednesday morning, I was having a conversation with a mom concerning the baptism of her baby and her two-year-old on the upcoming Sunday. She grew up in a small town here in Norway, was baptized and confirmed, and expressed a strong sense of belonging to the Church. Her ex-partner, the father of her children, was of an African background and raised Muslim, but was not very religious in the sense of practicing.

This mother was distressed. Her ex and his family had recently expressed criticism regarding the planned baptism, realizing that the children would then become members of the church. In contrast, she found her ex's religious tradition to be more present in the everyday lives of their children than her own. She considered baptism to be a significant ritual in her own family and a concrete, visible expression of her own faith.

As conversations unfolded, I realized that the main problem for the ex-partner and his family was the lack of a corresponding Muslim ritual to establish roots and initiate the children into their faith traditions. I was allowed to call the imam of the neighboring mosque, whom I knew quite well. The baptism family would be celebrating at a local café after church on Sunday, and after discussing this with the mother, I asked him whether he could officiate a sort of Muslim initiation rite there. As a result, the children were baptized in church and then celebrated through a Muslim ritual at the party, thereby establishing roots in both faith traditions.

In this case, I met a typical average practicing folk church member who had been baptized and confirmed in the church, attended church on Christmas Eve, visited the cemetery on Halloween, prayed once in a while, and identified with what she called Christian values. My impression was that she did not articulate her faith or practice Christianity intensely. However, she considered baptism to be not only a significant tradition in her own family but also a concrete, visible expression of her own faith and belonging.

This appeared to be the case more generally in Gamle Oslo, and I met with a somewhat similar understanding in many other situations as the local pastor. Parents of those to be baptized frequently had different faiths or life stances, folk church members were less vocal about their beliefs than others, and the ritual of baptism was perceived as a significant way of expressing their faith tradition and belonging.

I built a relationship with the local imam and mosque through interfaith dialogue and diapraxis. We began visiting each other's holy houses and celebrations, and we had volunteered together in the neighborhood. I took advantage of this common story, and based on an ecclesiology in the making, I recommended and contributed to this two-track solution.

Case 3: Who Is the Church, and What Is a Sponsor?

Today, I had a conversation with a baptism sponsor concerning a baptism this upcoming Sunday. Last week, I talked to his close friends, who are a couple preparing for the baptism of their second child. The person they strongly wanted as a sponsor had a minority background and had been raised Muslim. He was still religious, though without a clear-cut religious identity. He had been a very significant friend of this family during a rough time of their life, and it meant a lot to them to strengthen and confirm the relationship by making him a sponsor. The baptismal father and the additional sponsors came from a Christian-practicing family in the southern part of Norway.

I explained to the parents that the church regulations require that sponsors should be members of the Church of Norway, or another faith community that acknowledges children's baptism. I admitted that we accept sponsors of, for instance, a Pentecostal background, on the condition that they fully accept the validity of the baptism of the actual child. Furthermore, I acknowledged that I normally do not know anything about the faith or existential life stance of the sponsors in my church, except for their eventual church membership. It was thus probable that a few of them were secular or adhered to alternative religions, considering the religious landscape in our area.

I realized that this situation was sort of complicated. I asked for the sponsor's phone number and invited him in for a conversation. This young man was a teacher by profession, teaching social sciences and religion/life stance subjects, and was very knowledgeable about these matters. He was honored when asked by the parents to be a sponsor and wanted to contribute to the existential upbringing of their daughter.

I chose to accept him as sponsor but was harshly critiqued by some colleagues afterwards. I can understand this resistance, but I still consider my decision to be a defendable one.

In this third case, I found myself working through a dilemma related to the church regulations regarding baptism sponsors. Formally, there are two explicit criteria for a sponsor: the sponsor should be at least 15 years of age and a member of the Church of Norway *or* another faith community accepting infant baptism.[23]

Age is a quite simple criterion and normally does not cause any trouble. A few times, I have experienced parents suggesting that relatives younger than 15 to be sponsors. In these cases, I have suggested an arrangement with the actual youth as an informal sponsor in addition to the ones registered. Regarding the sponsor's view of baptism, in my view, there is no established practice to clarify this. As a pastor, I seldom meet the sponsors before the actual baptism service. They are always invited to the gathering with the parents on beforehand, but they very seldom attend. In the actual conversation, I always emphasize the importance of communicating the Christian faith to the baptized and offering knowledge, experiences, and relations to their local church. The reason for this is to present religious faith as a real option for children who are making their own existential choices later on. The responsibility of the sponsors is regularly mentioned in this context, and the "sponsor certificate" they receive in the service encourages them to take on this significant task. I always ask the parents in these preparatory gatherings prior to the baptism to describe their own religious backgrounds and upbringing and their actual faith or life stance. Nevertheless, the views of the sponsors

23. https://www.kirken.no/nb-NO/dap-i-den-norske-kirke/vare-fadder-for-et-dapsbarn/?gclid=CjwKCAjwrpOiBhBVEiwA_473dBpnKvlTVJWiC3nOJc3Cbpg GI6lHWzIaz73LeUPq2CidqyMloI1TGxoCBp4QAvD_BwE.

are almost never explicitly thematized. Only rarely does it come up, for instance, when parents ask whether it is acceptable that an actual sponsor is a member of a Pentecostal community practicing adult baptism.

It is likely that most baptism sponsors are not elected by the parents on the basis of their Christian faith and practice, but as a sign of love and trust. Relational significance as close relatives or friends might be decisive; sometimes, it might be a purely strategic network choice. In our days, I suppose this implies that most baptism sponsors are average folk church members with various degrees of faith and perceived church belonging. I am not interested in problematizing this practice any further than challenging the parents when we gather, as mentioned above. However, it is worth considering the implications of situations in which other faiths, or none at all, are represented by the sponsors and actually come to the fore.

In this context, I regularly experienced parents negotiating between having their children baptized or blessed. A couple of times, in accordance with my dean, I led a blessing ceremony instead. In the actual diverse context in Gamle Oslo, not only more religious diversity but also more explicit atheism than average seemed to be present, at least in more visibly active atheist groups. When parents wanted a sponsor to be a member of the Norwegian Humanist Association, I told them to make that person an informal sponsor and design an individual sponsor certificate that described the contribution desired by that particular sponsor.

Why did I make another decision in this actual case with the Muslim-raised sponsor? Was it because I knew the baptism parents well, or was it due to the Christian commitment of the father's family? Or, was it simply because I have many Muslim friends and identify more with a Muslim stance than a secular stance? Since Muslims are a stigmatized minority in our society, did I simply want the church to be more inclusive?

I am not sure why I made this decision. The actual case nevertheless made me reflect even further on the ecclesiological implications of such choices regarding baptismal theology and practice.

BAPTISM AND ECCLESIOLOGY

In a Lutheran church's practice of children's baptism, the ritual is of vital ecclesiological significance. Children's baptism strongly professes salvation by grace alone, and it is by baptism that we become members of the church.

Baptism is one of our two sacraments in the Lutheran church, and we understand the Word and Sacrament to be constitutive of the church: "The Church is the congregation of saints, in which the Gospel is rightly taught, and the Sacraments are rightly administered."[24] Some Lutherans assign priority to the Word and Sacrament, whereas others may emphasize the holy assembly.[25] What comes first in terms of significant constitution: the sacraments, the ministry, or the assembly? Is it the church, as the place where one can be included in the body of Christ and seek salvation through baptism and eucharist? Or is it the faith of the individual, as nurtured in church in the holy assembly? Orthodox and Catholic Christianity have traditionally emphasized ministry and sacraments, while Protestant traditions have focused on the Word received by the individual in faith or upon a gathering of true believers.

In this ecclesiological debate, the question of the relationship between the visible and the invisible churches also comes into play. How do we define the church community? Does it consist of those living in the parish, those who are baptized, those who feel they belong, or those gathering regularly or momentarily to worship? Do we conceive of the visible and the invisible church as two independent entities, or do we understand them as partially or totally overlapping?

In his book, *The Real Church*, Harald Hegstad takes Matthew 18:20 as a point of departure and emphasizes the empirical, visible church community as the real church.[26] Healy, in contrast, challenges an ecclesiological understanding that puts too much weight on the empirical community. Interestingly, his argument draws on the same paragraph of Matthew 18:20 but offers a different interpretation:

> Since the church does not exist as that kind of community (including a common life and language that are empirically describable), it is hard to see how that kind of community could be an essential aspect of the church, on earth at least. The body of Christ need not be, and historically often has not been, considered a community in anything like the modern sense. Jesus did not say, "Where two or three are gathered together, there is community." An emphasis upon watching our communal selves

---

24. https://bookofconcord.org/augsburg-confession/of-the-church/.
25. Tjørhom, *Kirken*; Kärkkäinen, *An Introduction to Ecclesiology*.
26. Hegstad, *The Real Church*, 17–20.

may distract our attention from what is far more important, for theology, the church, and the world.²⁷

Here, Healy problematizes an ecclesiological approach too focused on *communio,* or the empirical community, and indicates the danger of idealizing small and close-knit communities. As an extension of this, he challenges the extent to which ethnographic empirical ecclesiology actually can say anything general and normative about church as a defined community and its identity and mission.²⁸

However, Hegstad adheres to a nuanced perception of the empirical folk church community as porous and dynamic and claims that the ecclesiological debates around the folk church tend to assume a far too simple and clear-cut understanding of social groups and their reciprocal relationship and dynamics.²⁹

Taking our three baptism cases into consideration, I find all of them to be illustrative of the complex ecclesiological landscape of the folk church and how its external diversity highlights and intensifies the changing, blurry, and provisional character of the local folk church community. The six-year-old seemed to become increasingly aware of her own baptismal identity and church belonging when exposed to the religious artifacts and practices of her Muslim friends. As one who was baptized, she has been a church member since that time, but now, it is apparently conceived as a matter of genuine significance to her. The Muslim Christian family celebrating and initiating their children into two faith traditions forms part of the local church community, all of whom belong to the geographical parish. The Muslim-raised sponsor thus temporarily became a part of our local church when serving as a sponsor in the baptism service. These concrete baptism situations prompted me to reconsider my ecclesiological understanding, realizing how it is always in the making by being shaped and reshaped by the dialogue with insider and outsider voices. Of course, these voices are not always easy to distinguish from each other.

Ecclesiology is always in the making. Ongoing dialogue (and diapraxis) with inside and outside voices sparks questions about who and what the church is, which has become even more important in this actual context of religious diversity. Baptism is an ecclesiological practice

---

27. Healy, "Ecclesiology, Ethnography and God," 121.
28. Healy, "Ecclesiology, Ethnography and God," 189.
29. Hegstad, *The Real Church*, 114–15. Hegstad, "Kirken som fellesskap," 264.

combining theological radical openness and central clarity, like a few other practices. Baptism in our folk church is, on the one hand, a very exclusive ritual, taking place in the Sunday service and highlighting questions about membership and who is and is not a part of the church. The liturgy points to the necessity of God's grace and salvation and how we die and rise with Christ, which is content that is only meaningful to those accepting the Christian approach.

On the other hand, baptism practices in the Church of Norway are very inclusive in character, and they are still understood as a traditional ritual through which to introduce the newly born children to the community. Those who want themselves or their children to be baptized are welcome to participate; it is free of charge and any other conditions other than accepting church membership. The liturgy emphasizes baptism as the work of God, which is followed by the promise of God's grace, spirit, and salvation bestowed upon you. Then, it becomes the baptized individual's or their parents' decision regarding how to concretely respond to this practice.

Picking up on Urs von Balthasar's Healy's theo-dramatic theory mentioned above, every individual and community is independently responsible and free to shape their own role and response in this divine drama. For our folk church, this implies facilitating and moderating "ecclesiology as a process and conversational practice" (Watkins), thereby challenging members of different degrees of faith and belonging to respond. Baptism still represents a significant space in this sense.

The Swedish theologian Anne-Louise Eriksson has elaborated on Avery Dulles's models of the church and developed a folk church model called *besvarande gemenskap* (the responsive community). On this, she wrote the following:

> I would therefore like to speak of the church as a responding community. Through the world in which humans exist as individuals and congregations, we are addressed by God. Consciously or unconsciously, we respond in every moment in word and deed, through doctrine and life, to this appeal. Everyone does. But what makes us a Christian church is when people, firstly, perceive the address as God's address, and secondly, try to formulate an answer in community with all those who believe that God makes God self-known with God's will and love in Jesus Christ.[30]

30. Eriksson, "Besvarande gemenskap," 10–11.

Baptism, as a still widespread ecclesiological folk church practice, makes God's address to all people accessible to a broad range of our members and non-members as well. As a sacrament performed in the midst of the worshipping community, it facilitates the perception of the address as God's address. As a practice that takes place in the worship of the local community, it makes participation in the communal response to this divine address easier.

CONCLUSION

Drawing on the elaborated theo-dramatic theory of Urs von Balthasar and Nicholas Healy and the concept of ecclesiology as a process and conversational practice in Claire Watkins's work, I have reflected upon three concrete cases of preparing for a baptism in a context characterized by high religious diversity. I have tried to show how they have expanded my understanding of ecclesiology and the ecclesiological significance of this practice. Finally, taking advantage of Anne-Louise Eriksson's description of the church as a *responding community*, I have claimed that the practice of baptism has the capacity to facilitate this responding community in a quite inclusive way.

BIBLIOGRAPHY

Barstad, Anders. "Levekår i storbyene. Noen bydeler er særlig utsatte." In *Samfunnsspeilet* 2003/2. Statistisk Sentralbyrå, 2003.

Barstad, Anders, and Torbjørn Skardhamar. "Utviklingen av levekårene i Oslo indre øst." In *Samfunnsspeilet* 2006/2. Statistisk Sentralbyrå, 2006.

Bevans, Stephen. "Ecclesiology and Missiology: Reflections on Two Recent Documents from the World Council of Churches." *Dialog* 54 (2015) 126–34.

Cameron, Helen, et al. *Talking About God in Practice: Theological Action Research and Practical Theology*. London: SCM, 2010.

Dulles, Avery. *Models of the Church*. New York: Image/Doubleday, 2002.

Ekstrand, Thomas. *Folkkyrkans gränser: En teologisk analys av övergången från statskyrka till fri folkkyrka*. Stockholm: Verbum, 2002.

Eriksson, Anne-Louise. "Besvarande gemenskap." In *Folkkyrka nu? Samtal om utmaningar och möjligheter*, edited by U. Claesson, 8–11. Uppsala: Svenska kyrkan, 2012.

Graham, Elaine L. "The State of the Art: Practical Theology Yesterday, Today and Tomorrow: New Directions in Practical Theology." *Theology* 120 (2017) 172–80.

Healy, Nicholas M. *Church, World and the Christian Life: Practical-Prophetic Ecclesiology*. Cambridge studies in Christian doctrine 7. Cambridge: Cambridge University, 2000.

———. "Ecclesiology, Ethnography, and God: An Interplay of Reality Descriptions." In *Perspectives on Ecclesiology and Ethnography*, edited by Pete Ward, 182–99. Grand Rapids: Eerdmans, 2012.

Hegstad, Harald. *Folkekirke og trosfellesskap: Et kirkesosiologisk og ekklesiologisk grunnproblem belyst gjennom en undersøkelse av tre norske lokalmenigheter*. Trondheim: Tapir, 1996.

———. "Kirken som fellesskap: Lutherske folkekirker i forandring." In *National kristendom til debat*, edited by Jeppe Bach Nikolajsen, 253–66. Fredericia: Kolon, 2015.

———. *The Real Church: An Ecclesiology of the Visible*. Church of Sweden Research Series 7. Eugene, OR: Pickwick Publications, 2013.

Ideström, Jonas. *Lokal kyrklig identitet: En studie av implicit ecklesiologi med exemplet Svenska kyrkan i Flemingsberg*. Skellefteå: Artos & Norma, 2009.

Ideström, Jonas, and Tone Stangeland Kaufman, eds. *What Really Matters: Scandinavian Perspectives on Ecclesiology and Ethnography*. Church of Sweden Research Series 17. Eugene, OR: Pickwick Publications, 2018.

Kaufman, Tone Stangeland. "From the Outside, Within, or in Between?: Normativity at Work in Empirical Practical Theological Research." In *Conundrums in Practical Theology*, edited by Joyce Ann Mercer and Bonnie J. Miller-McLemore, 134–62. Theology in Practice 2. Leiden: Brill, 2016.

Kärkkäinen, Veli-Matti. *An Introduction to Ecclesiology: Ecumenical, Historical & Global Perspectives*. Downers Grove, IL: InterVarsity, 2002.

Myhre-Nielsen, Dag. *En hellig og ganske alminnelig kirke: Teologiske aspekter ved kirkens identitet i samfunnet*. Trondheim: Tapir, 1998.

Sandvik, Bjørn, ed. *Folkekirken: Status og strategier*. Oslo: Den norske kirkes presteforening, 1988.

Tjørhom, Ola. *Kirken—troens mor: Et økumenisk bidrag til en luthersk ekklesiologi*. Oslo: Verbum, 1999.

Ward, Pete, ed. *Perspectives on Ecclesiology and Ethnography*. Grand Rapids: Eerdmans, 2012.

Watkins, Claire. "Practicing Ecclesiology: From Product to Process: Developing Ecclesiology as a Non-Correlative Process and Practice Through the Theological Action Research Framework of Theology in Four Voices." *Ecclesial Practices* 2 (2015) 23–39.

Part III

Communication

12

Communicating about Baptism in Finland in the 2020s

LAURA KOKKONEN

NOT TOO LONG AGO, I received an invitation to attend a naming ceremony. The ceremony was being held at my friend's home for a three-month-old baby. Close family and a few friends, the latter of whom were asked to be the child's "godparents," were invited. The ceremony itself followed a similar pattern to any baptism I have attended in the past, since the naming ceremony is a secular ritual adapted from baptism. This time, however, the church was not invited to this celebration. In fact, an increasing number of new parents do not invite the church to take part in the baby's first official celebration and naming ceremony.

In light of such developments, this chapter discusses and seeks to understand the communication of baptism in Finland in the 2020s. Specifically, the objective is to identify the types of messages that are being presented about baptism through official church communication in Finland. The chapter begins by summarizing previous research and the baptism campaigns of the Evangelical Lutheran Church of Finland. The empirical part of this chapter provides a brief examination of the communication of baptism on the kaste.fi website of the Finnish Lutheran Church using the lens and method of discursive analysis.[1] In this sec-

---

1. As is typical for digital content, the site has been updated since the data collection

tion, the content of these sites is examined under the guiding question of how the Lutheran church is communicating about baptism, and how people are being addressed by the church. What kind of material does kaste.fi have, and what messages are conveyed? A broader discussion of how baptism is discussed and the image it conveys is then presented.

THE EVANGELICAL LUTHERAN CHURCH OF FINLAND

Historically, the Evangelical Lutheran Church of Finland is the largest church in Finland, with the majority of Finns being Lutherans. In Finland, the Lutheran church has an undeniably strong position in society, and Finns have a historically close relationship with the church. The number of church members has traditionally been remarkably high, with 90 percent of Finns being members of the Lutheran church until the 1980s, and 80 percent until the 2010s.[2] However, the church's dominance over Finns has evaporated in a brief time. At the beginning of 2022, only 66.5 percent of Finns belonged to the Lutheran church.[3] Traditionally, the church has acted as a center for life-cycle rites in Finland. Accordingly, the number of baptisms has been high, as has the percentage of the age group attending confirmation to validate the baptism in their teenage years. Also, marriages in the church used to be extremely popular and highly valued. Nevertheless, Finns' relationships with the church are getting colder, and Finns are attending these rites less and less. In other words, while Finns still enjoy the same life-cycle rites, these have become less connected to the church and its services.

According to Maarit Hytönen, the status of baptism in Finnish society and the Lutheran Church changed dramatically in the 2000s.[4] The statistics indicate that it was the standard to baptize a baby in Finland until the 2000s if one of the parents belonged to the church. In 2000, nearly 90 percent of parents had baptized their children. Baptisms have since declined quickly, which is also the starting point for this book, as it seeks to understand this trajectory more profoundly. The statistics indicate that an increasing number of parents have not chosen baptism for their children, with approximately 55 percent of Finns baptizing

---

and writing of this article.

2. Heino et al., *Kirkko vuosina 1980–1983*, 52; Palmu et al., *Haastettu kirkko*, 73.

3. *Kirkon jäsenyys.* On the reasons for resignation, see Äystö et al., "Miksi suomalaiset eroavat evankelis-luterilaisesta kirkosta?" and Niemelä, *Vieraantunut vai pettynyt?*

4. Hytönen, *Maailman tärkein tapahtuma*, 44.

their children in 2022.[5] The statistics follow the same trend in all Nordic countries, with the distinction that Finland has historically had the highest numbers of baptized citizens.[6]

The decrease in baptisms is related to the decrease in the number of church members, because one parent must belong to the church for the child to be baptized and become a member of the church. Of course, there have been many factors affecting the declining percentage of church members, besides unbaptized babies, in recent years. It is natural that leaving new generations outside the church has its effects, but there is also a notable number of adults who continue to resign. Some visible peaks can be identified during sudden events that arose in association with reputation crises, where even tens of thousands of people left the church in a matter of weeks.[7] In addition, interest in the non-religious lifestyle is growing, and one in four Finns did not belong to any religious community in 2018, and 40 percent classified themselves as a "non-religious person" in 2019, a number that continues to increase.[8] Naturally, church membership is also declining because of the aging population, as baby boomers are getting older, and fewer children are being born.[9] Since older generations are more religious than newer ones, the effect is obvious. In this vein, Kimmo Ketola has found that the most notable change in religiosity occurs between generations, since older age groups consider religion more important than younger age groups. This is evident when looking closely at the generations born before the 1950s, when three out of five considered religion necessary, while only less than one in five of the Y and Z generations born after the 1980s agreed.[10] Another phenomenon affecting the percentage of church members is immigration, mainly because immigrants often do not belong to the Lutheran church. This trajectory is more evident in

---

5. Jäsentilasto 1999–2022.
6. Statistics of the Finnish baptism can be found in Hytönen, *Maailman tärkein tapahtuma*, 44. Statistics of some Nordic churches are further discussed in the chapter by Skantz et al., and the situation in Finland by Salomäki.
7. Palmu et al., *Haastettu kirkko*, 83, 280.
8. Ketola, *Uskonto ja kulttuurin murros*, 38.
9. *Väestö ja yhteiskunta*.
10. Ketola, *Uskonto ja kulttuurin murros*, 43. The trend is similar throughout Europe; see Valk et al., *Teenagers Perspectives*.

some areas than in others; for example, in the capital of Helsinki, less than half of the population was Lutheran already in 2020.[11]

Although the church has had a strong position in Finnish culture and in the lives of its individuals, the high membership percentage has not necessarily reflected the religiosity of Finns or their enthusiasm for religious practice or attending church. This pattern can also be found in other Nordic countries. Despite the low attendance rates and limited religious commitment or belief, membership in the Evangelical Lutheran Church has long been associated with belonging to Finnish culture. It is not that Finns necessarily have negative images of the church; in fact, approximately five percent of Finns felt negatively about Finnish churches, according to a Gallup Ecclesiastica survey conducted in 2011.[12] Rather, when it comes to attending church activities, only two percent of Finns attend weekly, and six percent attend monthly.[13] Nevertheless, nearly two out of five Finns attend church services at Christmas.[14]

One valid concern about membership is whether Finns are losing their traditional *belief in belonging*.[15] Abby Day argues that belief in a group is more significant than belief in the Christian doctrine.[16] This type of belief is referred to as cultural Christianity, wherein members appreciate their Christian roots but do not hold onto the doctrines.[17] In Finland, it has been documented that cultural Christianity is disappearing, especially in some age groups; specifically, individuals aged 30 to 39 have increasingly detached from the church.[18] In other words, the meaning of the church has declined at both the societal level and in people's personal lives.[19]

11. *Jäsentietojen vuositilastot.*

12. Ketola et al., *Osallistuva luterilaisuus*, 81; Palmu et al., *Haastettu kirkko*, 52–54.

13. Salomäki, *Jumalanpalvelus, kirkolliset toimitukset ja kristilliset juhlapyhät*, 98.

14. *Kaksi viidestä suomalaisesta osallistuu joulukirkkoon.*

15. Bäckström, *Believing in Belonging*; Niemelä, *No Longer Believing in Belonging*. This phenomenon was originally referred to as belonging without believing, but was later rephrased as believing in belonging. This should be understood in light of the fact that 40 percent of Finns classified themselves as "See non-religious" in 2019. Ketola "Uskonto ja kulttuurin murros," 38.

16. Day, *Believing in Belonging*. Originally, this was reported by Davie, in *Religion in Britain Since 1945*, as "believing without belonging" and later *believing in belonging*.

17. Ketola, "Uskonnolliset identiteetit," 73. On cultural religion, see Demerath, "The Rise of 'Cultural Religion' in European Christianity."

18. Hytönen et al., *Johtopäätökset*, 254.

19. Ketola et al., *Osallistuva luterilaisuus*.

Based on the statistics surveyed above, Finns, along with other Nordics, are becoming more disengaged from established churches, and the effects seem to have hit baby baptisms, especially hard. However, babies do not play a decisive role in their own baptisms. With a longstanding tradition of baptizing almost every Finn, marketing baptism (on the part of the church) has not been necessary. There simply has not been a need to advertise baptism and lure people to the church. However, the reality has changed. The same concern applies to church marketing, or the lack of it, since, because of historical dominance, the church simply has not seen the need to promote itself.[20] This matter is further discussed in the following section.

COMMUNICATING WITH MARKETING AND BRANDING

Secularization has been a dominant pattern in explaining broader changes in belief in the study of religion.[21] Communication research in religious institutions in particular, however, benefits from a different perspective: the theoretical framework of consumption.[22] This framework suggests that neoliberalism has reinforced consumerism as the ethos of modern times or as a vector structuring our reality.[23] Consumer culture (or consumer society) refers to the widespread consumerism and consumption logic and orientation that has proliferated our societies.[24] One of its central phenomena is marketization. By extending both consumerism and neoliberalism, the global-market regime has come to encompass, to varying degrees, the entire scope of contemporary society.[25] In other words, marketing has entered (or been incorporated) into areas

20. For more details on the relationship between the church and marketing, see Kokkonen, *Negotiating with Branding*, and Moberg, *Church, Market, and Media*.

21. On the decline and other changes in actual spirituality and belief, see Casanova, *Public Religions in the Modern World*.

22. Gauthier et al., *Introduction: Religion in a Neoliberal Age*, 2–3; Gauthier et al., *Acknowledging a Global Shift*, 261–64; Moberg and Martikainen, *Religious Change in Market and Consumer Society*; Kokkonen, *Negotiating with Branding*.

23. Gauthier et al., *Acknowledging a Global Shift*, 266.

24. Featherstone, *Consumer Culture and Postmodernism*; Gauthier et al., "Introduction: Consumerism as the Ethos of Consumer Society," 4, 15; Miles, *Consumerism*, 1; Slater, *Consumer Culture and Modernity*. The application of this theory is discussed in more detail in Kokkonen's *Negotiating with Branding*.

25. Gauthier, *Religion, Modernity, Globalisation*, 182. According to Mautner (*Language and the Market Society*, 16), marketisation "means the process by which the laws of the marketplace are transferred to life worlds that were not originally organized along such lines."

that did not previously have an association with the market, such as homes, schools, and religious communities.[26]

My understanding is that the concrete forms of these larger cultural phenomena are marketing practices, and especially methods of branding. Theoretically, neoliberalism and the consumerist ethos inspired marketing and branding practices in multiple areas.[27] In established churches, marketing and branding are not meant to attract more members or lure people to join. For the Finnish Lutheran Church, reaching out to new adult members has never been as important as keeping existing ones. Instead, the aim may be to make religious commitment more stable and less vulnerable to external influences, enhance visibility and recognizability, and offer a desirable connection and membership benefits.[28] In this sense, the Lutheran Church has, for example, underlined its purpose and usability, which embraces the meaning of the church and therefore entangles membership deeply with meaning making.[29] What this means is that marketing and branding in churches do not need to be based on the motivation to create entirely new connections, but rather to maintain the existing members and take care of so-called "customer" relationships.

PREVIOUS RESEARCH AND BAPTISM PROJECTS OF THE FINNISH LUTHERAN CHURCH

As far as I know, the actual marketing and communication of baptism has not been examined from this point of view before in the Finnish context. In contrast, baptism itself has recently been studied both academically and in relation to baptism marketing within the church.

An extensive study of Finnish baptismal choices, perceptions, and theology was conducted under the editorship of Hytönen,[30] who was an important researcher on modern baptism in Finland. Hytönen also examined the meanings of both people's own baptisms and those of their children and estimated that baptism is especially associated with meanings related to community membership, traditions, and church

---

26. Moberg, *Church, Market, and Media.*
27. Kokkonen, *Negotiating with Branding.*
28. Cutright et al., *Finding Brands and Losing Your Religion?*; Kokkonen, *Negotiating with Branding.*
29. Kokkonen, *Negotiating with Branding.*
30. Hytönen, *Kasteen polulla.*

doctrine.[31] This research raised concerns about the future of baptism and suggested that both the church and individual congregations must actually invest in baptism and godparenting to present them in a positive, encouraging, and supportive way for members.[32]

This way of thinking has also been manifested in the projects that have been undertaken in the church. The work of Laine et al. summarized the projects related to baptism that were conducted between 2010 and 2020.[33] This chapter will not take a deeper look at these projects and campaigns, but will instead briefly summarize the key elements.

At the level of the national church, a project titled "Kaste ja kummius" (2018, Kirkkohallitus) was initiated that was related to baptism and godparenting. It included questionnaires to better understand the reasons behind individual baptism decisions. Through this project, the parents were asked what they needed to bring their children to be baptized. A stronger Christian identity among members was listed as a long-term goal.[34] "Kaste ja kummius" applied some common strategies of modern marketing, including influencer marketing through a video series launched on YouTube, which provided examples for godparents on what to do or where to go with their godchildren.[35]

It should be noted that all three cities in the capital area (Helsinki, Espoo, and Vantaa) as well as Tampere (Finland's second largest urban area) had also "noticed the rapid change in baptisms."[36] Essentially, these campaigns have been about offering baptisms with a low threshold (Aamukaste 2012 in Tampere and Kastepäivätapahtuma in Helsinki, Espoo, and Vantaa).[37] In addition to actual campaigns, parishes have distributed additional questionnaires to ask people their thoughts about baptism and have developed, for example, official certificates for the baptized and the godparents.[38]

---

31. Hytönen, *"Maailman tärkein tapahtuma."*

32. Hytönen, *"Maailman tärkein tapahtuma,"* 281.

33. Laine et al., *Kasteen ja kummiuden kehityshankkeet.*

34. "Kaste ja kummius -hanke: Tehtyä ja tulevia tarpeita"; "Kaste ja kummius -hanke."

35. See the video series "Kummin kanssa" on church's family channel "Kirkon kasvatus ja perhe."

36. Laine et al., *Kasteen ja kummiuden kehityshankkeet,* 140.

37. Laine et al., *Kasteen ja kummiuden kehityshankkeet,* 143–44.

38. Laine et al., *Kasteen ja kummiuden kehityshankkeet,* 142. During the editing of this article, a baptism campaign, (Ra)kastettu, was also organized in the capital region.

As these examples also show, the Lutheran Church has continuously sought to determine what its members wish the Church to be.[39] A customer focus based on gathering feedback and member satisfaction has often been at the center of these pursuits. Nonetheless, Laine et al. have noted that campaigning has not had any actual change when looking at the decline of baptisms, even though "the understanding of the members has deepened."[40]

An Easy and Memorable Party—
Communicating about Baptism in Kaste.fi

In this section, communication about the baptisms of the Finnish Lutheran Church will be reviewed based on the selected data and the method of discourse analysis. The Finnish Lutheran Church currently has a specific website on baptism, entitled Kaste.fi, which was founded in 2019.[41] Looking at this page, it can be observed that it addresses how the Lutheran church is communicating about baptism and how people are addressed by the church. In the chosen method of analysis, the key is the identification of discourses.[42] The discourse analysis thus begins by categorizing the data, which in this case would be the Kaste.fi webpage.[43] With the analysis, the data are reviewed, and central themes are located. In practice, the types of discourses that appear in the selected dataset are explored. In this case, how baptism is being communicated is what is studied, and the continuous themes and how they are presented are also explored. The focus is on language, specifically in terms of what is said and how it is argued.[44]

Even though I will not conduct a visual analysis here, a brief description of the webpage is useful in setting the scene. Visually, the internet pages appear fairly modern; the colors of the front page are blue and lilac, and there are photos of babies, parents, and the baptism ceremony. This visual section covers nearly the entire webpage with photos and key titles. At first glance, only a few short sections of text appeared on the pages.

---

39. Consider Jäsen360°, the membership analysis program, or Toiveiden kirkko (Church of Wishes), which was collected in Helsinki (2013).
40. Laine et al., *Kasteen ja kummiuden kehityshankkeet*, 140.
41. The Internet pages were reviewed in January of 2023.
42. Taira, *Taking "Religion" Seriously*, 26.
43. The writer has translated the texts from Finnish originals.
44. Jokinen et al., *Diskurssianalyysi*, 43, 338.

When moving the mouse, photos open as short key messages. The messages within them are examined in the following paragraphs.

The first message is "Baptism is about love," which explains how in the baptism, a child gets to experience a miracle and be loved as they are. The second message is about naming a child, and it describes the baptism ceremony as a place where the name is often revealed for the first time. The third is the memory list for organizing a baptism. Since this section is practical, it is not studied profoundly here. The fourth message has to do with godparenting, and it underlines that the relationship between a godparent and a child may be a lifelong friendship. The fifth message answers the question, "Why a Christening?" by showing that people form a safety net for a baby. In the next two messages, people's subjective experiences are reported. The first message is entitled, "A Christening surprised me," and in this case, a grandmother talks about the various forms of modern baptisms. The second one is titled "Felix's relaxed party," which explains how some parents initially thought about a secular naming ceremony but ended up with a baptism. The final theme focuses on the uniqueness of celebrations (or arranging the party so that it feels like your own), in which the idea of the Christening as a happy festival centered on the baby is embraced.

Since the messages on the front page are reviewed in this section, the themes will be reviewed throughout the remainder of this section. On the left, the webpage is divided into eight titles, which mostly overlap with the themes already listed. The titles on the sidebar are listed as follows: Why a baptism?; Unique christenings; Organizing christenings; What name?; Who's the godparent?; Christening music; and Questions and answers. Next, we take a closer look at the themes and pages that open up from the titles above.

Since the examples of the grandmother and Felix's relaxed party were not found in the sidebar when this article was written, but they were still visible in the pictures on the front page, they are described first. Subsequent topics are discussed in order according to the headings in the sidebar. Regarding the first video, a first-time grandparent describes the ceremony from her point of view. She describes how she is even impressed with how the priest was "young and modern," "had red fingernails," and was wearing "a knee-length dress." In this way, the new grandmother admires the modern priest. In the video for Felix's relaxed party, an example of casual baptism is provided, with one of the parents being a member of the church and the other not. After considering the naming ceremony, they decided to baptize, since it seemed "more festive," and the tradition felt important. On the day of the baptism, they report how the loved ones spent the entire day engaged in hobbies together, and the priest was invited to join them later in the afternoon.

Moving on to the sidebar of the kaste.fi webpages, in the first section, "Baptism is about love,"[45] the love of both close ones and God's love are emphasized: "At baptisms, loved ones gather together to wish for God to provide all the best in the child's life." Baptism is also phrased as being "about God's love." In addition, baptismal water is described as a protector. At the bottom of the page, like all other similar pages, there are a few thoughts from different individuals. On this page, the priests' thoughts are represented in terms of both a divine and a practical dimension: "Baptism is also an opportunity to gather a support network around you and ask for blessing and support in everyday life."

The next section explores why a Christening party should be considered.[46] Specifically, this section underlines the safety net of loved ones, the importance of the child, and the ecclesiastical nature of the celebration, but also the lack of formality, the people and the celebration, and the child's membership in their family and the congregation. The last sentence underlines how "at a Christening, loved ones gather together to wish for God to provide all the best in the child's life." In this sense, the Christian mission of baptism is mentioned last and only once. In the "Parents talk" section, a parent who does not belong to the church discusses the baptisms that occur on the parish premises. Another reveals how their child was baptized because both parents were baptized, but that the children can still decide their own faith later on.

The next section is about "Celebrating in your own way," which emphasizes uniqueness and the relaxed manner in which a baptism can be organized.[47] This section discusses how the church, as a site, brings forth a certain atmosphere of celebration and holiness. The comfort of the parish facilities and the choice of any flower color for the child ("instead of the traditional pink and blue") are emphasized, and it is explained how "the priest will listen to your wishes to make a memorable party." The idea that baptism is an "experiential" process is also discussed. Practical tips are provided and associated with a casual situation, which includes performances and readings of poems or passages from the Bible and other ways

---

45. kaste.fi, *Kaste on rakkautta.*
46. kaste.fi, *Miksi ristiäiset?*
47. kaste.fi, *Omannäköiset ristiäiset.*

of creating a welcoming atmosphere. It is even suggested that "you can even pour baptismal water at the base of the yard tree." In the individual examples, baptisms and same-sex "mini-weddings" are celebrated at the same time; songs by Elvis are played, and brunch is eaten.

At this point on the sidebar, matters related to organizing the party in practice appear.[48] This section is entirely related to the practical arrangements, thereby emphasizing the challenges potentially faced by new parents, the casual nature and individuality of a baptism, and the minimal use of money and effort. Again, various creative ways of remembering the event are proposed, such as collecting prayer stones or planting a tree seed. The individual examples describe how the traditional ritual organized in the church was found soothing. The section on how to name a child is also very practical,[49] as it provides information about naming practices and laws in Finland. In addition, it discusses the theological significance of how God calls a child by name in the baptism. The examples provide other concrete examples of the process of choosing a name.

The section about godparents ("Who's the godparent?") informs us of the role of trust and godparent practices in history.[50] It further addresses how the "godparent's spiritual task can also be fulfilled by praying for the godchild." This is the only time in this section when the so-called spiritual area is mentioned, since, otherwise, godparenting is explained in a more practical way. In the individual examples, people's beloved godparents are remembered. In addition, godparent webpages and a Godparents' Day are advertised, which was invented by the church and encouraged to be celebrated every year; in reality, it is simply an advertising campaign. The second and last section of the sidebar is devoted to music, which is also a very practical matter.[51] This section underlines "the playlist" of the ceremony and links to Spotify. The individual examples talk about pop, rock, and hymns. The last section is a Q&A, which is not explored in this article because of its scope. The Q&A answers numerous questions in detail on ten different themes.

It needs to be noted that the Kaste.fi web pages are not the only places at which one can find information about Lutheran baptism,

---

48. kaste.fi, *Ristiäisten järjestäminen*.
49. kaste.fi, *Mikä nimeksi?*
50. kaste.fi, *Kuka kummiksi?*
51. kaste.fi, *Ristiäisten musiikki*.

since the official church pages Evl.fi also have a section for baptism.[52] This article does not focus on the Evl.fi page, but it does contain many practical questions (and answers). At the same time, the section "What happens in baptism" may be the most theologically oriented in its explanation of the meaning of baptism, the baptismal formula, and the content of the priest's speech. Why such a parallel site exists and what the relationship between the sites is remains unanswered here, but it certainly raises some questions.

BAPTISM: EASY, ADAPTABLE, AND FUN

The messages on Kaste.fi are various, and one straightforward way to analyze them is to divide them into practice-oriented information and messages related to more abstract matters, such as the meaning, purpose, and spiritual aspects of baptism, as has been done above. From the perspective of marketing and branding, it seems obvious that the messages on the pages are well thought out and carefully selected to deliver a chosen image. The website paints a picture of a certain kind of baptism. This image is further discussed in this section.

The Kaste.fi baptism is essentially framed as an act of love. In fact, it is called a token of love, in the sense that the child comes to feel they are loved by God and their loved ones. The network of loved ones together with God is called a safety net, which is framed as a concrete support network for a new family with children. The membership of one's own family and local parish is emphasized at the baptism party when loved ones gather together. Godparenting is also emphasized as a meaningful and important relationship. Godparenthood is primarily framed as a social relationship, as the spiritual task of the godparents is mostly presented as a side plot. When specifically mentioned, the godparent's spiritual task to pray is considered only "an example" of one way to be a godparent. Various themes emphasize the importance of human relationships, and baptism as an act of love and godparenting are considered special kinds of relationships. Some overtones can be identified based on the messages presented here. First, when baptism is framed as an act of love, the implication is that any viewer should love their own child enough to baptize them. In addition, the idea of a safety net could be interpreted as a type of insurance for both the new parents and their babies.

---

52. "Ristiäiset."

A key message in the communication of Kaste.fi is that in the baptism, parents are free to do what they want: baptism is thus presented as casual, informal, and, most importantly, adaptable to (or accommodating of) the parents' wishes. It is often emphasized how people can choose what they want to do for the baptism ceremony, whether it be reading poems, throwing baptism water in the garden, or collecting prayer stones. Aside from prayers and hymns, Elvis is played, and the parents are encouraged to have a small, simple wedding ceremony at the same time. Effortlessness is emphasized, as there is no need to spend money, one's local parish can take care of everything, and parents hardly need to put in any effort at all. Baptizing a baby is thus construed as a simple and easy process.

In this sense, modern-day baptism ceremonies surprise older generations who are astonished by the free execution of a modern baptism ceremony. In this case, the ceremony's openness is emphasized, for example, by highlighting the possibility of gender-neutral colors. In addition, parents reveal how they came around to having a baptism after considering a secular naming party. The fact that a child is still able and free to decide about their own religion when they are older, even if they are baptized as a baby, is also noted. Priests, on the other hand, are presented as casual customer service agents who listen to the wishes of the parents. A priest in this sense is cool, nice, and modern. In the end, while God is mentioned here and there, the Christian meaning of the baptism is rarely explicit, and the ceremony is ultimately presented as just a memorable experience, especially for the parents.

A relevant question to ask at this point would be whether a "child's first official party" could be so informal and casual without the presence of the church. The site aims to answer this question by outlining what the church brings to the situation. The church (not only as a physical place but as more of an institution and ritual) is presented, for example, as an especially festive entity that provides a calming tone. In practice, the church can make the entire party effortless, since people can also have the ceremony away from their homes. This kind of communication corresponds to what the Lutheran Church does elsewhere in its communication, as it emphasizes the importance and purpose of the church in this respect. In this way, baptism communication emphasizes the underlying meaning and purpose of baptism. While the popularity of the church, especially baptism, has decreased, the site focuses on what baptism offers and presents baptism in a recognizable way. Again, one of the key themes is how easy and casual baptism is. It can be noted that a similar style of emphasizing a relaxed rite has, for example, been used in the Aamukaste campaign, which describes baptism as follows:

> Organizing this baptism could hardly be easier . . . It is worth taking your close friends with you to celebrate a big event and enjoy the cake and coffee offered by the congregation.[53]

As stated above, the Lutheran church rarely focuses on attracting just anyone to join, striving instead for the ideal of member satisfaction. Baptism, although technically a means of church membership acquisition, becomes more about member satisfaction. The current members of the church (the parents) are the ones who decide on their children's baptism, in which case their satisfaction is the focus.

VALUE OF MEMBERSHIP AS A GATEWAY TO BAPTISM

Some might maintain that the decrease in baptisms is a much more profound phenomenon and is largely intertwined with how the essence and importance of the church are valued more widely. The deeper issue regarding the church's diminishing status is thus reflected in the decline of baptisms.[54] It is hard to disagree here, as one can ask why people who question the church would even want to baptize their children. In the very first online seminar from which this book originated, Josephine Ganebo Skantz described how baptism is the basis of church membership.[55] As true as this may be, the marketing of baptism needs to convey a broader message, not only of the baptism itself, but also of the church. The relationship between baptism and membership is deeply connected to both the believer's identity and membership satisfaction. It can thus be assumed that satisfied members are more eager to baptize their children. The larger issue, then, becomes a matter of determining the overall message of the church and the kind of community into which the child is being baptized. Is it a community of faith? What is the key message, and what are the main values of this community? While baptism might no longer be "the thing" of the church, it can still serve as a gateway to membership in whatever organization the church frames itself to be in a broader way.

---

53. "Aamukaste."
54. Laine et al., *Kasteen ja kummiuden kehityshankkeita*, 140.
55. Churches in times of change, webinar 1.

Does such baptismal communication meet people's needs? First, the role of the godparent has been particularly emphasized in the sense that godparenting is construed as an important task. However, godparenthood is a somewhat secondary measure in this practice, and the godparent is not the party that decides on the baptism. Instead of godparents, parents decide on baptism, and in the surveys of parents of unbaptized children, the main reason for not baptizing was the desire to let the children decide for themselves later on. Since this justification is based on individual choice and the right to decide for oneself, changing the parents' opinions can be particularly difficult—even impossible— from the church's side.

People experiencing the value of membership are presumably more likely to baptize their children. In this sense, the Finnish "Kaste ja kummius" project listed strengthening the members' Christian identity as its long-term goal. It can thus be asked whether the Christian identity itself is sufficient to determine membership. When it comes to baptism, Hytönen examined the underlying meanings and found that practice is especially associated with community membership, traditions, and church doctrine. An interesting observation in Hytönen's research was that people's own experiences (of baptism) determined the future of Christian education.[56] It may be that the meaning of baptism is decided concretely in people's relationships with the church. It is difficult to intervene in this relationship through external means, such as advertising. While the church's brand can remind people of their relationship with the church and maintain a certain image, the church relationship is built, as the term suggests, in relation to the church, and in those situations in which one interacts with it. The importance of baptism also extends far into the future, and thus confirmation camps may be the next ones to see changes in participation numbers, as (non)baptism can certainly have a direct effect here.[57]

To conclude, I will return to the naming ceremony at my friend's house. What I did not expect was what followed the secular celebration. At the end of the naming ceremony, the new parents asked me if I could ask a familiar priest whether the child could still be blessed by the Lutheran church. Neither of the parents belonged to the Lutheran

---

56. Hytönen, *"Maailman tärkein tapahtuma,"* 281.

57. In 2019 800.000 youngsters born attended a confirmation camp followed by "confirmation" of membership of the church. Hytönen, *"Maailman tärkein tapahtuma,"* 200, 207.

church, so the child could not be baptized. It turned out that the new grandmother was troubled by this, even though she was merely known as a solid supporter of the Christian tradition of annual and life-cycle rites. As a sort of compromise, the new parents ended up having a Lutheran priest bless the child two months later. Did this serve as insurance against the existence of a Christian God, a means of pleasing the grandmother, or a way to connect with Finnish tradition and culture? In any case, this example shows that as the popularity and practices of baptism change, the church can be invited to participate in other ways, even alongside secular celebrations. It may very well be the case that the churches could more effectively illustrate their connection to Finns in ways other than baptism statistics.

BIBLIOGRAPHY

"Aamukaste." Tampereenseurakunnat.fi. https://tampereenseurakunnat.fi/palveluja/ristiaiset/aamukaste.

Äystö, Tuomas, et al. "Miksi suomalaiset eroavat evankelis-luterilaisesta kirkosta?" *Yhteiskuntapolitiikka* 87 (2022).

Bäckström, Anders. "Believing in Belonging: The Swedish Way of Being Religious." In *Urban Faith 2000*, edited by Riikka Ryökäs and Esko Ryökäs, 31–42. Helsinki: Helsingin yliopisto, 1993.

Casanova, José. *Public Religions in the Modern World*. Chicago: University of Chicago Press, 1994.

Churches in Times of Change. https://churchesintimesofchange.org/ressources-and-recordings-from-webinars.

Cutright, Keisha M., et al. "Finding Brands and Losing Your Religion?" *Journal of Experimental Psychology: General* 143 (2014) 2209–22.

Day, Abby. *Believing in Belonging: Belief and Social Identity in the Modern World*. Oxford: Oxford University, 2011.

Davie, Grace. *Religion in Britain Since 1945: Believing Without Belonging*. Oxford: Blackwell, 1995.

Davie, Grace. "Believing in Belonging: An Ethnography of Young People's Constructions of Belief." *Culture and Religion* 10 (2009) 253–78.

Demerath, N. J. III. "The Rise of 'Cultural Religion' in European Christianity: Learning from Poland, Northern Ireland, and Sweden." *Social Compass* 47 (2000) 127–39.

Featherstone, Mike. *Consumer Culture and Postmodernism*. London: Sage, 1991.

Gauthier, François, et al. "Introduction: Consumerism as the Ethos of Consumer Society." *Religion in Consumer Society: Brands, Consumers and Markets*, edited by François Gauthier and Tuomas Martikainen, 1–26. Farnham, UK: Ashgate, 2013.

Gauthier, François, et al. "Introduction: Religion in Market Society." In *Religion in the Neoliberal Age: Political Economy and Modes of Governance*, edited by François Gauthier et al., 1–18. Farnham, UK: Ashgate, 2013.

Gauthier, François, et al. "Acknowledging a Global Shift: A Primer for Thinking about Religion in Consumer Societies." *Implicit Religion* 16 (2013) 261–75.

Gauthier, François. *Religion, Modernity, Globalisation: Nation-State to Market*. London: Routledge, 2020.
Heino, Harri, et al. *Suomen evankelis-luterilainen kirkko vuosina 1980–1983*. Tampere: Kirkon tutkimuslaitos, 1985.
Hytönen, Maarit, ed. *Kasteen polulla: Kasteen ja kummiuden teologiaa ja käytäntöjä*. Vaasa: Kirkon tutkimuskeskus, 2021.
———. *"Maailman tärkein tapahtuma": Suomalaisten käsityksiä kasteesta ja kummiudesta*. Tampere: Kirkon tutkimuskeskus, 2020.
Hytönen, Maarit, et al. "Johtopäätökset." In *Uskonto arjessa ja juhlassa: Suomen evankelis-luterilainen kirkko vuosina 2016–2019*, edited by Hanna Salomäki et al., 251–66. Tampere: Kirkon tutkimuskeskus, 2020.
Jokinen, Arja, et al. *Diskurssianalyysi: Teoriat, peruskäsitteet ja käyttö*. Tampere: Vastapaino, 2016.
"Jäsentilasto." Kirkon jäsentilasto 1999–2022. kirkontilastot.fi. https://www.kirkontilastot.fi/viz.php?id=262.
"Jäsentietojen vuositilastot." helsinginseurakunnat.fi. https://www.helsinginseurakunnat.fi/artikkelit/vaestotilastot.
"Kaksi viidestä suomalaisesta osallistuu joulukirkkoon." Evl.fi. https://evl.fi/tiedote/kaksi-viidesta-suomalaisesta-osallistuu-joulukirkkoon/.
Kaste.fi. https://kaste.fi/.
"Kaste ja kummius -hanke." evl.fi https://evl.fi/plus/hankkeet/kaste-jakummius.
"Kaste ja kummius—hanke: Tehtyä ja tulevia tarpeita." https://evl.fi/documents/132 7140/51803182/Kaste+ja+kummius+toukokuu+2019.pdf/627c3220-ea9b-1a8f-498b-007d6cc2e5df?t=1558604395000.
"Kastepäivä." evl.fi https://evl.fi/plus/hankkeet/kaste-ja-kummius/kaste/.
Ketola, Kimmo. "Uskonto ja kulttuurin murros." In *Uskonto arjessa ja juhlassa. Suomen evankelis-luterilainen kirkko vuosina 2016–2019*, edited by Hanna Salomäki et al., 12–44. Tampere: Kirkon tutkimuskeskus, 2020.
———. "Uskonnolliset identiteetit ja uskomusmaailma moninaistuvat." In *Uskonto arjessa ja juhlassa. Suomen evankelis-luterilainen kirkko vuosina 2016–2019*, edited by Hanna Salomäki et al., 67–89. Tampere: Kirkon tutkimuskeskus, 2020.
———. "Luterilainen usko nykyajan Suomessa." In *Osallistuva luterilaisuus: Suomen evankelis-luterilainen kirkko vuosina 2012–2015: Tutkimus kirkosta ja suomalaisista*, edited by Kimmo Ketola et al., 47–87. Kirkon tutkimuskeskuksen julkaisuja 125. Tampere: Kirkon tutkimuskeskus, 2016.
Ketola, Kimmo, et al. *Osallistuva luterilaisuus: Suomen evankelis-luterilainen kirkko vuosina 2012–2015: Tutkimus kirkosta ja suomalaisista*. Kirkon tutkimuskeskuksen julkaisuja 125. Tampere: Kirkon tutkimuskeskus, 2016.
"Kirkon jäsenyys." Evl.fi. https://evl.fi/tietoa-kirkosta/tilastotietoa/jasenet.
Kokkonen, Laura. *Negotiating with Branding: the Adoption of Marketing in Established Lutheran and Orthodox Churches in Finland*. Helsinki: Faculty of Theology, University of Helsinki, 2022.
Laine et. al. "Kasteen ja kummiuden kehityshankkeet seurakunnissa vuosina 2010–2020." In *Kasteen polulla: Kasteen ja kummiuden teologiaa ja käytäntöjä*, edited by Maarit Hytönen, 140–49. Vaasa: Kirkon tutkimuskeskus, 2021.
Mautner, Gerlinde. *Language and the Market Society: Critical Reflections on Discourse and Dominance*. New York: Routledge, 2010.
Miles, Steven. *Consumerism: As a Way of Life*. London: Sage, 1998.

Moberg, Marcus. *Church, Market, and Media: A Discursive Approach to Institutional Religious Change*. London: Bloomsbury Academic, 2017.

Moberg, Marcus, and Tuomas Martikainen. "Religious Change in Market and Consumer Society: the Current State of the Field and New Ways Forward." *Religion* 48 (2018) 418–35.

Niemelä, Kati. *Vieraantunut vai pettynyt? Kirkosta eroamisen syyt Suomen evankelis-luterilaisessa kirkossa*. Tampere: Kirkon tutkimuskeskus, 2006.

———. "'No Longer Believing in Belonging': A Longitudinal Study of Finnish Generation Y from Confirmation Experience to Church-Leaving." *Social Compass* 62 (2015) 172–86.

Palmu, Harri, et al. *Haastettu kirkko: Suomen evankelis-luterilainen kirkko vuosina 2008–2011*. Tampere: Kirkon tutkimuskeskus, 2012.

"Pienelle parasta—koko ikäluokan kattavaa yhteydenpitoa lapsiperheisiin." helsinginseurakunnat.fi https://www.helsinginseurakunnat.fi/artikkelit/ pienelleparasta.

"Ristiäiset." Evl.fi. https://evl.fi/perhejuhlat/ristiaiset.

Salomäki, Hanna. "Jumalanpalvelus, kirkolliset toimitukset ja kristilliset juhlapyhät." In *Uskonto arjessa ja juhlassa. Suomen evankelis-luterilainen kirkko vuosina 2016–2019* edited by Hanna Salomäki et al., 90–132. Tampere: Kirkon tutkimuskeskus, 2020.

Slater, Don. *Consumer Culture and Modernity*. Cambridge: Polity, 1997.

Taira, Teemu. *Taking "Religion" Seriously: Essays on the Discursive Study of Religion*. Supplements to Method and Theory in the Study of Religion 18. Leiden: Brill, 2022.

Valk, Pille, et al. *Teenagers Perspectives on the Role of Religion in Their Lives, Schools, and Societies: A European Quarterly Study*. Münster: Waxmann, 2009.

"Väestö ja yhteiskunta." Stat.fi. https://www.tilastokeskus.fi/tup/suoluk/suoluk_vaesto. html#Väkiluvun%20kehitys.

13

On Communicating about Baptism

Perspectives from Baptism Projects in the Diocese of Lund

Lena Andersson

IN 2005, THE DIOCESAN Council in Lund, Sweden, distributed a survey to parishes to establish the issues that they believed needed the most support. One of these issues was baptism. As a consequence, the Diocesan Office in Lund worked on several baptism projects[1] together with the parishes during the years 2006–2015. The aim of these projects was to establish a deeper understanding of baptism on several levels, including a theological understanding of why someone chooses to baptize their child as well as why parents who are members refrain from baptizing their child. During the years of the project, findings, societal changes, and people's views on baptism added two additional target scenarios. One was to shift the downward trend in the baptism statistics, and the second was to uncover and remove those obstacles that resulted in parents choosing not to baptize their children, as well as those that

---

1. Lunds stift, *Rapport Dopstatistik och slutsatser*; Lunds stift, *Slutrapport Källa till liv—Pastoral handlingsplan för dop*; Lunds stift, *Slutrapport Dopet som rit - Höjd kvalitet i dopgudstjänsten rit*; Lunds stift, *Slutrapport Doptelogisk fördjupning*; Lunds stift, *Slutrapport Katekumenatet—Vuxenväg till tro*; Lunds stift, *Slutrapporter Fokus dop och Fokus dop 2*.

resulted in that unbaptized adults didn't discover baptism or influenced the decision not to be baptized.[2]

The situation in the Diocese of Lund in 2006 was that 89.1 percent of all children of church members had been baptized. For the entire Church of Sweden, the corresponding percentage for this group was 83.2.[3] Thus, baptism still held a strong position as part of the culture and of people's own traditions. When the projects were initiated, several church workers testified that they had never spoken about their baptism or reflected on questions of baptism together with their team. The parish workers expressed that it was as if the baptisms were treated as a routine—a bit like they were performed in an assembly-line fashion. They also said that they seldom talked about baptism in parish activities, that the communication regarding baptism was minimal, that no invitations to baptisms were sent out, and that baptism was seldom mentioned or made visible in the main church services. These issues were together identified as the main reason for the absence of dialogue and reflection. Generally, these stories led to a kind of awakening and greatly affected the work ahead. Therefore, early on into the projects, it was made clear that communication in all its forms was an important component of achieving the overall aim.

As the projects progressed, a shift was visible regarding how the parish workers related to baptism and who was allowed and even considered it possible to talk about baptism. In the beginning, the parish workers said that it was the priest who answered questions about baptism; they could not or dared not put into words what baptism implied. The parish workers were quite simply afraid to say the wrong things. When the projects were finished, almost all of them revealed at the evaluation that they now naturally and in their own words responded to questions about baptism, which generally included the following: Why should we baptize our child? I was never baptized as a child, and now that I am an adult, I am considering being baptized. Can you tell me what difference it would make? They also reported that it was now common for them to talk about baptism in church activities of various kinds, as well as in their private lives. Thus, compared to earlier circumstances, an increasing number of church workers dared to talk about and explain the meaning of baptism.

---

2. Lunds stift, *Slutrapport Fokus dop*, 10–11.
3. Svenska kyrkan, *Statistikdatabasen*.

This shift illustrated that a distinctly greater ownership of baptism communication had emerged.[4]

As a conclusion to the projects, three important perspectives regarding baptismal communication, both in terms of the single individual and the parishes' broader mission to tell and share, were made visible. These included the following:

- Everybody in the parish is involved in baptism.
- Being baptized means that one has a mission to communicate.
- The church does not own the image of baptism.

EVERYBODY IN THE PARISH IS INVOLVED IN BAPTISM

The projects showed that church workers held the unconscious attitude that those who contacted them about baptism had no major knowledge of baptism. For instance, some expressed statements like the following: "Those who contact us for baptism have strange expectations and perceptions that we must try to dispel or just ignore and then run our race. They have not understood what baptism is really about. They are a different kind of Christian than we who work in the church" (an interesting aspect, as previously mentioned, was that, at the same time, they themselves indicated that they had little understanding of the process). The church workers saw their mission partly as one of helping, and partly one of teaching something to "the other." That the person contacting them had something to contribute was not something that they considered. A clear difference thus emerged between "we in the church," which meant the church workers, and "those who contact us," who were the others. An insight that emerged here was that it would be important to make the church workers aware of the effects that this unconscious "us and them" thinking could have. Another objective was to make the church workers see the individual person and the baptismal family as resources. The project thus made it visible that when there is such awareness, a change can finally take place.

We also learned from the projects that there was rarely a consensus regarding baptism among the parish workers, that they seldom had conversations about faith, and that such interactions nearly never occurred between elected officials. This meant that there was some

---

4. Lunds stift, *Slutrapport Fokus dop 2*, 3

measure of ambiguity in the contact with the members because parish workers gave different views and pictures about baptism. For example, in one parish, priests had different views on where and when a baptism could take place. Some said that baptism could take place in different places and at different times: in the church, at home, in a lake, etc. Others said that it could only take place in the church and then in the main Sunday service. In some cases, this meant that those who wanted to baptize their child requested a specific priest, and in some cases, they refrained from baptizing.

A directive in the projects was to make vicars aware of the importance of initiating a process in which all church workers, volunteers, and elected officials participated. This was considered essential because they all meet many church members who participate in various activities or contact the church in a number of ways. Regarding the baptismal practice, a Swedish parish could be organized as follows:

- **The administrator** sends out invitations and is also the one who communicates with the parents when they book the baptism. After the baptism has taken place, the administrator registers the baptism in the Church of Sweden's membership register.
- **The child pedagogues** meet parents and children during various activities and bring up the matter of baptism.
- **The communicator** produces information material and is in contact with members and answers their questions via social media.
- **The matron** meets the parents when the parents wish to borrow a christening gown and is also the person who answers questions regarding the booking of the premises when wanting to throw a party or gathering after the baptism service.
- **The church caretaker** prepares the church room, receives the baptismal family, and takes care of many of the practical details during the baptism.
- **The musician** talks to the baptismal family about hymns and soloists and performs during the service.
- **The priest** meets the family before the baptism and has a conversation about the process, both regarding the church's view and the practicalities surrounding the baptism service. The baptism service is led by the priest, who is also the one who baptizes the subject.

- **The deacon** has the first conversation with a refugee family concerning conversion to the Christian faith.
- **The elected officials** make sure that there are sufficient resources for the parish to communicate, inform, and hold baptism services.
- **The church warden** meets with the congregation at church services and asks questions about baptism.

Thus, different functions in the church meet people before, during and after a baptism. This often means that the same person meets several of them. In the projects, we saw the importance of these functions, realizing that together and individually, they have a responsibility for baptismal communication. And that they need to communicate the theology and practice of baptism in a similar way. An additional dimension that needed to be considered was that the parish may also face questions about baptism that arise during spontaneous meetings, for example, in the grocery store, at a party, or out on the street. Some issues highlighted included the following: Why is baptism important for me, the congregation, the church, and God? What does it mean to belong to and serve a church that claims to have baptism as its foundation? What is my task? How should the parish communicate to people so that they see baptism as a resource in their lives? One thing that was revealed was that when the parish took time to reflect on baptism, a process was initiated whereby much of what they did was affected in such a way that the baptism became a living reality. Another point that emerged was that when many people joined the process and shared their experiences, it became evident that there were several points of view regarding baptism. The picture thus became multifaceted and complex. Such an environment, despite its diversity, usually leads to greater consensus in the congregation regarding baptism procedures. This, in turn, creates an openness toward the people who contact the parish regarding baptism and their different reasons and wishes.

BEING BAPTIZED MEANS HAVING A MISSION TO COMMUNICATE

During the projects, it was found that people rarely or never talked about their own baptisms, nor did they speak to others about what it meant to them to be baptized. Baptism was seen as a one-time event—a ritual that happened when they were children and something that did not affect their everyday lives. Based on this insight, the projects problematized this issue with questions such as the following: Does baptism make any difference to the individual, to the church, or to God? Can communication about baptism take place when understanding is so limited? Whose responsibility is it to talk about baptism?

In the Church of Sweden, this text from the Gospel of Matthew is read at every baptism: "All authority in heaven and on earth has been given to me. Go, therefore, and make disciples of all nations, baptizing them in the name of the Father and of the Son and of the Holy Spirit, and teaching them to obey everything that I have commanded you. And remember, I am with you always, to the end of the age."[5] This is known as the Great Commission. The first call is for communication: to go and make disciples of all people. All who are baptized are given this mission, just like Jesus's disciples, to go and spread the message of God. During the projects, it was discovered that there was a need to find ways to communicate so that everyone was able and felt comfortable talking about baptism. This was something that the church workers wanted. At gatherings, several of them had expressed that this was hard. The question, "What should I say?" was repeated quite often.

The strategy chosen for this part of the projects was the path of conversation. Initially, several methods were used to start conversations and deepen the participants' understanding of baptism. Conversations that were mostly based on one's own experiences, Bible stories, and the basic documents of the Church of Sweden were used in this regard. When people started to talk, it was made clear that everyone knew something about baptism, and most people knew quite a lot. They knew about other people's baptisms or the ones they had participated in or been involved with. Some knew things parents had told them about their own baptisms. Moreover, they also knew things through sermons, what they saw in the church rooms, and what they gleaned from different forms of media, exhibitions, and so on. Generally, the participants found that they had various sources to draw on when communicating about baptism. Therefore, they came to understand that when anyone communicates about baptism, it can be through his or her life and own experiences. Thus, another learning point here was the value of the personal story.

---

5. Kyrkohandbok för Svenska kyrkan, *Del I i urval på engelska franska spanska tyska*, 52 och NRSV, Matt 28:18–20.

CALL TO ACTION

In the projects, one strategy regarding individual communication resulted in some measure of encouragement, which was the call to action. The insight here was that everyone is an important communicator, and that if someone asks the questions "Why should our child be baptized?" or "Why should I get baptized?" it is important that they get an answer. One learning point from the projects was that there was not just one answer, and that each participant could use their own thoughts and experiences. When communication is between two people, a personal answer is often good enough. Generally, the person who asks wants to know what *you* think. If a baptized Christian cannot answer this basic question, who will? Another insight that emerged here was that it was important to take Jesus's mission seriously, and that every baptized person should take part in making baptism a buzzword and something that many people talk about. One way to achieve this was to use the classic and well-proven method of "word of mouth." In such cases, it is essential to use communication that is not only informative, but that also takes place in a mutual dialogue. A third point was that when a person begins to think, talk to others, and reflect on a personal level about their own baptism, this may lead to a decisive and deeper understanding of its significance. Talking and sharing are based on interpretive symbols and practices, and for many, the meaning of baptism became clearer through this process.

THE CHURCH DOES NOT OWN THE IMAGE OF BAPTISM

Tradition bearers and a variety of media[6] were analyzed in the projects to determine the content and agents of communication about baptism. The results showed that the Church of Sweden was only one of many agents who communicated about baptism in different ways and with different content. Thus, the church does not own the means of communication or even the information regarding baptism.

One conclusion of the project was that people essentially have their own experiences of baptisms, but they are also partly influenced by what they see in the media. This influence affects the impressions that they carry with them, whether unconsciously or consciously. Thus, church workers must assume that the people they meet already have certain images and understandings of what baptism is about. A second conclusion was that the church must consider what consequences this has for

---

6. Lunds stift, *Slutrapport Fokus dop 2*, 32

determining its communication strategies. Church workers need to reflect on questions like, "Are there images left out? What is our message? Who is part of the target group?"

The following sections include examples of how others outside of the church influence people's images of baptism.

Family, Friends, and Tradition

In the projects, parents were asked why they chose to baptize their children. A common answer was "because it's a tradition in our family." For these respondents, this tradition was still an important part of their culture and the social patterns that they followed. It was also clear that paternal and maternal grandparents, siblings, other family members, and close friends were often the first ones with whom they talked about baptism. For most, these conversations concerned practical matters. Some families had longstanding traditions around baptism that they wanted to preserve. Others had a christening gown that had been passed on through generations. On these gowns, some had embroidered the name of the child and the date of the baptism.

Royal Influencers

Royal baptisms have attracted a lot of attention in Sweden. They feature prominently in newspapers and on social media. Several such baptisms have been broadcast on television or live on the internet. News articles and features are full of interpretations and photos presented by journalists, reporters, and experts on royalty. In December 2017, Prince Gabriel was baptized. The Swedish daily *Expressen* wrote on its website, "Coziness, mischief and tears at the idyllic christening."[7] The prince was baptized in the Drottningholm church, which had been decorated to look like an idyllic winter scene. In one of the photos, the mother, Princess Sofia, was dressed in the Swedish national costume, and the father, Prince Carl-Philip, was dressed in military attire. A large number of guests were invited to the baptism. The *Expressen* even published a short film about the event. An event such as this one shows how the ceremony can be focused on the personal and the traditional at the same time. Such displays can encourage trends and give people a better

---

7. Expressen, *Mys, bus och tårar*, https://www.expressen.se/noje/kungligt/mys-bus-och-tarar-pa-idylliska-dopet/.

understanding of how a baptism should or can be carried out, which also leads to certain expectations from the church.

Social Media Changes the Game Plan

On social media, people share their lives with others. For instance, the Torsgården family has a vlog with 432,000 followers,[8] which is higher than the number of people who subscribe to Sweden's largest daily newspaper, *Dagens Nyheter*.[9] The wife and mother Helena vlogs about the family's everyday lives. On December 23, 2017, the family's firstborn child, Selma, was baptized. The vlog on that day was solely about this event.[10] Everything was nicely filmed and well organized, and the vlog started by describing the stress of organizing the laying table and preparing the cakes. After that, we see the family in the church for the ceremony, followed by guests enjoying coffee and cakes at the parish meeting house. Finally, we see Helena, Henrik, and Selma, all rather tired, sitting together on the family's settee and evaluating the whole day. They all seem to be very content that the day went so well, and they mention the priest's efforts and express gratitude for all the help they received. After just over six years, the vlog has been viewed almost 300,000 times, received almost 10,000 likes, and has been given 700 comments. When one views the vlog about the baptism, images of a big party, a large number of guests, fine clothes, gifts, and a traditional baptism all appear. This may be something that one consciously or unconsciously wants to replicate. However, those who do not have the resources to carry through something of this caliber might instead choose to refrain from baptizing their child altogether.

Baptism as a Concept

In Sweden, when you give a ship a name, you say that you have baptized it. There are more examples of how the word baptize is used in a variety of ways. You can read about schools, bridges, parks, and local trains being baptized.[11] While such practices have nothing to do with the church, people may still unconsciously come to connect a Christian

---

8. Familjen Torsgården, https://www.youtube.com/@HiiLen.

9. *Dagens Nyheter*, https://www.dn.se/ekonomi/digitalt-rekord-for-dagens-nyheter/.

10. Familjen Torsgården, *Selmas dop*, https://www.youtube.com/watch?v=5Q7pOYjwXmQ.

11. For example, see Malmö FF, *Skånetrafikens hyllning till Safari*, https://www.mff.se/skanetrafikens-hyllning-till-safari-doper-om-pagatagen/.

baptism with being given a name, and that it is thus synonymous with a name-giving ceremony.

There are also commercial interests in the practice of baptism. For instance, there are multiple examples of companies that use baptism in their commercial campaigns. A recent example is a Swedish gaming site that, during the FIFA World Cup, showed parts of a child's baptism in one of their ads.[12] In this ad, the child is baptized and then lifted up by the priest, who shows the child to the congregation. The priest goes on to take off his surplice, under which he is dressed in football clothes. Instead of holding the uplifted child, he now holds a victory trophy.

There are also some companies selling products related to baptism, including invitation cards, gifts, and dresses, and soloists can be hired from different agencies.[13] Such marketing products are essentially designed to affect people's understanding and experience of baptism.

Media Logic

When the church does something new and different regarding the subject of baptism, it sometimes grabs the attention of the local media. A feature article on drop-in baptisms conducted in the parish of Asarum is an example of this.[14] The local news program in Blekinge, which is shown on Swedish Broadcasting Television, reported the following on May 14, 2022: "Here in Asarum the children are baptized in assembly-line fashion. 'More easy going' and 'come as you are' was the message when the church in Asarum invited guests to drop-in baptisms on Saturday. Balloons, a bouncy castle, and coffee—and a total of five baptized children—led to a successful baptism festival."

TO VISUALIZE BAPTISM IN THE PARISH

In the Church of Sweden's Church Ordinance, it says, "The mission of the church is that everyone should be reached with the offer to be baptized."[15] When a parish is about to communicate with or inform

---

12. The advertising was affiliated with the FIFA World Cup 2022 and can no longer be found.

13. For example, see Kalasdekorationer, https://www.kalasdekorationer.se/sv/articles/149/dop-namngivning.

14. SVT Nyheter, *Här döps barnen*, https://www.svt.se/nyheter/lokalt/blekinge/har-dops-barnen-pa-lopande-band.

15. Kyrkoordning för Svenska kyrkan, *Inledningen till nittonde kapitlet*.

members of the church about baptism, the projects have shown that four considerations must be made. The first is that, before producing or analyzing the parish's current baptism material, it is wise to gather together to share knowledge and reflect on baptism. The objective here is to achieve a shared vision of what the parish wants to communicate. The second consideration is to try to understand just who the parishioners are. For example, it may be key to look at relevant statistics, family formations, and specific socioeconomic factors to establish whether there is an ongoing generational change or the development of new residential areas where more people will be moving in. Things like this affect the parish and have consequences for its communication. In this sense, when the parish wants to communicate with a certain group, it needs to analyze which arenas and channels the group uses. The third consideration is to acquire an understanding of why people do or do not choose baptism. Awareness of these different motives has consequences for how the church communicates, as it can affect the choice of words, photos, illustrations, and even layouts. A fourth consideration is how the church can shift its position in the equation through the following questions: *How can we help you when you wish to baptize your child? How can we help you when you wish to be baptized?* In this case, the church must put on the recipient's glasses and reflect on which questions, wishes, or requests are the most common. Such an approach also involves taking a critical look at and reflecting on whether the church has put up any unnecessary obstacles to baptism. Such obstacles can impact availability in a number of ways and include scheduling on certain dates and times and restricting the choice of church. The baptismal family or the person being baptized may want to influence the baptism service by choosing hymns, prayers, the active participation of children, soloists, and certain decorations, to name a few examples. This is not a matter of meeting insoluble demands, but rather about flexibility and explaining why things must be done in a certain way. It is also about taking the time to listen and taking people's requests seriously.

Generally, the church needs to communicate in a way that explains the process, helps people understand its significance, and also invites people to participate. At the same time, it is important to be aware that all communication is interpreted individually and is completely dependent on the recipient's frame of reference. What one person appreciates, another does not, and this will always be the case.

PART III: COMMUNICATION

Examples of Baptism Communication

INVITATIONS TO BAPTISM

Due to the Church of Sweden's Church Ordinance, members who have recently become parents must be informed of the possibility of baptism for the newborn child.[16] Most parishes send letters, with invitations to participate in a baptism, that they have produced themselves. There is also information on websites and parish magazines. Some parishes have produced folders that are distributed in childcare centers, in church, and in the parish meeting house. When parishes arrange drop-in baptisms, it is common to advertise such occasions in different media.

When the parish designs an invitation, they must think communicatively. The parish should consider questions such as the following: What do we want to tell and to whom? Who are we, and who is/are the recipient/recipients? In what ways should we invite people? Should it be through postcards, letters, Facebook, our website, films, telephone calls, or by being at the school, pub, or shopping mall?

One relevant finding from the projects was that association and identification are important, in the sense that the information sent out or supplied on the website should be from the local parish. It is therefore important to use photos of the baptismal font, the church room, the parish meeting house where the party or gathering can be held, the baptismal gowns, and the parish baptism gifts. The Church of Sweden, at the national level, has general information about baptism on its website, which can be used to complement the individual communication strategies of the parish in question.[17]

BAPTISM CANDLES AND CERTIFICATES

When someone is baptized in the Church of Sweden, it is common practice that a baptism certificate is handed out, as well as a baptism candle and a letter to the godparents. The parish should thus reflect on the following: what does the certificate say about baptism? To whom is it addressed? Is it designed in such a way that you can put it up on a wall, or is it meant to be kept in an envelope? What does the godparent certificate say about baptism and the task of being a godparent? What does the

---

16. Kyrkoordning för Svenska kyrkan, kap 19 §8.
17. Svenska kyrkan, *Dop*, https://www.svenskakyrkan.se/dop.

baptismal candle convey? Is it marked with a symbol? Does the recipient get a new one when it has burned down? If you are given a candlestick, is it in any way associated with the baptism?

Inside the Church

Churches are full of symbols, paintings, and other objects that provide information about baptism. In the projects, the parishes thought about how to use these objects to help people gain a deeper understanding of the meaning of baptism. For example, since the baptismal font is a strong symbol that reminds many of baptism, it should have a visible and well-thought-out placement in the church room. Water should always be kept in the font as a symbol of baptism being a constant and living thing. It should also be possible for church attendees to feel the water, as this then becomes not only becomes a visual experience but also a physical one, which can serve as a reminder of one's own baptism.

In many churches in the Diocese of Lund, there is what is commonly called a baptismal tree, which is often made from metal or a tree branch. The imagination is abundant, and there are objects such as fishnets, ladders, boats, paintings, Jesus figures, waterdrops, and hands.[18] When a baptism takes place, a symbol is hung on the tree with the person's name and the date of the baptism. The symbols vary, and the most common are angels, water drops, fishes, and fishing tackles.[19] Once or twice a year, the parish sends out invitations to a service in which those who have been baptized can receive their symbol. The presence of the baptismal tree makes it clear that baptisms take place, and that certain individuals have also been baptized. This is especially important, since most baptisms in the Diocese of Lund take place at individual baptism services and not at the main Sunday service.

Church Services

The projects highlighted the importance of considering how baptism is mentioned in common worship and other pastoral services. Questions

---

18. See, for example, *Jesus händer i Nättraby kyrka*, https://www.svenskakyrkan.se/nattrabyhasslo/nattraby-kyrka.

19. See, for example, *Dopängel i Burlövs församling*, https://www.svenskakyrkan.se/burlov/dopangel.

raised included the following: How do we tell people about baptism in our church services? How often is baptism mentioned in the sermon? What objects and methods can we use in the liturgy to make the message clearer and more inclusive? There are some parishes who hold services on the theme of baptism. On these occasions, the hymns, prayers, passages from the Bible, and the whole sermon are focused on baptism. In the church, they show, among other things, the parish's baptismal gowns and the gifts handed out at baptisms.

In the Church of Sweden's handbook, there is an order for celebrating a church service with a baptism reminder.[20] Through this process, baptism is visualized and made a part of the service. On such occasions, the event can begin by pouring water into the font. The whole congregation can then gather around the baptismal font. Members of the congregation will then be invited to touch the water, reminding themselves of their own baptisms, and to sign the symbol of the cross on their foreheads. Another way to go about this is by splashing water. In this case, a small tree branch can be dipped into the baptismal font and then used to splash water on the congregation.

Another insight that emerged from the projects was that the church also needs to reflect on how to communicate about baptism when it encounters people in other services, for instance, during confirmations and funerals. On these occasions, there are many people in attendance, and some of them do not usually join in other church activities, as they are not regular churchgoers, and some may not be baptized. When a baptism is confirmed, the parishes in the Diocese of Lund can make this connection visible in several ways. For instance, the confirmation service could commence with water being poured into the baptismal font. The candidate for confirmation and his or her godparent could walk in together during the procession. As another option, those to be confirmed could receive the sign of the cross on their foreheads with water.

Even at funerals, there are examples of how parishes could raise awareness about the significance of baptism. For instance, a baptismal candle could be placed next to the coffin. When a child or young adult has died, the baptismal candle that the deceased received at the baptism may still be there and can then be used.

The music and singing in the church service is also a way of communicating about baptism. To refine this aspect, the Diocese of Lund

---

20. Kyrkohandbok för Svenska kyrkan.

commissioned an oratory in 2008, which resulted in a newly created musical composition entitled, "The Living Water."[21]

Exhibitions

Arranging exhibitions on baptism in the parish, the church, or the parish meeting house is both a way of informing those who are not baptized about the process and reminding those who are baptized about its significance. Some parishes have fixed exhibitions in display cases showing objects connected to baptism. These objects could include baptism certificates, baptismal candles, baptism gifts, letters to the godparents, and even Barbie dolls that provide a visualization of the baptism ceremony. Some parishes hold temporary exhibitions in which they show christening gowns, gifts, photos of baptisms, roll-ups, and articles related to baptism. One particular parish sewed a gigantic christening gown that they hung from the roof. It was so enormous that you could actually step into the gown. The symbolism of clothing oneself with Christ became very evident in this case.

Giveaways

Some parishes in the Diocese of Lund have held giveaways with products handed out at baptisms. Such products could include onesies and bibs for infants printed with "Baptized."

Social Media

When an individual has been baptized, some parishes take photos of the child, the family, the relatives, and the friends who are present, which are then published on the parishes' Instagram or Facebook pages. This is a very modern way of announcing that someone has been baptized. Social media is also used to inform parishes about drop-in baptisms and church services that focus on baptism. The Diocesan Office has also used social media to encourage people to celebrate their baptism days. Specifically, they have started a Facebook group called "Let's celebrate our baptismal day."[22] On this page, members share stories of their baptism days and

21. Klaverdal/Falkenland, *Levande Vatten ett oratorium om dop*.
22. Lunds stift, *Let's Celebrate Our Baptismal Day*, https://www.facebook.com/

how they have celebrated the event. Short films have been produced by the Diocese, in which different people share their stories.²³

OTHER ARENAS

In conjunction with a nationwide arrangement in Malmö, a baptism walk was held on a Saturday in the city center, which was bustling with people. One objective of the walk was to help the participants experience how everyday environments can remind us of our baptism, and what it means to live in one's baptism. Malmö has several fountains and two canals, some of which were used as stops during the walk. The walk took the shape of a theatrical procession, and the participants walked together with Jesus to meet different people.²⁴ On the way to the last stop, someone was heard shouting in the distance. It was John the Baptist. People shopping stopped in their tracks and wondered what was happening. When the final act was performed, hundreds of spectators were able to experience Jesus being baptized.

CONCLUSION

As described in the introduction, the projects on baptism led to the insight that there are three central perspectives regarding baptismal communication. These three, "Everybody in the parish is involved in baptism," "Being baptized means that one has a mission to communicate," and "The church does not own the image of baptism," have been described in detail above.

Overall, the projects helped to clarify how the Diocese of Lund should and could continue to work to develop and deepen baptism. This work has been ongoing ever since.

BIBLIOGRAPHY

Burlövs församling. "Dopängel." https://www.svenskakyrkan.se/burlov/dopangel.
Dagens Nyheter. https://www.dn.se/ekonomi/digitalt-rekord-for-dagens-nyheter/.
Expressen. "Mys, bus och tårar." https://www.expressen.se/noje/kungligt/mys-bus-och-tarar-pa-idylliska-dopet/.

---

groups/112693625429143.

23. Lunds stift, *Lenas och Mats dopdag*, https://www.youtube.com/watch?v=peAYItZxudQ.

24. Gerdmar, "Replikmanus."

Familjen Torsgården. "Selmas dop." https://www.youtube.com/watch?v=5Q7pOYjwXmQ.
Familjen Torsgården. https://www.youtube.com/@HiiLen.
Gerdmar, Staffan. "Replikmanus: Dopvandring under Världens Fest i Malmö." 2012.
Kalasdekorationer. https://www.kalasdekorationer.se/sv/articles/149/dop-namngivning.
Klaverdal, Falkenland. *Levande vatten: Ett oratorium om dopet.* Oslo: Cantando musikforlag, 2008.
Lunds stift. *Projektrapport Utveckling av katekumenatet.* Lund, 2009.
———. *Rapport Dopstatistik och slutsatser.* Lund, 2006.
———. *Slutrapport Dopet som rit.* Lund, 2008.
———. *Slutrapport Dopteologisk fördjupning.* Lund, 2009.
———. *Slutrapport Fokus dop 2.* Lund, 2015.
———. *Slutrapport Fokus dop.* Lund, 2010.
———. *Slutrapport Källa till liv.* Lund, 2009.
Lunds stift. "Lenas och Mats dopdag." https://www.youtube.com/watch?v=peAYItZxudQ.
———. "Vi som firar vår dopdag." https://www.facebook.com/groups/112693625429143.
Malmö FF. "Skånetrafikens hyllning till Safari." https://www.mff.se/skanetrafikens-hyllning-till-safari-doper-om-pagatagen/.
Nättraby-Hasslö församling. "Konstverket Jesus händer i Nättraby kyrka." https://www.svenskakyrkan.se/nattrabyhasslo/nattraby-kyrka.
Svenska kyrkan. "Dop." https://www.svenskakyrkan.se/dop.
———. *Kyrkohandbok för Svenska kyrkan. Del I i urval på engelska franska spanska tyska.* Uppsala, 2022. (svenskakyrkan.se).
———. *Kyrkohandbok för Svenska kyrkan.* Uppsala 2018 https://www.svenskakyrkan.se/kyrkohandboken.
———. *Kyrkoordning för Svenska kyrkan.* Uppsala 2023. https://www.svenskakyrkan.se/kyrkoordningen.
———. "Statistikdatabasen."http://statistik.svenskakyrkan.se/statistik/.
SVT Nyheter Blekinge. "Här döps barnen." https://www.svt.se/nyheter/lokalt/blekinge/har-dops-barnen-pa-lopande-band.

14

Baptism in Times of Change
The Need for Targeted Marketing

Ingeborg Dybvig

> *The right word spoken at the right time is as beautiful as gold apples in a silver bowl.*

The above quote from Proverbs 25:11 shows how rhetoric always has a matter of finding the correct words at the right time. Today's rhetorical situations are set in a totally different reality, however. The Church of Norway has 3.4 million members, which is 63 percent of the Norwegian population.[1] These members represent different lives, needs, and expectations. They also have different knowledge of the church: some have in-depth knowledge, while others are distant, with a lack of interest or even prejudices. These individuals create a complex target group and represent a challenge for church communication departments in general. What should be said, to whom, and when? Which "right words spoken at the right time" can shape the message so that the church stands out as relevant, present, and inclusive of the people of today?

---

1. The Church of Norway, https://www.kirken.no/nb-NO/om-kirken/bakgrunn/kirkestatistikk/.

These questions point directly to the essence of communication and have posed a significant challenge to the Department of Communications in the Church of Norway over the last decade. The focus on more targeted communication in both physical and digital channels was initiated several years ago, which was boosted by the declining numbers for church ceremonies, such as baptism and confirmation, as well as church attendance in general. It was clear that the language, the communication formats, and the choice of channels must be able to reach the "modern member." Even though this work had already been started, the lockdown of the Norwegian churches in March 2020 due to the COVID-19 pandemic led to a much faster transformation and opened up a new type of ceremony linked to baptisms and weddings.

The focus in this article is on communication regarding baptism conducted by the Church of Norway. To give the best picture of the development of this specific type of communication, I will include the strategies and experiences from more general communications work for other church ceremonies. These are, in many ways, linked together, as the experiences from one area are often invaluable to those of another.

To fully understand the need for changes in baptism-related communications, one must also understand the recent changes within Norwegian society. I will, therefore, in more general terms, share a few glimpses of the Church of Norway's current situation and its changing role in society. Doing so I will illuminate how this situation makes it even more important to build trust with the population. I will examine the use of ethos as an appeal and explore the importance of trust in digital communication based on a more theoretical point of view.[2]

The work with communications throughout the pandemic provided important lessons, and these have further transformed the communication strategies employed after the pandemic. Since these developments provide a vital backdrop for understanding the more specific communications on baptism, I will look at the situation during the pandemic, highlight some findings from the church's own internal and external surveys on the use of digital content during the pandemic, and then describe how this knowledge is related to baptism communications today.

---

2. In a Master of Rhetoric thesis, I analyzed the concept of "an ethos of sympathy" and the importance of trust and did a comparative rhetorical analysis of selected baptism texts on the websites of the Swedish and Danish churches. See Dybvig, *Som epler av gull*.

PART III: COMMUNICATION

THE CHURCH OF NORWAY FACES A NEW REALITY

During the last few decades, the situation for the Church of Norway has dramatically changed. The Norwegian Constitution defines the church as the "people's church," and while this might have been a more accurate definition 20 or 30 years ago, when a vast majority of the population were members, today, the situation is different, as the membership percentage has decreased from 71 percent in 2015 to 63 percent in 2023.[3] There are several reasons for this decrease. In addition to those individuals who are actively leaving the church, there has also been a significant increase in immigration, mainly by non-Christians or at least not Lutherans, as well as a general decrease in the number of baptisms.

While more than 96 percent of children were baptized in the Church of Norway in 1973, this number decreased 54 percent in 2022.[4] There are large geographical variations in these numbers, ranging from 64 percent in the diocese of Møre on Norway's west coast down to 23 percent in the diocese of Oslo. Even though there are some more positive examples, for instance, in that every year, nearly 1,200 teens are baptized before their confirmation, and that the number of drop-in baptisms is increasing[5], the general tendency of a decrease remains clear.

With 65 percent of the population identifying as members, the Church of Norway can still claim to be the largest faith community in the country. Nevertheless, society is still increasingly secular and diverse. Knowledge of Christianity, the church, and its ceremonies is in general quite low. A future forecast made in 2019 indicated that the numbers will most likely continue to decrease, falling from today's 3.5 million to 3.3 million members in 2039.[6]

It is through baptism that one becomes a member of the Church of Norway. The decrease in the number of baptisms therefore threatens the church's status as the people's church. Against this background, this article addresses the following question: *Could a more strategic and consistent communication approach stop this decrease?*

After providing a theoretical background, my analysis starts with a brief overview of how today's status of the church affects its members' trust and decreases its relevance. I will then outline the development of the

---

3. Statistics are obtained from the Church of Norway's register of members.
4. Statistics Norway, https://www.ssb.no/statbank/table/12025/tableViewLayout1/.
5. Statistics from The Church of Norway, 2022.
6. Brunvoll, *Utviklingen av antall medlemmer i Den norske kirke*.

church's general digital communication strategy before moving to more specific baptism communications. I will also investigate the general communications work before, during, and after the pandemic. The experiences linked to these communication efforts have proved relevant for how more specific communications regarding baptism have been shaped after the pandemic and in the development of a strategy moving forward.

INSIGHTS FROM RHETORICAL THEORY

In a previous study of digital baptism texts on the national websites for the Church of Sweden and the Evangelical Lutheran Church in Denmark, I identified the importance of three ethos appeals: a simple style, an expression of the values of community and presence, and the use of accurate, persuasive speech.[7] This insight demonstrated the need for targeted and strategic communications based on the appropriate use of language.

Today, one of the biggest challenges for the church is to fight back a lack of interest and become more relevant to people's lives. Even though the digital reality and the new opportunities it has created are quite recent, it is possible to use Aristotle's classic terms of persuasion, ethos, and pathos to understand this situation. While an ethos appeal focuses on a speaker's character and the ability to build trust in the audience, a pathos appeal relies on the use of emotions to create sympathy in the audience.[8]

Historically speaking, the church built its communications on pathos. This pathos tradition, with a strong focus on emotions and preaching closely connected to faith, fear, mercy, heaven, and hell, has played a vital role within the church. In the last decade, the reality has completely changed, however, as a much more secular and diverse society has opted to make the individual choice of belonging to the church, which is often decided in the negative. The church cannot take Christian knowledge and a longing to belong for granted. It must prove itself relevant and interesting to its members today.

Trust is therefore vital, and a strong ethos builds trust.[9] Ethos is about credibility and character and can be related to a person or an organization.[10] In this vein, Cicero connected ethos with pathos and intro-

---

7. Dybvig, *Som epler av gull*.
8. Aristoteles, *Retorik*.
9. Wisse, *Ethos and Pathos*, 32.
10. Hoff-Clausen, *Online Ethos*, 51.

duced an "ethos of sympathy,"[11] in which goodwill and the rhetor's attitude toward his audience stand in the center. These two elements are vital to convincing an audience and generating sympathy.[12] The church knows that it has the world's most important message. Even so, this knowledge is insufficient. Ethos is dynamic and not constant, and trust is challenged every time a rhetor establishes contact with its audience. In other words, ethos is also decided by the receiver's attitude and its knowledge and experience with the rhetor.[13] To reach out more effectively, the rhetor must also convince the audience that he or she is worthy.

The opposite of sympathy is antipathy, which refers to a strong feeling of disgust or reluctance. I claim that the main enemy of the church is indifference, not antipathy.[14] The challenge for the church today is that the strong initial ethos it originally owned, created by sympathy, knowledge, and belonging, has been changed into an "ethos of indifference." This is established when the audience is unclear, the messages are indistinct, and the language and visual devices are random. The reasons for these changes are in many ways obvious, but increased diversity, a growing polarization, and a stronger privatization of religious belief are just a few.

THE NEED FOR AND USE OF DIGITAL CHANNELS IN THE CHURCH OF NORWAY

The last decade has seen enormous growth in digital communication. A wide range of channels provides many opportunities to pursue more professional and targeted marketing, and churches all over the world have invested in digital communications as a result. At the same time, as a digital rhetor, the church must build its own reputation and trust to make its audience listen and act appropriately. It must also be aware of the challenges. These are linked to issues regarding ethics,[15] and how it is essentially difficult to determine whether key messages are actually reaching their target groups.

The Church of Norway has had a digital presence for years, which was built on the need to be present where people are present—and people

---

11. Cicero, *Om talekunst*, 126.
12. Wisse, *Ethos and Pathos*, 32ff; Miller, *Expertise and Agency*, 210.
13. McCroskey, *An Introduction to Rhetorical Communication*, 182.
14. Dybvig, *Som epler av gull*, 7–8.
15. Ethical dilemmas linked to the use of social media channels have become part of an important discussion. Even so, this issue remains outside the scope of this article, and it is therefore not further discussed here.

are online. Even so, presence as such has not been the main reason here, as the ultimate goal has been to share the good news of Jesus Christ and show how this message can be relevant today. In other words, the broader objective is to build knowledge, sympathy, and trust.

The Church of Norway created a national Facebook account in 2014, but without a clear content strategy. Since 2015, the understanding of the importance of a professional digital presence has steadily increased. A more detailed communication and digital strategy was approved by the Church General Synod in 2017[16] and by the National Council of the Church of Norway in 2018.[17] By 2020, the church's online presence had gradually become stronger and more targeted on the official website, kirken.no, and on different social media platforms. The content was linked to faith, prayers, and church ceremonies.

In 2017, the church introduced a digital wall on which to pray and light a candle.[18] It also started to explore online services and interactive prayers. There was a wide range of campaigns targeted toward young parents to promote baptism and toward young teens to promote confirmation. These were used in both digital and printed media on the national and local levels.

COMMUNICATIONS ABOUT BAPTISM BEFORE THE PANDEMIC

The slow but still steady decrease in baptisms gave way to a new mobilization. An increasing number of church employees at both the national and local levels looked for new ways of communicating. This mobilization included several different actions: an analysis of church statistics, a survey distributed among parents on attitudes and expectations, an increased focus on internal communication and motivation, different resources to employ locally, and additional national communication measures. A printed magazine called "Dåpsløftet" was issued four times between 2015 and 2018.[19]

16. The Church Synod, KM 12/17, https://www.kirken.no/globalassets/kirken.no/om-kirken/slik-styres-kirken/kirkemotet/2017/saksdokumenter/km_12_17_kirkens_digitale_satsing_og_medlemskommunikasjon.pdf.

17. The National Council of The Church of Norway,KR 72/18, https://www.kirken.no/globalassets/kirken.no/om-kirken/slik-styres-kirken/kirkeradet/2018/desember/kr_72_0_18_okt-digital-satsing-i-den-norske-kirke.pdf.

18. The Church of Norway, https://be.kirken.no/.

19. Dåpsløftet, https://www.kirken.no/nb-NO/om-kirken/for-medarbeidere/dapslo

The first national activity was an advertisement on baptism in "Spedbarnsboken," a book with relevant information and commercial ads given to all young parents. In 2014, the diocese of Stavanger arranged a special seminar on how to stop the decline in baptism numbers. Among the measures taken were an increased number of baptism services and more targeted communication. Lademoen church in the diocese of Nidaros became the first in Norway to invite potential members to a drop-in baptism in May 2015, inspired by similar efforts in Sweden, at which eight people were baptized. Since then, several congregations all over the country have included drop-in baptisms in their programs. The Bishops' Council also saw the need to focus on the importance of baptism. In the autumn of 2019, they published an official text, "The Gift of Baptism," followed by a dedicated booklet on baptism in February 2020.[20]

The members and their expectations were also put into focus. A national member survey conducted in 2019 explored their needs, expectations, and attitudes toward the church.[21] One question asked was, "If you had a baby today, would this baby be baptized?" Nearly eight in 10 members answered yes. To be able to move these persons from a passive yes in a survey to real action, the church needed to remain in touch with people in different ways and through different channels, both of a digital and physical nature.

New communications materials were therefore produced, mainly to be used for the local promotion of baptism, which included videos, still photos, brochures, templates for social media posts, and printed advertisements. There was also a stronger focus on how to answer questions about and requests for baptism, how to plan and communicate about baptism ceremonies for a longer period to increase the choice of dates, and how to meet and greet families attending a baptism. This was in many ways the beginning of a more receiver-oriented and member-focused communication strategy.

When the national website www.kirken.no was established in 1997, it did not have a clear content strategy or target group. The site tried to communicate with employees, volunteers, and members at

---

ftet--mobilisering-til-dap/.

20. Bispemøtet, *Livstegnet*.

21. The Church of Norway, "Membership Surveys." The one referred to is from 2019, but the same results were obtained in the two following surveys conducted in 2020 and 2021. See https://www.kirken.no/nb-NO/om-kirken/bakgrunn/kirkestatistikk/medlemsundersokelse/.

the same time. Information about baptism played an important role from the beginning, but the messages were not particularly receiver oriented. The general focus was on the theology of baptism, which was communicated in an internal Christian language that was difficult for many to understand.

In 2015, the church's intranet was launched, and at the same time, the website changed its focus from employees to members. This opened up a pathway toward a more targeted and simple communication style, with a stronger focus on church ceremonies and how to communicate them to members. In recent years, the receiver orientation has become even stronger. The angle of the stories, and especially the language, has been revised several times to ensure that the receiver gets the information needed. Finding the most appropriate language when the church talks about baptism remains an ongoing challenge. The descriptions of baptism on www.Kirken.no were traditionally more poetic and theological than easy to understand. Terms like "baptism is God's gift" or "when you are baptized, you become a member of God's family" might give meaning to those who attend church on a regular basis but appear meaningless to others. The current strategy is to use very simple and concrete entrance texts, since surveys show that information on *where*, *when*, and *how* is more important than *why*. The next layer can then include information about *what* baptism is and *why* it is important.

Based on surveys on people's attitudes toward baptism, we know that tradition is important, and that in many cases, the parents disagree regarding baptism. Websites can therefore offer knowledge, insight, and arguments to mitigate such issues.

COMMUNICATIONS DURING THE PANDEMIC: WHAT DID THE CHURCH OF NORWAY DO?

Church communication during the pandemic was based on a general approach. Even so, the experiences obtained during this period played a role in the development of baptism communication moving forward.

When COVID-19 closed the country and church buildings on March 12, 2020, the Church of Norway broadcast a digital service from the Oslo Cathedral on Facebook less than 24 hours later. This was possible due to the strategic digital communications work conducted in previous years. The service was one of the starting points for a national landslide of digital church presence, wherein the content was produced both nationally and locally. This content consisted of online prayers, short services, concerts, and evening devotions. There was an immediate response, almost like an explosion, and the number of followers on Facebook and Instagram beat all previous records. This made it clear once again that in a time of crisis and uncertainty, people turn to the church for comfort.

The external campaign work was intensified on many different platforms. Digital paid ads were placed in Norway's largest newspaper *VG* and in different social media channels. There was also a strategic focus on search engine optimalization to come first in the Google searches made by the public looking for information on the different church services and offers.

While the authorities granted special exceptions for funerals, many of the already planned baptisms and weddings were postponed or cancelled. However, the church saw an opportunity here. Soon, it became clear that the lockdown not only created a need for a digital presence, but also a strong urge for more bespoke offers, like outdoor gatherings as well as alternative shorter church ceremonies that were more bespoke. A baptism was performed with the priest and the baby, the parents, and maybe two witnesses. Such an approach was merely designed to offer an alternative during a crisis, but the positive feedback was immediate: families reported back that these small and private ceremonies felt more intimate, they could participate more actively, and they could also have more control over the time and place. Some said they would never have chosen baptism if the only option was a traditional service on a Sunday morning.

Internally, the church offered webinars at the national level on different themes surrounding baptism, including how a local church could communicate about this ceremony and how to use the church building and the symbols in the room as part of this communication. The church also strengthened its support for the local churches by upgrading the content linked to baptism in the national "Bank of Resources,"[22] with more illustrations, photos, templates for posters, advertisements, videos, and posts for social media content.

---

22. The Church of Norway, *Ressursbanken*, https://ressursbanken.kirken.no/nb-NO/.

COMMUNICATION AFTER THE PANDEMIC

The pandemic gave rise to new opportunities and led to greater innovation within the local church. All employees entered an unknown territory and were forced to communicate with members and meet their congregations in new ways. The lower barrier to trying out new ideas may have sometimes led to failure, but it also allowed for the opportunity to try again, which facilitated important insights and experiences, especially those linked to the importance of flexibility, bespoke offers, and targeted communication. This opened up new pathways for creativity, both in terms of how to offer a church community in a time of crisis and how to communicate and reach out to the population. These experiences proved invaluable in later years.

Before the pandemic, the church questioned the quality of an online community. It could, of course, never replace a physical service. Do you *attend* a digital service, or do you *watch* it? Are you present inside, or are you only a voyeur outside? Early on in the pandemic, we experienced the importance of interactivity, both physically and digitally. During the lockdown, it became clear that it was possible to build a feeling of a community through digital channels. It was possible to "meet" people online, and those who participated in online services wanted to tell us that they did so by sending hearts, giving a thumb-ups, or just commenting "thank you" or "I'm here." It seemed as if those members who normally very rarely attended church, to a greater extent, found more ways to be a part of a church community when it was digital. This gave way to new thinking about how the church communicates and how different campaigns should be targeted.

Being present on different channels builds trust, and this was also the case with the different campaigns that were launched. From a communication strategy point of view, the paid ads were successful, at least with respect to the number of views and clicks. The best ad had more than 3.1 million views, a response far above the benchmark for comparable marketing.[23] It was obvious that these ads should therefore be continued. The choice of digital channels has also provided new opportunities for targeted messaging. For instance, it is possible to channel social media posts on baptism toward those who are interested in baby equipment.

In addition, the new, more bespoke services were highly appreciated. There are no specific statistics, but many families who had a

---

23. Schibsted Partnerstudio, Oslo/Norway, 2020.

more tailormade baptism on a certain time and day that they preferred provided very positive feedback. On a more general level, one could say that people are more accustomed to flexible offers, have higher demands, and are not willing to accept a "one size fits all" attitude in today's society. It may be challenging to meet these expectations, but at the same time, the wish for more alternatives could be looked upon as an opportunity for the church.

A NATIONAL CAMPAIGN ON DROP-IN BAPTISM

For the first time, the Church of Norway had a national campaign on drop-in baptism from May 27 to June 10, 2023. This was well prepared and anchored within the church landscape. Over the previous few years, drop-in baptisms had become more popular, and even though communications materials to support this had been developed on a national level, marketing was conducted strictly on the local level. The idea was that a coordinated national campaign would attract more attention and give an extra push to local marketing.

The campaign was planned in extensive detail, and the results were good: 208 babies, children, teenagers, and adults were baptized in simple ceremonies around the country. The oldest was 83, and the youngest was only a few weeks old. More than 80 drop-in ceremonies were advertised in this period on the Church of Norway's "Skjer i kirken," which is a country-wide online calendar of church activities.[24] The number of drop-in offers might not seem high, and some church's experienced that no one came. The feedback from these employees as still positive, though, as the offer created news stories, and it became the "talk of the town."

The campaign's slogan "Helt enkelt, like stort," which translates into something like "Simple yet amazing," captures the essence of these ceremonies. Even though they are flexible and simple, people find them meaningful and substantial, and many congregations planned to repeat the offer.

The campaign strategy was developed and implemented by the Department of Communications, which wanted to pursue a more holistic approach. Therefore, the campaign included paid measures in different media channels as well as increased visibility in all channels, meetings, and other platforms. The strategy included the scope, clear goals, and what the church ultimately wanted to achieve. A specific strategy was

24. Skjer i kirken, www.skjerikirken.no.

developed with different measures for internal communications and media approaches, as well as a simple guide to use in the local church.

The overall goal was, of course, to increase the number of baptisms, but this was not the direct objective of the communications campaign. To truly stop the decrease, people need to know that baptism is an option. The purpose was to increase the knowledge of simpler and easier baptism ceremonies and to ensure that the church had room for everyone. There was also the goal to create more opportunities for parents or guardians who had postponed or canceled a baptism and to improve the church's reputation as inviting and inclusive. Increased visibility of the church was more important than the number of clicks, and it was this approach that influenced the choice of channels.

The main target groups were parents or guardians of children between one and six, 14–15-year-olds, and their parents/guardians. There was also a focus on young adults between 18–30 years. It was important to tell these groups that it was never too late to receive baptism. The main channels for the sponsored messages were Snapchat, TikTok, Instagram, and Facebook. The key channels overall were the church's national website www.kirken.no, the online calendar www.skjerikirken.no, and the national accounts on Facebook, Instagram, TikTok, and LinkedIn. Together, these channels reached a large number of the population, but Snapchat and TikTok were the most important in reaching the younger target groups.

The campaign consisted mainly of nationally coordinated posts and advertisements on these channels, which consisted of videos, animations, and still photos with the Church of Norway logo and short captions that were easy to read within a few seconds. A series of supporting messages and captions were developed to simplify local marketing. These focused on baptism as a tradition and a way of belonging, that it gives room for a new beginning and puts life into a greater context, and that it could be offered on weekdays with or without a celebration. Additionally, specific internal messages were developed to advise and assure employees and volunteers.

Synergies proved important. During the campaign period, a more general communication approach regarding baptism was very visible in all channels. For instance, posts about the baptism candle, which is a tradition in the church, and the newly baptized were welcomed, as were stories on what it means to be a witness. The national website focused on stories and insights into baptism. The theology of baptism was not part of the campaign, even though it was possible to find more information on this on the church website.

The core message to the media was that the church offers baptism to everyone at any time. A national press release was sent out at the end of May 2023, focusing on the when, why, and how. The local churches were also provided with templates for news stories and printed and digital advertisements. This resulted in many news stories from all over the country. Norway's main TV news program, Dagsrevyen on the national broadcasting network NRK, had a several-minute-long story on the weekend of the Pentecost, where they interviewed people who chose to participate in drop-in baptisms, a bishop, and a priest. This news story was afterwards spread on the church's social media channels (with permission from NRK), and it had a direct impact. Many said that after this news story, they checked whether their local church offered drop-in baptism. In Sagene Church in Oslo, 10 persons were baptized, eight of whom came the Sunday after the news story was aired.

In addition to the news stories, several priests and other church employees wrote articles about drop-in baptisms and the "new" offer. An example is Torkel Irgens, a priest in Rønvik in Bodø, Northern Norway, who published an article in his local paper under the title "Baptism— a blessing for life" (my translation), where he outlines that the baptism is open to everyone and describes the local drop-in opportunity.[25] This article was combined with social media posts and more physical events, including a stand in a local shopping mall and an open panel discussion on baptism. On the first Saturday in June 2023, a little boy, a three-year-old girl, and a woman of 65 were baptized. The church has since decided to offer a drop-in baptism event once every semester.

Engagement in digital media is about action, user views, clicks, or comments. In this sense, the campaign created a lot of engagement: it received 3.8 million viewings in total, and the posts had two million unique viewers on Snapchat, Instagram, and Facebook combined. An impressive 26,000 clicked on www.skjerikirken.no and looked at the drop-in baptism offers.[26] These clicks were not part of the campaign goal, but they might have had a positive effect moving forward.

The engagement on Snapchat was most impressive. Compared with the estimated coverage of the target group of young parents/guardians

---

25. Irgens, "Dåpen—en velsignelse for livet."
26. Report from Mediacom, June 2023.

(age 22–35) of 80 percent, the actual coverage reached 95 percent. This means that 526,000 unique users have seen the posts.

Drop-in baptism has been seen as more suitable for cities than the countryside. When we look at the results, we see no difference. Several city congregations had no drop-ins, while some congregations in smaller places had many.

PERSPECTIVATION: FROM ETHOS TO REPUTATION

Religion and marketing are both forms of meaning making. Religion and marketing are both parts of identity creation.[27]

As described above, there are many challenges inherent in building the credibility of a faith community through communication. This is among the many elements linked to an increasingly diverse society and people's differing expectations and demands. Despite these challenges, the classic rhetorical elements are as relevant today as they were in the times of Aristotle and Cicero.

An ethos of sympathy could be translated into a more modern expression of reputation. All companies and organizations today live by their reputations. As rhetors—or communicators—we need to have a clear communication goal in mind. Even the church must redefine its "brand" from time to time. If it does not, it becomes more difficult to be relevant. If the church cannot reach its members, there will be no one with whom to share the church's good news.

Ethos appeals may be translated into four types of communication advice.[28]

Communicate with a Simple Language and Style

It is important to analyze the situation, context, and people's needs before choosing the target group and shaping the message. Essentially, one must be aware of the values that should be highlighted, and the right language and style through which to do so.

It is vital to choose the words carefully and present the main points in a style that best suits the message. Essentially, these words need to be simple. A church's language can easily exclude more than it includes. Today, many of the religious figures of speech are meaningless to a large part

---

27. Vinther, *Omdømmehåndtering*, 13.
28. Dybvig, *Som epler av gull*, 41–43.

of the population. It might be easy for the church to use an expression like, "When you are baptized, you become a member of God's family," or, "Baptism is a gift," but these phrases might be difficult to understand for most people today. The choice of words should not require a certain level of knowledge of the Bible or Christianity.

Messages Must Be Targeted

Who is the most important target group? This is also a key question within the church. If you do not know who you are talking to, it is difficult to shape the most appropriate message and generate the impact you want. Even if the church always wanted to reach out to all, it was not possible to have everyone as the main target group at the same time. A defined target group makes it much easier to adjust the message and the choice of words, and also to choose the right channels. If the church wants to increase the number of baptisms, the target group is most likely younger parents within the age range of approximately 25–45 years. How can we get in touch with them, and which channels are the best? These questions need answers.

Communicate Consistently

The quote at the beginning of this section indicates that both religion and marketing may create meaning and build identity. For instance, trying to hide moral dilemmas or theological disputes that are unpopular within the population may lead to an understanding that the church is unreliable or deceptive. In this sense, the struggle to be seen as relevant may lead to a loss of reputation. To balance this may prove difficult, but it needs to be addressed.

A Holistic Communication Strategy Is Key

Both the digital and the more traditional rhetoric of our time will benefit from ancient *evidentia* strategies, meaning that all elements used must point in the same direction. Text, images, and other visual material must be seen as a unified entity so that they strengthen and support the same message. This holistic approach toward all the content in a campaign or on a website is also part of being consistent and building trust and reputation. For instance, using third-party stories on baptism on a website is both an important ethos strategy and an effective communication choice to build trust. There are also many good examples of how personal testimonies can support the main message.

CONCLUSION: A NEW FORM OF COMMUNICATION ON BAPTISM?

To recall, the main research question of this article was the following: could a more strategic and consistent communication approach stop the decrease in baptisms?

Several congregations have reported a cease in the decrease and even an increase in the number of baptisms. On a national level, 27,971 were baptized in the Church of Norway in 2022. This is higher than the year before, when 27,073 were baptized.[29] At the same time, the birth rate was lower in 2022, at 51,480, compared to 56,060 the year before.[30] We do not know the exact reasons for this increase. One could be the pandemic, since a larger number of those between one and three years old were baptized.[31] It could also be a stronger level of knowledge regarding baptism or simpler and more intimate ceremonies.

Unfortunately, we have no survey data that reveal whether this or other campaigns have changed the target groups' attitudes and actions. It is not possible to prove that the campaigns have actually affected the number of baptisms. Even so, we know that from a longer perspective, campaigns can change attitudes. A better understanding of the church's offerings may change attitudes, which may then lead to actions. Good campaigns remind the audience of the church, and they may lead to further discussions on baptism or other church ceremonies.

As described earlier, drop-in baptism existed before the pandemic. When the country and the churches opened their doors after the pandemic, the phenomenon had increased, but there were no specific statistics to document this. Only emergency baptisms and baptisms performed in private homes are registered, in addition to those that take place during the Sunday ceremonies. The church has only been able to know the number of drop-in baptisms by asking the congregations directly. Most baptism ceremonies are part of the traditional Sunday service, followed

---

29. Statistics Norway, Statbank Table 12026.
30. Statistics Norway, Statbank Table 06913.
31. Statistics from the Church of Norway, 2022.

by Saturdays with some peaks on other weekdays, which are mainly linked to holidays (Easter, Pentecost, and Christmas).[32]

Many would argue that the church in general has the most important message in the world. It has a 2,000-year-old tradition of communication, but this fact does not automatically make the church a good communicator today. Our times demand a clear strategy and "the right speech at the right time." With all the changes in society, the increased diversity, the huge selection of offerings, and the struggle for attention, the need for targeted communication is greater than ever before. To be able to navigate this situation, the church must know who it is communicating with. If not, it is difficult to find the most appropriate language and style, and it becomes even more challenging to find content that meets the needs of the audience. Generally, such a lack of knowledge leads to lost opportunities.

In addition, it is almost impossible to communicate efficiently without trust. To build trust, it is important to know and understand the complex rhetorical situation that the church is currently in. The rhetor (in this case, the church) needs to define its main audience among many possible audiences and be brave enough to focus on the chosen one. Trust can then be increased by finding the right language for a specific message. By doing this, an ethos of sympathy can be built.

In the past few years, the Church of Norway has developed targeted campaigns for those groups of members who do not use the church on any regular basis. There has also been a new approach toward 13–14-year-old teenagers who are planning to have their confirmation but are not baptized. Ultimately, flexibility and close cooperation are important factors in moving forward. A key factor in this field is cross-country, interdisciplinary ownership and cooperation.

The baptism is not only about the actual ceremony; it is also about the process before the ceremony. All church employees have important roles, including the person answering the phone call or email from a dad searching for information to the deacon or the priest. On a national level, the church offers a wide range of targeted and tailormade marketing material, which includes videos, ads, images, and texts, for use in different media and platforms. Ultimately, the church must continue to focus on receiver orientation, generate curiosity within its target

---

32. Statistics from The Church of Norway's register of membership, 2022.

groups, offer a wide range of opportunities, and remain available and flexible to ensure its future success.

BIBLIOGRAPHY

Aristoteles. *Retorik*. Copenhagen: Museum Tusculanum, 1991.
Bispemøtet. *Livstegnet: Et hefte om dåpen*. Oslo: Den norske kirke, 2020.
Brunvoll, Helge. *Utvikling av antall medlemmer i Den norske kirke*. Oslo: Report for the Church of Norway, 2019.
Cicero, M. T. *Om talekunst: De Oratore I-III: Tre dialogar skrivne til broren Quintus*. Oslo: Aschehoug, 2012.
Cicero, Marcus Tullius. *Retorikk og filosofi*. Oslo: Det Norske Samlaget, 1995.
Dybvig, Ingeborg. *Som epler av gull i skåler av sølv er ord som blir talt i rett tid. Kirkens bruk av ethosappeller i digital kommunikasjon for å bygge troverdighet*. Master's thesis, Aarhus Universitet/Roskilde Universitet, 2020.
Ellinggard, Stein. *Frelst i en fei?!: En kritisk undersøkelse omkring bruken av drop in-dåp i Den norske kirke fra 2015-2020*. Oslo: Den norske kirke, 2021.
Hoff-Clausen, Elisabeth: *Online Ethos. Webretorik i politiske kampagner, blogs og wikis*. Frederiksberg: Samfundslitteratur, 2008.
Irgens, Torkel. "Dåpen—en velsignelse for livet." *Avisa Nordland*, June 1, 2023.
McCroskey, James C. *An Introduction to Rhetorical Communication*. Boston: Allyn & Bacon, 2001.
Miller, Carolyn R. *Expertise and Agency. Transformations of Ethos in Human-Computer Interaction*. Raleigh: North Carolina State University, 2004.
Vinther, Ole: *Omdømmehåndtering i en kirkelig organisasjon—en studie av identitet, kommunikasjon og omdømme i Sjømannskirken*. Master oppgave i strategisk ledelse og økonomi, Tromsø: Handelshøyskolen and UIT, Norges Arktiske Universitet, 2016.
Wisse, Jakob. *Ethos and Pathos—from Aristotle to Cicero*. Amsterdam: Hakkert, 1989.

Part IV

Theology

15

The Meaning of Baptism in Our Time
Resources for a Contemporary Lutheran Baptismal Theology

HARALD HEGSTAD

THE NUMBER OF INFANT baptisms in Nordic Lutheran churches is declining. This development is not only a consequence of a growing immigrant population, with religious affiliations other than the Lutheran majority churches, but is also because a growing number of church members choose not to baptize their children. In many cases, this does not imply a rejection of baptism, but rather that the child can decide for itself when it gets older. This development and its contributing factors are thoroughly analyzed in other chapters in this book.[1]

Churches have addressed this development with various measures, including communication and marketing strategies.[2] Good communication is not just a matter of determining how a message is communicated. It also depends on what is communicated: whether the message is clear and understandable, and whether it seems convincing and plausible to the recipients. When tradition alone loses importance as an independent

---

1. See the chapters by Josepine Ganebo Skantz and Andreas Sandberg, Tore Witsø Rafoss, Karen Marie Sø Leth-Nissen, and Hanna Salomäki.

2. See the articles by Laura Hanna Kokkonen, Ingeborg Dybvig, and Lena Andersson.

reason for choosing baptism, religious and theological aspects may become even more important in this context. In this particular situation, renewed engagement with the theology of baptism has thus become a pressing issue. Therefore, churches must now ask how their inherited theologies might be interpreted in these new circumstances.

Before turning to my proposal, I will point to some aspects of a more traditional interpretation of baptismal theology that might be problematic in the present context.

BAPTISM AS A CONTROVERSIAL ISSUE

Baptism has traditionally been a controversial issue among churches and confessional traditions. This is especially the case when considering the relationship between churches that baptize infants and those that reject infant baptism. In the Nordic context, advocates of so-called "believer's baptism" are primarily represented by churches in the Baptist and Pentecostal traditions.

Disagreement regarding baptismal theology has not only been connected to when baptism is to be conducted in a person's life, but also to the understanding of what is happening in baptism. While Lutherans (together with Catholics and Orthodox) have a strong sacramental understanding, Baptists and Pentecostals have traditionally been associated with a more symbolic approach. While a sacramental understanding implies that baptism is a means of conveying the gifts of salvation, a symbolic understanding sees baptism as a confirmation or confession of what has already been given elsewhere.

One important aspect of these doctrinal differences is how the status of the unbaptized child is understood. In Lutheran theology, the concept of original sin has played an important role as an argument for why infants need to be baptized. Baptist theology has not seen this as a reason for baptizing infants, as they have understood small children to be already covered by Christ's work.

Disagreements in baptismal theology and practice have often taken a polemical form, in which churches have defended their position while criticizing the position of others. This controversial context has, in many cases, led to a certain one-sidedness in various versions of baptismal theology. Lutheran theology is no exception to this. The defense of infant baptism against Baptist criticism has led to a tendency to identify the entire practice of baptism with infant baptism. Defense of a sacramental position vis-à-vis a symbolic one has often led to a strong emphasis on what happens in the act of baptism itself, thus downplaying the process by which the event is a part. The use of original sin as an argument for the need for baptism for infants has often been interpreted as an expression of a negative and pessimistic anthropology.

In recent decades, there has been a remarkable development in ecumenical relations. This includes convergences in sacramental and baptismal theology. This development is documented in bilateral and multilateral documents, of which the Faith and Order document *Baptism, Eucharist and Ministry* from 1982 (hereafter the BEM) is the primary example. In such documents, churches strive to say as much as possible in common before moving on to issues where differences still exist. This development is not only important for inter-church relations, but should also be an impulse to reconsider more confessional doctrinal interpretations. Different understanding of baptism is not only a matter of disagreement between churches and confessional traditions but is also a reality within Lutheran churches. The widespread tendency to let children "decide for themselves" whether they want to be baptized shares some similarities with the traditional Baptist position of "believer's baptism." Furthermore, mixed marriages between Lutherans and spouses from traditions with different baptismal theologies mean that differing positions on baptismal theology and practice are also an internal matter.

A CRISIS OF PLAUSIBILITY

Traditionally, the vast majority of infants were baptized in Nordic countries. Generally, there was a common understanding that the newborn child should be baptized as soon as possible to avoid temporal and spiritual dangers. While being unbaptized used to be an anomaly, this is no longer the case. The normality of not being baptized or not having one's child baptized might be seen as a challenge to claims made regarding the difference that baptism makes. Is it really plausible for people in a pluralistic context to see unbaptized children as outside the grace of God and on their way to damnation? Is not every created person a child of God?

In its baptismal liturgy, the church makes bold claims about the gifts of baptism. Baptism is said to cleanse one from sin, save one from death, and give one the Holy Spirit. However, such a change is not easy to confirm on an empirical level. At least when understood as a radical and instantaneous transition, such claims might be too strong to be taken seriously. Furthermore, the understanding of baptism as a means of cleansing sin might seem to imply too harsh a judgment of unbaptized infants. Is this all that can be said about a child whose parents view as pure and perfect? Is the child necessarily a lost sinner who only the church is able to save through a sacramental act? In the baptismal liturgy of the Church of Norway, which was in use until 2011, the child who was about to be baptized was introduced as "born with humanity's sin and guilt."[3] In the liturgy presently in use, harsh statements like this have been replaced by affirmations of the child's value as created in the image of God, as in the following prayer: "Eternal God, you give life to all beings and have created us in your image: We thank you for NN. She/he/they is/are precious in your eyes. Keep her/him/them in your care and give her/him/them a home in your church."[4]

The latter liturgical adjustment raises fundamental questions about the relationship between creation and salvation. What does the salvation provided in baptism add to what has already been given in creation?

BAPTISM AS A SACRAMENTAL SIGN

In the following, I argue that a renewed reflection on baptism as a sacramental sign might serve as a key to resolving some of the problems mentioned above. In these reflections, I turn to important insights found in Martin Luther's baptismal theology.[5]

The understanding of baptism as a sacramental sign goes in the Western tradition back to Augustine of Hippo. For Augustine, the sacraments are understood as a piece of creation that, by the Word of God, becomes a sign of the reality of God. As a sign, the sacrament does not merely point to something absent; by the power of the Spirit, it is connected to the reality it signifies.[6]

In medieval theology, sacramental theology follows two different tracks: one that understands the sign more symbolically, and one that interprets the sign more realistically. Together, these tracks continue into reformation theology.[7] While Zwingli followed the symbolic track,

---

3. *Gudstjenestebok for Den norske kirke*, vol. 2, 18 (my translation).
4. These liturgies are available at https://ressursbanken.kirken.no/ (my translation).
5. This is further developed in Hegstad, *Dåpen*.
6. Wenz, *Einführung in die evangelische Sakramentenlehre*, 13–20; Dokka, *Som i begynnelsen*, 306.
7. Wenz, *Einführung in die evangelische Sakramentenlehre*, 20–21; Hägglund, *Teologins historia*, 134–41.

Luther positioned himself in the realistic camp. A vital difference between these positions is how the relationship between the sign and what the sign signifies is understood.

A way of framing such differences is through the semiotic theory of the American philosopher Charles S. Peirce (1839–1914), who distinguished between three categories of signs: icons, symbols, and indexes. What distinguishes these types of signs is the ways in which they are determined by the objects they denote. A sign is an icon when it shares the characteristics of the object or has a certain likeness with it. A sign is an index when it participates in the object it signifies in its individual existence. In contrast, a sign is a symbol when it is only related to the reality it signifies by habit; thus, there is no real connection between a symbol and that which it denotes.[8]

While the Zwinglian understanding clearly falls within an interpretation of the sacramental sign as a symbol, a Lutheran position might be viewed as holding the sacramental sign as an index.[9] In particular, this seems to be a reasonable interpretation of the baptismal theology of Martin Luther. For Luther, baptism is a sacrament that actually brings salvation, and not just illustrating or confirming it. In the section on baptism in Small Catechism, this is expressed in the following way:

> What gifts or benefits does baptism grant? Answer: It brings about forgiveness of sins, redeems from death and the devil, and gives eternal salvation to all who believe it, as the words and promise of God declare.[10]

This effect of baptism is thus not a result of the outer form of the sign as such, but of the sign as connected to the reality it conveys through the Word of God, which is itself connected to the sign:

> How can water do such great things? Answer: Clearly the water does not do it, but the Word of God, which is with and alongside the water, and faith, which trusts this Word of God in the water. For without the Word of God the water is plain water and not a baptism, but with the Word of God it is a baptism, that is, a

---

8. Peirce, *Peirce on Signs*, 251–52.

9. Andrew Robinson also argues for understanding sacraments in the Peircian sense of an index, as "a sign that actualizes what it signifies, *where what it signifies is the gift of participation in the divine life.*" See Robinson, *Traces of the Trinity*, 71. His use of this insight does, however, follow different paths than those presented in the present article.

10. Kolb and Wengert, *Book of Concord*, 359.

grace-filled water of life and a "bath of the new birth in the Holy Spirit," as St. Paul says to Titus in chapter 3 . . .[11]

Here, Luther clearly presupposes Augustin's definition of a sacrament, which he also quotes in a passage in the Large Catechism:

> Therefore it is not simply a natural water, but a divine, heavenly, holy, and blessed water—praise it in any other terms you can—all by virtue of the Word, which is a heavenly, holy Word that no one can sufficiently extol, for it contains and conveys all that is God's. This, too, is where it derives its nature so that it is called a sacrament, as St. Augustine taught, "Accedat verbum ad elementum et fit sacramentum," which means that "when the Word is added to the element or the natural substance, it becomes a sacrament," that is, a holy, divine thing and sign.[12]

As a sacramental sign, baptism takes part in the gifts of salvation as an effective sign. This happens in a real, but not a complete, sense. As a sign, it is also a promise of something that has yet to be fulfilled. As such, baptism may be understood as both an event and a process. This becomes evident in Luther's emphasis on baptism's role in the life of the baptized:

> What then is the significance of such a baptism with water? Answer: It signifies that the old creature in us with all sins and evil desires is to be drowned and die through daily contrition and repentance, and on the other hand, that daily a new person is to come forth and rise up to live before God in righteousness and purity forever.[13]

Thus, baptism not only signifies what is given in the event of baptism, but also the lifelong sanctification of the baptized and, finally, the resurrection of the dead. The realization of the promise is in this life always anticipatory and thus waiting for its eschatological fulfillment. As Luther says in "The Babylonian Captivity of the Church":

> Here again you see that the sacrament of baptism, even with respect to its sign, is not a matter of the moment, but something permanent. Although the ceremony itself is soon over

---

11. Kolb and Wengert, *Book of Concord*, 359.

12. "Fourth Part: Concerning Baptism"; 17–18. Kolb and Wengert, *Book of Concord*, 458.

13. Small Catechism from "The Sacrament of Holy Baptism," Kolb and Wengert, *Book of Concord*, 360.

the thing it signifies continues until we die, yes, even until we rise on the last day.[14]

In this way, it can be said that "the eschatological righteousness is sacramentally present in baptism."[15]

Understanding baptism as both an event and a process for Luther leads to his rejection of the idea that other acts interpreted as sacraments might add something to what has already been given in baptism. Confirmation, penance, and ordination are the same in that they do not contain any extra spiritual quality. A Christian never needs anything more than baptism, but only to return to baptism and make use of the gifts already received there. Repentance is, therefore, not something that replaces baptism, but instead represents a return, as there "is nothing else than a return and approach to baptism, resume, and practice what has earlier been begun but abandoned."[16]

Understanding baptism as an effective sign also means that it is understood as a *promise*—a promise whose fulfillment has already begun but awaits its final realization. As a promise, it invites belief. In faith, the gifts of baptism are received, and as Luther writes, "Thus it is not baptism that justifies or benefits anyone, but it is faith in that word of promise to which baptism is added."[17] This does not mean that faith might replace baptism or make baptism superfluous. On the contrary, "faith must have something to believe—something to which it may cling and upon which it may stand."[18]

While Luther's understanding of the baptismal sign clearly falls within Peirce's category of the sign as an index, he is also concerned with baptism being construed as an icon. This is expressed in Luther's insistence on immersion as the ideal way of performing baptism. For baptism to function as a sign, its outer form has to come as close as possible to the reality it signifies. Thus, through immersion, baptism becomes an iconic sign of being buried and resurrected by Christ (cf.

---

14. Luther, *Luther's Works*, vol. 36, 69.

15. Josefson, *Luthers lära om dopet*, 61; "Den eskatologiska rättfärdigheten är sakramentalt närvarande i dopet" (my translation).

16. Large Cathecism, "Fourth Part: Concerning Baptism," 79; Kolb and Wengert, *Book of Concord*, 466.

17. Luther, *Luther's Works*, vol. 36, 66.

18. Large Cathecism, "Fourth Part: Concerning Baptism," 29; Kolb and Wengert, *Book of Concord*, 460.

Romans 6). The closer the performance of the sign comes to the reality it signifies, the more clearly the sign speaks.[19]

FROM POLEMICS TO CONVERGENCE

While Luther's theology of baptism is quite dynamic and includes a conceptualization of baptism as both an event and a process, this is not the case in Article 9 on baptism in the Augsburg Confession. Here, the confession simply states that baptism "is necessary for salvation, that the grace of God is offered through baptism, and that children should be baptized." In addition, the Anabaptist view that "children are saved without baptism" is condemned.[20]

The focus here is on baptism as an event. This does not, of course, exclude the process perspective, even though it is not explicitly mentioned. At the same time, it might be assumed that this focus has contributed to a certain one-sidedness in later Lutheran baptismal theology. In the polemics against Baptist theology, baptism's character as conveying salvation in the act of baptism has been stressed in a way that has downplayed the processual element and thus also the understanding of baptism as a sign.

An example of this rather one-sided understanding of baptism as an event can be found in a booklet by the Norwegian theologian Leiv Aalen (1906–1983). According to Aalen, a basic problem with the Baptist position is its view that God may give salvation through the Word independently of baptism. In Aalen's view, baptism is an exclusive means of salvation, which implies a rejection of the possibility of taking part in salvation before baptism or independently of it. Faith before baptism is thus not a saving faith, but only a faith *seeking* salvation. Since the salvation given in the event of baptism is complete, all that is needed after baptism is for the baptized to *make use* of the gifts already given. Here, it seems that God's work is primarily located in the event of baptism. In contrast, what happens before and after the event is interpreted as humans' preparations for and response to this event.[21]

---

19. This is further developed in Dokka, *Som i begynnelsen*, 137–38.
20. Kolb and Wengert, *Book of Concord*, 43.
21. Aalen, *Dåpen og barnet*. In spite of this strong emphasis on the event of baptism, Aalen does not draw the conclusion that unbaptized children cannot be saved. More details on Aalen's position can be found in Hegstad, "Dåpen som hendelse og prosess," 187–88.

Aalen's interpretation of baptism as primarily an event appears in an ecumenical context as a rather extreme one-sidedness. This corresponds to the polemical context vis-à-vis Baptist theology, in which Aalen's understanding is developed. In my view, an understanding of the baptismal sign, which also includes a process perspective, is easier to fit into an ecumenical conversation.

This becomes apparent when considering the BEM document. Here, baptism is referred to as "the sign of a new life through Jesus Christ." According to the BEM, baptism allows for participation in salvation and also points to the continued life of the believer, as well as eschatological fulfillment in the kingdom of God. On the one hand, baptism "initiates the reality of the new life given in the midst of the present world" and "gives participation in the community of the Holy Spirit." On the other, it "is related not only to momentary experience, but to lifelong growth into Christ," and "it is a sign of the Kingdom of God and of the life of the world to come."[22]

Even if the term sacrament does not play a central role in the BEM, it is fair to say that the document still reflects a sacramental understanding of baptism as an effective sign that conveys salvation. This position might be seen as a reflection of the development from a purely symbolic to a more sacramental understanding of baptism in many traditions. The most remarkable has been the attempt by Baptist theologians to recover a "Baptist sacramentalism." According to one of the proponents of this view, "Baptism is a sacrament; it is a means of grace; it is a human event through which a divine act is promised to occur."[23] Such an understanding of baptism as an act of God has also made it easier for Baptists to accept the validity of infant baptisms.[24]

A similar development from a symbolic to a sacramental understanding of baptism might be found in Methodist theology. In the document "By Water and the Spirit" from the United Methodist Church, the concept of the sign is used to interpret baptism and eucharist as acts of God: "United Methodists believe that these sign-acts are special means of grace. The ritual action of a sacrament does not merely point to God's

---

22. BEM par. 2, 7, 9, and 18.

23. Colwell, *Promise and Presence*, 133. Cf. Cross and Thompson, *Baptist Sacramentalism*, 2.

24. Cf. Terje Hegertun's article in this volume.

presence in the world, but also participates in it and becomes a vehicle for conveying that reality."[25]

A similar understanding of baptism as a sign was also an important factor behind the agreement between the Church of Norway and the Methodist Church in Norway. In the document "Nådens fellesskap" ("Community of Grace") from 1994, the view that baptism is an effective sign is used as a key to the understanding of baptism. Here, baptism is understood as an "effective sign," meaning it is a ritual act conveying community with the Triune God. God's act in baptism is not isolated from the baptismal event, but is rather continued throughout the whole life of the baptized. An interesting aspect of this document is that it not only discusses what God does after baptism, but also before. For the Methodists, this is linked to the idea of prevenient grace, while Lutherans interpret this variation within the framework of the theology of creation. However, both agree that God graciously relates to humans before baptism.[26]

Against this background, it is worth noting that the Norwegian bishops' meeting in a theological document on baptism, orients their understanding from the concept of the sign, an approach that is reflected in the title "Sign of Life" (Norwegian: "Livstegnet"). Here, baptism is interpreted as an effective sign, which gives way to that which it signifies. At the same time, baptism is a promise that points toward its final fulfillment in the future. This is also how the bishops explain the discrepancy between the liturgical claim that baptism frees one from sin and death and the empirical reality of living in a world marked by sin and death. Even if salvation is given in an anticipatory way in baptism, it still awaits final fulfillment.[27]

BAPTISM AND THEOLOGY OF CREATION

Developing an understanding of baptism as sign is not only fruitful for an ecumenical convergence on the meaning of baptism, but also for resolving some of the plausibility problems related to baptism in today's Nordic context that are described above.

---

25. "By Water and the Spirit: A United Methodist Understanding of Baptism," par. 21.

26. *Nådens fellesskap*.

27. Bispemøtet, *Livstegnet*, especially par. 2 and 3.

An important question to consider is the content of the theology and liturgy of baptism that is implicitly or explicitly communicated regarding the unbaptized and life before baptism. The traditional justification of infant baptism by means of the doctrine of original sin might lead to the impression that baptism is based on a completely negative picture of humans before baptism. Such an understanding does not sufficiently take into account the notion that all humans are created by God, and that their value as created in the image of God is primary to any effect sin and evil might have on their life. The theological basis of baptism must include the theology of creation. The primary reason for baptism is not human sinfulness, but rather human createdness. In baptism, God's love for both humanity and the individual human is confirmed. What happens in baptism stands in continuity with what God has already done in the life of the person being baptized. This includes the gift of life itself, as well as all good things that have happened to the person. These works also refer to the process that has brought the person to baptism. Whether this is called prevenient grace or God's creative work, these acts are all performed by the same God, who acts in baptism.

Understanding baptism as a sign might, from this perspective, mean that it not only points to what happens after baptism, but also to what has occurred before. Baptism is thus a sign of God's creative activity and salvific will, not only for the person baptized, but for all of humanity. It is a sign that God wants the best for all of God's creation. In one of his hymns, the Norwegian hymn writer Svein Ellingsen makes an interesting connection between baptism and the sign of the rainbow, which, according to Genesis 9, was a sign that God would not destroy the earth again, as "the water of baptism reflects the covenant of the rainbow."[28]

This also has consequences for how we interpret the salvation given in baptism, as well as the relationship between creation and redemption. Salvation does not entail the replacement of creation, but rather the fulfillment of creation and the freeing from everything that destroys it. Salvation is thus not about becoming anything else but human; on the contrary, it means realizing one's authentic humanity. This is expressed in the Christological basis of baptism, insofar as being baptized is to be united with Jesus, the true human. That salvation does not replace creation does not mean that salvation is not needed. God's good creation is

---

28. "Dåpsvannet gjenspeiler regnbuens pakt" (my translation), *Norsk salmebok 2013*, no. 209. The link between baptism and the flood in the times of Noah is found in 1 Peter 3:20–21.

threatened and distorted by sin, suffering, death, and separation from the creator. This is not just a theological proposition, but part of our daily experience. For people who live their lives in a world marked by evil and destruction, baptism is a sign of God's loving intentions for the world's future. The sign of baptism thus does not only take the form of a general promise, but is rather applied to the individual who is baptized. In baptism, the baptismal candidate is addressed by his or her individual name, and God confirms God's love for the individual person and gives a promise of salvation to that specific individual.

The link between baptism and creation also connects baptism to life in general, and not just in terms of the "religious" aspects. Besides being a sacrament, baptism has traditionally played the role of a *rite de passage* in families and societies. Often, families have chosen baptism not primarily because of the religious content, but rather because it has been seen as a valuable tradition. There are also various ideas and practices connected to baptism that are not based on strict doctrinal ideas, such as the interpretation of baptism as a name-giving ceremony.

Churches have often expressed a critical attitude toward such ideas and practices, insisting instead on the priority of a "correct" theological interpretation. However, these different perspectives should be understood as complementary rather than conflicting. Rather than attempting to "correct" popular interpretations and practices, the church should include these contributions when constructing its theological framework of communication.

A SACRAMENT OF HOPE

Baptismal liturgies include bold statements, including those stipulating that God frees us from the power of sin and death. Such declarations are, of course, difficult to confirm through experience. In this sense, the baptized person is as vulnerable to sin and death as before. However, as a sign, baptism not only speaks about the present, but also about the future. It thus inaugurates a process that continues throughout life until its eschatological future.

This means that baptism is a sacrament of *hope*. As such, it points to God's faithfulness in the present and in the future, even in the face of death. "The light of baptism endures beyond life's end," says Svein Ellingsen, in a popular baptismal hymn.[29] This correspondence is expressed in

29. "Dåpens lys forblir når livet slukner" (my translation), *Norsk salmebok 2013*,

the reading of 1 Peter 1:3 in both the baptismal and funeral liturgies of the Church of Norway: "Blessed be the God and Father of our Lord Jesus Christ! By his great mercy he has given us a new birth into a living hope through the resurrection of Jesus Christ from the dead."[30]

As a sign pointing forward, baptism points to the continued life of the baptized. What is given in baptism has to be received in faith and lived out in daily life. For persons baptized as infants, this means being introduced to the practices and beliefs of the faith into which one has been baptized. Baptism also entails the challenge and authorization of service in the church and society.

Understanding baptism as a process does not devaluate baptism as an event. Even if it is part of a process, it is still the turning point and event that the baptized always return to when seeking to identify their hope and faith.

SALVATION AS GOD'S WORK

Understanding baptism as a sign means that it is a sign of God's saving activity. It is not baptism that saves; rather, it is God. Baptism is a tool that God is using to transmit God's grace to humans, and it is given by the church to bring this grace close to people. When the Augsburg Confession states that baptism is "necessary for salvation," this should be interpreted as a necessity for the church, not for God. While the church has to baptize its members to remain true to God's calling, God is free to convey grace in whatever way God chooses.[31]

This has consequences for how we see the relationship between baptized and unbaptized persons. Believing that God, in a special way, has given grace to those who have been baptized should not be followed up with negative statements about those who have not been baptized. We do not have any certain information regarding their actual relationship with God or their eternal destiny. What we do know is that God loves all people and has gracious intentions for everyone, independent of status and beliefs (cf. 2 Tim 2:4). The special promise of salvation given in baptism does not invalidate these general intentions.

---

no. 586.

30. Bible quotations are from the New Revised Standard Version.

31. This necessity has been characterized by Kirsi Stjerna as a "good necessity." See Stjerna, "Seeking Hospitable Discourse on the Sacrament of Baptism," 95–96.

PART IV: THEOLOGY

A SIGN OF UNITY

An important aspect of baptism is its role as an inclusion into the church. This is not just inclusion in an organization, but into the church as the body of Christ. This means that all who are baptized are baptized into the same body of Christ and, ultimately, into the same church. There is only "one baptism," as Paul states in Ephesians 4:5. Baptism is thus a sign of the unity of the church. As with other gifts delivered in baptism, this is given at that time but not fully realized. Baptism thus implies a challenge to churches in making this unity visible. It is a tragic reality that conflicts regarding baptismal theology and practice have often been a source of division among Christians. Mutual recognition of other churches' baptisms and convergence in baptismal theology is therefore, in itself, an essential tool for Christian unity. Rather than being a sign of division, churches should strive to make baptism a sign of unity.

Baptism's role as inclusion into the church is the element that most clearly differentiates between baptized and non-baptized. As a community, the church is distinguished from other religious entities or from those who do not belong to any religion. Nevertheless, the church is part of humanity and committed to its unity. This unity is given in our common dignity, as created in the image of God and in the eschatological redemption of the world. Faith in this future obliges the church to work for unity in the present world. As a sign of the eschatological future, baptism points toward the unity of all humanity, when God is "all in all" (1 Cor 15:28). As such, the church is the first fruit of redeemed humanity, and baptism is thus a sign of that redemption.

BIBLIOGRAPHY

Aalen, Leiv. *Dåpen og barnet: Barnedåp eller "troendes dåp"?* Oslo: Lutherstiftelsen, 1945.
Bispemøtet. *Livstegnet: Et hefte om dåpen.* Den norske kirke, 2020.
"By Water and the Spirit: A United Methodist Understanding of Baptism." The United Methodist Church, 1996.
Colwell, John E. *Promise and Presence: An Exploration of Sacramental Theology.* Milton Keynes, UK: Paternoster, 2005.
Cross, Anthony R., and Philip E. Thompson. *Baptist Sacramentalism 2.* Milton Keynes, UK: Paternoster, 2008.
Dokka, Trond Skard. *Som i begynnelsen: Innføring i kristen tro og tanke.* Oslo: Gyldendal akademisk, 2000.
Gudstjenestebok for Den norske kirke. Bd. 1-2. Oslo: Verbum, 1992.
Hägglund, Bengt. *Teologins historia: En dogmhistorisk översikt.* 5. upplagan. Lund: Liber, 1981.

Hegstad, Harald. *Dåpen: En nådens kilde.* Oslo: Verbum akademisk, 2019.
———. "Dåpen som hendelse og prosess." *Teologisk Tidsskrift* 5.3 (2017) 176–94. https://doi.org/10.18261/issn.1893-0271-2017-03-02.
Josefson, Ruben. *Luthers lära om dopet.* Stockholm: Svenska Kyrkans Diakonistyrelses Bokförlag, 1944.
Kolb, Robert, and Timothy J. Wengert, eds. *The Book of Concord: The Confessions of the Evangelical Lutheran Church.* Minneapolis: Fortress, 2000.
Luther, Martin. *Luther's Works.* Vol. 36. Philadelphia: Fortress, 1959.
Nådens fellesskap: Rapport fra samtalen mellom Metodistkirken i Norge og Den norske kirke. Oslo, 1994.
Norsk salmebok 2013. Stavanger: Eide, 2013.
Peirce, Charles S. *Peirce on Signs: Writings on Semiotic.* Chapel Hill: University of North Carolina, 1991.
Robinson, Andrew. *Traces of the Trinity: Signs, Sacraments and Sharing God's Life.* Cambridge: James Clarke, 2014.
Stjerna, Kirsi. "Seeking Hospitable Discourse on the Sacrament of Baptism." *Dialog: A Journal of Theology* 53 (2014) 92–100.
Wenz, Gunther. *Einführung in die evangelische Sakramentenlehre.* Darmstadt: Wissenschaftliche Buchgesellschaft, 1988.
World Council of Churches. *Baptism, Eucharist and Ministry.* Faith and Order Paper 111. Geneva: World Council of Churches, 1982.

16

"I Consecrate You, Water"
Arctic Baptismal Practices and Indigeneity under Climate Change

Sigríður Guðmarsdóttir

THE OLDEST LAW BOOK in Iceland, *Grágás* (which spans the ninth to the thirteenth centuries), contains instructions for an emergency baptism when traveling with a sick child.[1] The guidelines consist of three general directions, all of which are important to this chapter. First, while fresh water would have been preferred for the baptism, according to *Grágás*, it was also possible to baptize in the ocean or even in snow. Second, the individual performing the baptism of the child was expected to engage in a baptismal exorcism by marking crosses into the snow three times, one for each person of the Trinity. Finally, the person baptizing was to address the water itself: "I consecrate you, water" (Icelandic: *Eg vígi þig, vatn*).[2] The ancient practices of talking to water in the liturgy and making a cross in the snow vanished from later canon law. *Kristinréttur*, the Christian canon law of the thirteenth century, makes a special note of telling people that moisture, ice, and snow do not themselves make a baptism, unless the snow or ice was melted beforehand into water.[3] In this chapter, the Icelan-

---

1. Finsen, *Grágás*, 5; Dennis et al., *Grágás*, 25.
2. Finsen, *Grágás*, 5.
3. Bernharðsson et al., *Járnsíða og Kristinréttur*, 145.

dic memory of snow crosses and sea baptisms functions as a cosmological metaphor for the sacredness of the stable form of water. The glaciers and sea ice that cover a good portion of the Arctic can be honored, fought for, and remembered for its significance. After all, they are rapidly vanishing from our world—like the church ritual from *Grágás*.

Our time is one of various human-made environmental crises, and these long-term climate changes are significantly affecting the water systems. Glaciers are melting in the circumpolar regions, as well as the Himalayas. Gas emissions are causing sea levels to rise, which in turn leads to storms and the disappearance of sandy beaches and islands, which may eventually fall underwater. In other places, the scarcity of water has led to intense droughts and forest fires, displacement, poverty, health issues, and the loss of biodiversity. The poet Andri Snær Magnason has reflected on the melting ice of the Arctic region during climate change from an Icelandic perspective, expressing how "Glaciers are frozen manuscripts that tell stories just like tree circles and sedimentary deposits; from them, you can gather information and create a picture of the past."[4] Magnason has constructed his own metaphor of the glacial manuscripts that resembles the ancient manuscripts of the Icelanders, which contain an important part of the history of the Nordic people. Accordingly, Magnason asks us to read these glacial texts as sites of cultural memory, through which it is possible to make meaning of past experiences, as well as our present circumstances, under climate change. The vanishing glaciers, in Magnason's view, are places to which we belong and relate as species. Magnason writes:

> When it comes to discussing issues that affect all water on Earth, all of Earth's surface, the planet's entire atmosphere, the issue's enormity absorbs all meaning. The only way to write about the subject is to go past it, to the side, below it, into the past and the future, to be personal and also scientific, and to use mythological language. I need to write about things by *not* writing about them. I need to go backward to move forward.[5]

Water is the indispensable natural element of baptism. Can baptismal practices thus be viewed as "a glacial manuscript," or a code in water? If Magnason is right, and we need to connect to our local and personal pasts to understand the future, how does this search for meaning impact

---

4. Magnason, *On Time and Water*, 179.
5. Magnason, *On Time and Water*, 10.

practical and liturgical theology? How can baptismal practices speak to meaning making in the context of climate change? Can baptismal practices function as a liberating praxis?

What happens in the Arctic affects the entire world. Its impact is heavily experienced by Indigenous peoples who rely on semi-domesticated animals, fisheries, and other livelihoods intricately linked to wildlife and climate, such as Inuits and Sámi reindeer herders. When presenting Nordic eco-theological questions in the Arctic context, the focus is on those parts of the region that are located closest to the glacial meltdown—and not only the sovereign states that usually have their centers of power located further south. By turning the geographical focus toward the Arctic north, two interesting themes emerge. The first is the growing sense of intercultural indigeneity, whereby the Sámi and Inuit cultures become more visible than in other parts of the Nordic countries.[6] The second refers to the process through which, while thinking eco-theologically about baptismal practices in the Arctic (and elsewhere), one remains attentive to the wounds of colonialism. The Arctic speaks to us about the general impact of colonialism, and the need to decolonize old and new histories of oppression is emerging with a new force now, while Truth and Reconciliation committees (TRC) continue to investigate colonial policies and injustices against the Sámi people in Norway, Sweden, and Finland.[7] Given the complicity that majority churches in Nordic countries have shown with respect to colonial projects, learning about the hard truths of the colonial exploitation of Indigenous people and minorities in the Arctic should lead to some kind of theological reckoning from the churches for these groups.[8] Given that climate change has disproportionally high impact on the lives of Indigenous peoples, theological statements on the environment need to take indigeneity into consideration. When it comes to baptism in Nordic countries, what would such a decolonization of baptism look like?

---

6. In this chapter, I write "Indigenous" with a capital I when referring to specific peoples and their cultures and languages, who have suffered colonial settlement and had their own cultures and languages suppressed. See the definition in the UN Declaration on the Rights of Indigenous Peoples, from 2007. What counts as Arctic is debatable, but in this chapter, I use the definition of the Arctic Monitoring and Assessment Program (AMAP) of the Arctic Council from 1998. See Inuuteq Holm Olsen, "Greenland, the Arctic," 82–83.

7. Johnsen, "Negotiating the Meaning of 'TRC,'" 19–40.

8. Sjöberg and Sara, "When justice," 107–21.

The chapter comprises three sections, each of which is framed by the ancient prescriptions for emergency baptism, according to *Grágás*. The first section of the chapter discusses baptism as an ecological source from the perspectives of international liturgical and ecological theology. Indigenous baptismal practices from Sápmi inform the two remaining sections and guide the way in which I reconsider the baptismal traditions of my native culture in Iceland. While the second section explores the practices of the baptismal sign of the cross, the third focuses on the tradition of the sacred springs.

ECO-THEOLOGICAL PERSPECTIVES

I have pointed out elsewhere that a sacramental understanding of water can go hand in hand with contemporary concerns regarding water scarcity and water pollution.[9] My conclusion there was that the rigorous abstraction of turning water into spiritual water often resulted in disdain for the water in the waterworks and the town supply. Thus, when baptismal theologies turn their attention to water as such (or the lack thereof), theology becomes political, and baptismal waters become an issue of social justice.[10] In this chapter, I continue these eco-theological explorations into liturgical theology, but from an Arctic standpoint.

As Magnason reminds us, climate change is happening disproportionally quickly in the Arctic with the meltdown of glaciers and sea ice. Magnason's metaphor traces the interconnections between the textual histories and the landscapes that shape us as people of a particular place. Theologians are gradually becoming aware of the importance of learning from the wisdom, stories, and sustainable practices of Indigenous peoples to address such challenges.[11] Theologian Mary Elizabeth Moore has pointed out the ambiguity associated with Western people turning to Indigenous groups for guidance in light of the colonial trauma afflicted on Indigenous people and asks, "How can people in non-indigenous cultures value and learn from indigenous people? The challenges of those traditions to most Western worldviews are so vital that we need to find ways to learn without objectifying and to collaborate without dominating or colonizing."[12]

---

9. Guðmarsdóttir, "Water as Sacrament," 110–17.
10. Guðmarsdóttir, "Water as Sacrament," 7.
11. Moore, "Responding," 13–14.
12. Moore, "Responding," 13.

Fighting for the preservation of sacred waters is a part of Indigenous struggles for land and water worldwide. Glossing over colonial history only deepens the historical and intergenerational trauma. Thus, baptismal waters convey an ambiguous heritage, wherein coerced baptism and missionary activities have too often gone hand in hand with political, economic, and extractive purposes. Given the trauma of colonialization, of which Moore reminds us, it is important not only to recognize the importance of Indigenous worldviews to ecological thinking, but also to reflect further on the colonial projects of extraction. Christian identity construction through baptism has come at a great cost, resulting in the loss of Indigenous land, autonomy, and culture. Moore's answer to her own question of ambiguity is to quote Indigenous writers, such as the botanist Robin Wall Kimmerer, at length in her chapter, and try to listen carefully to Indigenous perspectives, instead of extracting value from them and the land to which they belong.[13] In a similar vein, Kimmerer speaks about the importance of paying close attention to living on ancestral lands with life forms other than the human. She speaks about the mystery of becoming attentive to a river, realizing that it has been in this bed for a long time, and listening to the sounds of water. She wonders if one could ever know a river. Instead, she suggests that it would be helpful to focus on the drops.[14]

In the spirit of Kimmerer, I would like to point to baptismal practices in the Arctic that underscore living, running water, and the relationship between baptism and creation. Somehow, we need to learn to be more attentive to water. From the perspective of Fennoscandia, the historian Solveig Wang explains how indigeneity does not necessarily follow an argument regarding who was first to a country. Rather, it centers on the power balance in interactions between different ethnic groups in each place.[15] While all the Nordic countries have strong historical roots in the Lutheran traditions through national majority churches, the view from the Arctic may allow for alternative ways of portraying baptismal practices than the one that emerges from the Nordic south. My native country, Iceland, is the only Nordic (and Arctic) country that does not have an Indigenous population, but which was settled in the ninth century AD by people of Norse, Celtic, and Sámi

---

13. Moore, "Responding," 14.
14. Kimmerer, *Braiding Sweetgrass*, 298.
15. Wang, *Decolonising Medieval Fennoscandia*, 5.

origin and later colonialized by Denmark-Norway.[16] By placing my discourse on baptismal practices in the Arctic, I am thinking about the cultural memories of different peoples, while simultaneously recognizing the difference between my own Icelandic roots and the Indigenous trauma of the Sámi and Inuits, which is not my own.

The theologian Cláudio Carvalhaes (who has Brazilian and Indigenous roots) has argued that "[b]aptism is not only and solely a function of the church, not only the liturgy confirming the gospel, but a connected symbol to the sacred wisdom of the whole life of the community."[17] Carvalhaes describes an experience from a community in the Nogales desert in Mexico, in which the communal pool would have three functions: a water reservoir, a baptismal font, and the community's swimming pool. For Carvalhaes, baptism plays a double role in establishing both unity and division. He portrays baptismal practices as the unity of Christian identity in cosmic and sacramental relations with the earth as *imago dei*. Likewise, he argues that baptismal practices disrupt structural sins. Baptism, seen as a possibility to break from old habits of exploiting the earth, should thus become a focal point from which Christian people address issues of social justice.[18]

Is baptismal water extra (i.e., exceptionally) ordinary or extraordinary? As Carvalhaes focuses on the baptism that unites people in preserving the earth, the theologian Harald Hegstad writes about the double character of baptism as an event and as a process.[19] Hegstad discusses Luther's teachings on the sacramental sign of baptism and argues that the interpretation of the sign is present in both modes (i.e., as an event as well as a process).[20] Hegstad argues that Lutheranism has too often focused too strongly on the event of baptism and neglected the ongoing life in the Spirit given at baptism—that is, what happens before and after baptism.[21] Hegstad argues that there is a convergence between the Methodist sensibility regarding baptismal life and the way in which creation theologies have been developed in Lutheranism.[22] When these two perspectives, consisting of Carvalhaes's insistence on baptismal practices

16. Pálsson, *Úr landnorðri*.
17. Carvalhaes, *What's Worship?* 48.
18. Carvalhaes, *What's Worship?* 49, 54.
19. Harald Hegstad, "Dåpen," 176–94.
20. Hegstad, "Dåpen," 190.
21. Hegstad, "Dåpen," 191.
22. Hegstad, "Dåpen," 192–93.

being understood as unifiers and disrupters of oppressive structures and Hegstad's interpretation of the sacramental sign of baptism as an event and process, are posed next to one another, the communal and creational aspects of baptismal practices emerge. If one interprets baptism not only as an historical event in the life of the believer, but also as the continuation of a life-long process, one might ask when that process starts. Is it at the event of baptism itself? May we envision the systems of snow, glaciers, oceans, and running waters from which the baptismal water emerges as a part of the baptismal process?

THE SIGN OF THE CROSS AS A PROCESS AND DIALOGUE WITH NATURE

The baptismal ritual in Grágás entailed making the sign of the cross in the snow. Using examples from Sápmi and Iceland, in this section, I interpret the practices of making the sign of the cross as a dialogue with the nonhuman world, and as such, a part of a life-long process that has deep connections to baptism. Making the sign of the cross has been an important part of baptismal liturgy since the early third century. In the *Apostolic Tradition*, one of the oldest Christian liturgies preserved today, the preparation for baptism would happen on the day before baptism, when the bishop would ask the baptismal candidate to renounce evil and afterwards breathe through their nostrils and make the sign of the cross.[23] Christians in patristic times used the cross outside the formal liturgy for protection and blessing of the food, especially the bread.[24] The church fathers would exhort people to make the sign of the cross frequently on their own foreheads and integrate the practice into their everyday lives as a continuation of the ritual blessing in the baptismal liturgies.[25] Moving from ancient Mediterranean church history to the Medieval Arctic, making the sign of the cross was called *signing* in Icelandic and *velsigning* in Norwegian. Signing was a prescribed ordinary ritual in medieval times. Every person was supposed to make the cross on their foreheads upon waking up and before eating and drinking. One would then "walk every day, armed by the sign of the holy cross."[26] Icelanders would also make use of breastplate prayers (lat. *lorica*) during

---

23. Bradshaw, "The Gospel," 144–46.
24. Lupton, "The Sign," 99–110.
25. Lupton, "The Sign," 101.
26. "Jóns saga," 208–9.

the Middle Ages and are the only Nordic nation to have integrated this Celtic tradition into their religious practices.[27]

The Sámi historian Siv Rasmussen has pointed out that the seventeenth-century Protestants who came to Sápmi made a special note of how often Sámi people crossed themselves.[28] The theologian Lovisa Mienna Sjöberg has discussed the religious customs of ordinary life that are in North Sámi called *sivdnidit*, which translates as both "to create" and "to bless."[29] Sjöberg decided to describe these customs as "religious praxis" and argues that focusing on praxis rather than dogmatic systems helps to destabilize the dichotomy between nature and culture and between primitive and civilized religion.[30] For Sjöberg, categorizing *sivdnidit* as praxis rather than religion also serves to account for those practices that are a part of a Christian worldview, but not exclusively so.[31] According to Sjöberg, *sivdnidit* is an important component of Sámi rituals and a part of Sámi baptismal education for protection and comfort in difficult circumstances.[32]

The Sámi politician and author Karen Marie Eira Buljo described similar Sámi traditions of making the sign of the cross on the child before leaving it to sleep, as well as putting the Gospel of John or a page from the hymnal into *komsa* (North Sámi: portable cradle) for protection.[33] The Sámi theologian Tore Johnsen characterized the sacramentality of nature in Sámi spirituality and argued that *luonddu láhjit* in North Sámi (North Sámi: the gifts of nature) and *Ipmila láhjit* (North Sámi: the gifts of God) are used synonymously for the sustainable practices of receiving food from nature, fish, reindeer, and berries. Johnsen maintains that blessing by the sign of the cross was also practiced as a ritual for felling a tree or catching a ptarmigan.[34] Johnsen recites the story of a reindeer herder who learned *sivdnidit* from his parents, and that every time he slaughtered a reindeer, he should cut the antlers and do the sign of the cross three times for each person of the Trinity.[35] When asked, the herder said that this

27. Óskarsdóttir and Ingólfsson, "Dýrlingar," 119–21.
28. Rasmussen, "Samisk integrering," 203–4.
29. Sjöberg, "Att leva," 7.
30. Sjöberg, "Att leva," 15–16.
31. Sjöberg, "Att leva," 15–17.
32. Sjöberg, "Att leva," 101.
33. Buljo, "Samiske skikker," 30.
34. Johnsen, *Jordens barn*, 22–24.
35. Johnsen, *Sámi luondduteologiija*, 19–20.

was how he was taught to give thanks for the gift of meat as a blessing for the reindeer and for the future well-being of the flock. This sacramental understanding of the gifts of nature is therefore vastly different from the colonial resource politics of extraction.

Icelanders also used the sign of the cross for protection. According to nineteenth-century ethnographic sources, making the sign of the cross over the cradle of unbaptized children was common, because these individuals were considered to be in special danger from the hidden people, who could exchange human babies for their own.[36] The practice of crossing oneself before putting on a clean shirt is known to this day. Women would bless the sheep after milking them, and it was customary to make the sign of the cross on the door of the sheepcote before closing the door of the house in the evening.[37] Icelanders were known to cross-cut the heart when slaughtering livestock at home and cut a cross into the liver, as well as make the sign of the cross on the blood-catching trough before slaughtering the animal.[38] The trough gathered the blood for the blood pudding, which is still a stable part of the diet. They would then make the sign of the cross on all doors in the evening and on the fire in the open stone fireplace, as well as over the water spring outside.[39]

Icelanders and Sámi people have both linked the sign of the cross to food practices. Thus, Sámi and Icelandic religious praxis functions in a Christian framework as ritual expressions for blessing, protecting, comforting, establishing relations, and giving thanks to God and creation.

THE SACRED SPRINGS

In contrast to other Nordic regions, baptism outside the church is still a widespread practice in Iceland and Northern Norway. It was common for laypeople in the eighteenth and nineteenth centuries in Sápmi to baptize children, and the custom varied between the ethnic and cultural groups who lived in the area. For Sámi nomads, emergency baptisms were customary, and the pastor would confirm the baptism

---

36. "The hidden people" are called *huldufólk* in Icelandic, *ulddat* in North-Sámi, and *hulder* in Norwegian.
   For information about the Sámi *ulddat*, see Sjöberg, "Adams barn," 22–33. For the *hulder* in Northern Norway, see Kristiansen, "Om å være," 79–92.

37. Jónsson, *Íslenskir þjóðhættir*, 367.

38. Jónsson, *Íslenskir þjóðhættir*, 90. The National Museum of Iceland, "Questionnaire: Slaughtering."

39. The National Museum of Iceland, "Questionnaire: Light and Fire."

later, when the parents brought the child to church.[40] Lay baptism is still common in northern Norway, especially among Laestadians.[41] If the baptisms in Sápmi were mostly home baptisms, the same can be said about Iceland, where most children in the nineteenth century were baptized at home by the local pastor a day or two after birth and before the midwife went home.[42] Baptisms in Iceland are still evenly divided between home and church. In the summertime, baptism often takes place outdoors and frequently in locations of historical importance to the baptismal families.

In the South Sámi context, the Sámi theologian Bierna Bientie has stressed the spatial element of baptismal practices and how they are connected to geographic and cultural contexts. Bientie describes the waterways as part of *eatneme* (South Sámi: Mother Earth), and the springs as expressions of God´s generosity. For Bientie, Sámi baptismal practices are deeply focused on protection for the child, identity, and belonging more than the traditional Lutheran doctrine of the forgiveness of sin.[43] Bientie maintains that water is central in Sámi baptismal practices, and many take great care to get water from local water sources with symbolic ties to the family.[44] Bientie describes a Sámi baptismal liturgy wherein the water is poured down near the fireplace after the service, and the baptismal prayer gives thanks for water and the Holy Spirit. From a North-Sámi perspective, Buljo has said that the water needs to be poured out after the service with great care, outside, close to the holiest part of the dwelling, which is the fireplace of the tent or house.[45] The one who pours out the water blesses it in the name of the Holy Trinity.

The medieval Nordic tradition of looking at all waters as holy waters because of Jesus's baptism in Jordan is well documented. The sermon on Epiphany appears both in the Icelandic and Norwegian versions of the *Book of Homilies* (both from the early thirteenth century). The Icelandic version is shorter and succinctly states that the Lord asked John the Baptist to baptize him in the River Jordan, to hallow all water and all pools, and

---

40. Anderzén, "Dåp och dåppraxis," 46.

41. Evjen, "Hjemmedåp i det flerkulturelle Nord-Norge," 69–80. Laestadianism is a pietistic revival movement, named after Lars Levi Laestadianus, that originated in nineteenth-century Sápmi.

42. Jónsson, *Íslenskir þjóðhættir*, 263.

43. Bientie, "Sørsamisk dåpsliturgi," 69.

44. Bientie, "Sørsamisk dåpsliturgi," 71.

45. Buljo, "Samiske skikker," 30.

to "make all waters holy, so that they would be appropriate for baptism, wherever in the world the baptism takes place." The sermon continues in a typological fashion, indicating that the drops of the baptismal water flowed from Jesus's body; they were in fact the sins of all later generations. "We were not yet born, yet, we were already washed in baptism," the sermon exclaims.[46] If the two *Books of Homilies* concur in their statement that all water and all pools are already holy because of Jesus's baptism, the same idea of the holiness of water occurs in *Landnáma*, the book of the settlement of Iceland (written in the early twelfth century). *Landnáma* tells the story of Auður the Wise One, who was a Christian woman of Norse origin from the Hebrides Islands. On Auður´s deathbed in Hvammur, Iceland, she instructed that the burial was to take place down by the sea, so that her grave would be cleansed daily by the water. Since Christianity was not an organized religion in Iceland at the time of Auður´s death, there was no possibility for a burial on consecrated ground, and the sea was considered universally holy.[47]

The medieval connections to the cosmological holiness of water lead us back to holy water as the ocean, rivers, glaciers, and baptism. In Iceland, geothermal water has its own hallowed baptismal stories. According to the Icelandic stories of Christianization (*Kristni saga*, written in twelfth or thirteenth centuries), the representatives of Icelanders made the political decision for all to become Christian in the year 1000. However, those new baptismal candidates did not want baptism in the chilly waters of the parliamentary site Þingvellir. Those traveling home from Þingvellir to the northern and eastern part of the island were baptized in Reykjalaug (English: *Steam Pool*) in South-Iceland, which was later called Vígðalaug (English: *Hallowed Pool*), while those heading west were baptized in Krosslaug (English: *Cross Pool*) in Lundarreykjadalur in West Iceland.[48] Thus, the cultural memory of Christianization in Iceland connects baptismal practices to geothermal hotsprings. Vígðalaug does not only form a link to the story of Christianization in Iceland, but also to the historical event of the Reformation. The execution of the last Catholic bishop in Hólar with two of his sons took place in the vicinity of Skálholt, and their bodies were washed in Vígðalaug before their burial.[49]

46. Einarsson et al., *Íslensk hómilíubók*, 116; Indrebø, ed., *Gamal homiliebok*, 58–59.
47. Bryan, *Icelandic Folklore*, 95; *Landnáma*, 55.
48. Vésteinsson, *Vígðalaug*, 205–18; G. Ólafsson, *Fredlysta fornlämningar*.
49. Vésteinsson, *Vígðalaug*, 205.

The eighteenth-century geologist Eggert Ólafsson distinguished between two kinds of geothermal water in the springs: *hverir*, which are boiling and bubbling hot pools, and *laugar*, which are the still pools, with clear water warm enough to bathe in and wash clothes.[50] Keeping in mind Carvalhaes's description of the community pools in Brazil, which were also used for washing and baptizing, a similar arrangement seems to have been in place in Iceland, where the warmth of the geothermal water would make up for the colder climate. Both geothermal springs in Krossalaug and Reykjalaug have, to this day, been considered to exhibit healing powers. The same goes for baptismal water in general, and elderly people still wash their eyes in the water after a baptism. There used to be a strong belief that the pastor had to pour the water into the eyes of the children at a baptism so that they would not be able to see the hidden people.[51] This harkens back to the Sámi practice of pouring the water respectfully out near the fireplace of the tent, and there are accounts of Icelanders pouring the water inside the house for protection; others poured the baptismal water over the ridge of the house as a blessing ritual.[52]

Pastors in contemporary Iceland recount baptismal practices wherein the water is poured to the ground of newly built houses, and there is a recent example of parents from different places who blended the water from their own birthplaces in the font before the baptism as an identity marker for the child and their families.[53] Some bring water from the Icelandic Highland to the baptism,[54] while others ask the local pastors to join the family on a tour to the Highland to baptize.[55] Rev. Vigfús Ingvar Ingvarsson from the eastern part of Iceland was asked to baptize an individual close to a warm natural spring near a glacial river. The context behind this choice is that two glacier rivers were being dammed to create

---

50. E. Ólafsson, *Ferðabók I*, 72–73.
51. Jónsson, *Íslenskir þjóðhættir*, 264.
52. Jónsson, *Íslenskir þjóðhættir*, 264.
53. Rev. Halla Rut Stefánsdóttir (pastor in Hofsós, Northwest Iceland) in a discussion with the author in March 2023. The author, herself a young pastor at the end of last century, has spoken to parishioners who poured baptismal water over the roofs of their houses for protection in Westfjords, Iceland.
54. Rev. Magnús Erlingsson (pastor in Ísafjörður, Westfjords, Iceland) and Rev. Dr. Sigurður Árni Þórðarson (pastor emeritus in Reykjavík) in discussion with the author in January 2023.
55. Rev. Sigurður Rúnar Ragnarsson (pastor emeritus in Neskaupsstaður, East-Iceland), January 2023.

reservoirs for a power plant, which in turn would produce electricity for an aluminum factory. Rev. Ingvarsson thus wrote the following:

> I baptized a child at Lindur, which is a warm spring that vanished in the Háls-lagoon, when the dam at Kárahnjúkar was made. The baptism took place next to the spring, and we took the water from it. It was deeply meaningful to the parents and the others who attended. This was on the 19th of August 2006, and in addition to being a baptism, people experienced the ritual, I think, as the consecration of this land, where beautiful vegetation had been sentenced to go under the glacial water. They would also experience it as an acknowledgment or admonition that the land is sacred and as a farewell ritual for this place.[56]

The damming of the rivers took place only a few weeks after the baptism. Given the message in both the Icelandic and Norwegian *Book of Homilies* that since all waters and springs are already sacred because of Jesus's baptism, Kimmerer's point, that we never fully know a river, leads us to suggest that Christian baptismal theology should also acknowledge that our sacred rituals have a depth and cultural memory that is connected to water in myriads of ways.

CONCLUSION: TALKING TO WATER AND MAKING CROSSES IN THE SNOW

In this chapter, I have heeded Magnason's advice to go "backwards to move forward" when speaking about climate change.[57] If a glacier is a "frozen manuscript," what, then, can be said of baptismal practices? What can we decode from such rituals about our past and present? By insisting on the Arctic context in this discussion of baptism, I am not claiming that these practices are necessarily unique to the Arctic. Nor am I claiming that religious gestures and traditions are only connected to Christian baptismal rituals, or that baptismal practices everywhere in the European Arctic are the same. Instead, I am proposing here to let the practical wisdom of the peripheral narratives, images, and practices in the Arctic take precedence, because these kinds of perspectives are usually neglected when speaking about baptism in Nordic countries.

---

56. The National Museum of Iceland: "Questionnaire: Admonitions and Beliefs," my translation.

57. Magnason, *On Time and Water*, 10.

Given our environmental context, do our rituals and practices provide any sense of meaning, values, or beliefs that can be used to address these emergencies? When I read the ancient narrative in *Grágás* of crosses in the snow and emergency baptisms in the ocean, I wondered what the world would look like if we learned to talk to water, like the ancient law prescribes. When Kimmerer tells us that we may not know the river but can listen to it and taste the blessing of its watery drops, we might heed that advice in our sacramental rituals. If the laws of Grágás prepared us for baptism in a state of emergency, how do we prepare and interpret the Christian sacraments in the hour of our need? The baptismal gestures of making the sign of the cross for thanksgiving and protection reflect on a universe where all is connected, including humans, animals, other life forms, and inanimate beings, in the many forms of water, such as snow, ice, the sea, running fresh water, and geothermal springs. Rituals make meaning, and the interconnected universe that is decoded from these glacial manuscripts provides a possibility for action. As Pastor Ingvarsson shows us in his powerful account of baptism in a place about to be sunk under water for industrial purposes, baptismal practices can also serve as environmental laments. May we therefore say with dread and hope, "I consecrate you, water," to all endangered waters of the earth and ask for the courage to do something about it?

BIBLIOGRAPHY

Anderzén, Sölve. "Dåp och dåppraxis: Nordskandinavien i 1700 og 1800 tallet." *Dåp og død: Din inngang og din utgang*, edited b Skarstein, 23–48. Vadsø: Vadsø Museum-Ruija kvenmuseum, 2003.

Árnason, Jón, ed. *Íslenskar þjóðsögur*. Vol. 1. Leipzig: Hinrichs, 1862.

Bernharðsson, Haraldur, et al. *Járnsíða og Kristniréttur Árna Þorlákssonar*. Reykjavík: Sögufélag, 2005.

Bientie, Bierna. "Sørsamisk dåpsliturgi med utgangspunkt i det samiske." *Praktisk kirkelig teologi nedenfra*, edited by Stig Lægdene, 69–74. Tromsø: Kirkelig utdanningssenter nord, 2008.

Bradshaw, Paul. "The Gospel and the Catechumenate in the Third Century." *Journal of Theological Studies* 50 (1999) 143–52.

Bryan, Eric Shane. *Icelandic Folklore and the Cultural Memory of Religious Change*. Leeds: Arc Humanities, 2021.

Buljo, Karen Marie Eira. "Samiske skikker / tradisjoner i tilknytning til gudstjenestefeiring." *Vi bekjenner at jorden hører Herren til*, 30–36. Oslo: Den norske kirke, Samisk kirkeråd, 1999.

Carvalhaes, Cláudio. *What's Worship Have to Do With It? Interpreting Life Liturgically*. Eugene, OR: Cascade Books, 2018.

PART IV: THEOLOGY

Dennis, Andrew, et al. (transl.), *Laws of Early Iceland: Grágás, the Codex Regious of Grágás, with Material from Other Manuscripts*. Vol. 2. Winnipeg: University of Manitoba, 1980.

Einarsson, Sigurbjörn, et al., eds. *Íslensk hómilíubók: fornar stólræður*. Reykjavík: Hið íslenska bókmenntafélag, 1993.

Evjen, Bjørg. "Hjemmedåp i det flerkulturelle Nord-Norge." *Dåp og død: din inngang og din utgang*, edited by Sigrid Skarstein. Vadsø: Vadsø museum og Ruija kvenmuseum, 2003. 69–80.

Finsen, Vilhjálmur, ed. *Grágás: Islænderenes lovbog i fristatens tid*. Trans. Vilhjálmur Finsen. Vol. 1. Copenhagen: Det nordiske literatur samfund, 1852.

Guðmarsdóttir, Sigríður. "Water as Sacrament: Tillich, Gender and Liturgical Eco-Justice." *Dialog* 53 (2014) 110–17.

Hegstad, Harald. "Dåpen som hendelse og prosess." *Teologisk tidsskrift* 6 (2017) 176–94.

Indrebø, Gustav, ed. *Gamal norsk homiliebok Cod AM 619 4*. Oslo: Kjeldeskriftfondet, 1931.

International Labor Organization (ILO). *Convention 169 on Indigenous and Tribal Peoples*. 2019.

Johnsen, Tore. *Jordens barn, solens barn, åndens barn: kristen tro i et samisk landskap*. Oslo: Verbum, 2007.

———. "Negotiating the Meaning of 'TRC' in the Norwegian Context." In *Trading Justice for Peace: Reframing Reconciliation in TRC Processes in South Africa, Canada and Nordic Countries*, edited by Sigríður Guðmarsdóttir, et al., 19–40. Cape Town: AOSIS, 2021.

———. *Sámi luondduteologiija: Samisk naturteologi på grunnlag av nålevende tradisjonsstoff og nedtegnede myter*. Tromsø: The Arctic University of Tromsø, 2005.

Jónsson, Jónas. *Íslenskir þjóðhættir*. Reykjavík: Ísafoldarprentsmiðja, 1961.

Kimmerer, Robin Wall. *Braiding Sweetgrass: Indigenous Wisdom, Scientific Knowledge and the Teachings of Plants*. Minneapolis: Milkweed, 2015.

Kristiansen, Roald E. "Om å være from og fremsynt." In *Religion i kontekst: Bidrag til en nordnorsk teologi*, edited by Roald E. Kristiansen, 79–92. Oslo: Norges forskningsråd, 1996.

Lupton, Brendan. "The Sign of the Cross in the Dialogues of Gregory the Great." *Downside Review* 138 (2020).

Magnason, Andri Snær. *Time and Water: A History of Our Future*. London: Serpent's Tail, 2020.

Moore, Mary Elizabeth. "Responding to a Weeping Planet: Practical Theology as a Discipline Called by Crisis." In *Practical Theology and the Environment*, edited by Pamela McCarroll and HyeRan Kim-Cragg, 7–20. Basel: MDPI, 2023.

The National Museum of Iceland: Sarpur: A Cultural-Historical Database. "Questionnaire: Light and Fire in Customs and Folklore: 302/1961-2 Ólafur Daníelsson (1895) Hvalfjörður." 1961. https://sarpur.is/Adfang.aspx?AdfangID=555580.

———. Sarpur: A Cultural Historical Database. "Questionnaire: Invocations and Beliefs Connected to Churches. 17249/2009-2 Vigfús Ingvar Ingvarsson (1950) Egilsstaðir." 2009. https://www.sarpur.is/Adfang.aspx?AdfangID=551398&fbcl id=IwAR25Y52xAaAoZSjW6MHux92DByoz8Z2nVDtSirFf4ACAEMPu3DS7n RKkjhY.

———. Sarpur: A Cultural-Historical Database. "Questionnaire: Slaughtering Livestock at Home and Slaughter Practices. 14/1960-1: Magnús Björnsson (1889 in Skagafjörður)." Reykjavík: The National Museum of Iceland, 1960. https://sarpur.is/Adfang.aspx?AdfangID=555580.

Olsen, Inuuteq Holm. "Greenland, the Arctic and the Issue of Representation: What Is the Arctic? Who Has a Say?" In *The Arctic and World Order*, edited by Kristina Spohr and Daniel S. Hamilton, 77–91. Washington, DC: Foreign Policy Institute, 2020. https://transatlanticrelations.org/wp-content/uploads/2020/12/The-Arctic-and-World-Order.pdf.

Ólafsson, Eggert. *Ferðabók Eggert Ólafssonar og Bjarna Pálssonar um ferðir þeirra á Íslandi árin 1752-1757* [The Travel Journals of EÓ and BP 1752–1757]. Vol. 1. Reykjavík: Ísafoldarprentsmiðja, 1943.

Ólafsson, Guðmundur. *Fridlysta fornlämningar i Borgarfjörðurs härad Island*. Reykjavík: Uppsala Universitet, 1991.

Óskarsdóttir, Svanhildur, and Árni Heimir Ingólfsson. "Dýrlingar og daglegt brauð í Langadal. Efni og samhengi í AM 461 12mo [Daily and divine affairs in Langidalur. The content and context of AM 461 12mo]." *Gripla* 30 (2019) 107–53.

Pálsson, Hermann and Paul Edwards, trans. *The Book of Settlements, Landnámabók*. Winnipeg: University of Manitoba, 1972.

Pálsson, Hermann. *Úr landnorðri: Samar og ystu rætur íslenskrar menningar*. Reykjavík: Bókmenntastofnun, 1997.

Rasmussen, Siv. "Samisk integrering i norsk og svensk kirke i tidlig nytid: En komparasjon mellom Finnmark og Torne lappmark." Ph.D. diss. Arctic University of Norway, Tromsø, 2016.

Simpson, Jacqueline, ed. *Icelandic Folktales and Legends*. Stroud: Tempus, 2009.

Sjöberg, Lovisa Mienna. "Adams barn tillsammans i klimatskrisens tidearv: Några reflektioner kring de osynligas plats i skapelsen." *St. Sunniva* (2022) 22–33.

———. "Att leva i ständig välsignelse: En studie av sivnidit som religiös praxis." PhD diss., University of Oslo, 2018.

Sjöberg, Lovisa Mienna, and Mikkel Nils Sara. "When Justice has Borders: Some Reflections on National Borders in Relation to the TRC in Norway" In *Trading Justice for Peace? Reframing Reconciliation in TRC Processes in South Africa, Canada and Nordic Countries*, edited by Sigríður Guðmarsdóttir et al., 107–21. Cape Town: AOSIS, 2021.

Steingrímsson, Sigurgeir, and Peter Foot. (eds.). "Jóns saga ins helga." *Biskupa sögur I.* Íslensk fornrit XV. Vol. II, 173–316. Reykjavík: Hið íslenska fornritafélag, 2003.

Vésteinsson, Orri. "Vígðalaug í Laugardal." *Árbók hins íslenska fornleifafélags* (2000–2001) 205–18.

Wang, Solveig. *Decolonising Medieval Fennoscandia: An Interdisciplinary Study of Norse-Saami Relations in the Medieval Period*. Berlin: de Gruyter, 2023.

17

Naming and Belonging
Some Aspects of Baptism in the Sámi Tradition

LOVISA MIENNA SJÖBERG

> *Gullet mu, gáiddus rittut,*
> *guldalehket, álbmogat*
> *mat lehpet gáidagasas!*
> *Hearrá rávkkai mu*
> *juo ovdal go mun riegádin,*
> *son attii munnje nama*
> *go mun ledjen vel eadnán goatus. Jes. 49:1*

Listen, O isles, unto me; and hearken, ye peoples, from far: Jehovah hath called me from the womb; from the bowels of my mother hath he made mention of my name. Isa 49:1

RELIGIOUS HISTORY IN SÁPMI (which is an area that stretches across the borders of four countries in the Arctic North) is a story about colonialism, struggles for justice, and theological negotiations. Although the study of religious history is far more common than attempts to interpret different Sámi traditions within a theological frame, in this chapter, I suggest that the Christian tradition of baptism in Sápmi, having long roots and representing some distinctiveness, has something to offer to conversations about baptism in general.

Today, most of Sápmi is Lutheran, and the region shares the same multiple pathways of faith and secularism as are found in the Nordic countries in general. However, the Finnish and Russian sides of Sápmi are also influenced by the Orthodox Church. The national borders between Norway/Sweden/Finland and Russia are vertical, while the internal, regional Sámi borders are horizontal, often defined by differences in language and the direction of migration routes used by the reindeer herding population.

Baptism in Sápmi, as we know it today, came with Lutheranism in the seventeenth and eighteenth centuries, and it was first and foremost a way to document people. Building churches and chapels was a way to claim land in areas where national borders had not yet been established. Churches were often built at meeting places for trade, tax collection, and court hearings. This administrative system also changed burial practices, which became a means of keeping a record of the population in widespread areas.

The Sámi people had (and some still have) migration routes crossing national borders, as their reindeer herds have seasonal pastures on both sides of the border. These ways of life presented challenges to the authorities in the respective nationstates. There were probably other rituals connected to name giving before Protestantism arrived in Sámi areas, but since there are few written sources from these times, we do not know much about them. We do know that Sámi names were replaced during the sixteenth and seventeenth centuries, probably due to the intensification of missionary efforts. Specifically, the Sámi names were replaced by Biblical or European names, probably more or less through pressure from the authorities.[1]

To define baptism in this chapter, I have chosen a document published by the World Council of Churches in 1982, also called the Lima Document. Since it is an ecumenical document broad enough to include many different baptism traditions and, at the same time, focuses on what is common ground for many organized Christians in the world today, it might suit us as an overall definition. One of the remarks in

---

1. Rasmussen, "Navn I Det Nordlige Sápmi," 149–70.

the document indicates that baptism does not include a Christian name giving, and the church shall not suggest names other than the local names in the area, even though such practices may be common in some places. This suggests that more or less forced name giving is still an issue today in some places. In addition, I have made use of Martins Luther's "Comfort for Women Who Have Had a Miscarriage," written in 1542, the version of which has been translated into English and published in *Devotional Writings II* in 1968. For the studies on Sámi naming traditions, I have primarily made use of Siv Rasmussen's and Håkan Rydving's research, in addition to my own. To shed light on the traditional stories about *eahpáraš* (unbaptized dead children), I have mainly used the writings of the Sámi thinker and author Johan Turi.

This chapter focuses on the task of name giving in Sámi tradition, which is an important aspect of the baptism ritual that has extensive roots. Name giving is also important in other traditions in Sápmi, which might provide us with clues about how we can best reflect upon baptism today, both in Sámi society and elsewhere. Sámi naming traditions might add something to reflections around baptism in general, but in this chapter, I connect the task to the mourning associated with the loss of an unborn, dead-born, or unbaptized child. I suggest that parts of Sámi traditions may give additional comfort to those of us who have lost a child who had little or no time among us.

UNBAPTIZED CHILDREN AND WORDS OF COMFORT

In all human societies, some children have been stillborn, either at full term or before. Moreover, some children have died during birth. There have also been cases where the mother or the parents could not provide for the child, after which the child was put to rest by the family itself or someone else after birth. In addition, in our times, we now have the choice of abortion. In a Christian context, these various phenomena entail that not all children have the opportunity to be baptized. If baptism is what connects us to God and saves us in eternal life, what happens, then, to unbaptized children? This issue has been an additional burden for mothers, and probably many fathers, in their grief. The fear of having a child who will not reach eternal life with God is probably why Luther wrote about these situations in a small text to comfort mothers in their grief. In short, comfort should be found in the idea that this situation is under the governance of God, and we must put our trust in God to deal with such difficulties:

> A final word—it often happens that devout parents, particularly the wives, have sought consolation from us because they have suffered such agony and heartbreak in childbearing when, despite their best intentions and against their will, there was a premature birth or miscarriage and their child died at birth or was born dead. One ought not to frighten or sadden such mothers by harsh words because it was not due to their carelessness or neglect that the birth of the child went off badly. One must make a distinction between them and those females who resent being pregnant, deliberately neglect their child, or go so far as to strangle or destroy it . . . Therefore, one must leave such situations to God and take comfort in the thought that he surely has heard our unspoken yearning and done all things better than we could have asked.[2]

Taking Sámi tradition into account might add something to Luther's words of comfort, thereby helping mothers and parents to cope with these difficult situations.

BAPTISM AND CONFLICTING NAME-GIVING TRADITIONS

Name giving is not considered to be the most significant part of the sacrament of baptism, at least not in today's official documents. In previous times, there had been efforts to change the local and/or Indigenous names into Christian or more Western names. This happened in Sápmi and probably also in other Indigenous locations. We know that between the sixteenth and the nineteenth centuries, local Sámi names more or less disappeared or were changed.[3] I have not found theological explanations for the church's ambition to make people choose names other than those they were accustomed to. While name giving is not formulated or discussed as a central part of the sacrament of baptism, much effort has historically been put into changing names in the context of Christian baptism.

The World Council of Churches' document on baptism does not mention name giving as an important part of baptism, despite its aim to

---

2. Luther, "Comfort for Women Who Have Had a Miscarriage," 247–50.
3. Rydving, "On the History of the Sami Family Name System," 11–32.

include many different practices. However, in one of the remarks, it is underlined that the church should not in any way put pressure on anyone to give a Christian name instead of a local name. The statement reads: "A name which is inherited from one's original culture roots the baptized in that culture, and at the same time manifests the universality of baptism, incorporation into the one Church, holy, catholic and apostolic, which stretches over all the nations of the earth."[4] This suggests that the practice is still common in some places, and that the name also gives the receiver a sense of belonging to a place and a community. In a way, this statement gives the impression that name giving is not connected or does not have to be connected to the sacrament of baptism; the name itself does not or should not matter. In Sámi tradition, however, name giving has been and probably still is one of the most important aspects of baptism.

PATTERNS OF NAME-GIVING IN SÁMI TRADITION

Patterns of name giving in contexts beyond the naming of humans might be a productive pathway through which to consider the significance and meaning behind naming a child. Name giving is one of the first tasks given to mankind in the second creation story of the Bible, wherein Adam gave a name to all the animals and plants. One might therefore wonder how this task shaped the relationship between human beings and the rest of creation for the times to come.

In Sámi tradition, naming the natural surroundings is a way of sorting and categorizing things, but sometimes from a starting point other than the biological one. Often, the name contains information about the specific relationships the named one has with humans. The reindeer, an important animal in Sámi contexts, is not categorized in terms of being a biological animal. Instead, it has several different names based on the kind of relationship it has with human beings. Some of the names in Northern Sámi[5] are *goddi* (a wild reindeer), *boazu* (a reindeer in a herd that has a relationship with humans), and *heargi* (a reindeer trained to pull a sledge). The categories are flexible, and it is possible to extend one category to another, although this requires a shift in the named's relationship with humans over time. We find the same structure in naming one's surroundings according to what kind of activities or uses connect them to people

---

4. World Council of Churches, *Baptism, Eucharist and Ministry*, 6.

5. In this chapter, when referring to the Sámi language, I mean the dialect of Northern Sámi.

at different times, which in turn might result in the same place having several names.[6] Some of the names are connected to activities that change with the seasons. This way of name giving functions alongside and in addition to more fixed names, such as those referring to what that particular lake, mountain, or valley is called. There are also specific places named after people who have died nearby. Thus, name giving says something about relationships between humans and the landscape, as well as humans and other beings, and also about human activity in general.[7]

Traditionally, some animals have had many names, particularly those representing possible danger. Such naming practices form the way people talk or even think about animals.[8] Such names can be connected to an activity, such as hunting, but also to efforts to pay respect and resist challenging the forces of creation. An example here would be the traditional hunting of a wolf. Hunting a wolf was a dangerous task; it was done while skiing, and the wolf was eventually killed with a spear. The hunter had to be trained both mentally and physically to be able to complete the hunt. A part of the preparation and preferred state of mind during the hunt would be to think about the wolf under a name that differs from the one that is common in the local language or dialect. If the wolf's name was *gumpe*, for example, you would try to think of other names it may have as you planned the hunt and skied after it. The hunt connects you to the wolf, and as it may come to know what you are thinking, it is essential that you both honor the wolf and at the same time protect yourself. Besides thinking about it by a different name, you should also think of nine different ways of killing it and leave the method you aim to use as the last option. Of course, this is also a way to ensure that you do not rush into an unpredictable situation and expose yourself to a dangerous animal. Generally, this type of naming process sheds some light on how important names have been and even continue to be in Sámi tradition.[9]

Talking about the animal or the hunt then requires that you know several other names and also how to handle your relationship with the wolf, an animal that in previous times had the potential to threaten your livelihood. We find the same pattern in discussions about epidemic diseases. Epidemic diseases were powerful, and small communities

6. Sjöberg, *Att leva i ständig Välsignelse*.
7. Sjöberg, *Att leva i ständig välsignelse*; Sara, *Knowing, Recognizing and Describing a Terrain*; Rydving, "Visible and Invisible Landscapes."
8. Sara, *Gumpe, sápmelaš ja boazu*; Sjöberg, *Att leva i ständig välsignelse*.
9. Sara, *Gumpe, sápmelaš ja boazu*.

were often at risk of extinction. For example, Ole Andreas Thomassen explained how smallpox (*boahkkodávdda*) itself does not want that name to be used, but rather prefers, *smávvačalbmi* which directly translates to *small eye*. To use the more honorful name *smávvačalbmi* will protect you, if not from the disease itself, then from its harsher symptoms.[10] Thus, a name in these traditions is not just a representation of something; it is also a part of the particular being. In this sense, a human name does not just represent you; it is also a part of you.

So, what might it mean in this tradition to give a child a name? First, it might give the child a connection and a sense of belonging. Unlike the case of a wolf or a dangerous disease, the relationship to the child is one you want to nurture and maintain.

A CHILD IS BORN, AND A DAUGHTER/SON HAS BEEN GIVEN

Traditionally, in Sápmi, a child would be named after one or more of its relatives. There has been a strong belief that the child also inherited some of a deceased person's characteristics and qualities. The child was also given a *nammašiella* (name-*šiella*), often a small item made of silver or other metal. This object protected the name and the child as well. In our times, it is still common to give a *šiella* as a gift in connection with baptism.[11] Nowadays, the object is often a special type of silver ball with small rings attached to it, and it is still thought to protect the child, which is especially significant given that newborn children are fragile and need all the protection they can get. The name gives the child a sense of belonging to their own history and family and establishes a connection to ancestors and the living family. It also gives the child a place and space in the human sphere and the broader sphere of living beings. The name can also protect the child if it receives the right one.

In earlier times, a child or even an adult who became ill could be re-baptized and given a new name to facilitate recovery. Since the named individual would have inherited some of the identity or qualities of the one he or she was named after, it is possible that one could fall ill when receiving the wrong name. The relationships between the dead and the living were assumed to be close. In this respect, the name connected the

---

10. Thomassen, *Lappenes forhold*, 155–56; Sjöberg, *Att leva i ständig välsignelse*.
11. Fjellström, *Lapskt silver*.

individual to the family and ancestral community.¹² If a name was connected to violence or other negative traits, there was a risk that it would fall out of that particular family tree. Today, it is more common to name a child after a living relative. Just as a baptism in the church offers a bigger global community, in the Sámi tradition, a name establishes a connection to one's ancestors and becomes a part of the acts and deeds conducted by the *gáibmi* (or namesake) during their lifetime.

There are also other important aspects of name giving, one of which has to do with becoming a part of human society.

STORIES OF *EAHPÁRAŠ*

One type of story in which both baptism and name giving are important is that about the so-called *eahpáraš*. In the past, it would sometimes be the case that the mother or parents, for various reasons, would leave a child to die by hiding it somewhere in the landscape. This dead child is called an *eahpáraš* in Sámi language, which in Scandinavian is referred to as a *myling/utbor*. The dead child will reveal itself close to its hiding place where it was left to die, since it has no peace in death, the dead child is screaming and crying.¹³ The phenomenon of parents causing death to their newborns, in one way or another, has probably existed more or less all over the world in pre-contraception and abortion times and is also thematized by Luther.¹⁴ In the Sámi tradition, the dead child or *eahpáraš* is caught between two spheres of life, which is a dangerous place to be. Anyone in contact with this being also risks becoming sick or stuck in between the worlds, which would incline one toward insanity.¹⁵ In the Sámi tradition, the world consists of at least two spheres, one of which is invisible. As long as we live, we belong to the visible sphere. The other sphere is always there as a second layer.¹⁶ In the other sphere, there are inhabitants, including both humanlike beings and animals, as well as those who have deceased. The *eahpáraš* is someone who is stuck between these two spheres. To avoid this unwanted state, a child needs to receive a name that reveals his or her belonging. The only way to bring some rest to a crying and screaming child is to baptize it,

12. Rasmussen, "Samisk integrering i norsk og svensk kirke i tidlig nytid."
13. Utsi, *Sámi Muitalanárbevierru*; Sjöberg, *Att leva i ständig välsignelse*, 218ff.
14. Luther, "Comfort for Women Who Had a Miscarriage"
15. Utsi, *Sámi Muitalanárbevierru*; Gaski et al., *Min njálmmálas árbevierru*.
16. Rydving, "On the History of the Sami Family Name System," 2.

meaning, in this context, to give it a name under the protection of God. In most stories, this is done by reading the Lord's prayer backward or in three different languages and then giving the *eahpáraš* a name.[17] It is explained that this cannot be a human name, but rather one associated with a sharp object, like the edge of an ax or a needle. Why it has to be a name of an object might be because the *eahpáraš* cannot be a part of the human society or the living sphere, and a dead object does not belong to the living sphere. But it might as well be remains of old traditional human names in Sápmi. We know that some of the older names that disappeared referred to objects like a *juoksa* (crossbow).[18] In this situation, the *eahpáraš* could also be commanded to come back to the earth, where it would hopefully then rest in peace.

In these stories about baptism, the main point is to be given a name in accordance with the Trinity. The name gives one peace and a place or a context to belong to. Who or what, then, is the *eahpáraš*, or other children who, for different reasons, are not a part of our living community? In 1910, Johan Turi provided an explanation for what an *eahpáraš* is.[19] Turi describes how to behave if an *eahpáraš* is encountered in a particular place. In one particular encounter, some people who were brave enough dared to stop and asked the dead child whom they had found and why it was crying. The *eahpáraš* told them that someone had put him/her there, and that he/she now wanted a name. If the person was bold, he or she could then proclaim, "I baptize you in the name of the three persons. In God the father, the son, and the Holy Spirit, Adam or Eve is your name" (my translation).[20] Then, the person would continue by reading the Lord's prayer and blessing, ending with "Sleep in God's peace until judgment day arrives, and you will stand before the highest king."[21] Turi's story can be read as a way of conceptualizing the *eahpáraš* in relation to human society. Although the *eahpáraš* in Turi's story is not given a specific family or ancestral line, it is nevertheless given a place in the human sphere and community. It is given the names of the first human beings, with a promise to rise on the last day and stand in front of the creator, as everybody else would be expected to. Whether the idea that the *eahpáraš* belongs to human society was a new thought or in fact just a new version of another

17. Utsi, *Sámi Muitalanárbevierru*; Sjöberg, *Att leva i ständig välsignelse*.
18. Rydving, "On the History of the Sami Family Name System."
19. Turi, *Samene og noaidekunsten*, 73.
20. Turi, *Samene og noaidekunsten*, 73.
21. Turi, *Samene og noaidekunsten*, 74 (my translation).

story, where it is understood that older names refer to humans and not dead objects, is not possible to sort out in this chapter. Regardless, Turi's version provides a clear answer to the question of how to relate to the child. It belongs to us, as it is human.

Considering Turi's story in relation to Luther's words of comfort, it seems that Turi also holds the opinion that the child is under God's administration, and the decision is his. However, he also adds something here. Giving the child a name, or giving a name in line with the Trinity, is actually a way to baptize (*gásttašit* in Sámi). In this sense, the child is connected to the human sphere, even though it is not among those who are alive. There is great comfort in knowing that the child is a part of us, and that it belongs to our human society. The name can be given by anyone who knows the Lord's prayer; it does not have to be the parents, although it might be. If the child is named by a parent, it also has the opportunity to become a part of the family and deceased relatives through its name. In this way, we make our dead or unborn children a part of us and a part of our society. This ritual might also include children who are aborted by free choice. What is not decided through this act is whether the child unites with Christ and his people (as formulated in the Lima Document); instead, the question of belonging in this respect is left to God to decide. From a human perspective, we have, through name giving, offered a place to such children in our society.

SOME ASPECTS OF RESEARCH ON RELIGIOUS HISTORY IN SÁPMI

The first extensive written sources to describe the Sámi religion show how baptism was conducted both in church and at home. Whether home baptism was a way to wash away the Christian baptism and secure another name, we do not know, as the source material is limited.

In Sápmi, the transmission of knowledge has mostly been conducted through oral and practical means. Written language was constructed and developed through translations of parts of the Bible and other central Christian texts from the seventeenth century onwards. The first written sources on the Sámi religion also appeared in the seventeenth century and were mostly written by Lutheran missionaries and clergymen, who took a negative approach to interpreting the Sámi religion. Apart from missionary accounts and similar texts, there are court documents and travel accounts that shed further insight on Sámi society and its religious life over the last few centuries. Each study that mentions religious practices in the past should, for these and similar reasons, be read through a critical lens.[22] The first texts (with very few exceptions) originally written in the Sámi language and produced within the Sámi society came to light in the late nineteenth century and onwards. During the same period, assimilation politics, often legitimized by studies in racial biology and related disciplines, grew stronger, and in the late twentieth century, the greater part of the Sámi population had lost their Sámi language.[23]

There has been some critical discussion among researchers of religion in Sápmi about the focus on representatives of the majority society. In traditional research, Sámi individuals are often described as passive respondents to the politics and decisions made by others. There has also been increasing interest in studying traditional Sámi religion rather than Sámi Christianity, even though we know that the first Sámi priest was consecrated as early as the late sixteenth century.[24] Another discourse that has influenced research on the religious past of the Sámi has been the categorization, and sometimes deconstruction, of practices as being either Sámi or Christian, but never both. Recent research has challenged descriptions of both the present and the past, thereby attempting to move toward an improved understanding of how religion, when explained as a pure institution, says more about modern understandings of what religious systems are than about religion as it is and has been lived in everyday life.[25] Although power relations were extremely asymmetrical in the past, the fact that there are now Sámi institutions, Sámi parliaments, reindeer herding practices, and language(s) that never died shows that Sámi society has been resilient. This could also be the case with other religious traditions and practices, even though they may have changed over time.

Based on the document on baptism from the World Council of Churches, it is not an essential part of baptism that one receives a Christian name, nor does the document suggest that the name giving act is a part of the sacrament of baptism; rather, it is an act that connects the one being baptized to the local community.[26] In Nordic contexts, it is common to talk about baptism in terms of name giving, even though this is

22. Mebius, *Bissie*.
23. Sjöberg, "Kristendomens historia på norsk och svensk sida av Sápmi."
24. Sjöberg, Kristendomens historia på norsk och svensk sida av Sápmi."
25. Rydving, "Samisk Kyrkohistoria," 31–42; Sjöberg, *Att leva i ständig välsignelse*.
26. World Council of Churches, *Baptism, Eucharist and Ministry*.

not a central part of the process. Whether or not this view has its roots in the older Nordic tradition is unknown. In Sámi tradition, however, the act of naming is important both to the sacrament and in establishing a connection with one's family, local community, and human society.

SOME FINAL REFLECTIONS AND WORDS OF COMFORT

Baptism is a sacrament that goes back to the New Testament. Although Christians have different opinions about whether name giving should be connected to this sacrament, it is still a sacrament that unites Christians of different confessions all over the world. In Sámi tradition, the name giving act is of special interest, since names are not only something to call other people, but also a part of who they are. Your name connects you to your relatives and gives you a place in the human sphere and society. To be given a name is a part of becoming a human being, a part of something bigger than yourself. When children are born and for some reason or another end up not being a part of our living world, there is comfort in knowing that the child can still be a part of our human community and even a part of one's family, as long as a name is provided. Whatever happens after that, as both Luther and Turi suggest, should be left to God to decide. After all, he is the creator of us all.

While baptism has been used as a part of colonial practices, it has, through the centuries, also been common in Sápmi to baptize children as well. A way to adjust ourselves to the fact that Sámi interpretations and lived theology have had an almost non-existent effect on theological discussions in general is to write, and by that shed some new light upon Sámi Christian traditions in all their variations. In this sense, certain Sámi traditions might be a resource for mothers and fathers (or others) in grief. Maybe it can add a little something to Luther's words of comfort, and maybe we can also apply such insights to our aborted children, if we want to. Name giving is under our jurisdiction, as it was a task given to the first human beings (1 Mos. 2:19). Through the confession that unbaptized children, or the aborted, are a part of our human society, we can leave Adam or Eve, or whatever name we choose to give the child, as a sign of belonging. We can then put the child to rest in peace in the hands of God, our creator. After all, he knew the name of the child long before it was even born.

PART IV: THEOLOGY

BIBLIOGRAPHY

Fjellström, Phebe. *Lapskt silver: Studier över en föremålsgrupp och dess ställning inom lapskt kulturliv. 1. Textdel*. Skrifter, Uppsala: Landsmåls—och folkminnesarkivet, 1962.

Gaski, Harald, et al. *Min njálmmálas árbevierru: máidnasat, myhtat ja muitalusat*. Karasjok: Davvi girji, 2004.

Luther, Martin. "Comfort for Women Who had a Miscarriage" *Luther's Works: Devotional Writings II*. Vol. 43. Philadelphia: Fortress, [1542] 1968.

Mebius, Hans. *Bissie: Studier i samisk religionshistoria*. Östersund: Jengel, 2003.

Rasmussen, Siv. "Navn i det nordlige sápmi på 1500-1600-tallet: Eller historien om navnene som forsvant" Rapport, Bd. 1, 149–70. Uppsala: NORNA, 2015.

Rasmussen, Siv. *Samisk integrering i norsk og svensk kirke i tidlig nytid - En komparasjon mellom Finnmark og Torne Lappmark*. 189–220. Tromsø: Universitetet i Tromsø, 2016.

Rydving, Håkan. "On the History of the Sami Family Name System." Minoritehtagielaid namat - njálmmalaš ja čálalaš oktavuođain. *Dieđut* 1 (2021) 11–32.

Rydving, Håkan. "Samisk kyrkohistoria: en kort översikt med fokus på kvinnor som aktörer." *Kyrkohistorisk årsbok*, 31–42. Uppsala: Svenska kyrkohistoriska föreningen, 2011.

Sara, Mikkel Nils. *Gumpe, sápmelaš ja boazu: boazusámi čilgehusat ja muitalusat gumppe ja guođoheami birra*. Guovdageaidnu: Sámi allaskuvla, 2003.

Sara, Mikkel Nils. "Knowing, Recognizing and Describing a Terrain. Examples from Nomadic Reindeer Herding." Keynote speech (Unpublished), Sámi allakuvla, 2010.

Sjöberg, Lovisa Mienna. *Att leva i ständig välsignelse. En studie av sivdnidit som religiös praxis*. Oslo: Universitetet i Oslo, 2018.

Sjöberg, Lovisa Mienna. "Kristendomens historia på norsk och svensk sida av Sápmi." Oslo: Teologisk tidskrift, 2020.

Thomassen, Ole Andreas. *Lappenes forhold*, edited by Peder Arild Mikalsen et al. Gáivuona: Sámi giellaguovddáš, Gáivuona suohkan, 1999.

Turi, Johan, and Per Turi. "Samene og noaidikunsten: den første samiske boken om den åndelige arven = Sámit ja noaidevuohta: vuosttaš sámi girji vuoiŋŋalaš árbbis." *Lappish Texts*. Nittedal: Tre bjørner, 2014.

Utsi, Mai Britt. "Njálmmálaš árbevierut álbmoga vuoiŋŋalašeallima govvideaddjin, erenoamážit gufihtarárbevierru." *Cafe Boddu: essayčoakkáldat* B.3 (1998).

Utsi, Mai Britt. *Sámi muitalanárbevierru ja mo luohti luovvana muitalusas*. Tromsø: Universitetet i Tromsø, 1998.

World Council of Churches. *Baptism, Eucharist and Ministry*. Faith and Order Paper 111. Geneva: World Council of Churches, 1982.

18

A Future with Hope

New Perspectives on Baptism in Times of Planetary Emergency

Anna Karin Hammar

> *For surely I know the plans I have for you, says the* Lord, *plans for your welfare and not for harm, to give you a future with hope.*[1]

My family is no different from many other families in the Church of Sweden. We, as grandparents, might be immersed in the church and the Christian tradition, but the next generation has a somewhat looser relationship in this regard, even though they may still baptize their children. Having the privilege of baptizing one's grandchildren provides a reason for reflection. What kind of world and future can they expect? In the planetary emergency we are in the midst of, what are the prospects for their future on Earth? What is the meaning of baptism in times like these?

Questions as these have inspired me to return to the work I did in my doctoral dissertation on baptism, with more specified questions. How can we interpret baptism in this time of planetary emergency in a way that will give new generations hope?

---

1. NRSV, Jeremiah 29:11.

Both Catholic and Protestant traditions have strongly emphasized original sin and the guilt already of the newly born baby. Reflecting on this it struck me that theology of baptism in the Western paradigm has been essentially backward looking.[2] It focuses on the sinful past and claims to liberate the baptized individual from the guilt of original sin. In the Protestant tradition, this focus has paradoxically led many people to perceive themselves as sinful, rather than liberated. The proclaimed need for liberation from sin, already in the newborn babies, has opened the door for the idea that the world as such is inherently sinful. When we look around and see competition, greed, and military aggression we may conclude that this is how humans are meant to be, even though the Jewish and Christian traditions have seen creation as good and the human beings as made to live in cooperation, empathy, and just peace.

In this chapter, I will explore perspectives within the theology of baptism that may help us to a more forward-looking theology of baptism, stressing the gift of baptism as an invitation to live in sacred communion with all living beings and a calling to responsibility for the future of life on earth.

In the Greek language of the New Testament, there are two words for "new." If you buy a new car (maybe an electric one these days), you would use the word *neos*, which refers to something completely new. In contrast, if you take a bath during the summer, you might feel like a new human being. In this case, the Greek language would use the word *kainä* (*kainos*). In my search for new perspectives within the realm of the theology of baptism, I prefer to use the word *kainä*. A new story of this kind is often more rooted in an older one, and if it is older than modernity and industrialization it may be situated within a more holistic worldview. In these times of planetary emergency, we may find inspiration by picking up aspects of a more holistic worldview that is compatible with nature.

I am a systematic theologian, living in the global North, and more specifically in Europe, and in Sweden, thereby belonging to a Western theological tradition that traces back to St. Augustine (354–430). Still in this chapter I would like to present a theopolitical and theopoetic position on baptism that draws inspiration from other, mainly Orthodox, theological traditions.[3]

---

2. I am in this article limiting my scope to the baptism of children.

3. In my attempt to write theopoetic theology I understand theology as closer to poetry than to for example law or mathematics.

I start with a contextual analysis of the present situation with regard to the planetary emergency, and I continue by elaborating on the need for a new narrative for the relation between humanity and the rest of creation.

I then proceed to explore themes and theological resources that I used in my doctoral dissertation from 2009, such as a trinitarian theology of creation, the mystery and sacrament of creation, and the baptism of Jesus.[4] The trinitarian theology of creation that I propose undergirds the other themes and perspectives that I raise.

A CONTEXT OF PLANETARY EMERGENCY

The human domination over nature and its ecosystems, as well as the exploitation of the poor and pauperized of the Earth, may be described as a system of separation and superiority.[5] The Western world—often including the Western church—has developed with the help of these separations during several hundred years. In theology the separation between God and the world is upheld by portraying God as predominantly otherworldly. The separation between human beings and other species, comprising the entirety of nature, is upheld by belittling human dependency upon all of creation. The superiority of human beings in relation to nature and ecological systems is a master narrative of the Western world, a dominant paradigm that has served many of us well. Still, today it must be challenged.[6] Millions of people are already climate refugees and victims of ecological breakdowns.

We in the global North are transgressing both planetary and social boundaries that are vital to a good life for all of humankind. We are expecting the poor, and often pauperized, of the Earth, to be chiefly responsible for the failures of an economic system that does not respect the needs of all before the enrichment of the few and the destruction of nature and the climate.

The sociologist Max Weber (1864–1920) talked about the development of modernity as a disenchantment of the world.[7] Objectification and exploitation have replaced the feeling of wonder and praise, and the

---

4. Hammar, *Skapelsens mysterium*.

5. Percy, "A New Story for Earth."

6. Barca, *Forces of reproduction*. See also the writings of the philosopher and sociologist Bruno Latour (1947–2022).

7. Weber, *Wissenschaft als Beruf*, http://www.textlog.de/2321.html.

world has stopped singing. Today, we can hear the Earth crying out loud due to the mismanagement of many humans. Can the world start singing again, evoking once again a sense of awe and wonder in modern people in the global North? With this awe and wonder, can humility also be inspired, which would bring us closer to the humus of the Earth?

A NEW NARRATIVE

The British author and climate journalist George Monbiot writes that it is the storytellers who rule the world.[8] Increasingly influential authors and politicians argue that the present story of modernity, ending up in misusing the Earth at any cost, must be replaced by a new story. The Swedish author and former minister of the Swedish government, Isabella Lövin, explicitly argues for the need of a new story about humanity and finds inspiration in the notion of the oceanic feeling described by Romain Rolland in his letters to Sigmund Freud. Lövin writes, "The Oceanic feeling is everywhere. It is rapture, humility, connectivity, and the feeling of being a part of all that is alive."[9]

From another arena the economist Kate Raworth, working in Oxford and Cambridge, tries to enfold a new circular economic narrative, commensurable with the limits of nature and social needs.[10] Within the field of law, the concept of rights of nature and "earth jurisprudence" shapes a new narrative that assigns rights to ecosystems, floods and rivers, mountains, and forests. For human rights to be guaranteed in the long run, the ecosystems of the Earth also need to have rights.[11]

What, then, about us theologians? How do we contribute? In 1975, the World Council of Churches embarked on a programmatic adventure in Nairobi in search of a *Just, Participatory and Sustainable Society*.[12] This programmatic pilgrimage continued in 1983 in Vancouver, with an emphasis on *Justice, Peace and the Integrity of Creation*.[13]

Feminist theologians like Rosemary Radford Ruether (1938–2022) in the Catholic tradition and Sallie McFague (1933–2019) in the

---

8. Monbiot, *Out of the Wreckage*, 1–29.
9. Lövin, *Oceankänslan*, 227.
10. Raworth, *Doughnut Economics*.
11. Cullinan, *Wild Law*; Hallgren & Thiel, *Naturlagen*.
12. Lossky et al., *Dictionary of the Ecumenical Movement*, entry "Just, Participatory and Sustainable Society."
13. Lossky et al., *Dictionary of the Ecumenical Movement*, entry "Justice, Peace and the Integrity of Creation."

Protestant tradition articulated early the need for a new narrative of care of the Earth.¹⁴ Even earlier, in Sweden, at the beginning of World War II, the famous author Elin Wägner (1882–1949) wrote about peace not just on the Earth but also *with* the Earth.¹⁵

Among the first to start searching for alternative narratives in the Western hemisphere were the Indigenous theologians and among them Tink (George) Tinker from the Osage nation, who, building on Indigenous people's tradition, affirms a worldview of life in harmony with the Earth.¹⁶

More recently, the ecumenical patriarch Bartholomew of Constantinople, known as the "Green Patriarch," has contributed to a new story that accounts for the ecological disaster the world has experienced over the last fifty years. The contributions of the old Orthodox tradition are, with the help of his writings, being interpreted anew for our time.¹⁷

In *Laudato si´*, Pope Francis composed a new contribution to Catholic social teaching, in which a narrative was advanced that emphasized both planetary boundaries, especially the climate, and the situation of the poor.¹⁸ *Laudato si´* was published in time for the Paris Climate Summit in December 2015, which united the world around the goal of not transgressing a 1.5 degree increase in global warming. In *Laudato si´*, Pope Francis also turned to Saint Francis (1181/1182–1222), just like Lynn White in 1967 had suggested in a well-known article that classic interpretations of Christian traditions were responsible for the ecological crisis.¹⁹ For Lynn White the only exception was Saint Francis and hence when pope Francis chose his name he became a response to Lynn White's expressed desire.

More could be said here about these new narratives emerging from different corners of the Earth, but for now, I will turn more specifically to the theology of baptism and how my findings in this field may contribute to care for the Earth and the emergence of new perspectives, maybe even a new narrative.

---

14. Ruether, *Gaia and God*; McFague, *The Body of God*.

15. Wägner and Tamm, *Fred med jorden*.

16. Tink (George) Tinker played a significant role in the 1987 *WCC Integrity of Creation* conference in Granavollen, Norway.

17. Chryssavgis, *Creation as Sacrament*; Chryssavgis, *On Earth as in Heaven*.

18. Pope Francis, *Laudato si*.

19. Pope Francis, *Laudato si*, 10–12 in particular. White, "The Historical Roots."

PART IV: THEOLOGY

MY JOURNEY TOWARD
A TRINITARIAN THEOLOGY OF CREATION

I was walking in the snow at Sidensjö outside Örnsköldsvik in the middle of Sweden, on the occasion of being invited to speak about creation at a weekend seminar exploring environmental issues in relation to the Bible, when it suddenly struck me that I myself was included in the notion of creation. While "nature" is a word we often use for what we see around us, or walk into, and "environment" is something that surrounds us, "creation" has a deeper and more inclusive meaning. The theological word "creation" has a contribution to make to the oneness of the Earth community. Creation includes humans, trees, animals, birds, fishes in the lakes, oceans, and all other such entities that belong together.

In addition, creation includes an idea of how all on Earth depend upon the Creator God and one another. We, as human beings, are co-created beings with all that exists on Earth, and therefore we all are related to the Creator of all.[20]

Having gained this sudden insight I came to notice that there is a great difference between the Nicene Creed and the Apostles' Creed in how they articulate the process of creation. In my church, the Church of Sweden, the Apostles' Creed is always used at baptisms and often in Sunday mass. Much of Western Protestant theology is structured along the lines of the Apostles' Creed, with an emphasis on the Father as the Creator. This often implies that the first article is a step that Christians have in common with all of creation, but what is more specifically Christian is somewhat different and more restricted to the second and third articles of the creed, and thus more applicable to Christians alone. The Nicene Creed, in contrast, suggests a different understanding. The Nicene Creed professes that the Father, Son, and the Spirit are together the Creator and are thus fundamental to both creation and creativity:[21]

> I believe in one God,
> the Father almighty,
> **maker of heaven and earth,**
> **of all things visible and invisible.**

---

20. Hammar, *Att finna Gud i en snigel*, 17–18.

21. Cf. Gunton, *The Promise of Trinitarian Theology*; Gunto also used the expression of trinitarian creation theology.

I believe in one Lord Jesus Christ,

---

through him all things were made.

I believe in the Holy Spirit, the Lord, **the giver of life**.[22]

The Nicene Creed embraces the Trinity as the source of creation and all that is created. The Spirit is the giver of life, present not only at the beginnings of the evolution, but also in the midst of it, as the world was in the beginning, is now and ever shall be.

With Christ, the Nicene Creed echoes Colossians 1:16, "for in him all things in heaven and on Earth were created . . . all things have been created through him and for him" (NRSV). The Nicene Creed opens up for a trinitarian theology of Creation, which does not separate creation and salvation.[23] This trinitarian theology of creation embraces humankind and all creation as the dwelling place of Godself. It is not just the origin that is from God, and not just the future that is in God's hands, but rather, the Triune God is the divine indwelling in all that exists on Earth. God is our present creative reality, present everywhere in the universe, and not least on the beloved planet Earth. A trinitarian theology of creation based on the Nicene creed is my main attempt to explore baptismal theology in the context of planetary emergency.

Hence, I wish I could shout to the grandchildren and their parents: "Do not give up, and do not close your ears to the cries from the Earth. Listen to all who die in the mass extinctions of living species, listen and know that the Creator is not far away, waiting to fill our actions for life with energy to revoke the wrongdoings of modernity, to stop the deadly game of the fossil fuel industry, and to change the blatant misconceptions of the economic and financial systems, instead of respecting the safe space of the economy between the planetary and the social boundaries. The presence of the Triune Creator God is the hope of humankind for ecological conversion, the hope for healing and salvation. The source of awe and wonder, opening in us voices of praise and reverence, making us walk gently on Earth in respect for all that is alive. The world can start singing again. The re-enchantment of the world is a possibility."

---

22. *Nicene Creed*, United States Conference of Catholic Bishops, https://www.usccb.org/prayers/nicene-creed.

23. Hammar, Skapelsens mysterium, 16, 196-223.

Is this not too idealistic? Is not the ruling Protestant story on how the world has fallen and remains in the hands of evil more realistic and accurate? Is there really hope to expect from present realities? Are there not more reasons to believe that there is hope beyond death rather than in the here and now?

But let me return to the trinitarian theology of creation and especially its contributions to a revised anthropology in relation to the Western master narrative. Being created by God, the human person is co-created with all Earth inhabitants. As part of this co-creation, we encounter the problem of evil in the world. Does the human being have a special responsibility here? The trinitarian theology of creation that I am a proponent of does not deny evil. It is worth noting, however, that no creed, whether Apostolic or Nicene, mentions evil. Evil and destruction are rather seen as the backdrop against which the Triune God is creating and revitalizing life on Earth. Evil and destruction constitute the background against which God is calling creation into cooperation against the destruction.

Good and evil are not equal, according to the early church. By using the word "destroying" instead of the word "evil," Saint Irenaeus implies that the destructive force, the devil, can destroy what God creates, but the devil can never create anything itself, and can instead only destroy what God has created as good: " . . . it is only God who creates: the devil can only prey on what God produces. He can destroy; he can put to death, but he can never create."[24]

The re-enchantment of the world that I call for should against this background not be seen as idealistic, otherworldly praise, but rather a praise of resistance against the forces of destruction. By praising the Triune God, we may hold onto life as more powerful than death, compassion more powerful than ignorance, and cooperation more powerful than competition.

CONSEQUENCES OF A BAPTISMAL THEOLOGY OF CREATION

What consequences does the view of good and evil described above have for our understanding of baptism? First, I will point to the *anthropological basis* for baptismal theology. Are we all created good, and can destruction only serve as second in command to God's good creation? Are we

---

24. Wingren, *Man and the Incarnation*, 39.

baptizing babies because they are evil, and if not, are they good? Why do we even baptize, as St. Augustine asked when, as a practical theologian, he observed the practice of baptizing children and hence drew the conclusion that they too must have acquired original sin.[25] Baptism did not start with a theory of original sin; it started with a practice, and the argument later unfolded in the Western church that we baptize children because of original sin and, more specifically, to remove the guilt acquired. Hence, the question remains: what kind of anthropology does baptism imply?

My tentative reply is to see baptism in the name of the Father, the Son, and the Spirit, as being baptized to the Triune God, to the source of the identity of the human person. The human person is then affirmed and embraced as a child of God and as a unique and beloved person in a sacred communion of co-created beings.

Paradigmatic for this kind of trinitarian baptismal theology of creation is the baptism of Jesus. It is a vital paradigm of baptism in the early church and still in Orthodox traditions. Alexander Schmemann (1921–1983), theologian and interpreter of the Orthodox world to the West, referred to the baptism of Jesus as the first (public) appearance in the cosmos of the Holy Trinity as Father, Son, and Spirit.[26] The link between the baptism of Jesus and Christian baptism is visible in engravings on twelfth-century baptismal fonts in Sweden. In Orthodox churches, and particularly those in the Middle East, the baptism of Jesus is often shown as happening close to the baptismal font. So even in Catholic churches in southern Europe. I will further develop this rich paradigm of baptism later, but here I only mention that the voice of being loved, as Christ heard it at his baptism, is heard each time a person is baptized in the name of the Father, the Son, and the Holy Spirit.[27] There are more reasons for baptism than original sin and its guilt. One is to be embraced by the love of the Triune God upon all and in all of creation.

---

25. St. Augustine wrote the following about children who are baptized: "If they were hurt by no malady of original sin, how is it that they are carried to the Physician Christ, for the express purpose of receiving the sacrament of eternal salvation, by the pious anxiety of those who run to him?," "Chapter XIII He refutes Those who Allege that Infants are Baptized Not for the Remission of Sins But for the Obtaining of the Kingdom of Heaven," NPNF1-05, St. Augustine, *Anti-Pelagian Writings, Book I, A Treatise on the Merits and Forgiveness of Sins, and on the Baptism of Infants*, by Aurelius Augustin, Bishop of Hippo, Addressed to Marcellinus, AD 412.

26. Schmemann, *Av vatten och Ande*, 45.

27. Hammar, *Skapelsens mysterium*, Chapter 5.

Searching for alternatives to the binary alternatives of good and evil I turn to the work of the French Protestant philosopher Paul Ricoeur (1913–2005). With him I would like to argue that the basic characteristic of the human person is neither that she is good, nor that she is evil, but that she is *fragile*.[28] The human person is, from the beginning, dependent on how she is respected and treated. Among the many species of creation, the human person is the most vulnerable and least genetically programmed. An elk knows what it is to be an elk from day one, but a human person needs to learn a lot in this regard. Hence, culture and religion play such a great role in the life of human beings,[29] thereby shaping the narrative into which the human person is to be fostered. Would it be best if this was a narrative of competition and greed, or one of cooperation and compassion? A baptismal narrative grounded in a trinitarian theology of creation might have a lot to contribute to the latter.

GOD'S PRESENCE IN ALL OF CREATION

The relevance of baptism is not limited to anthropological questions, as it has consequences for how we understand God's presence in all of creation. We are shaped as human beings in an interplay with the Triune God, whose presence flows through the world. In baptism, the human being becomes a sister and brother to the wolf, the elk, the cat, and the Danish-Swedish farm dog. The trinitarian theology of creation that I argue for counts on God's creative presence in all processes of life and in all aspects of the creation process that are still at work.

When a child is baptized in the name of the Father, the Son, and the Holy Spirit, this earth opens up as an inhabited Earth, and the identity of the human person is linked to the Triune God. Baptism reveals a miracle of creation and evokes hope of liberation for humankind, which in this case is represented by the candidate to baptism. The water that springs forth in baptism is filled with and embraced by God's triune stream of love through the world, simultaneously creating the universe and caring for one single person as if she was the only one. In baptism she is not alone. Together with the reindeer and the roe deer, the lark and the sparrow, the woods and the seas, and the floods clapping their hands in the face of God's creating and liberating presence, a human being is baptized into a love that creates the world.

28. Ricoeur, *The Conflict of Interpretations*.
29. See Kurkiala, *När själen går i exil*.

This is why we grieve the loss of biodiversity and a vast number of species on Earth. What is taking place now is called the sixth mass extinction in the history of Earth.[30] When we, in the name of the Father, the Son, and the Holy Spirit, are baptized into the affinity and connectedness that fills the world, our pain grows for how we deal with life on Earth. With the Triune God, we grieve the destruction of life.

In the early church, the Triune God was understood as giving birth to the universe in its dance of giving and receiving *perichoresis*.[31] The love of the Triune God, in its community of being One, overflows and creates the world. In baptism, we are acknowledged as partners in this dance of creativity, compassion, and cooperation. Accordingly, instead of talking about a theology of baptism that is constructed mainly on the paradigm of the Apostles' Creed, we can affirm the Nicene paradigm and talk about God as the Triune Creator.

MYSTERY AND SACRAMENT OF CREATION

When I defended my dissertation on baptism, a professor of astronomy asked me why I had not dwelled more on the function of the water itself. I did not have a reply then, but I would have argued today that the Christian tradition cannot speak of water alone, but rather of water and Spirit. Without the dynamic interplay between water and Spirit, we cannot understand the new narrative that can be developed from Christian sources in cooperation with the social and natural sciences.

The origins of water are still debated in the natural sciences. Water is likely to have appeared in the evolution of Earth by "itself," or, as often astrophysics suggests, from ice crystals in the area of Jupiter, from which it was transported to Earth.[32] Whatever the understanding of its origin (it all seems like a mystery in the natural sciences as well), water is fundamental to life and our existence on Earth as a community. When a child is baptized in water and Spirit, it is baptized into the mystery and sacrament of creation. Water is created like the child, the sun, and

---

30. World Wild Life, https://www.worldwildlife.org/stories/what-is-the-sixth-mass-extinction-and-what-can-we-do-about-it.

31. LaCugna, *God for Us*, 270ff.

32. https://news.agu.org/press-release/scientists-theorize-new-origin-story-for-earths-water/#:~:text=Many%20scientists%20have%20historically%20supported%20a%20theory%20that,as%20a%20unique%20chemical%20signature%20of%20water%20sources.

the moon, and the Spirit is the creativity holding it all together, which allows us to unfold and grow in the triune love of God.

The mystery of creation is an Eastern and Oriental Orthodox way of talking about what the Western tradition refers to as the sacrament of creation. Based on the Catholic notion of the German term *Ur-Sakrament*, I point to in my thesis that the foundational sacrament might be creation itself. For the German Jesuit Karl Rahner (1904-1984), it was the church, and for the Dutch Dominican Edward Schillebeeckx (1914-2009), it was Jesus Christ. At the beginning of the 21st Century Mathai Kadavil, an Indian Catholic theologian, proposed a way of viewing creation as Ur-Sakrament.[33]

What, then, would a sacramental worldview mean in the context of baptism? A sacramental worldview is connected to the sacraments as the *epiphania* of the invisible reality surrounding us and within us. We are surrounded by the Triune Creator God, and this makes baptism reveal a mystery that Hindus, Jews, Muslims, Agnostics, and many more religions have in common, which is the sacrament of creation. It is often taken for granted in Western Protestant theology that the world surrounding baptism is a profane one, while holiness is attributed to the sacrament of baptism only within the realm of the church.[34] However, this distinction between the sacred and the profane leads us straight to denial of the holiness and sacredness of creation. Instead I want to distinguish between sacrament and sacramentality. It is not just the church that is filled with the presence of the Triune God, but rather the entire world, and there is only one God present in the whole world.

The presence of the Holy One, of the Triune God, in the world can be understood in different ways. In addition, the absence of God in the world can be interpreted positively as an actual understanding of God and how God is. The all-transcendent God can be described by the notion of *theism*, very much present beyond death and the world, but not in the world. The different understandings of the relationship between God and the world can be exemplified by the three notions of *theism*, *pantheism*, and *panentheism*. Theism implies a distant Creator God who once created the universe and set it into motion. The transcendence of God is understood as otherworldly and beyond death. Pantheism, in

---

33. Kadavil, *The World as Sacrament*; Hammar, *Skapelsens mysterium*, 52–53.

34. This difference between the holiness of the sacrament and the secularization of the world (i.e. the world as profane) is most visible in the Western world in the throwing away of edible food.

my view, implies that all of creation is holy, and that God is ultimately only this-wordly. In this sense, there is nothing to expect beyond death and the world. Panentheism, which is the alternative preferred by many contemporary theologians, including myself, means that God is present everywhere in the world, but also beyond this world and beyond death.[35] As Sallie McFague (1933–2019) has expressed, "Everything that is is *in* God and God is *in* all things and yet God is not identical with the universe, for the universe is dependent upon God in a way that God is not dependent on the universe."[36]

There is still a distinction between the Creator and the created in this understanding, but not in a way that will undo the holiness of the Triune God that is present in the world as the inherent value and dignity of all. The sacramentality of creation is not founded on an abstract notion of holiness, but rather on the creativity of the Triune Creator God, who is immersed in our lives both as human beings and as species. The holiness of this world is dependent upon the presence of the Triune God and the close relationship between the Spirit and matter.

There is a thin distinction between Spirit and matter in a panentheistic understanding of God. However, they are never separated. This fits well with the understanding of contemporary science of matter as energy transformed.[37] Spirit and matter cannot be separated, but neither are they fully identical. The violation of woods and oceans, or of a sparrow that falls to the ground, is also a violation of the presence of God, or the Holy One. The killing of one human person is a violation of the dignity of the image of God, and therefore a violation of God's self.

The Orthodox theologian John Chryssavgis, working closely with the ecumenical patriarch Bartholomew, has described the Orthodox tradition in a way surprisingly similar to Sallie McFague:

> The distinction between divine essence and divine energies defines the relationship—both intimate and separate—between Creator and creation. In other words, nothing exists or survives outside the embrace of God, everything is directly related to God, inasmuch as all of creation is a reflection of and contains the trace of the divine Creator. At the same time, God´s essence remains totally transcendent and undetermined.[38]

35. https://plato.stanford.edu/entries/panentheism/.
36. McFague, *The Body of God*, 149.
37. Radford Ruether, *Gaia and God*, 38–39.
38. Chryssavgis, *Creation as Sacrament*, 44.

My own inspiration for a theology of baptism hence comes from feminist theologians as well as Orthodox theologians. Baptism manifests connectivity and serves as a kind of embrace of the universal communion of life. A life-giving stream becomes visible in baptism, which appears as the mystery and sacrament of creation. The presence of the Triune God in the world, acting in baptism, sustains the entire creation, the whole communion of life and all of humanity. The story about the baptism of Jesus (Mark 1:9-11; Matt 3:13-17; Luke 3:21-22; John 1:29-34) links the creation story in Genesis 1 with the baptismal commission in Matthew 28, as well as with the new birth in water and Spirit in the John 3.

The litugical historian Gabriele Winkler connects the old Syriac and Armenian Orthodox tradition "*Imitatio* of the baptism of Jesus on the Jordan with the *Johannine* concept of rebirth of the water and the Spirit. At the same time, there is a flashback to the morning of creation (Gen.1-2) and so one can speak of *a Genesis mysticism* here."[39]

The linkage between the baptism of Jesus and baptism in the early church is thus established in creation by the Triune God. The baptism of Jesus connects the baptism of a child today with the morning of creation through the creative presence of the Triune Creator God. Hence a trinitarian theology of creation is fundamental also to baptism as mystery and sacrament of creation.

THE BAPTISM OF JESUS—BEING BAPTIZED INTO A NEW NARRATIVE WITH A CALLING FOR LIFE

Baptizing a child into a new story of connectiveness in the world is a great gift of the global church to the salvation of the planet. Within the realm of a trinitarian theology of creation, salvation is still needed, but this is a salvation rooted in the whole creation of God, and with the awareness that God often saves by creating new conditions for life. In the present times of planetary emergency, the issue at stake is therefore not so much the salvation of the individual soul after death, but rather the salvation of the Earth and the whole Earth community, represented in baptism by the baptismal candidate and the community, the water, and the presence of the Triune God. As the Gospel of Mark 16:15 reads, "And Jesus said to them, 'Go into all the world and proclaim the good

---

39. Winkler, *Das Armenische Initiationsritual*, 444. Original wording: "*Imitatio* der Taufe Jesu am Jordan mit der *johannäischen* Konzeption einer Wiedergeburt aus dem Wasser und dem Geist. Dabei wird zugleich auf den Schöpfungsmorgen zurückgeblendet (Gen 1-2) und so kann man hier von einer *Genesis-Mystik* sprechen."

news to the whole creation'" (NRSV). In baptism, the child is forever welcomed into a communion of all beings, thereby received as a blessed member of the Earth communion.

By linking the baptism of Jesus with the baptism of the child or adult in the Christian tradition, the early church emphasized the forward-looking aspects of being baptized and the calling of the baptismal candidate. Baptism in the name of the Triune God, a process that was first revealed at the baptism of Jesus, welcomes the child into an Earth community of equals. As co-created, human beings live in mutual connectivity with the entirety of creation. In baptism, the child is given a calling to live in that communion of co-created beings that is immersed in the presence and love of the Triune God. This narrative carries the potential of overcoming the separations and superiorities of modernity. The Catholic priest and cultural historian Thomas Berry (1914–2009) expressed it well:

> The world is a communion of subjects, not a collection of objects; it is a communion of subjects each with their own intrinsic value, interiority, and subjectivity, not a collection of objects simply or primarily for human use, taking.[40]

In baptism, the child is given a particular calling for life: to be the disciple of Jesus Christ, which means walking on Earth with the light footsteps of Jesus Christ, seeing the lilies in the field with his eyes, and listening with his ears to the cries of sisters and brothers, be they humans or other co-created beings and manifestations.

The baptism of Jesus is a calling to resist destruction and an anointing to care for the poor and marginalized. Christ, the Messiah, the anointed One, was anointed by the Holy Spirit to resist destruction and to care for all who were downtrodden. Today, in times of planetary emergency, the panda and the Baltic porpoise also belong to the downtrodden. As a disciple of Jesus Christ and also anointed by the Holy Spirit, the baptized person is called to resist like Jesus resisted, and to care like Jesus cared.

In the Orthodox church in Finland, Scandinavia, and other locations around the world, the blessing of the water is a deep tradition linked to the baptism of Jesus, *Epiphania*, and the Christian baptism. The blessing of water can be seen as a calling for all of humankind in general and for the church in particular. The Earth community's dependency on fresh water is crucial to life on Earth. Blessing the water is the gift of

---

40. Berry, *Evening Thoughts*, 23.

baptism, which is also a calling to respect the integrity of creation.[41] In the water of Jordan, all water is blessed.[42] The calling of a blessing and not a cursing of the world—and by extension the waters of the Earth—is bestowed upon the baptized person as a calling for life.

Following Jesus Christ as a disciple in times of planetary emergency implies being called to praise the Triune God with all of creation in gratefulness for the gift of life and for belonging to a sacred communion of life. Indeed, baptism is the promise of belonging to this communion of life, no matter what.

We could therefore pray in conjunction with baptism in the Church of Sweden, also remembering the baptism of Jesus, "Reveal to us the Mystery of your Baptism—one Water and one Communion of Life."[43] Following Jesus Christ in times of planetary emergency implies downsizing our ecological footprints on Earth and enjoying the gift of life and the communion of life without transgressing planetary borders and social limits. Furthermore, following Jesus Christ in times of planetary emergency implies resisting false narratives about the endless exploitation of the planet and its people. For this to happen, we need new narratives.

I started this investigation into the significance of baptism for the planetary emergency by trying to develop a more forward-looking and constructive perspective with the help of traditions of the church which have not hitherto been in focus in the Nordic and Lutheran countries. Now, I would like to tell my grandchildren: "Look for your place in the new narrative! There is a place that is especially yours, which was presented to you for the first time when you were baptized in Lena Church, not far from Uppsala, Sweden."

Bethany Beyond the Jordan on the East Bank of the Jordan River is the place where Jesus most likely was baptized.[44] Jesus was baptized at the lowest possible point on Earth. To our grandchildren, the River Jordan, therefore, whispers, "Always remember that deeper can nobody fall on this Earth than into the hands of the Triune God." And as the flood continues: "Never be afraid of looking at things from below!"

Having said that, it is time to summarize the main findings of this chapter.

41. Hammar, *Skapelsens mysterium*, 148.
42. McDonnell, *The Baptism of Jesus in the Jordan*, 68, 148–49.
43. Hammar, *Skapelsens mysterium*, 223.
44. Here, in 2030, many pilgrims from around the world will commemorate the 2,000 years that have passed since Jesus was baptized.

A new more forward-looking perspective on baptism grounded in the recognition of a sacred communion between God and all that exists, can contribute to a new narrative in relation to modernity. Many are searching for this new narrative and the Christian church could recognize this search as God´s creativity at work in the world. A child baptized into the sacred communion of life can enjoy the company of many more, searching for responsibility, or response-ability, in times of planetary emergency.[45]

BIBLIOGRAPHY

Barca, Stefania. *Forces of Reproduction: Notes for a Counter-Hegemonic Anthropocene.* Cambridge Elements. Cambridge: Cambridge University Press, 2020.

Berry, Thomas. *Evening Thoughts: Reflecting on Earth as Sacred Community, a Collection of Essays by Thomas Berry.* Edited by Mary Evelyn Tucker. San Francisco: Sierra Club, 2006.

Chryssavgis, John. *On Earth as in Heaven: Ecological Vision and Initiatives of Ecumenical Patriarch Bartholomew.* New York: Fordham University, 2012.

Chryssavgis, John. *Creation as Sacrament: Reflections on Ecology and Spirituality.* London: T. & T. Clark, 2019.

Cullinan, Cormac. *Wild Law: A Manifesto of Earth Justice.* 2nd ed. Cambridge: Green, 2011 (2003/2002).

Francis, Pope. *Laudato si´: On Care for Our Common Home.* Vatican: Editrice Vaticana, 2015.

Gunton, Colin E. *The Promise of Trinitarian Theology.* Edinburgh: T. & T. Clark, 1991.

Hallgren, Henrik, and Pella Larsdotter Thiel. *Naturlagen. Om naturens rättigheter och människans möjligheter.* Stockholm: Volante, 2022.

Hammar, Anna Karin. *Skapelsens mysterium, Skapelsens sakrament. Dopteologi i mötet mellan tradition och situation.* Uppsala: Uppsala universitet, 2009.

Hammar, Anna Karin. *Att finna Gud i en snigel—om tro, hopp och naturens rättigheter.* Stockholm: Proprius, 2021.

Kadavil, Mathai. *The World as Sacrament: Sacramentality of Creation from the Perspectives of Leonardo Boff, Alexander Schmemann and Saint Ephrem.* Studies in Liturgy 20. Leuven: Peeters, 2005.

Kurkiala, Mikael. *När själen går i exil.* Stockholm: Verbum, 2019.

LaCugna, Catherine Mowry. *God for Us. The Trinity and Christian Life.* 1973. Reprint, New York: HarperCollins, 1991.

Lossky, Nicholas, et al. *Dictionary of the Ecumenical Movement.* Grand Rapids: Eerdmans, 1992.

Lövin, Isabella. *Oceankänslan, om behovet av en ny berättelse.* Stockholm: Natur & Kultur 2022.

McDonnell, Kilian. *The Baptism of Jesus in the Jordan. The Trinitarian and Cosmic Order of Salvation.* Collegeville, MN: Liturgical, 1996.

McFague, Sallie. *The Body of God. An Ecological Theology.* London: SCM, 1993.

---

45. Response-ability, credit to the feminist scholar Donna Haraway in *Staying with the Trouble*, 2016.

PART IV: THEOLOGY

Monbiot, George. *Out of the Wreckage: A New Politics for an Age of Crisis*. London: Verso 2017.

Percy, Mary Ann. "A New Story for Earth." *Western Friend*, November 2019. https://westernfriend.org/magazine/on-separation/a-new-story-for-earth/

Radford Ruether, Rosemary. *Gaia and God: An Ecofeminist Theology of Earth Healing*. San Francisco: HarperSanFrancisco, 1992.

Raworth, Kate. *Doughnut Economics: 7 Ways to Think Like a 21st Century Economist*. White River Junction, VT: Chelsea Green, 2017.

Ricoeur, Paul. *The Conflict of Interpretations: Essays in Hermeneutics*. Evanston, IL: Northwestern University Press, 1974.

Schmemann, Alexander. *Av vatten och Ande*. Uppsala: Bokförlaget Pro Veritate, 1981.

White, Lynn, Jr. "The Historical Roots of our Ecological Crisis." *Science* 155 (1967) 1203–7.

Wingren, Gustaf. *Man and the Incarnation: A Study in the Biblical Theology of Irenaeus*. Edinburgh: Oliver & Boyd, 1959.

Winkler, Gabriele. *Das Armenische Initiationsrituale. Entwicklungsgeschichtliche und liturgievergleichende Untersuchung der Quellen des 3. bis 10. Jahrhunderts* (Winkler Arm), Orientalia Christiana Analecta 217. Rome: Pont. Institutum Studiorum Orientalum, 1982.

Wägner, Elin, and Elisabeth Tamm. *Fred med jorden*. Stockholm: Bonniers, 1940.

19

A Baptismal Theology for Imperfect People with Unfinished Faith

Niels Henrik Gregersen

THEOLOGIES OF BAPTISM USUALLY ask the question, "*What* is baptism, and what is its meaning?" Another and likewise important question is, "*Who* is the one to be baptized, and what are the life horizons and hopes of those to be baptized?" These two sets of questions are interlinked, of course, for the meaning of baptism can never be abstract. Rather, a baptism always means *something to somebody* in a specific life story.

In this essay, I propose to combine the following two questions: What *happens* in and after baptism, and what is the *array of meanings* of baptism. These questions are considered specifically for the one who is to be baptized, for the ones who carry or accompany the baptismal candidate to baptism, and for the welcoming community who baptizes the child. I thus put weight on the *who* question and will argue that we cannot, and should not, set up a model for the one and only "correct" way of approaching the sacrament of water and Spirit. Rather, we must recognize that people come to baptism with a variety of personal backgrounds, expectations, and life horizons.

Reflections on life situations, and on the different ways of being a Christian, are important in a majority church like my own, the Evangelical Lutheran Church in Denmark, with a membership (by baptism) constituting 72 percent of the population, around 4.3 million people.[1] I assume, however, that a life-historical perspective is relevant to consider for all Christian churches, particularly those in minority settings.

People are different, and this applies to children, youth, and adults. The child to be baptized may barely have survived its birth, having come into the world through a preterm birth. Perhaps it has been born into a life story involving uncertain social conditions. Other children have been floating into existence more or less effortlessly through the birth pangs and woes of their mothers, and strong and caring parents and families may surround the newborn child. Experiential conditions vary considerably, but a constellation of fragility and gratitude is an experience underlying all baptisms of children. When teenagers and adults come to be baptized later in life, they may do so with even more differing life trajectories and horizons, but I assume that we would again find a combination of a sense of fragility of existence and a sense of gratitude for life, in addition to an expressed wish to connect with God. In one sense, baptism is always about seeking refuge and embracing it in the face of uncertainties. In another sense, the meaning(s) of baptism will be more specific for those who have reached the threshold of reflection by asking questions, seeking answers, and somehow finding anchorage in the divine promise of baptism: "Remember, I am with you always, to the end of the age" (Matt 28:20, NRSV).

MORE THAN SINNERS: THE INDISPENSABLE PERSPECTIVE OF CREATION THEOLOGY

All too rarely, the question asked is what kind of person is coming to a baptism. What is lacking from the perspective of systematic theology are more sustained reflections on the theology of creation. Nevertheless, there must be an inner connection between being created "out of pure, fatherly, divine goodness and mercy, without any merit or worthiness in me" and being embraced by Christ in baptism, "that is, a grace-filled water of life" and a bath of a "new birth in the Holy Spirit."[2]

---

[1]. In 2022, 56.2 percent of the total population in Denmark was baptized within their first life year. However, out of the 40,849 baptisms in total, ca. 8,700 were youth baptisms, usually prior to confirmation (in 2022, this approach was chosen by 66.5 percent of youngsters), while about 800 were baptized later in life. See Folkekirkens Videns- og Uddannelsescenter, *Kirkestatistik*, https://www.folkekirken.dk/om-folkekirken/folkekirken-i-tal/daab.

[2]. Martin Luther on the first article of faith resp. on baptism in Small Catechism,

Correspondingly, relevant to any baptismal theology are reflections on the life-cycles of human development from newborns to toddlers and further on into early adolescence, one's middle years, and old age.[3] A broader consideration is needed here, since facets of the meaning of baptism will no doubt change over a lifetime.

The standard procedure for explaining the meaning of baptism, at least in mainstream Western theology, has been to start out with the Augustinian view of original sin. Coming from the doctrine of original sin as the horizon that explains the need for baptism, the answer to the proper meaning of baptism would be as follows: it is the sinner who is baptized, and in baptism, we receive the forgiveness of our sins. This answer is not wrong, but it is not very complete, either.[4]

If we identify the *proprium* of baptism in the removal of original sin, we can perceive baptism as a remedy for returning to an equilibrium state zero from the state minus of inherited sin. However, this would imply a neglect of the divine welcome to humans in the state plus of creation and to think too lowly about baptism. Baptism is a state plus plus offered by the unambiguous divine promise of embrace and by the giving of the Holy Spirit.

A clearer picture emerges, I think, if one understands the relationship between creation and baptism as follows: just as any human being has been carried into time and space by the Father's creative benevolence, so, too, is one to be baptized carried by the grace of Christ and Spirit into God's own eternal life. "The Lord preserves your exit and your entrance," as it is said in the baptismal ritual in the Danish church[5]. Baptism is about creation *and* salvation, and just as salvation already begins in the midst of creation, eternal salvation is about the salvation of the life stories of creation.

ON BEING GOD'S CHILD:
THE UNFINISHED BUSINESS OF CREATION

The child carried to baptism by the parents is therefore not only the child of a family clan, but also God's child. In the Bible, God is called

---

Kolb and Wengert, *Book of Concord*, 354 and 359.

3. See Kelcourse, ed., *Human Development and Faith*.

4. A critique of this inherited view can be found in Ratschow, *Die eine christliche Taufe*, 66–100.

5. *Ritualbog*, 61.

the "Father of all": humans have "one God and Father of all, who is above all and through all and in all," just as in baptism, there is "one Lord, one faith, one baptism" (Eph 4:5–6). In this light, those who are baptized cannot make a copyright claim on the title of being the "child of God," for this title belongs to every child welcomed into God's world of creation. It is also true of every adult, although not all adults are God's best children. It was thus to the (unbaptized) children that Jesus said, "It is to such as these that the kingdom of God belongs. Truly I tell you, whoever does not receive the kingdom of God as a little child will never enter it" (Mark 10:14–15).

As Harald Hegstad has rightly pointed out, salvation is not "a substitution for or an abrogation of creation, but on the contrary a salvation of what has been created."[6] I would add that if anything is unfinished, it is human life stories. The one to be baptized is always a person under growth, in extension and conversion, and in creativity and reconnection. Thus, as the child develops, it will grow into the many contexts of life in God's world of creation, whereby the child will be given many roles and functions and, accordingly, will become a person with multifarious identities. The same is true for the adult, who nevertheless has the cognitive advantage over the child by being well acquainted with the tailwinds and resistance of existence (in theological language: "misery"). In addition, since the adult has already participated in many social role-plays, the adult usually knows more about what it is like to live below par in the destruction of the life possibilities of others, as well as those of oneself (in Christian language: "sin"). At best, the adult has also come to realize his or her own limitations and may have discovered that any human being will end up in the great nothingness unless one connects with God's eternal source of life.

Grown-ups know a lot by experience, and those who are baptized as children therefore have much to learn from those who have struggled with life through hard-won insights. Among other things, they can learn about what it can mean to be surprised by God in one's middle years or late in life. Any such witnesses of experience and conversion are worth listening to, whether or not others have taken different paths in life. Nevertheless, adults still have very much to learn from children as well, not the least of which is from their immediate trust in life.

---

6. Hegstad, *Dåpen*, 57.

YOU ARE WHAT YOU ARE CONNECTED TO: ON BELONGING AND REDEMPTION

I suggest that infant baptism and adult baptism are both about belonging. What happens in baptism is that the person being baptized is becoming embedded with Christ and, through him, with the life of God. *You are what you are connected to!*

Thankfully, human beings are not only what they are in themselves, but also their limited and rather broken life stories. As human persons, we are more than just the sum of our thoughts and opinions, and of our beliefs about God or ourselves. We are *always more than we think and believe*. Just as birth means to be drawn into the networks of creation, baptism means to be drawn into God's eternal life. As such, baptism is a further divine plus, which is superimposed upon the divine plus of a creaturely existence already willed and nourished by God, and freeing and redeeming it in the process.

In the Pauline tradition, baptism is called the "water of rebirth and renewal by the Holy Spirit" (Titus 3:5). By being united with Christ, the baptized person is given the Holy Spirit. If anything connects us with Jesus's own baptism by John in the River Jordan, it is the life-renewing power of the Spirit. Baptism, however, does not make the baptized person a completely new and different creature. Any Christian is like anybody else created "out of nothing"—that is, "out of divine love"—and is "re-birthed" and "re-newed" by the Holy Spirit. In baptism, a human person is restored to become a new creature, which happily carries within it and enlivens the old creature (i.e., the person whom God, in his creative imagination, has brought into the world in the first place). Creatures coming into the world at birth thus come to full fruition in the rebirth and renewal of baptism. In old Danish, being "saved" or *frelst* means to get a "free throat" (i.e., to be freed from captivity), and in German, salvation is called *Heil*, which means becoming whole and healthy again. To become a Christian is thus to become a true human once again.

The purpose of baptism is thus to set free God's own creatures from the chains of sin and thereby allow and assist the rejuvenated creature in growing into faith, hope, and love. The baptized person, therefore, has the spiritual freedom to be unfolded into a myriad of roles and identities. Many of these identities are provisional and have a *good secular value* in themselves. It may be to play tennis or being a bodybuilder; it may be to develop into a connoisseur of food and wine, to pursue a modeling career, to identify with a particular gender identity, to be interested in art history, or to be a member of a fan club. Anything is allowed as long as one does not hurt anyone, including oneself. Whatever roles people have or take, the grace offered in baptism makes everyone equal in Christ.

The *base identity* of baptism is given in advance, so one need not worry about it. Still, one can draw nourishment from it so that one may build up a variety of additional identities, learn to resist the powers of evil, and smile at the follies and burdens of the world-and-oneself. The materiality of the created world is eminently plastic, opening up many pathways of life, but there is always somebody to care for—children, beloved ones, friends and strangers, lilies, flowers, societies, and ecosystems. The ethical call of baptism follows from the union with Christ, who is present in the least of fellow creatures—those in hunger, thirst, or other needs. Borrowing from Matthew 25:31–46, "Whatever you do—or do not!—to the least my brothers and sisters, you do—or do not!—do for me."

Baptismal faith is the awareness of being part of a sustained base identity in Christ, but the identity of being a Christian can also accommodate the depressing experience that one's own personal acts and choices of identity can begin to disintegrate and crumble when we come of age. At some point, the person to whom God has given the spirit of freedom (also the freedom to test the spirits of our own design) must begin to relax and accept what has become her or his destiny. In the end, one must accept the inevitable process toward amnesia and death, while looking forward to being drawn up anew, without having a cognitive knowledge of exactly how and when. All of this is part of baptismal life as a lifelong spiritual process of struggle and rejuvenation.

FROM DEEP INCARNATION TO DEEP BAPTISM

The longitudinal perspective is central to baptismal theology, as we saw. Let us now further explore the theological meaning of baptism on the vertical and spatial axes. In the incarnation of Christ *and* in baptism, God, the "highest," is mingling with the entire world of creation, and in doing so, combining "high" and "low." Here, there is a route to follow from the idea of "deep incarnation" to the depth and scope of the baptismal event.[7]

---

7. See Gregersen, ed., *Incarnation*; Gregersen, "Deep Incarnation and Chalcedon."

A central point of baptismal theology is that Christ has conjoined himself with the baptized person in a permanent way. In light of this, the practice of re-baptism is a distrust of the divine promise of being there for us to the end of days. This divine "being there for us," however, presupposes that Christ is already present in the corporeal world. Thus, having incarnated himself in the world of "flesh" (John 1:14), Christ is already intimately connected with all layers of creaturely existence—from social and organismic life down to the material constituents of any embodied existence. As we know today all living bodies are made up of cells; in turn, organismic life is made up of material particles, which break down into quarks. In biblical language, this is called "all flesh" (in Hebrew, *kol-bashar*), which includes the moister of "clay" and "earth."

In the elements of baptism, we see the same coordination of the bodily and material aspects of reality. First, we have the human "earthlings" who are baptized, for the name "Adam" is derived from the Hebrew *adamah*, which means soil or earth. This earthliness is a signature of both the "old Adam" and the "new Adam" of Christ—that is, any subsequent Christ-formed existence (Romans 5-6). Second, in baptism, we have the natural element of "water," which cleanses us from dirt and sin. Third, we have the Holy Spirit, who is associated with the element of "air." The root meaning of the Greek *pneuma* is thus wind and air.[8] The divine *pneuma*, or Spirit, is dissipated by sparkles of the divine "fire," too, as we find it in Pentecost (Acts 2). In this sense, all four basic "elements" of antiquity (earth, water, air, and fire) are present in what happens in baptism.

What is added to the natural elements is the divine Word of promise, which—unlike the natural elements—is an unambiguous pronunciation of divine grace "for us" and ready to be absorbed over a lifetime. Moreover, with the Word of promise (Christ) comes the gift of the Holy Spirit. The combination of the earthbound perspective with the divine Word of the gospel and the Holy Spirit is central to the emotional and cognitive aspects of baptism.

WE LIVE AT A DEEPER LEVEL THAN WE THINK: THE GOSPEL FOR THE SUBCONSCIOUS LIFE

Baptismal life is about being united with Christ and being part of the extensive Body of Christ, one divine-human body with many members

---

8. *The Brill Dictionary of Ancient Greek* lists "wind" and "air (as element)" as the primary meanings of the figurative terms "breeze" and "breath."

(1 Cor 12). To receive one's base identity in Christ is to receive a shared identity beyond human distinctions between "high" and "low," or "child" or "adult," since the identity of being united with Christ has validity, no matter how much or little the individual human person is capable of living in faith, hope, and love. There is a key distinction to note between the *validity* of baptism, which stands firm by the divine Word, and the *use* of baptism in our lives. If we could imagine a baptized person living fully devoid of trust, expectation, and warmth, we would know what it would mean to live in a total separation from God, at least as seen from a human perspective. This is hardly even thinkable.

Children, youngsters, and adults live at a deeper level than they think and understand. The practice of infant baptism reflects an ecclesial awareness that the grace of baptism is fully as much about the "subconscious" as it is about a "conscious" awareness of divinity. Imagine that faith existed only by virtue of our conscious awareness; we would then fall out of the grace of baptism as soon as we fell asleep. Furthermore, the grace of baptism would not make sense to the intellectually disabled, who may not understand the creed, but "only" the repetitive rituals, music, and praise. Likewise, one might imagine that love exists only when we love in an emotionally self-transparent manner and with a trusting orientation toward Christ; then, human engagements of love would be infused with the risk of forgetting the ones to be loved in overeager attempts to think of God. However, love is most often pre-reflective: "Whoever lives in love lives in God, and God in him" (1 John 1:4). Similarly, if we overemphasize the role of human awareness and self-reflection, the divine promise of baptism would no longer be valid if we were to slip into states of dementia as elderly persons.

Hypercognitive and hyperemotional approaches to baptism are therefore highly problematic. If baptisms are conditioned by a composed and self-transparent human "confession," the uncomprehending children and cognitively less gifted adults could at best be called the "not-yet" Christians; similarly, demented people and those in comas would have to be seen as "no-longer" Christians.

I have here presented a human as well as a theological argument against the claim that only an adult baptism by confession is a "genuine" baptism. We need a more inclusive understanding of what it means to be part of the community of believers, which is not just a cognitive community and not just an emotion-based community; rather, it is a deep community of faith, hope, and love. In the end, love is the greatest, if we are to believe Paul (1 Cor 13:13).

THE SACRAMENT OF BAPTISM IS MORE THAN A BLESSING AND MORE THAN A CONFESSION

When Lutherans, in line with the Catholic tradition, speak of baptism as a "sacrament," they understand the baptismal event as a "means of grace." Here, baptism is not the end state of Christian existence, but the channeling of a divine-human life that finds its end in the kingdom of God. Moreover, what the sacramental traditions emphasize is that the divine promise "to be with you, to the end of the age" (Matt 28:20) stands firm and remains valid, even despite the ethical shortcomings and cognitive impairments of the disciples of Christ. The point of baptism, however, is that the embodiment in Christ, and the presence of Christ and Spirit in the believer, cannot but lead to life-stories marked by faith, hope, and love.

In the sacramental view, baptism is something more than a freely chosen ecclesial act of blessing, just as it is also something more than a mere act of personal confession. Ecclesial rites of blessing the children (whom God has already blessed by bringing them into the world) are meaningful and even beautiful. In the same way, a person's surrender to God in an outspoken confession is central to the life of churches, as the future of Christianity depends on people who do not shy away from committing to God and strive to live a Christ-formed life.

The sacramental view of baptism, however, does not reduce baptism to church ceremonies of blessing or to personal acts of confession. This would mean to capitalize either the Church or the believing Subject, while decapitalizing God as the father, son, and spirit. Under the hand, God is reduced to a religious background condition for freely rewritten church rituals or to a trampoline to be leveraged for the intensity of "my own" personal faith. In the sacramental view, it is God who acts in baptism, since it is Christ who has instituted the practice and made his promise to be with the baptized for all the days of the world (Matt 28:20).

BAPTISM AS A SACRAMENT: LUTHER ON THE LIFE-CYCLIC DEPTH OF BAPTISM

I do not share the view that Luther was right in everything he said, and that contemporary theologies of baptism should not draw on any other resources besides Luther alone. Nevertheless, Luther's strength was and is that he maintained the focal point of baptism: it is the Lord of the church who has instituted baptism, and baptism is therefore a mandate that the church itself cannot do with as it pleases.

Luther knew well that his own theology of baptism was in line with the preceding Catholic tradition. As phrased by Augustine, "The word comes to the element and creates the sacrament."[9] Luther continues this tradition in his emphasis that, in baptism, God bestows grace on the future lives of the baptized. Baptism takes place through the Word of Christ, who unites Himself with water (the "element" in the narrower sense) and is vividly present in the entire act of baptism ("elements" in its broader social sense).

The natural elements and the instituting words of baptism become a sacramental unity. In the words of Luther's "Large Catechism" of 1529, "To be baptized in God's name is to be baptized not by human beings but by God himself."[10] First comes God, and then comes the church! Baptism is thus not an arbitrary ecclesial act devised by well-meaning pastors, but an act in which God is the enduring subject. Similarly, it is not our fluctuating faith that justifies baptism, but rather God's faithfulness: "My faith does not work baptism; rather it receives baptism. Baptism does not become invalid if it is not properly received or used, as I have said, for it is not bound to our faith, but to the Word."[11]

In other words, the church baptizes in the confidence that Christ, by his word and promise, has conjoined himself with the child and will therefore bring about faith. This is the first and the most essential act. The manifestations of faith are second and subsequent, as they become a part of the life in faith, hope, and love. The meaning of baptism is thus a spiritual process that lasts a lifetime, and faith, hope, and love each play their own roles. Baptism is valid by virtue of God's promise, but only beneficial when received by faith. In this way, Luther develops a theology of baptism that begins in God's word but ends in the response of faith, thereby establishing a *reciprocal relationship* between the calling God and the human response: "Yes, I will." In this sense, baptism is a new covenant. The tension between baptism as an accomplished act ("perfective") and baptism as a continuous and unfinished process ("imperfective") lies like

---

9. Quoted in Martin Luther's "Large Catechism," in Kolb and Wengert, *Book of Concord*, 458.

10. Kolb and Wengert, *Book of Concord*, 457.

11. Kolb and Wengert, *Book of Concord*, 463.

a basso continuo in Luther's theology of baptism. In his early "Sermon on Baptism" from 1519, Luther linked baptism (in German, *Taufe*) to the depth of being (in German, *Tiefe*).[12] Luther has an awareness of the preconscious depth of baptism, but he also views baptism as a life-historical process. The baptized person is fully immersed in the water of baptism in order to die as a sinner, but he or she must also be drawn up as in a resurrection. The event of baptism takes only a moment, but its meaning, "the spiritual baptism," takes a lifetime to unfold.[13] Baptismal life is fulfilled only at death, when there is no stable ego left, and only our immersion in the fluid Body of Christ remains.

The strength of Luther's theology of baptism, in my view, is that he does not presuppose the idea of the perfect human believer. On the contrary, Christians must learn to give up their ideals of perfectionism. One can therefore interpret Luther's anthropology as a *rejection of perfectionism* as the eighth mortal sin, a sin that medieval theology never discovered and therefore never overcame. "You must accept that you will never be perfect!"—so I would paraphrase Luther's teaching on sin. However, you must also "accept that you are accepted!"—so I (with Paul Tillich) will paraphrase Luther's concept of justification by faith.

THE DANGER OF FAITH PERFECTIONISM: WHAT LUTHER FAILED TO SAY AND DO

From a contemporary perspective, I see an open wound in Luther's theology of baptism, despite its value. Inadvertently, Luther may have paved the way for a perfectionist concept of faith.

A recurrent motto in Luther's theology is, "If you believe, then you have. If you doubt, you are lost." In Luther's context, this was a liberating message insofar as the anxious person did not have to worry about his or her own level of perfection. We are embraced "on account of Christ" (*propter Christum*), and not on account of our faith, but "through faith" (*per fidem*), as stated in the Augsburg Confession, Article 4.[14] The emphasis on the external word of God can be interpreted as a means of overcoming the two-fold danger of overestimating one's own state of faith or (more often today) being ashamed of one's too small and wavering faith.

---

12. Luther, "Sermon," 29.
13. Luther, "Sermon," 30–31.
14. Kolb and Wengert, *Book of Concord*, 41.

In the centuries to come, however, Luther's emphasis on faith as the hinge of it all gave room for an unhealthy focus on one's own state of faith. This led either to the desire for a pure doxastic faith, as developed in the Orthodox period (and in today's fundamentalisms), or to the desire for an intensified faith, which was prevalent in the era of pietism (and in today's hyperemotional religiosities).

In today's psychologizing climate, the emphasis on faith as the only expression of the human side of baptism easily leads to feelings of inadequacy and shame, since many modern Christians doubt whether they "believe enough" or are sufficiently "authentic" and therefore come to doubt whether they are at all acceptable as "real Christians." In this situation, the constant reference to the wholeheartedness of faith ("if you believe, you have; if you don't believe, you're lost") underhandedly becomes an act of self-justification by one's own faith. Luther took no time to distinguish between human forms of faith, between firm and vacillating faith, or between intuitive faith, skeptical faith, and articulate faith. Today, however, we have to develop a more variegated understanding of faith. The gospels might be a starting point for reflections on weak states of faith. As described in Matthew 28, Christ gave his commission to baptize to disciples with wavering states of faith and doubt. When the eleven disciples went to Galilee to the mountain where Jesus had summoned them, "they saw him, they worshiped him; but some doubted" (Matt 28:17). It was to these disciples that Christ said, "All authority has been given to me. . ." The so-called "baptismal command" was not addressed to disciples who were secure in their faith; rather, it was an encouragement to begin a life of faith as disciples of Christ. Similarly, we have "the children's gospel" (Mark 10:13–16), in which we hear about how the far-from-perfect disciples wanted to hinder the children and even rebuked their parents. In this case, Jesus intervened: "Let the little children come to me; do not stop them," for "whoever does not receive the kingdom of God as a little child will never enter." In the gospels, it is hard to find clear-cut divisions of people into "believers" and "nonbelievers." The same people appear sometimes as both, the disciple Peter perhaps being the best example of a vacillating believer. Ultimately, faith is all about beginning again and often from scratch.

FAITH, HOPE, AND LOVE: A SKETCH FOR A MORE INCLUSIVE THEOLOGY OF BAPTISM

Since Augustine in the fifth century, Western theologians have referred to the forgiveness of original sin as the *proprium* of infant baptism. Correspondingly, the proper task of the sacrament of penance was the forgiveness of sins after baptism.

Since the eighteenth and nineteenth centuries—with Reimarus, Schleiermacher, and Kierkegaard—the Augustinian idea of an original sin as something biologically inherited from Adam (and Eve) became increasingly problematic. Consequently, "sin" tended to become associated with individual evil acts and hence moralized.[15] In the twentieth century, theologians therefore proposed new ways to reformulate the intention of the concept of original sin. For example, the Danish theologian Regin Prenter translated the term original sin as a "personal sin" (a sin rooted in the depth of human strivings), thereby establishing some distance from the view that sin is "transferred through propagation."[16] In the vein of Friedrich Schleiermacher, liberation and feminist theologians have likewise reinterpreted the idea of universal sin as a "structural sin" of human sociality, thereby pointing to ways of overcoming the social aspects of original sin.[17]

Nevertheless, I think it is fair to say that these reinterpretations of original sin have not been able to find widespread resonance in the contemporary Danish church, especially not among laypeople. We see this in current Danish discussions of the official baptismal liturgy, particularly regarding the prayer preceding the baptismal act. The *Ritual for Baptism* from 1992 (going back to 1912) reads as follows:

> We thank You, Heavenly Father.
> that through Your only begotten Son,
> You have given this Holy Baptism
> in which You make us your children
> and give us the Holy Spirit
> with the forgiveness of sins and eternal life . . .

This liturgical prayer makes no reference to the removal of original sin, but the current Danish debate concerns whether an Augustinian doctrine

---

15. Pannenberg, *Systematic Theology II*, 231–35.
16. Prenter, *Creation and Redemption*, 286–88.
17. Suchocki, *The Fall to Violence*.

of original sin is nonetheless presupposed in the line "in which You make us your children." In other words, the following question arises: is the hidden meaning of the ritual that baptism is the exclusive condition for being a child of God, while unbaptized children are considered to be living under divine wrath? This is not how the prayer is understood by the parents who bring their children to baptism, but critics have argued that such an exclusivist view is nonetheless presupposed in the prayer.

My own proposal (sent to the public hearing on liturgy in 2017) is to change the wording as follows: "In which You receive us as your children." This formulation expresses the sacramental view that God is active in baptism and that baptism offers a new state—a new *plus* superimposed on the *plus* of already being a child created out of divine love—without implying any negative consequences for the many children of this world who are not baptized.

Discussions like these will be part of the newly established Baptismal Commission of the Evangelical Lutheran Church in Denmark, which began its work in June 2023 and will end by 2027. The commission has been called to "modernize" the baptismal ritual within the general framework of the Lutheran confessions while expressing a clear "sacramental view of baptism."[18] Whatever the advice of the Commission will be in detail, and to what extent the existing ritual will be revised and authorized, the Commission will most likely not affirm that the removal of the original sin is the only proper task of baptism.

In today's Danish discussions, we find two proposals for a baptismal theology, both of which seem to question the sacramental understanding of baptism as a means of grace.

The first strategy is to say that the sacrament of baptism is nothing but a *blessing ceremony* of the church, stating that all people are under God's grace in advance, with or without baptism. Baptism is nothing but an affirmation of the already-created human being, told by the blessing ceremony of the church that it is good enough as it is. In this view, *nothing happens* in baptism, which is reduced to a solemn *declaration* that God loves the child, for which the parents now receive the church's word. In as much as I have argued above for the strong bond between creation, incarnation, and baptism, I remain critical of the reduction of the sacrament of baptism to a celebratory blessing of a newborn life.

---

18. See the presentation and the members of the Baptismal Commission from the Danish Governments' Ministry of Ecclesiastical Affairs, https://www.km.dk/aktuelt/singlevisning/kommission-skal-overveje-modernisering-af-folkekirkens-daab/.

Another strategy is the so-called confessional baptism in charismatic circles, which has been inspired by Baptist traditions. In this view, the validity of the baptismal act depends on the specific cognitive and emotional awareness of the one who has chosen to be baptized. Therefore, a division is produced between a little flock of those who take their faith seriously, while the remainder of the church, including those baptized as children, are viewed as deficient Christians.

This situation calls, in my view, for the formulation of a theology of *baptism for imperfect people with unfinished faith*. First, there is a need for greater coherence between creation theology and baptism theology, for it is God's own children who are baptized on the promise of Christ. What happens in baptism is that the person, already carried at birth into the world of creation by divine generosity, is now carried into a union with Christ for eternal life. Second, as mentioned above, new interpretations of the doctrine of original sin are called for. Children are *not* biologically born as children under divine wrath. Nevertheless, every human person—whether it be a child or an adult—lives with selfishness deep at the root of their motivational structure. Already infants, who do not immediately receive food and warmth, react with aggression against the mother's breast. In similar ways, forms of inner aggression continue to show up in most adults, regardless of whether they are baptized.

Third, a new and expanded understanding of baptism as a lifelong process is needed. Christians rarely live with a fixed and finished faith. Rather, Christian life is determined by the triad of faith, hope, and love and is always in states of imperfection. Here, the Danish hymn writer, pedagogue, and theologian N. F. S. Grundtvig (1783–1872) helped to rediscover the importance of the "image of God" for a future ecumenical and Lutheran theology. According to Grundtvig, faith, hope, and love are "actually as old as the human race," thus far from being something brand-new that first came into being with Christianity.[19] A human person is more than a sinner, for she or he is and remains created in the image of God, even after the "fall."

This Grundtvigian view opens up a broader repertoire in the personal pathways into the Christian faith. Sometimes it is the searching faith, sometimes it is the hope (for others and for oneself), and, still at other times, it is love that becomes the entry point to the church. In faith, hope, and love, there is thus a *deep continuity* between the

---

19. Grundtvig, *Human Comes First*, 356.

"natural" human being and the Christian. Faith, hope, and love are thus precisely the primordial aspects of human flourishing to which baptism gives both strength and direction.

In Grundtvig, we therefore also see a further development of understanding baptism as a *two-sided* covenant. First, every human being is created in the image of God. It is therefore the person created in God's image who comes to baptism to connect with the divine light and say "no" to the powers of darkness. Already by natural powers, the baptismal candidate can renounce "the Devil and all his deeds." Second, the baptismal candidate now meets Christ's graceful invitation to baptism and accepts the pathway extending all the way with Christ. Nevertheless, this may require experiences of grace in one's previous life, before baptism. Third, by the sacramental act of baptism, humans are united with Christ and empowered by the Holy Spirit; they are thus given a new capacity to live a Christ-formed life in faith, hope, and love.[20]

In this light, the difference between infant baptism, youth baptism, and adult baptism is not very significant, as they are all equal pathways to baptism. Theologically, we should acknowledge that many different paths of life precede baptism, for every human being is created and willed by God before being baptized. This is true both for the child and for the adult who has struggled with life for a long time and who may have learned important lessons along the way.

THE CRYSTAL OF BAPTISM: WHO IS PART OF THE COMMUNITY OF FAITH, HOPE, AND LOVE?

All theology must begin where God begins—namely, by creating the world and placing human beings in that world. In his "Small Catechism," Luther asks the question of what creation means. His response is, "I believe that God has created me together with all that exists. God has given me body and soul; eyes, ears, and all limbs and senses; reason and all mental faculties... And all this is done out of pure, fatherly, and divine goodness and mercy without any merit or worthiness of mine at all!"[21]

We hear nothing here of humans as children of wrath. Creation begins in a plus and not in a minus state. We are not thrown into an alien world by an alien God but are instead borne into existence by a God of divine benevolence and care. Church fathers older than Augustine went

---

20. Grundtvig, *Human Comes First*, 249–63.
21. Kolb and Wengert, *Book of Concord*, 254–55.

further than Luther did. In his *Apology*, Tertullian (c. 200) wrote that "every soul is born a Christian."[22] Gregory of Nyssa (c. 380) made a similar declaration in his *Great Catechism*, in that every human being is born with the "original grace" that makes humans seek God.[23]

Luther was content to say that every creature is accompanied by God's good will. He also emphasized that human life is never lived alone. Human existence is encompassed and extended by the natural and social spheres of life (field, family, home, etc.), and any human life is limited in time, ultimately by death. Next to this good but limited finitude, we live a selfish existence in a broken world. However, Luther did not say anything about this in his exposition of the first article of faith, but only in the exposition of the second article about Christ and redemption. Here, Christ is the divine Lord who "has redeemed me, a lost and condemned human being."[24] What, then, is the relationship between God's good creation and sin when we come to baptism? Baptism is a physical, spiritual, and social event. Baptism is bodily because the promise of God connects one with the element of water, and we become connected with Christ as the "body of Christ" (1 Cor 10). Baptism is spiritual because, in it, we are connected to God's life-giving and renewing Spirit, who always understands the depths of humanity from within (1 Cor 2). Baptism is deeply social, too. Baptism is a social event (usually) taking place in a local church with the congregation as witnesses and fellow believers, dreamers, and lovers.

Since one cannot baptize oneself, there are at minimum two present at every baptism: the baptizer and the baptized. However, baptism is also an incorporation into the universal church. Therefore, baptism is not primarily about membership in a national church or any other particular church community. Baptism is about being united with God, the Father, the Creator, who, from the moment of birth, is involved with every human being—indeed, with all living flesh. The way into God is through incorporation into the body of Christ. However, just as Christ is never *solo*, without a congregation, the body of Christ is never without *flesh*—that is, without an extensive world of social and biological creatures.

In baptism, we are incorporated into the communion of faith, hope, and love with all Christians and with all others who wish to live in faith, hope, and love. In biblical terms, the universal church includes not only other Christians, but also Adam and Eve, Abel and Cain, Noah

22. Tertullian, *Apology*, chapter 17.
23. Gregory of Nyssa, *The Great Catechetical Discourse*, chapters 8 and 16
24. Kolb and Wengert, *Book of Concord*, 355.

and his sons Shem, Ham and Japheth, and Abraham and Sarah and their children (Heb 11:4–12), as well as Job and all the others who have suffered and prayed during history. As the Hebrews put it, "All of these died in faith without having received the promises, but from a distance they died without having their promises fulfilled; they had only seen and greeted their fulfillment from afar. They confessed that they were strangers and foreigners on the earth, for people who speak in this way make it clear that they are seeking a homeland" (Heb 11:13–15). The church, understood as the community of all believers, hopefuls, and lovers, does not begin with the Christian church, but instead goes back to the prehistory of humankind.

It may be worth recalling that Abraham is called the "father of faith" by Paul, and that Jesus says that the poor Lazarus will find peace and blessedness "in the bosom of Abraham." However, neither of them was baptized. We may ask further: does not the Virgin Mary belong to the community of believers, even though she was a non-baptized? Of course! It seems that no theologian has the right to set up baptism as a "condition of salvation," thereby setting limits to divine love and grace.

Baptism is a means of grace but not necessarily the only one. In theological tradition, even Augustine spoke of baptism by desire and longing (e.g., *On Baptism Against the Donatists* IV, 21). Likewise, Luther spoke of the baptism of blood, that is, by martyrdom. In a long letter, entitled "On Rebaptism to Two Pastors" from 1528, he could say without further ado that all the innocent children that Herod murdered during the infanticide in Jerusalem were beautified through their martyrdom.[25]

Instead of looking for the "proprium" of baptism, meaning what only baptism can do for a person, I propose to understand baptism as a *crystal* with many prisms that each contain a little of what the Christian faith is all about: the affirmation of creaturely existence, forgiveness of sins, union with Christ, gift of the Spirit, and promise of eternal life. There is, however, always a difference between the crystal and the light that shines through it, the latter of which is Christ. The crystal with its prisms shines only as long as the light shines, but the light also shines outside the crystal.

---

25. Luther, *Von der Wiedertauffe*, 156.

BIBLIOGRAPHY

Gregersen, Niels Henrik. "Deep Incarnation and Chalcedon: On the Enduring Legacy of the Cappadocian Concept of 'Mixis.'" In *Herausforderungen des klassischen Theismus, Band 2: Inkarnation*, edited by Thomas Marschler and Thomas Schärtl, 253–87. Münster: Aschendorff, 2020.

Gregersen, Niels Henrik, ed. *Incarnation: On the Scope and Depth of Christology*. Minneapolis: Fortress, 2015.

Grundtvig, N. F. S. *Human Comes First: The Christian Theology of N. F. S. Grundtvig*. Translated by Edward Broadbridge. Aarhus: Aarhus University Press, 2018.

Hegstad, Harald. *Dåpen: En nådens kilde*. Oslo: Verbum, 2019.

Kelcourse, Felicity B., ed. *Human Development and Faith. Life-Cycle Stages of Body, Mind, and Soul*. 2nd ed. St. Louis: Chalice, 2015.

Folkekirkens Uddannelses—og Videnscenter. *Kirkestatistik*. https://www.folkekirken.dk/om-folkekirken/folkekirken-i-tal/daab.

Kolb, Robert, and Timothy J. Wengert, eds. *The Book of Concord: The Confessions of the Evangelical Lutheran Church*. Minneapolis: Fortress, 2000.

Luther, Martin. "Sermon on the Holy and Blessed Sacrament of Baptism." In *Luther's Works* Volume 35: *Word and Sacrament*, edited by E. Theodor Bachmann, 29–43. Minneapolis: Fortress, 1960.

———. "Von der Wiedertauffe an zween Pfarheern." *Martin Luthers Werke* Band 26, 144–72. Weimar: Böhlaus, 1928.

Montanari, Franco, et al., eds. *The Brill Dictionary of Ancient Greek*. Leiden: Brill, 2015.

Pannenberg, Wolfgang. *Systematic Theology*. Vol. 2. Translated by Geoffrey W. Bromiley. Grand Rapids: Eerdmans, 1994.

Prenter, Regin. *Creation and Redemption*. Translated by Theodor I. Jensen. Philadelphia: Fortress, 1967.

Ritualbog. Gudstjenesteordning for Den Danske Folkekirke, København: Det Kgl. Vajsenhus', 1992.

Suchocki, Marjorie Hewitt. *The Fall to Violence: Original Sin in Relational Theology*. New York: Continuum, 1995.

Ratschow, Carl Heinz. *Die eine christliche Taufe*. Gütersloh: Gerd Mohn, 1972.

20

Baptism as an Ecclesiological and Ecumenical Demarcation

An Orthodox Reading from the Finnish Context

Pekka Metso *and* Ari Koponen

This chapter focuses on the common statement on baptism (2022) issued by the Finnish Orthodox Church and the Evangelical Lutheran Church of Finland. The statement is noteworthy not only as a major ecumenical achievement by the local Finnish (or Nordic) bilateral ecumenical dialogue, but more broadly, for its mutual recognition of baptism between a local Orthodox church and a local Lutheran church, at the level of common theological statement, which is a rarity. In addition, formal Orthodox–Lutheran ecumenical dialogues are uncommon among local Orthodox churches, while the results of global dialogue between Orthodox churches and the Lutheran World Federation (since 1981) do not often affect local levels.[1]

As the starting point of this chapter, we recognize that attitudes toward ecumenicity and demarcations of church membership vary within the Orthodox tradition itself. While in Finland, it has become natural for the Orthodox to maintain close ecumenical contacts, even to the point

---

1. On ecumenical engagements and dialogues between Orthodox and Lutheran traditions on local and global levels, see Kalaitzidis et al., *Orthodox Handbook*, 319–542.

of recognizing the validity of Lutheran baptism, many Orthodox in other local contexts may have severe doubts about undertaking ecumenical engagements in the first place. The lack of proper ecumenical education and the rigidity of certain anti-ecumenical sentiments among the Orthodox may even lead to a point where rebaptism is required when an individual Christian coming from a different church tradition wants to embrace Orthodoxy. Despite the fact that he or she may have already been baptized in another Christian church according to its baptismal tradition, such as a Lutheran, Anglican, Evangelical, or Catholic church, rebaptism may be required when entering the Orthodox church. While most Orthodox churches are seriously committed to ecumenical work and formally reject rebaptism on official levels, there is a significant variety of practices and realities when the churchliness of another Christian denomination and the validity of their sacraments are evaluated in the multiple contexts of lived reality throughout the Orthodox church.[2] As Alkiviadis Calivas (following John Ericson) aptly put it, the existing practices of how converts are received by Orthodoxy are conflatious and obscure.[3]

As a recent development, the question of rebaptism has also emerged in Finland. This matter was discussed in September 2023 between the Finnish bishops and the Ecumenical Patriarch Bartholomew during his visit to Finland. Archbishop Leo, the head of the Finnish Orthodox Church, described as problematic a deviation from the local tradition in Finland, in which some people, received into the Orthodox church through the sacrament of anointing, traveled to Greece to be rebaptized. The Patriarch confirmed that the prevailing Finnish practice, which involves accepting through anointing into the Orthodox church those who have already received triune baptism elsewhere, is canonically correct and identical to the practice of the church of Constantinople.[4] In November 2023, following the patriarchal visit, the synod of the Finnish Orthodox bishops issued a pastoral letter on rebaptism, titled *One Lord, One Faith, One Baptism* (in Finnish, "Yksi Herra, yksi usko, yksi kaste"). According to the letter, baptisms performed outside the Orthodox church are valid and "considered 'Orthodox baptisms' because there is no other baptism than that which the Lord has entrusted to His Church. Denying their baptisms is denying the work of the Holy Spirit; it is denying

---

2. Calivas, *Liturgy*, 143.
3. Calivas, *Liturgy*, 154.
4. "Suomen piispojen tapaaminen."

the tradition of the Church."⁵ The current discussion about (re)baptism among the Finnish Orthodox underlines the ecumenical relevance of the Orthodox–Lutheran joint declaration on baptism.

The overall aim of this chapter is to provide an ecumenically credible analysis of the declaration, as seen through Orthodox lenses. First, we begin with a brief description of the Finnish ecumenical setting from the point of view of the Finnish Orthodox church. Second, we analyze the Finnish Lutheran–Orthodox baptismal declaration. Third, we give the declaration a broader theological reading, which is facilitated by present-day interpretations of baptism from the perspectives of Eastern Orthodox ecclesiology. Finally, we end with some conclusions on the significance of the declaration and the ecumenical perspectives it opens up.

FINNISH ORTHODOX PERSPECTIVE ON ECCLESIOLOGICAL READINGS OF BAPTISM

The cultural and historical borderline between Western and Eastern Christianity runs from Mediterranean Egypt and the Greek peninsula through Balkan Eastern Europe and Baltic countries, extending all the way to the Arctic Ocean. Located in the northern end of that line is Finland, a historically unique Nordic region of interface between Catholic and Protestant traditions of the West and Orthodox Christian tradition of the East. By the twelfth century, the Catholic church had extended from the west into the territory of present-day Finland through the crusades of the Kingdom of Sweden, while the Orthodox church was introduced from the east through missions of the Kyivan Rus' state of Novgorod. Due to the sixteenth-century Reformation, the Catholic tradition dramatically tailed off in Finland and was substituted by the Lutheran tradition. For over 500 years, Lutheranism has been the predominant form of Christianity in Finland. Today, about 3.7 million Finns, 67 percent of the nation's population, belong to the Evangelical Lutheran Church (2021).⁶

In Finland, unlike in other Nordic countries, Eastern Orthodoxy constitutes an endemic Christian minority. Currently, there are some 59,000 registered members of the Finnish Orthodox church (2021). With barely just 1 percent of the population, it is, however, one of the nation's biggest religious minorities in addition to Muslims, Roman Catholics and Pentecostals. In contrast to other religious minority

---

5. "Yksi Herra," 7.
6. Hietamäki and Metso, "Finland"; Statistics Finland, "Population."

groups, the Orthodox Church of Finland has a special legal status, similar to the Lutheran church: it has been recognized as a national church, secured by legislation since 1918.[7]

On the one hand, the Finnish Orthodox church is bound to a complex minority-majority reality with various social, cultural, political and existential impacts. Important factors historically affecting the life of the Finnish Orthodox faithful—and the entire Orthodox community—include the dominance of mixed marriages among the Orthodox population, the prevalence of baptism of children born in mixed marriages into the Lutheran church, conversions from the Orthodox church to the Lutheran church, and a generally weak awareness of the Orthodox tradition, both among the majority population and the Orthodox themselves. Nurturing relationships with the dominant Lutheran church has been vital for the prosperity of the broader Orthodox church in Finnish society.[8]

At the same time, the Finnish Orthodox church epitomizes the full capacity of Eastern Orthodox tradition and ecclesial structure in its canonically defined jurisdiction. As an autonomous local Orthodox church under the Patriarchate of Constantinople (since 1923), it belongs to the global communion of Orthodox churches. This wider communion is even registered in Finnish civil law. The opening section of the Law on the Orthodox church states that the Bible, tradition, dogma, and canons of the broader Orthodox church form the bases of the national Orthodox church.[9]

Regarding ecumenical interaction, the peculiar glocal nature of the Finnish Orthodox church (simultaneously a Finnish minority church and a member of the global Orthodox church family) is reflected, firstly, in its aim to foster good ecumenical relations with the Lutheran church. The two churches share a common societal and cultural environment and are bound to similar realities, which include their vulnerability to changes affecting the role of religion in society and among individuals.[10] In addition to the manifold everyday contacts and shared lived reality between the two churches, an official Lutheran–Orthodox dialogue has been ongoing since 1989.[11] For another, as a local church in communion

---

7. Sohlberg and Ketola, "Religious," 48–49; Laitila, "History"; Pietarinen, "Churches," 39–40; Statistics Finland, "Population."

8. Laitila, "Suspicion"; Pietarinen,"Churches," 40–41.

9. Finlex, "Laki," §1.

10. Hietamäki and Metso, "Finland"; Vogelaar, "Intriguing Dialogue."

11. On the history of the dialogue until 2007, see Metso, "Evaluation"; Toiviainen,

with other Orthodox churches, the Finnish Orthodox church is bound to fidelity to Orthodox tradition. As a result, the possibilities and limitations of domestic ecumenical engagements of the Finnish Orthodox Church are evaluated with fidelity to pan-Orthodox understanding.[12] Within the limitations of such "ecclesial restrictions" of the Finnish Orthodox church, the two churches issued the *Joint Declaration on Baptism* in 2022. Instead of being a straightforward mutual recognition of baptismal theology, the document focuses more on common witness to baptism in the era of changes affecting commitment to Christian tradition. With the rather concise declaration, a theological commentary was issued as background material.[13] The commentary complements the declaration with a theological reading of the biblical and doctrinal bases of the two churches regarding baptism.

Conscious engagement of the local dialogue with supra-national church traditions was defined in the 1989 communiqué of the first round of the national Finnish Lutheran–Orthodox dialogue as follows:

> Now the question is one of dialogue on a Finnish basis between the two Finnish national churches. At the same time, the churches in question represent not only Finnish Christianity but also the churches' doctrinal legacy. It is a question of a meeting of the Eastern and Western traditions.[14]

It is precisely this "doctrinal legacy" that discloses a spectrum of prevailing interpretations of baptism for different needs of ecclesiology in the Orthodox church. As the Orthodox responses to BEM indicate, the question of "the relationship between unity of the church and baptismal unity" lies at the heart of Orthodox ecclesiology and ecumenical theology.[15] As pointed out by the Ecumenical Patriarchate of Constantinople, "it is not possible to seek a 'consensus' on baptism . . . without the existence of an agreement on the road to salvation and deification,

---

"Discussions." For other assessments of the dialogue, see Karttunen, "Kristittyjen yhteys"; Metso, "Suomen"; Metso, "Yksimielisyyden kohdat."

12. See, for example, Metso, "Evaluation," 191.

13. The declaration and the theological background material are published in English translations in *Baptism and Salvation*, which we refer to for documentation in this article.

14. *Finnish*, 9.

15. Thurian, "Inter-Orthodox," 125. Other Orthodox responses also emphasize the fundamental cohesion between baptismal unity and church unity. See Thurian, "Russian," 8; Thurian, "Alexandria," 2; Thurian, "Romanian," 6; Thurian, "America," 16–17.

which presupposes an agreement on ecclesiology."[16] In modern Orthodox ecclesiology, baptism is seen, on the one hand, as an uncompromising boundary that identifies Orthodoxy as the only genuine form of Christianity (e.g., leading even to re-baptism, which is formally rejected by the Orthodox church), and, on the second hand, as something elusive by nature, especially regarding ecclesiological boundaries when examining the correlation between baptism and church (which are vulnerable to diverse ecumenical visions, thereby challenging from within the rigid interpretation mentioned above). Consequently, while Orthodox ecclesiology might sound triumphalistic, in the words of the internationally renowned Finnish Lutheran scholar Veli-Matti Kärkkäinen, in its solid understanding of the Orthodox church as the manifestation and safeguard of church unity, the church itself is at the same time keenly concerned with reestablishing the unity of all Christians.[17]

ANALYSIS OF THE FINNISH LUTHERAN–ORTHODOX COMMON STATEMENT ON BAPTISM (2022)

Assessing the accomplishments of over three decades of the Finnish bilateral Lutheran–Orthodox dialogue, it is quite easy to conclude that there were no previous milestones comparable with the joint declaration of baptism in 2022. There are two topical reasons for publishing a document that signal strong mutual devotion between the two churches in dialogue. First, there is a strong will of commitment to the achievements of the twentieth-century international ecumenical work on baptism at the national level. Second, resulting from changes in religiosity over the past few decades, there is a shared concern by the two Finnish churches about the decrease in the number of baptisms and the general observance of Christianity in present-day Finland.

The first reason becomes evident in the beginning of the background material to the joint declaration, where Finnish dialogue is linked with the international ecumenical context. The two churches here describe their conscious adherence to the BEM document's call for explicit mutual recognition of baptism. Alongside BEM, the Finnish churches note that the urge for the mutual recognition of baptism was potently repeated in *The Charta Oecumenica* (2001), issued by the Conference of European Churches and the Council of the Bishops' Conferences of

---

16. Thurian, "Constantinople," 4.
17. Kärkkäinen, *Introduction*, 227–28.

Europe of the Catholic church. There is also a link with the International Lutheran–Orthodox Joint Commission's "consensus on the sacrament of baptism as part of becoming and growing as a Christian," which was achieved in 2004. Furthermore, the Finnish churches' will of mutual recognition regarding baptism echoes the multilateral *Magdeburg Declaration* (2007), in which German churches of various major traditions, Evangelicals, Protestants, and Orthodox included, expressed their shared basic consensus on baptism.[18]

The second reason for the document's emergence is related to the societal challenges "regarding the transmission of the Christian heritage" due to the ongoing shifts and changes of religiosity.[19] Both churches are currently losing members, and the number of baptisms is in decline. Many Finns in the Lutheran and Orthodox churches are weighing their relationship with Christianity, pondering questions relating to their faith and beliefs and making decisions on whether or not to pass on Christian traditions to their children.[20] It is evidently these changes of religiosity and their effects on church affiliation that are referred to in the joint statement as unfamiliarity with "the life-giving content of the baptism" for many and the need "to learn more about it."[21] Ultimately, the churches seem to acknowledge that the internal mission among their existing members is currently more vital than a mission outside the church.[22] The circumstances of the context and present-day realities are loudly pronounced in the declaration. Its core content is, therefore, in the first place, societal.

In addition to confluences arising from the context of the churches' everyday coexistence, there is also a theological substance matter regarding convergences and disagreements on baptismal theology and the administration of baptism. There are three main themes that we detected that help to recapture the theological core of the joint declaration and its appendix.

---

18. *Baptism and Salvation*, 35–36. In addition to the international links, recent domestic ecumenical developments also form a basis for the joint declaration, namely *Baptism is the Sign of a Common Faith* (2020, in Finnish), a publication by The Finnish Ecumenical Council.

19. *Baptism and Salvation*, 34.

20. For more on the present-day Finnish religious landscape and trends in church membership, see Sohlberg and Ketola, "Religious," 47–64.

21. *Baptism and Salvation*, 34.

22. For a grass-roots level example of common Lutheran-Orthodox witness, see Huttunen, "Witnessing."

First, the two churches share a conviction, based on Christian anthropology and sacramental theology, that a human being is born into this world as distanced from God, but through baptism this estrangement is abolished and replaced by a new way of being in connection with the Triune God. In the sacrament or mystery of baptism, a person becomes a "partaker of salvation" in Jesus Christ, whose incarnation, public ministry, death, and resurrection constitute the "salvific work of the Triune God."[23] Furthermore, "baptism saves the human being from this sin and mortality by letting the recipient partake in Christ's saving death and resurrection." Thus, the churches have indicated that there is a remarkable change that takes place in and through baptism, which is a birth to a renewed humanity in closeness to God. This new baptismal ontology, as it could be described, does not entail only participation in Christ but also the dynamic manifestation of the new life it brings about in the baptized. "As a confessing member of this community," baptized Christians live a new, grace-filled life in Christ.[24] The two churches state thus that living as a Christian is an integral part of the personal experience of humanity saved in Christ, given in baptism as the unique and fundamental gift of God.

The fundaments of baptismal theology are rooted in the New Testament and expressed accordingly in the baptism rites of the two churches. Key points of biblical reference consist of the Johannine and Pauline crystallizations of baptism as a source of eternal life with God (cf. John 3:5 and Col 2:12). Both churches' baptismal rites traditionally include exorcism and creed as manifestations of joining Christ. Exorcism, however, currently has a less explicit role in Lutheran practice, to the extent that "the average parishioner is unlikely to notice it," while in the Orthodox church, baptism is performed by threefold immersion, "representing Christ's three days in the tomb." In contrast, the Lutheran church adheres to baptism by affusion. Furthermore, the Orthodox church sees a link between the sacrament of baptism and the baptism of Christ in Jordan. Specifically, the baptism of Christ in the Jordan River (i.e., theophany or epiphany) is understood as an act of the Triune God of redeeming and baptizing all of humanity in Christ. This kind of extensive reading, with strong connotations of the theology of creation, is echoed in certain prayers of the Orthodox baptismal formula.[25] Although there are

23. *Baptism and Salvation*, 33.
24. *Baptism and Salvation*, 37.
25. *Baptism and Salvation*, 36–38.

dissimilarities in the outspokenness of liturgical expressions between Lutheran and Orthodox baptismal rites, they are nevertheless seen to convey congruent theological understandings, both of which are aligned with New Testament baptismal theology.

Second, there is some agreement on the pneumatological aspect of baptism, as a person receives the gift of the Holy Spirit in baptism. This is evidenced in excerpts from the baptismal formulas of both churches, which enable us to conclude that "the Holy Spirit is described as being active in baptism itself." Nevertheless, there is a major difference in the respective understandings of the role of the Holy Spirit in the broader sacramental practice linked to baptism. Unlike in the Lutheran church, the Orthodox church gives special importance to the sacrament of anointing as "the gift of the Holy Spirit," which is administered immediately after baptism.[26] The Finnish Orthodox church has underlined the importance of linking baptism with anointing in her response to the BEM.[27] As an indication of Lutheran responsivity toward Orthodox views and practices, it is noted that there is a growing awareness of "the connection between this post-baptismal prayer and the gift of the Holy Spirit" in some local churches (e.g., in the Evangelical Lutheran Church in America). In addition, the Lutheran church suggests that laying on hands in the Western rites of confirmation can be paralleled with the sacrament of anointment.[28] There is, however, no reference to how the Finnish Orthodox church perceives such a juxtaposition.

Third, baptism is perceived ecclesiologically as an entry into the communal life of the church. In baptism, "a person is born again by the power of God, but not in isolation from other baptized Christians." The ecclesiological character of baptism is witnessed in numerous New Testament passages (1 Cor 12:13; Eph 2:20–22; Col 1:18; 1 Pet 2:9–10).[29] The background material of the joint declaration conveys an understanding that in the Orthodox church, baptism is pronouncedly seen to take place inside the pneumatological mystery of the church. According to this type of perception, baptism is presented as an entry to a transformative and sanctifying ecclesial life. As partakers in the life of the church through

---

26. *Baptism and Salvation*, 39–40.
27. Thurian, "Finnish," 28–29.
28. *Baptism and Salvation*, 39–42.
29. *Baptism and Salvation*, 43.

baptism, gifts of the Spirit are administered personally to each baptized Christian in the sacrament of anointing.[30]

Based on their shared understanding of the ecclesiological nature of baptism, both churches express a commitment to *one* baptism, as outlined in the Nicene creed. At the same time, it is attested that divisions among Christians challenge the theology of oneness of baptism and its role as a fundament for church unity. Due to their different ecclesiological footings, "the Lutheran Church can speak more easily than the Orthodox church of the worldwide church in the sense that the universal church of Christ is made up of Christians of different denominations around the world." The difference is demonstrated in the "traditional [Orthodox] conviction" that the Orthodox church is the one, holy, Catholic and apostolic church. Despite the rigid exclusiveness of Orthodox ecclesiology, the Finnish Orthodox church receives converts from the Lutheran church through the sacrament of anointing, not by rebaptism. Likewise, there is no rebaptism for a person moving from the Orthodox church to the Lutheran church. Rather, he or she is received in an occasional service through their confession of the Christian faith.[31]

Drawing from their adherence to the faith of the New Testament and the tradition of undivided Christendom, there exists a fundamental mutual understanding of baptism between the two churches. This common theological foothold enables churches to recognize the validity of each other's baptism. Even though "the Orthodox Church also mostly refrains from evaluating the efficacy of the sacraments administered outside it, confining itself to identifying whether they are consistent with or lacking in terms of the Orthodox Church's tradition," the Finnish Orthodox church clearly considers baptism in the Lutheran church to bear sufficient validity to recognize its efficiency. This can be seen as a positive expression of awareness regarding the tension between canonical and charismatic boundaries of the church, referred to in the background

---

30. *Baptism and Salvation*, 39–41. A similar understanding of the nature of the rite in the historical-sacramental reality of the church is detected in the baptismal statement of the international commission: "The Orthodox see a fundamental parallel between participation in the sacraments of the Church and the history of salvation realized in history."

31. *Baptism and Salvation*, 43–46. Patristic and canonical grounds for receiving converts to Orthodoxy without rebaptizing them are presented by Finnish Orthodox bishops in their 2023 pastoral letter. See "Yksi Herra," 2–4.

material as a perspective arising from the contradiction between the theology of one church and the reality of many denominations.[32]

LEVELS OF BAPTISMAL DEMARCATION IN ORTHODOX BAPTISMAL THEOLOGY

This section explores the multi-faceted layers of baptismal demarcation, yet with a serious commitment to ecumenical openness rooted in both traditional baptismal theology and modern ecumenical engagements of the Orthodox church. We will focus on three levels or themes of baptismal demarcation: liturgical-philosophical, ecclesiological internality–externality, and canonical.

Liturgical-Philosophical Level

In the liturgical tradition of the Orthodox church, baptism is depicted as the common source for all Christians of their life in Christ and communion with God. This sacramental reading is based on the theology of creation, which locates baptismal grace within the wider framework of God's creative, life-giving, and sustaining Word. For example, the liturgical tradition acknowledges non-baptized catechumens as belonging to the church without being members of it.

The question of church membership obviously entails multiple interpretative levels: it can be regarded as an administrative and jurisdictional matter, as well as an issue of mystical or existential significance, as indicated by the notion of "belonging to a Church."[33] Theologically and ecumenically, the primary level of belonging is naturally expressed in baptism, which not only joins the individual into the community but also marks the beginning of the new life in Christ. In this sense, baptism

---

32. *Baptism and Salvation*, 46. As an insightful reflection on Orthodox ecumenical involvement and commitment rooted in Finnish Orthodox context, see Huttunen "Local," 756–58. The criterion for recognizing baptisms of non-Orthodox traditions and denominations is encapsulated by Orthodox Church of America in her response to BEM: "For the Orthodox, the content of the credal confession of faith made at baptism" forms the basis "of receiving as already baptized those coming to her communion from certain groups while insisting upon baptism for those coming from other groups, whose "baptism" she is unable to recognize." See Thurian, "Orthodox Church of America," 16–17.

33. It is fair to say that Orthodox ecclesiology has been grounded on the Patristic "indefinability" of the church itself, wherein a precise definition is lacking precisely because the Church is the ontological reality that arises the possibility of the church in question in the first place. See Huovinen, *Images*, 20 and 32.

is the ontological event of becoming a Christian, and the subsequent life of a Christian displays and refers continually back to this event.

The "inner" logic of membership has different connotations, however, when applied to the question of determining the extent to which those outside the officiated and visible sacramental boundaries of the Orthodox church should be viewed in terms of membership. As the Finnish Orthodox scholar Harri Huovinen has remarked, the classical Patristic authors treated membership in a dual sense: as belonging to the Church and as a process whereby the idea of "membership" seems to function in more fluid terms.[34] In modern Orthodox theology, there have been several attempts to formulate *ecclesia extra ecclesiam* (a term employed by Sergius Bulgakov)—that is, the mystical and universal scope of the body of Christ.[35] Bulgakov acknowledged that there is "a potential ecclesiality in one or another way," which correlates to the visible Church. Though Bulgakov had particular ecumenical issues in mind, his formulation can serve as a theologoumenon through which the sacramental "potentiality" of different Christian groups could also be treated with tolerance precisely by the "obscure" nature of their membership.[36] A similar view can be found in the thought of a pre-eminent ecumenical Orthodox figure of twentieth century, Dumitru Staniloae. He spoke of "open sobornicity," which crudely translates into a tolerant and open-ended view of ecclesiology, or a process of "churching" in history.[37]

The structure of the Orthodox liturgy, in a broader sense, depicts the initiation process into Christianity. The two parts of liturgy—the liturgy of the catechumenate and the liturgy of the faithful—represent the sacramental fulfillment of baptism in the eucharist. The recognition of Christ's own baptism as that of the whole of human nature provides the occasion to broaden the demarcation of Christian identity into

---

34. Huovinen, *Images*, 43.

35. Bulgakov, *Bride of the Lamb*, 271. In a dialogue between Anglican and Orthodox churches in 1927, Bulgakov suggested that both the essence and membership of the church are ultimately indefinable, but still simultaneously grounded on the unity of tradition. Bulgakov, "Outlines," 27.

36. There are also views that translate this idea of "pre-sacramental potentiality" into a process of fulfilment, as in the case when an already baptized individual joins the Orthodox Church. For example, metropolitan Anthony Bloom and Ilarion Alfeyev write that re-baptism is not necessary (as long as the original was conducted properly) since by joining the apostolic body of the Church, the sacrament "gets filled with grace." See Hovorun, *Scaffolds*, 98.

37. Bordeianu, "Staniloae," 250.

cosmic proportions.[38] While this cosmic notion is emphasized in the background material, especially by the Orthodox, it is not employed in the actual joint statement.

The cosmic dimension is significant in its disclosure of the underlying theological question of how baptism supplements, or even relates to, the theology of creation. Even the catechumens (i.e., the non-baptized) can be conceived to be "pre-members" of the church via their transfigured humanity in Christ, in addition to their intention of becoming Christians. In Orthodox theology, the transfigured nature of Christ displays the aim and purpose of human life. Usually, this apparent dialectic is "solved" by interpreting the actual salvation as the core aspect and the purpose of Christian life as a counter-process of the Fall. However, the ontological demarcation between the non-baptized and the baptized can appear secondary since it rests ultimately on the salvific work of Christ (and, more precisely, on their "potentiality"). Thus, it can be the case, while certainly not the intention, that disregarding the theology of creation and transfiguration may steer the understanding of baptism toward the administrative sense of membership in the Church. Consecutively, this can result in "resolving" the obscurity of membership by strictly accommodating it within the jurisdictional sacramental boundaries of the historical Church.

Level of Ecclesiological Internality–Externality

The theology of creation, linked with the eschatological recapitulation in Christ, brings about a certain vagueness to sacramental theology, at least regarding practical (-theological) attempts to differentiate most of Christianity from Orthodoxy (exemplified, for example, in how Orthodox churches address the question of the validity of a baptism performed by ordinated women in non-Orthodox churches). Thus, the logic of ideal orthodoxy in Orthodox ecclesiology is not applicable as such to prevailing ecumenical reality, nor even between different Orthodox jurisdictions themselves. Therefore, the manner in which baptism is treated by Orthodox churches in bilateral dialogues explicates the dynamics of internality and externality in modern ecumenical contexts.

In the responses of different Orthodox churches to the BEM document, it seems that, regarding baptismal identity, both the proper act of baptism and its connection to the apostolic faith are stressed. This in

---

38. *Baptism and Salvation*, 38.

itself displays a demarcation between externality and internality, since at the ecumenical level, the ontological aspect of ecclesial being is stressed, yet the particular economic reality is still acknowledged. Nevertheless, the response of the Finnish Orthodox church is illuminating for the purpose of this article. The shared apostolic faith precisely in baptismal font provides a fertile starting point, not necessarily the closing point between the traditions. It may be noted that most of the responses stress that baptismal unity cannot be conceived apart from the unity of all the sacraments and thus the plenitude of the Church.

The ecumenical reality of the Lutheran and Orthodox churches in Finland is explicated and affirmed in the joint declaration as an already-present factual situation. This is remarkable in itself, especially when keeping in mind that Orthodox practices of baptism vary greatly and not only when the need for re-baptism is considered, particularly in the case of someone coming from outside the Orthodox church, but also between different local Orthodox churches.

The Finnish joint declaration on baptism is therefore an example of a local bilateral agreement, which recognizes both its ecumenical and international background as well the necessity for theology to accommodate the economic reality with certain fundamental theological presuppositions. In this way, baptismal theology is a crucible of theological common ground that does not need to be relativized in the name of economy but rather theologically confronted in the same manner that the theology of creation is always interacting with the sacramental and soteriological theology. Thus, the baptismal theology can point the way forward both as an act and a process, wherein the process of becoming a Christian is also considered important, and not only in terms of what happens after the singular act of baptism.

Level of Canonical Tradition

In the canons of the Orthodox church, the question of orthodoxy in relation to baptism is perceived, perhaps surprisingly, in a quite tolerant way. The church recognizes baptisms performed not only by schismatics, but also by a number of heterodox groups. Interestingly, such a relaxed position is rarely seen in present-day readings when the Orthodox church reflects Christian identity and ecclesiology in the prevailing ecumenical reality. We argue that instead of strictness, there is a certain innate theological creativity in baptismal theology suggested by canonical tradition.

This kind of tolerance should be discovered anew, despite its "obscurity," which in turn finds clarity precisely in terms of fluid interpretations of membership and the supplements from the theology of creation.

This approach naturally requires an interpretative reading of canonical texts, since they are by nature aimed at concrete and historical problem-solving. The Apostolic Canons refer to baptism as the sacrament of grace, which is generally not to be repeated.[39] The baptism itself is valid if it is conducted in a "proper" manner and according to "substance and form." This definition is followed by an analysis of how baptisms from non-Orthodox churches should be viewed. The apostolic continuity and ministry are underlined as disclosing the authenticity of the sacraments.

Given this general framework, local canon traditions testify to the concrete dilemma of letting schismatics and heretics back into the church. For example, in the year 314, the local synod of Ancyra was responsible for addressing the issue of deniers of Christ in persecutions and other deviating practices of Christians of that time. Baptism, or re-baptism, is not mentioned at all, and it seems that the confessional and practical deviations were viewed simply as a matter of pastoral reprimand and the need for penance.[40] In the council of Laodicea in Asia Minor (343), only the heretics needed a sacramental renewal in order to gain entry into the Church, and in some cases only the chrismation is mentioned as a method of re-entry.[41] The same relatively relaxed position can be interpreted in the later canons of Constantinople in 861, where only schismatic positions could be redeemed simply by "returning to their own bishop."[42] Only since the eighteenth century, due to rigid reading of the canonical tradition caused by growing anti-Catholic sentiments among the Orthodox, did an absolutist interpretation of the boundaries of the church and the validity of baptism gradually become a mainstream current in Orthodox theology and practice.[43] This latter development is deemed by the Finnish Orthodox bishops to be a

---

39. *Ortodoksisen kirkon kanonit*, 94–98.

40. For example, the Canon VIII of Nicea displays a reasonable degree of tolerance towards Novatian schismatics re-enter the Church.

41. *Paikallissynodien kanonit*, 30. Even adherents to "Trinitarian" heresies, such as Arians and Apollinarians, were seemingly only chrismated upon re-entering (Canon 7 of Constantinople, Percival 274–75). In this case, the "form" of baptism was correct, being thrice immersed in water, whereas the heterodox who had not participated in this form were in need of another baptism.

42. *Paikallissynodien kanonit*, 103.

43. Calivas, *Liturgy*, 156–72.

"deviation from the ecumenical and general Orthodox tradition."[44] As Cyril Hovorun notes, the varied responses of the early Church toward schismatics reflect the growing pains of understanding what membership meant in the context of the invisible church.[45]

CONCLUSION: OBSCURITY AND TOLERANCE OF BAPTISMAL GRACE

The above analysis of the Finnish Lutheran–Orthodox joint declaration on baptism and our observations of baptismal demarcations in Orthodox theology give ground to the following conclusions.

First, we find the possibility of issuing a joint statement on baptism illuminating in itself. As the theological background of the joint statements indicates, the underlying ecclesiologies and understandings of the church are different in the Lutheran and Orthodox traditions. Nevertheless, this is not seen as an obstacle to acknowledging the baptism of the other church as valid. This willingness to mutually recognize these baptisms reveal an acknowledgment of the economic reality in Finland. In addition, it shows how the definitions between baptism and other theological concepts can be constructed on the basis of their relative obscurity. Furthermore, it shows creative adherence to previous national and international ecumenical commitments, as well as an ability to reflect theology in dialogue with others in a common context that accounts for the sociological realities of the time.

Second, the joint statement offers a valuable opportunity to delve into disagreements and fundamental convergences between Lutheran and Orthodox churches. Both parties agree on the unity of the sacrament of baptism and the baptismal rite. From the BEM process, we can learn that it is typical in the Orthodox church to emphasize certain elements in the rite of baptism as essential for a common understanding of baptism.

---

44. "Yksi Herra," 4.

45. Hovorun, *Scaffolds*, 15. To be fair, there has been some criticism that the very idea of the invisibility of the church undermines the reality of the "church incarnated" and lets the empirical diversity act as a vehicle for philosophical unclarity. Nevertheless, it is clear already from the biblical texts, at least on the level of narrative, that a mystical aspect of Christian community is somehow related to the mystery of God in Christ. As Hovorun notes, "Polarization between the real and ideal in the church weakens the incentive for the Christians to grow and to become mature." *Scaffolds*, 18.

These include triple immersion,[46] exorcism,[47] and linking baptism with chrismation.[48] Differences regarding these elements in Orthodox and Lutheran traditions are also discussed quite extensively in the background material of the Finnish joint declaration.[49] However, the Finnish Orthodox church does not highlight them as distinguishing factors, leaving it open how crucial they eventually are perceived to be. The obvious consensus nature of the joint statement suggests that dissimilarities between rites are not seen for both Orthodox and Lutherans as an obstacle to explicating common ground in baptismal theology. While churches bring forth important elements of their own rites that convey the theology of baptism and subsequent ecclesiology, neither seems to presuppose that baptism can only be celebrated exclusively according to their rite nor within their own ecclesiological tradition. The Orthodox understanding of uniformity in baptismal rites is explicated in more detail in the pastoral letter of 2023, in which the Finnish Orthodox bishops state that it is not possible to set exact requirements for the rite of baptism performed outside the Orthodox church, for example, regarding triple immersion.[50] Differences in baptismal rites undoubtedly reflect deeper ecclesiological understandings; nevertheless, they also show fertile tolerance toward understanding the other tradition. Consequently, baptismal demarcations can be seen as wider and porous than ecclesiological or confessional boundaries. This is especially noteworthy regarding the Orthodox counterpart, due to its tense attitudes toward ecumenical theology, which is oftentimes detected among local Orthodox churches.

Finally, based on the Finnish Lutheran–Orthodox readings of baptism, we detected a certain tolerance in obscurity (or obscure tolerance) regarding membership of the church. Ecclesiological demarcations may serve as a helpful corrective, especially when contemplated within a dialogue that seeks, first of all, to enhance a common understanding, instead of being seen as an opportunity to palisade each (especially Orthodox) ecclesiological fundament on an ecumenical platform. The Finnish Lutheran–Orthodox joint declaration and its background material demonstrate that both churches share common ground in their understanding of the sources of authenticity of the church as rooted in

---

46. Thurian, "Bulgarian," 16–17.
47. Thurian, "Alexandria," 2.
48. Thurian, "Romanian," 6.
49. *Baptism and Salvation*, 37–42.
50. "Yksi Herra," 5.

apostolic tradition, which, at least in some regards, has shown itself to be relatively tolerant toward the *ecclesia extra ecclesiam*. Thus, it may be that the apostolic deposit of faith can serve as a fruitful and cross-fertilizing theme for their dialogue in the future.

BIBLIOGRAPHY

Baptism and Salvation. Lutherans and Orthodox in Dialogue. Suomen evankelisluterilaisen kirkon julkaisuja. Kirkko ja toiminta 134. Helsinki: Kirkkohallitus, 2023. https://julkaisut.evl.fi/catalog/Tutkimukset%20ja%20julkaisut/r/4342/view mode=infoview/qsr=Saatavuus%3A%20ladattava%20tiedosto%20(PDF).

Bordeianu, Radu. "Dumitru Staniloae and the West." In *Orthodox Constructions of the West*, edited by George Demacoupoulos et al., 240–53. New York: Fordham University, 2013.

Bulgakov, Sergius. *The Bride of the Lamb*. Trans. Boris Jakim. Grand Rapids: Eerdmans, 2002.

———. "Outlines of the Teaching about the Church." http://www.sobornost.org/Archives_Bulgakov-Outlines-of-the-Teaching-about-the-Church_Dec1926-Jan1927.pdf.

Calivas, Alkiviadis. *The Liturgy in Dialogue. Exploring & Renewing the Tradition.* Brookline: Holy Cross Orthodox, 2018.

Finlex. "Laki ortodoksisesta kirkosta 10.11.2006/985." https://www.finlex.fi/fi/laki/ajantasa/2006/20060985.

The Finnish Lutheran–Orthodox Dialogue. Conversations in 1989 and 1990. Documents of the Evangelical Lutheran Church of Finland 4. Helsinki: Church Council for Foreign Affairs, 1993.

Hietamäki, Minna, and Pekka Metso. "Finland." In *Christianity in Western and Northern Europe*. Edited by Kenneth R. Ross et al. EUP Edinburgh Companions to Global Christianity 8. Edinburgh: Edinburgh University Press, 2024.

Hovorun, Cyril. *Scaffolds of the Church: Towards Poststructural Ecclesiology.* Eugene, OR: Cascade Books, 2017.

Huttunen, Heikki. "Local Ecumenism from Orthodox Perspectives." In *Orthodox Handbook on Ecumenism. Resources for Theological Education*, edited by Pantelis Kalaitzidis et al., 755–60. Oxford: Regnum, 2014.

———. "Witnessing in a Secular Situation: Reflections on the Orthodox Church of Finland." *Ortodoksia* 49 (2002) 194–207.

Huovinen, Harri. *Images of Divine Participation: A Reappraisal of Fourth Century Views on Church Membership*. Studia Patristica Fennica 18. Helsinki: Societas Patristica Finnica, 2022.

Kalaitzidis, Pantelis, et al. *Orthodox Handbook on Ecumenism. Resources for Theological Education*. Oxford: Regnum, 2014.

Karttunen, Tomi. "Kristittyjen yhteys ja Kirkon näkyvä yksys yhteisenä luterilais-ortodoksisena tavoitteena." *Reseptio* 1 (2020) 44–49.

Kärkkäinen, Veli-Matti. *An Introduction to Ecclesiology. Historical, Local, and Interreligious Perspectives*. 2nd ed. Downers Grove, IL: InterVarsity, 2021.

Laitila, Teuvo. "Suspicion, négligence et respect: les relations entre l'Église luthéranne et l'Église orthodoxe en Finlande après la Seconde guerre modiale." *Istina* 53 (2008) 365–79.

Metso, Pekka. "Evaluation on the Dialogue between the Evangelical Lutheran Church of Finland and the Orthodox Church of Finland." *Reseptio* 1 (2009) 191–203.

———. "Suomen ortodoksisen kirkon ja Suomen evankelis-luterilaisen kirkon dialogi vuodesta1989 nykyhetkeen. Ekumeeninen konteksti, dialogin arvio ja tulevaisuudennäkymät." *Reseptio* 2 (2016) 69–90.

———. "Yksimielisyyden kohdat ja perusteet tähänastisessa dialogissa." *Reseptio* 1 (2020) 37–43.

Ortodoksisen kirkon kanonit selityksineen. Trans. Antti Inkinen. Kuopio: Ortodoksisen kirjallisuuden julkaisuneuvosto, 1980.

Paikallissynodien kanonit. Translated by Antti Inkinen. Kuopio: Ortodoksisen kirjallisuuden julkaisuneuvosto, 1983.

Percival, Henry. *The Seven Ecumenical Councils.* Edited by Paul A. Böer Sr. Charleston: Veritatis Spledor, 2013.

Pietarinen, Rauno. "Churches in Minority and Majority Situations and the Related Perception of Ecumenism." In *Orthodox Handbook on Ecumenism. Resources for Theological Education*, edited by Pantelis Kalaitzidis et al., 37–41. Oxford: Regnum, 2014.

Sohlberg, Jussi, and Kimmo Ketola. "Religious Communities in Finland." In *Religion in Daily Life and in Celebration. The Evangelical Lutheran Church of Finland, 2016– 2019.* Church Research Institute Publication 65, edited by Hanna Salomäki et al., 45–66. Helsinki: Church Research Institute, 2021. https://julkaisut.evl.fi/catalog/ Tutkimukset%20ja%20julkaisut/r/4289/viewmode=previewview.

Statistics Finland. "Population 31.12.2021 by Religious Community." https://pxdata. stat.fi/PxWeb/pxweb/en/StatFin/StatFin__vaerak/statfin_vaerak_pxt_11rx.px/ table/tableViewLayout1/.

"Suomen ortodoksisen kirkon toimessa olevien piispojen tapaaminen Hänen Kaikkipyhyytensä, Ekumeenisen patriarkka Bartolomeoksen ja tämän seurueen kanssa 11.9.2023. Muistio." https://ort.fi/sites/default/files/2023-09/Piispojen%20 tapaaminen%20patriarkka%20Bartolomeoksen%20kanssa%2011.9.2023%20 %281%29.pdf

Thurian, Max. "Bulgarian Orthodox Church." In *Churches Respond to BEM*. Official Responses to the "Baptism, Eucharist and Ministry" text 2, edited by Max Thurian, 13–23. Geneva: World Council of Churches, 1986.

———. "Finnish Orthodox Church." In *Churches Respond to BEM*. Official Responses to the "Baptism, Eucharist and Ministry" text 2, edited by Max Thurian, 24–29. Geneva: World Council of Churches, 1986.

———. "Ecumenical Patriarchate of Constantinople." In *Churches Respond to BEM* . Official Responses to the "Baptism, Eucharist and Ministry" text 4, edited by Max Thurian, 1–6. Geneva: World Council of Churches,1987.

———. "Greek Orthodox Patriarchate of Alexandria." In *Churches Respond to BEM*. Official Responses to the "Baptism, Eucharist and Ministry" text 3, edited by Max Thurian, 1–3. Geneva: World Council of Churches, 1987.

———. "Inter-Orthodox Symposium on Baptism, Eucharist and Ministry." In *Churches Respond to BEM*. Official Responses to the "Baptism, Eucharist and Ministry" text 1, edited by Max Thurian, 122–29. Geneva: World Council of Churches, 1986.

———. "Orthodox Church of America." In *Churches Respond to BEM. Official Responses to the "Baptism, Eucharist and Ministry" text 3*, edited by Max Thurian, 15–25. Geneva: World Council of Churches, 1987.

———. "Romanian Orthodox Church." In *Churches Respond to BEM. Official Responses to the "Baptism, Eucharist and Ministry" text 3*, edited by Max Thurian, 4–14. Geneva: World Council of Churches, 1987.

———. "Russian Orthodox Church." In *Churches Respond to BEM. Official Responses to the "Baptism, Eucharist and Ministry" text 2*, edited by Max Thurian, 5–12. Geneva: World Council of Churches, 1986.

Toiviainen, Kalevi. "The Discussions between the Evangelical Lutheran Church of Finland and the Orthodox Church of Finland, 1989–2007." *Reseptio* 1 (2009) 204–10.

Vogelaar, Huub. "An Intriguing Ecumenical Dialogue: Lutheran-Orthodox Encounters in Finland." *Exchange* 42 (2013) 267–301.

"Yksi Herra, yksi usko, yksi kaste—Paimenkirje jo kastettujen kirkkoon liittämisestä." https://ort.fi/ru/wp-content/uploads/2023/11/Paimenkirje-kasteesta.pdf.

APPENDIX

Learning Points from the Joint Nordic Lutheran Project "Baptism in Times of Change"

THE FOLLOWING RECOMMENDATIONS ON baptism in the contemporary Lutheran folk churches is the result from a joint Nordic research project, conducted 2020–2022 by a group of national researchers (see more at www.churchesintimesofchange.org). The recommendations were presented for discussion with a larger group of engaged practitioners, academics, representatives from the LWF communion office, and church leaders in the Nordic area on 19th-20th January 2022. Our hope is that this will contribute to the development of how baptism should be viewed and practiced in a time of change in the Nordic Lutheran folk churches.

The recommendations take as point of departure the themes identified in the annotated bibliography, identifies challenges and relevant questions, and points to examples or 'good practices' in relation to baptism, without necessarily entailing endorsement from all participants in the consultation. Furthermore, the recommendations are not binding policies for participating churches as each national group needs to continue working on how they will use the recommendations in their own context and constituency. In short, the recommendations are best viewed as learning points from a joint study and discussion.

Thus, a main outcome of the joint research process and the consultation is the following list of refined and critiqued recommendations, brought back to the participating churches by the national groups.

APPENDIX: LEARNING POINTS FROM "BAPTISM IN TIMES OF CHANGE"

A. CHURCH IN WIDER SOCIETY (STATISTICS, QUALITATIVE ASPECTS, SOCIETAL CHANGE)

Churches are recommended

1. to consider the profound social changes transforming our societies as a renewed call to be churches in mission.
2. to view our Nordic societies as inviting us to theologize contextually.
3. to explore contemporary idioms in dialogue with biblical and traditional symbols in order to make Christianity relevant to people in modern society.
4. to learn to be churches in a pluralistic society sharing public space and working together with people of other faiths and convictions.

B. THEOLOGY (LUTHERAN, ECUMENICAL, CONTEMPORARY)

Churches are recommended

5. to work with theologies of baptism in ways that are accessible and understandable.
6. to develop a rich and comprehensive understanding of the gifts of grace and discipleship received in baptism as giving us new relationships to participate in God's mission in the world.
7. to develop the relationship between baptism and all of creation including the wider human family as well as the ecological environment.
8. to develop an understanding of baptism not exclusively related to infant baptism but including baptism of children, youths, and adults.
9. to work with the understanding of baptism together with ecumenical partners.

C. COMMUNICATION (MEETING MEMBERS, EDUCATION, CAMPAIGNS)

Churches are recommended

10. to improve dialogue-oriented communication on baptism, including the theological aspects of baptism.
11. to communicate about baptism in a way that emphasizes belonging, community, and relationship.
12. to equip members to consider their own baptism as a 'mission to communicate'.
13. to develop programs to teach Christian faith for baptized and non-baptized.

D. PRACTICE (LITURGICAL DEVELOPMENT, NEW FORMS OF BAPTISMAL PRACTICE)

Churches are recommended

14. to explore greater variation in baptismal practice, e.g. special baptismal services, drop-in services, and services outside the church building.
15. to reflect on the role of and provide resources for godparents.
16. to explore ways to relate to multifaith families and parents opting for delayed baptism, affirming that the child 'belongs to the kingdom of God'.
17. to develop liturgies and hymns suitable for various ages and circumstances.
18. to constantly review and revise the liturgical language and practices of baptism.

www.ingramcontent.com/pod-product-compliance
Lightning Source LLC
Chambersburg PA
CBHW071146300426
44113CB00009B/1101